How the Internet Works

Sixth Edition

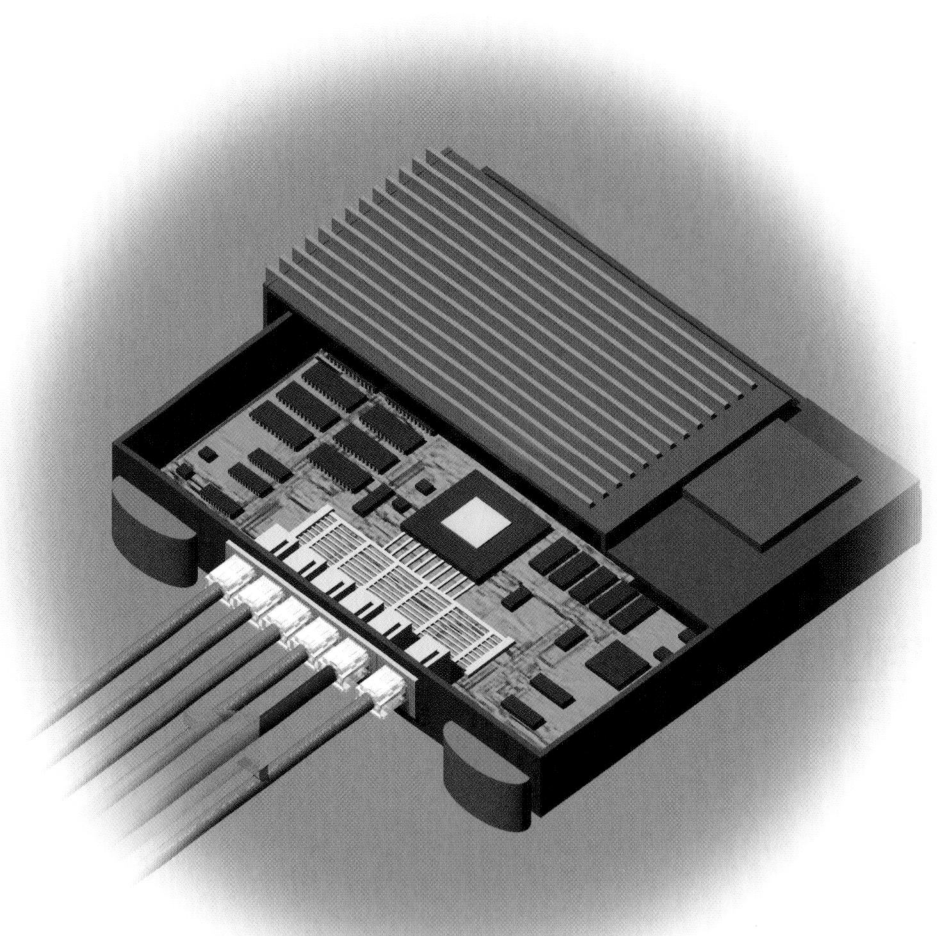

How the Internet Works

Sixth Edition

Preston Gralla

201 W. 103rd Street
Indianapolis, IN 46290

How the Internet Works, Sixth Edition

Associate Publisher	Greg Wiegand
Acquisitions Editor	Stephanie J. McComb
Development Editor	Nicholas J. Goetz
Managing Editor	Thomas F. Hayes
Project Editor	Karen S. Shields
Production Editors	Megan Wade Amy Jay
Indexer	Erika Millen
Technical Editor	Chris Faust
Illustrator	Michael Troller
Team Coordinator	Sharry Lee Gregory
Page Layout	Gloria Schurick

International Standard Book Number: 0-7897-2582-7

Library of Congress Catalog Card Number: 20-01087727

Printed in the United States of America

First Printing: September, 2001

04 03 02 4 3 2

Trademarks

Warning and Disclaimer

Acknowledgments

THIS book, like the Internet, is a collaborative work. My name might be on the cover, but I am far from the only person involved in its creation.

Development editor Nick Goetz managed to pull together all the elements of a complex project, all the while keeping a cool head, improving the illustrations, and offering editorial insight and help. And acquisitions editor Stephanie McComb was instrumental in getting the book off the ground, and as always, was a pleasure to work with.

The illustrator for the book, Michael Troller, deserves much thanks. Not only did he create new illustrations from scratch specifically for this book, he redid all the ones from past books and made this edition a more coherent, richer, more visually pleasing experience.

Thanks also go to illustrators of past editions: Mina Reimer, Sarah Ishida, Shelly Norris, and Stephen Adams. And many thanks to the entire team at Que who produced the book, including Karen Shields, Megan Wade, Amy Jay, Gloria Schurick, and Erika Millen.

Thanks also have to go to the many, many people I interviewed for this book. People from Quarterdeck Corporation, Chaco Communications, Progressive Networks, White Pine Software, Microsoft, Netscape, Headspace, SurfWatch Software, WebTV, Accrue, VDONet Corporation, America Online, Yahoo!, Hilgraeve, Fairmarket, eWallet, and Nuborn Technologies are only a few of the folks who gave their time to help me understand the nitty-gritty of how various Internet technologies work. Tim Smith from ZDNet offered me vital help as well.

I gleaned much information from the many FAQs and similar documents widely available on the Internet. I'd like to thank the anonymous authors of those documents, whoever they are.

Many thanks go to Chris Faust, the technical editor for the book, who did a superb job of ensuring that I always got the information right.

Finally, big thanks have to go to my wife, Lydia. She put up with those occasional glassy-eyed looks that were replies to simple questions like, "Did you leave your keys in the refrigerator again?" She also endured my extreme absent-mindedness while I was figuring out ways to explain how firewalls, ISDN, or Web robots work when I should have been concentrating on more immediate matters.

Tell Us What You Think!

AS the reader of this book, you are our most important critic and commentator. We value your opinion and want to know what we're doing right, what we could do better, what areas you'd like to see us publish in, and any other words of wisdom you're willing to pass our way.

As an associate publisher for Que, I welcome your comments. You can fax, e-mail, or write me directly to let me know what you did or didn't like about this book—as well as what we can do to make our books stronger.

Please note that I cannot help you with technical problems related to the topic of this book, and that due to the high volume of mail I receive, I might not be able to reply to every message.

When you write, please be sure to include this book's title and author as well as your name and phone or fax number. I will carefully review your comments and share them with the author and editors who worked on the book.

Fax: 317-581-4666

E-mail: `feedback@quepublishing.com`

Mail: Greg Wiegand
Associate Publisher
Que
201 West 103rd Street
Indianapolis, IN 46290 USA

Introduction

IN the course of cruising the World Wide Web and clicking a link, have you ever wondered, "How does that work?" Or perhaps this question popped into your mind while you were transferring a file to your computer via FTP, or reading a newsgroup message, or when you first heard about technologies such as spam, cookies, and firewalls. Maybe you've wondered how a message sent from your computer travels through the vastness of cyberspace and ends up in the right e-mail box halfway across the world. Have you ever wanted to know how search tools find the exact piece of information you want out of the millions of pieces of information on the whole Internet? How can you listen to music and view animations while surfing the Web?

This book is designed for everyone interested in the Internet. Its guiding principle is this: No matter how much of a cyberpro you are—or how much of a novice—there's a lot you don't understand about the Internet. Here's just one small example. I have a friend who has made his living with companies involved with the Internet for many years. He's a complete cyberpro who lives and breathes the Internet. One day, he almost whispered to me, "I don't like to admit this, but I don't know what a proxy server is. How does it work, anyway?"

He's not alone. The Internet changes so quickly and the technology advances so rapidly that it can seem almost impossible to keep up with all of it. If you're like just about everyone else involved in the Internet, your questions are similar to those of my friend. You'll find your answers here.

In Part 1, "Understanding the Internet's Underlying Architecture," I explain the underlying basics of the Internet: who runs it, how TCP/IP works, how to understand Internet addresses and domains, and similar topics. Here's where you'll find out about things such as routers and how the client/server architecture underpins virtually every aspect of the Internet.

Part 2, "Connecting to the Internet," depicts the various ways you can connect your computer to the Internet. Here's where to turn if you're interested in any of the following topics: how a cable modem, a digital subscriber line (DSL), or ISDN works; how online services connect to the Internet; how you can connect by satellite to the Internet; how "palmtop" computers, such as 3COM's Palm, can browse the Web; how a modem works; how you can access the Internet from your own home network; and a host of similar subjects.

Part 3, "Communicating on the Internet," covers every aspect of Internet communications. It shows how e-mail and newsgroups work, how IRC chat works, what e-mail "spam" is and what you can do to prevent it, how instant messaging works, and how you can use the Internet to make telephone calls anywhere in the world.

Part 4, "Using the World Wide Web," covers what has become by far the most popular part of the Internet—the World Wide Web. You'll learn virtually every aspect of how the Web works. It delves into how browsers work, how Web server software works, and how Hypertext Markup Language (HTML) works. This section also covers the ways in which the Web is becoming integrated directly into your computer, how Web pages are published and organized on a site, and every other aspect of the Web that is likely to be of interest to you.

Part 5, "Using Common Internet Tools," takes a close look at common Internet tools. Here's the place to learn about basic tools and services, such as telnet, and what happens when you use FTP to download a file to your computer. You'll also learn how search engines and search tools work. And it's the section of the book that covers cutting-edge Internet technology. You'll find out about how push technology works, how the Java and ActiveX programming languages work, how JavaScript works, how agents can silently do your bidding for you, and how the Common Gateway Interface (CGI) works, which is a little-known but vital part of the Internet.

Part 6, "Enjoying Entertainment and Multimedia on the Internet," shows you how some of the most exciting parts of the Internet work—the various multimedia technologies. Whether you want to know how virtual reality or animations work, how streaming video works, how videoconferencing works, or how similar technologies work, you'll find it all here.

Part 7, "Shopping and Doing Business on the Internet," covers intranets, how the Internet works with the outside world, and how you can shop online. You'll see how companies use Internet technologies to build their own private networks, called *intranets*. And you'll take a close look at the underlying technologies that let you shop on the Web, which accounts for billions of dollars a year in sales.

Finally, Part 8, "Protecting Yourself on the Internet," covers security concerns. It explains the controversial cookie technology that lets Web servers put bits of information on your hard disk and use that information to track you. It explains how the even-more controversial FBI system called Carnivore can in essence wiretap people's use of the Internet to read their e-mail, watch their Web browsing, and more. This part also shows how firewalls work, how viruses can attack your computer, and how cryptosystems allow confidential information to be sent across the Internet. It delves into how hackers can attack Internet service providers (ISPs) using so-called "smurf attacks," and how they can attack your computer as well. And it covers the issue of pornography on the Internet and shows how parental-control software can prevent children from seeing objectionable material.

So, come along and see how the vast Internet works. Even if you're a cyberpro (and especially if you're not), you'll find out a lot you never knew.

P A R T

UNDERSTANDING THE INTERNET'S UNDERLYING ARCHITECTURE

FOR the first time ever, the world is at your fingertips. From your computer, you can find information about anything you can name or even imagine. You can communicate with people on the other side of the world. You can set up a teleconference, tap into the resources of powerful computers anywhere on the globe, search through the world's best libraries, and visit the world's most amazing museums. You can watch videos, listen to music, and read special multimedia magazines. You can shop for almost anything you can name. You can do all this by tapping into the largest computer network in the world—the Internet.

The Internet isn't a single network; it is a vast, globe-spanning network of networks. No single person, group, or organization runs the Internet. Instead, it's the purest form of electronic democracy. The networks communicate with one another based on certain protocols, such as the Transmission Control Protocol (TCP) and the Internet Protocol (IP). More and more networks and computers are being hooked up to the Internet every day. Tens of thousands of these networks exist, ranging from university networks to corporate local area networks to large online services such as America Online and CompuServe. Every time you tap into the Internet, your own computer becomes an extension of that network.

The first section of this book is spent defining the Internet. It also examines the architectures, protocols, and general concepts that make it all possible.

Chapter 1, "What Is the Internet?," examines how the Internet runs. You'll look at who pays for the high-speed data backbones that carry much of the Internet's traffic and at the organizations that ensure that standards are set for networks to follow so the Internet can run smoothly. You'll also look at the various types of networks connected to the Internet.

Chapter 2, "How Computer Networks Send Data Across the Internet," explains how information travels across the Internet and describes how hardware such as routers, repeaters, and bridges sends information among networks. It also shows how smaller networks are grouped into larger regional networks—and how those large regional networks communicate among themselves.

Chapter 3, "How TCP/IP Works," covers the Internet's basic protocols for communications. You'll learn a little about basic Internet jargon, such as TCP/IP (short for Transmission Control Protocol and Internet Protocol). This chapter also explains how those protocols work and how special software such as Winsock enables personal computers to get onto a network originally designed for larger computers.

Chapter 4, "Understanding the Internet's Software Structure," looks at the Internet's client/server architecture. *Servers*—also called *hosts*—are powerful computers that perform functions such as delivering information or Web pages, hosting databases, and handling e-mail. A *client* is your own computer and the software that sits on it, such as a Web browser or piece of e-mail software. Clients request information from servers, which do the heavy-duty processing and then send the information back to the client, which displays the information.

Chapter 5, "How Internet Addresses and Domains Work," takes the mystery out of the Internet's often confusing addressing scheme. You'll learn about Internet domains and addresses and will even be able to make sense of them. More than that, you'll learn how domain servers are capable of keeping track of all the locations on the Internet and translating addresses such as `www.zdnet.com` into Internet IP addresses such as `134.54.56.120`. You'll also learn how some computers are assigned new IP addresses by special servers every time they connect to the Internet.

Chapter 6, "How Routers Work," details how the most basic piece of hardware on the Internet—a router—works. *Routers* are combinations of hardware and software that perform the job of ensuring that all data is sent to the proper destination. Think of routers as traffic cops of the Internet. They use the IP addresses the name servers have translated to route the data. Routers look at the addresses and then send the data to the next-closest router to the destination and so on, until the data is finally delivered. They use *routing tables* to determine how to route the traffic, and they can also adjust the routes as the traffic on the Internet changes, thus ensuring that the data is routed in the most efficient way possible.

Chapter 7, "How Internet File Types Work," gives you an understanding of the most common types of files you'll come across when you browse the Net. Compressed files, video files, graphics files—you'll learn about almost every type of file you might encounter.

Whether you're a newbie or cyberpro, this section teaches you the basics of the Internet.

CHAPTER

1

What Is the Internet?

ONE of the most frequently asked questions about the Internet is: Who runs it? The truth is that no centralized management of the Internet exists. Instead, it is a collection of thousands of individual networks and organizations, each of which is run and paid for on its own. Each network cooperates with other networks to direct Internet traffic so that information can pass among them. Together, these networks and organizations make up the wired world of the Internet. For networks and computers to cooperate in this way, however, a general agreement must take place about things such as Internet procedures and standards for protocols. These procedures and standards are laid out in requests for comment (RFCs) that are agreed on by Internet users and organizations.

A variety of groups guide the Internet's growth by helping to establish standards and by educating people on the proper way to use the Internet. Perhaps the most important is the Internet Society, a private, nonprofit group. The Internet Society supports the work of the Internet Activities Board (IAB), which handles much of the Internet's behind-the-scenes and architectural issues. The Internet Engineering Task Force (IETF) is responsible for overseeing how the Internet's TCP/IP protocols evolve. For information about the IETF, go to `www.ietf.org`.(See Chapter 3, "How TCP/IP Works," for details on TCP/IP protocols.)

The World Wide Web Consortium (W3C) develops standards for the evolution of the fastest-growing part of the Internet, the World Wide Web (find it at `www.w3.org`). The W3C is an industry consortium run by the Laboratory for Computer Science at the Massachusetts Institute of Technology (MIT).

Private companies oversee the registering of Internet domains, such as `www.zdnet.com` or `www.quepublishing.com`. These companies, called *registrars*, all must cooperate with one another to ensure that only one person or company can own a particular domain and that all the domains work properly. The registrars compete with one another as well in allowing people and businesses to register domains. Registering a domain costs money, and the registrars compete on cost and on giving extra services to those who buy domains.

Although all these types of organizations are important for holding together the Internet, at the heart of the Internet are individual local networks. These networks can be found in private companies, universities, government agencies, and online services. They are funded separately from each other and in a variety of manners, such as fees from users, corporate support, taxes, and grants. Many Internet service providers (ISPs), which provide Internet access for individuals, have networks as well. Individuals who want to access the Internet pay ISPs a monthly connection rate, so in that sense, everyone who uses the Internet helps pay for it.

The networks are connected in a variety of ways. For efficiency's sake, local networks join in consortiums known as *regional networks*. A variety of leased lines connect regional and local networks. The leased lines that connect networks can be as simple as a single telephone line or as complex as a fiber-optic cable with microwave links and satellite transmissions.

Private companies who make money by selling access to their lines build *backbones*, which are very high-capacity lines that carry enormous amounts of Internet traffic. Government agencies, such as NASA, and large private corporations pay for some of these backbones. The National Science Foundation also pays for some backbones.

How the Internet Comes Together

Organization of networks Because the Internet is a loose organization of networks, no single group runs it or pays for it all. Instead, many private organizations, universities, and government agencies pay for and run parts of it. They all work together in a democratic, loosely organized alliance. Private organizations range from small, homegrown networks to commercial online services, such as America Online and CompuServe, and private Internet service providers (ISPs) that sell access to the Internet.

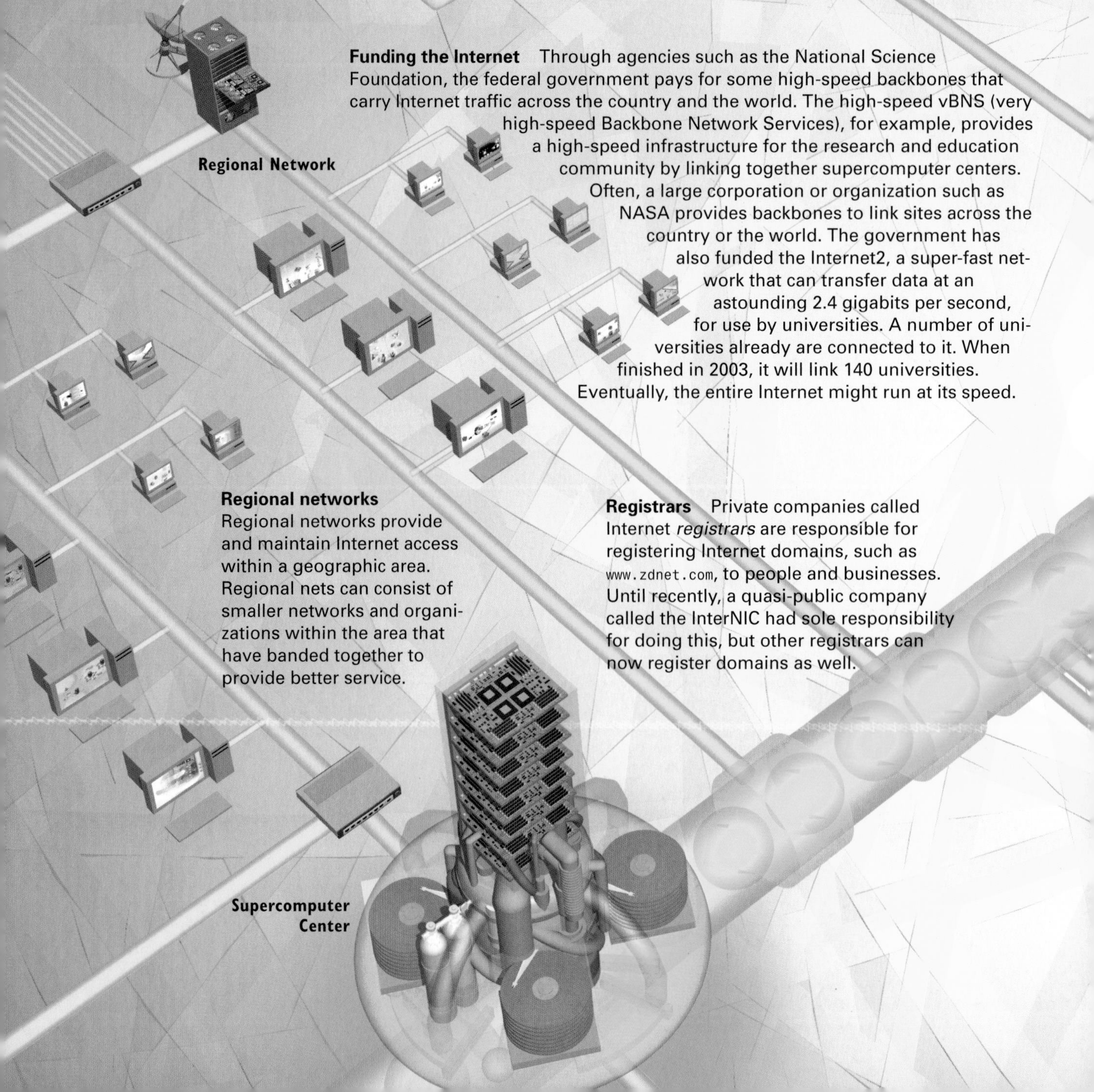

Funding the Internet Through agencies such as the National Science Foundation, the federal government pays for some high-speed backbones that carry Internet traffic across the country and the world. The high-speed vBNS (very high-speed Backbone Network Services), for example, provides a high-speed infrastructure for the research and education community by linking together supercomputer centers. Often, a large corporation or organization such as NASA provides backbones to link sites across the country or the world. The government has also funded the Internet2, a super-fast network that can transfer data at an astounding 2.4 gigabits per second, for use by universities. A number of universities already are connected to it. When finished in 2003, it will link 140 universities. Eventually, the entire Internet might run at its speed.

Regional Network

Regional networks Regional networks provide and maintain Internet access within a geographic area. Regional nets can consist of smaller networks and organizations within the area that have banded together to provide better service.

Registrars Private companies called Internet *registrars* are responsible for registering Internet domains, such as `www.zdnet.com`, to people and businesses. Until recently, a quasi-public company called the InterNIC had sole responsibility for doing this, but other registrars can now register domains as well.

Supercomputer Center

Internet service providers ISPs sell people monthly connections to the Internet. They run their own segments of the Internet and also might supply long-distance connections called *backbones*. Telephone companies are another source of long-distance connections for the Internet.

Internet Society The Internet Society is a private nonprofit organization that makes technological and architectural recommendations that pertain to the Internet, such as how TCP/IP and other Internet protocols should work. This body guides the direction of the Internet and its growth.

InterNIC The InterNIC is responsible for maintaining the domains registered through registries. It tracks the connections between Internet addresses, such as `125.34.24.21`, and domain names, such as `www.zdnet.com`.

CHAPTER

2

How Computer Networks Send Data Across the Internet

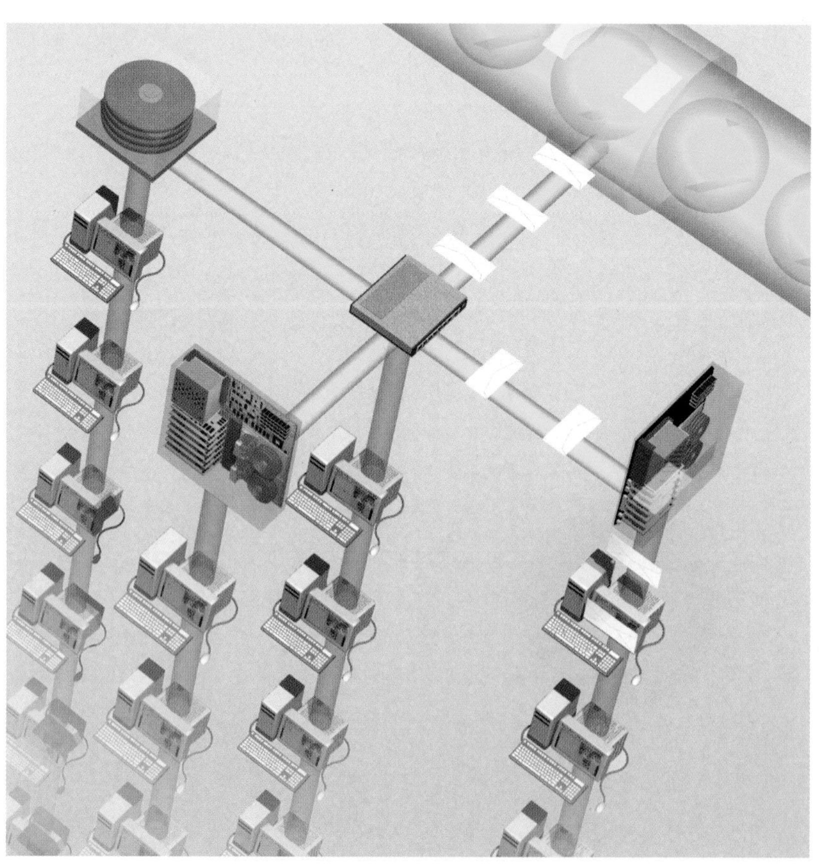

YOU might take for granted that when you send a piece of information across the Internet, it will always reach its intended destination. However, the process of sending that information is remarkably complex.

When you send information across the Internet, the *Transmission Control Protocol (TCP)*—the language computers use when communicating over the Internet—first breaks the information up into *packets*, smaller blocks of information that also contain a variety of data that helps the packets travel across the Internet. Your computer sends those packets to your local network, Internet service provider (ISP), or online service. From there, the packets travel through many levels of networks, computers, and communications lines before they reach their final destinations, which might be across town or around the world. A variety of hardware processes those packets and routes them to their proper destinations. This hardware is designed to transmit data between networks and makes up much of the glue that holds the Internet together. Five of the most important pieces of hardware are hubs, bridges, gateways, repeaters, and routers.

Hubs are important because they link groups of computers to one another and let computers communicate with each other. *Bridges* link local area networks (LANs) with one another. They enable data destined for another LAN to be sent there, while keeping local data inside its own network. *Gateways* are similar to bridges, but they also translate data from one type of network to another.

When data travels across the Internet, it often crosses great distances, which can be a problem because the signal sending the data can weaken over the distance. To solve the problem, *repeaters* amplify the data at intervals so the signal doesn't weaken.

Routers play a key role in managing Internet traffic. Their job is to ensure the packets always arrive at the proper destination. If data is being transferred among computers that are on the same LAN, routers often aren't necessary because the network itself can handle its internal traffic. Routers come into play when the data is sent between two different networks. Routers examine packets to determine their destinations. They take into account the volume of activity on the Internet, and they send the packet to another router that is closer to the packet's final destination. For more information on routers see Chapter 6, "How Routers Work."

All this hardware connects the many networks that make up the Internet. At the most local level of networks are corporate local area networks. Midlevel networks hook these LANs together using high-speed telephone lines, ethernet, and microwave links. A *regional* network is a midlevel network in a geographic area. A *wide area network (WAN)* is another type of midlevel network. A WAN consists of an organization with many networked sites linked together.

When a packet travels from a computer on a LAN in a midlevel network to a computer somewhere else on the midlevel network, a router (or a series of routers) sends the packet to its proper destination. However, if the destination lies outside the midlevel network, the packet is sent to a network access point (NAP), where it is sent across the country or the world on a backbone. High-speed backbones such as the vBNS (very high-speed Backbone Network Services) can transmit enormous amounts of data—155 megabits (millions of bits) per second (Mbps). Even faster backbones are being built that will transmit data at an astonishing 9.6 billion bits per second.

How Networks Link to the Internet

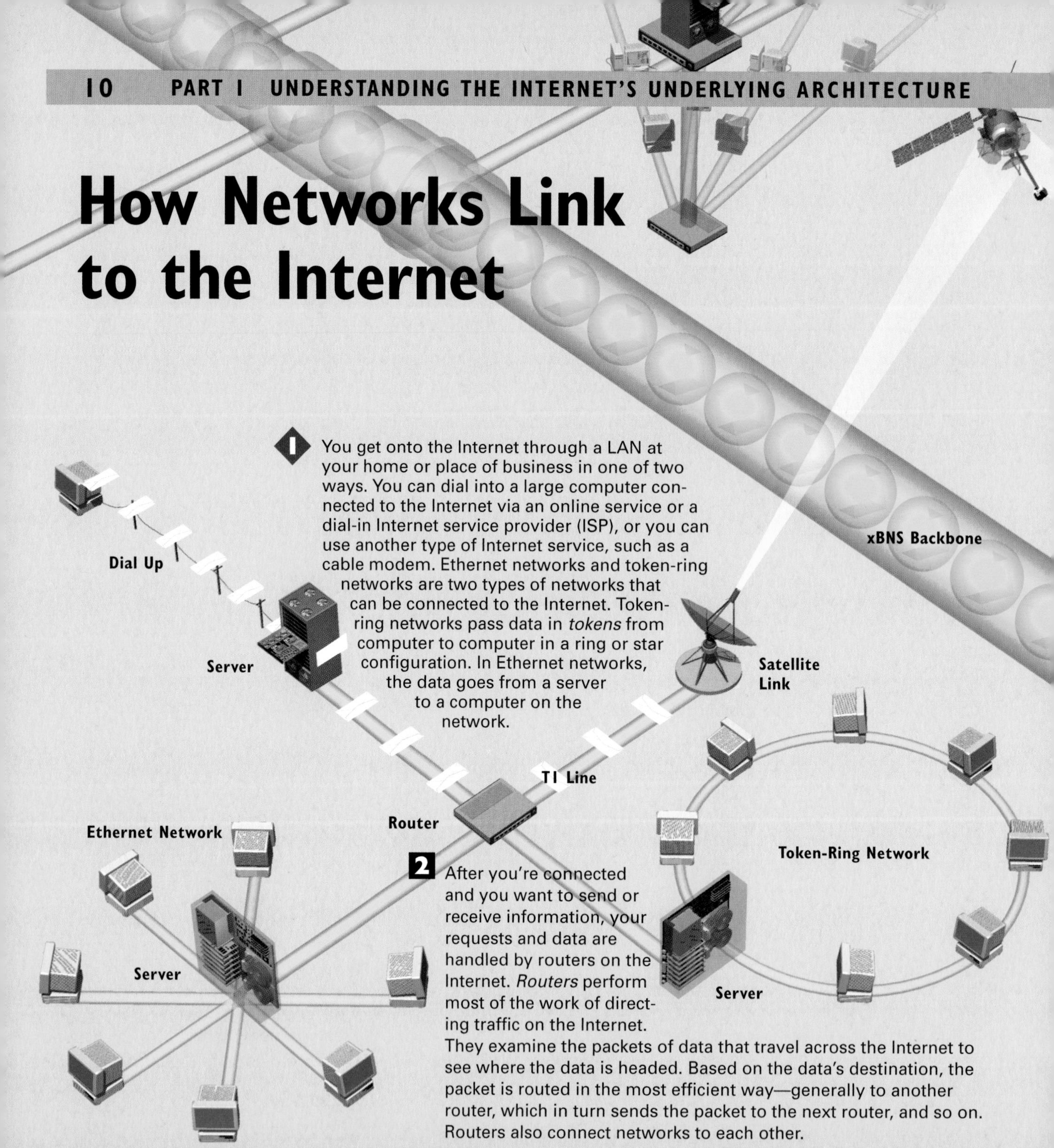

1 You get onto the Internet through a LAN at your home or place of business in one of two ways. You can dial into a large computer connected to the Internet via an online service or a dial-in Internet service provider (ISP), or you can use another type of Internet service, such as a cable modem. Ethernet networks and token-ring networks are two types of networks that can be connected to the Internet. Token-ring networks pass data in *tokens* from computer to computer in a ring or star configuration. In Ethernet networks, the data goes from a server to a computer on the network.

2 After you're connected and you want to send or receive information, your requests and data are handled by routers on the Internet. *Routers* perform most of the work of directing traffic on the Internet. They examine the packets of data that travel across the Internet to see where the data is headed. Based on the data's destination, the packet is routed in the most efficient way—generally to another router, which in turn sends the packet to the next router, and so on. Routers also connect networks to each other.

3 The data can be transferred between networks in a number of ways. Dedicated telephone lines can transmit data at 56Kbps (kilobits per second). An increasing number of T1 leased telephone lines carry data between networks. A T1 link can carry data at 1.544Mbps. Higher-speed T3 links, which can carry data at 44.746Mbps, are being used as well. If you dial into an ISP from home, you might connect at a lower speed than at your office, where you might have higher-speed connections such as a T1 or 56Kbps line. However, a variety of high-speed options are available for connecting to the Internet at home, such as cable modems or high-speed Digital Subscriber Line (DSL) connections.

4 A variety of other methods transfer data between networks. Satellites can be used to send and receive information, as can fiber-optic cables, special Integrated Services Digital Network (ISDN) telephone lines, and high-speed DSL connections.

5 The networks in a particular geographic area are connected into a large regional network. Routers pass information within that area from network to network.

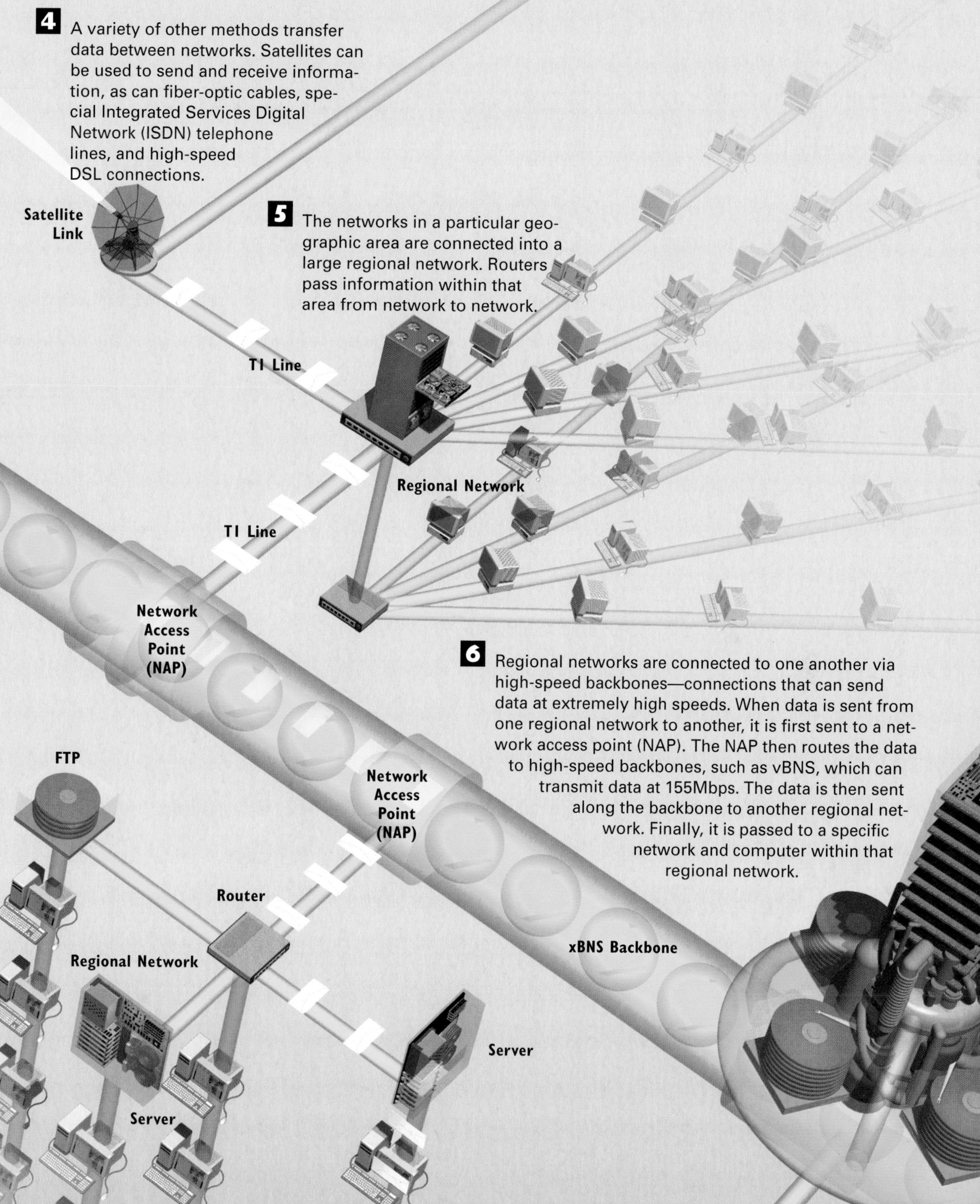

6 Regional networks are connected to one another via high-speed backbones—connections that can send data at extremely high speeds. When data is sent from one regional network to another, it is first sent to a network access point (NAP). The NAP then routes the data to high-speed backbones, such as vBNS, which can transmit data at 155Mbps. The data is then sent along the backbone to another regional network. Finally, it is passed to a specific network and computer within that regional network.

CHAPTER 3 How TCP/IP Works

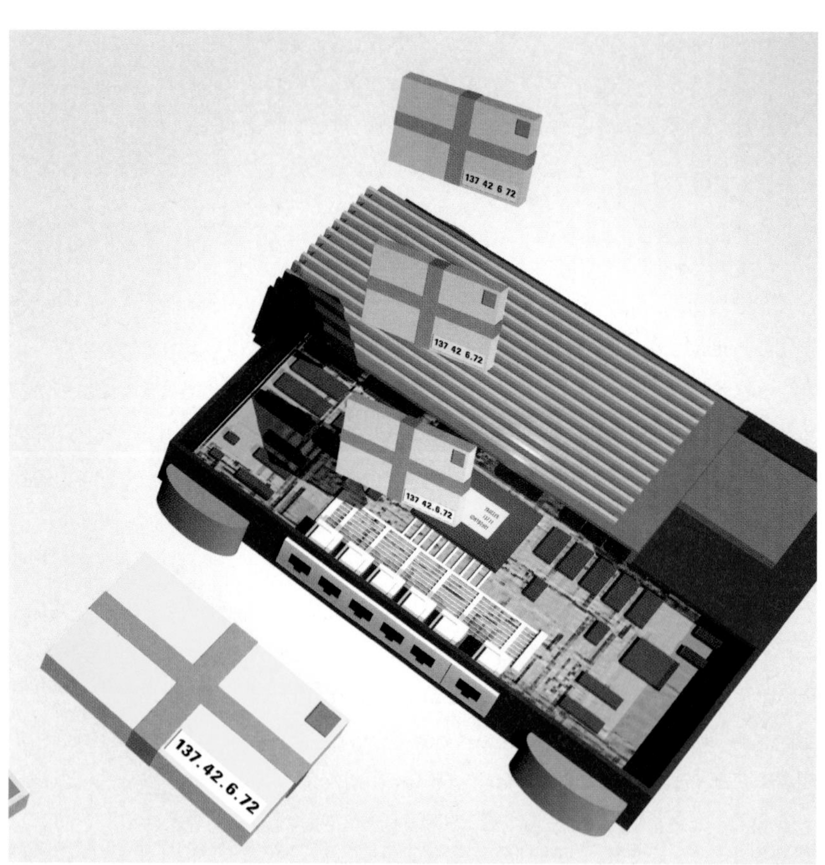

A seemingly simple set of ideas makes it possible for computers and networks all over the world to share information and messages on the Internet: Break up every piece of information and message into pieces called *packets*, deliver those packets to the proper destinations, and then reassemble the packets into their original form after they've been delivered so the receiving computer can view and use them. That's the job of the two most important communications protocols on the Internet—the Transmission Control Protocol (TCP) and the Internet Protocol (IP). They are frequently referred to as *TCP/IP*. TCP breaks down and reassembles the packets, whereas IP is responsible for ensuring the packets are sent to the right destination.

TCP/IP is used because the Internet is what is known as a packet-switched network. In a *packet-switched network*, there is no single, unbroken connection between sender and receiver. Instead, when information is sent, it is broken into small packets, sent over many different routes at the same time, and then reassembled at the receiving end. By contrast, the telephone system is a circuit-switched network. In a *circuit-switched network*, after a connection is made (as with a telephone call, for example), that part of the network is dedicated only to that single connection.

For personal computers to take full advantage of the Internet, they need to use special software that understands and interprets the Internet's TCP/IP protocols. This software is referred to as a *socket* or a *TCP/IP stack*. For PCs, the required software is called Winsock. Many versions of Winsock are available for PCs. For Macintoshes, the software is called MacTCP. In both cases, this software serves as an intermediary between the Internet and the personal computer. Personal computers can take advantage of the simplest, most rudimentary parts of the Internet without using Winsock or MacTCP—for example, you can't view Web pages without it or listen to music over the Internet, among many other things. For full access to the Internet, TCP/IP stacks are necessary.

There are two primary ways that a computer can connect to the Internet and then use these protocols—through a direct connection via a local area network (LAN), cable modem, or DSL line; or by dialing in using a modem. To connect via LAN, cable modem, or DSL line, a computer needs a network card. To communicate with the network and the Internet's TCP/IP protocols, the network card requires a hardware driver—software that mediates between the network and the network card. When the computer instead dials in to the Internet by using a modem, the computer must use one of two software protocols: either Serial Line Internet Protocol (SLIP) or Point-to-Point Protocol (PPP). These protocols do the job of communicating with the Internet's TCP/IP protocols.

SLIP and PPP are designed for computers connected to the Internet over a serial connection via a modem. In general, the newer PPP provides a more error-free connection than does the older SLIP. Computers can also dial in to the Internet without using TCP/IP stacks, SLIP, or PPP. However, they won't be capable of tapping into the full power of the Internet, most specifically, the World Wide Web. To make full use of the Web, you need a computer that is part of the Internet, which requires a TCP/IP stack. The SLIP or PPP must then be used when dialing in to an ISP for Web access.

How the Internet's Basic TCP/IP Protocols Work

1 The Internet is a packet-switched network, which means that when you send information across the Internet from your computer to another computer, the data is broken into small packets. A series of switches called *routers* send each packet across the Net individually. After all the packets arrive at the receiving computer, they are recombined into their original, unified form. Two protocols do the work of breaking the data into packets, routing the packets across the Internet, and then recombining them on the other end: The Internet Protocol (IP), which routes the data, and the Transmission Control Protocol (TCP), which breaks the data into packets and recombines them on the computer that receives the information.

2 For a number of reasons, including hardware limitations, data sent across the Internet must be broken into packets of fewer than about 1,500 characters each. Each packet is given a header that contains a variety of information, such as the order in which the packets should be assembled with other related packets. As TCP creates each packet, it also calculates and adds to the header a *checksum*, which is a number that TCP uses on the receiving end to determine whether any errors have been introduced into the packet during transmission. The checksum is based on the precise amount of data in the packet.

3 Each packet is put into separate IP *envelopes*, which contain addressing information that tells the Internet where to send the data. All the envelopes for a given piece of data have the same addressing information so they can all be sent to the same location to be reassembled. IP envelopes contain headers that include information such as the sender address, the destination address, the amount of time the packet should be kept before discarding it, and many other types of information.

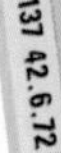

6 When all the noncorrupt packets are received by the computer to which the information is being sent, TCP assembles them into their original, unified form.

5 As the packets arrive at their destinations, TCP calculates a checksum for each packet. It then compares this checksum with the checksum that has been sent in the packet. If the checksums don't match, TCP knows that the data in the packet has been corrupted during transmission. It then discards the packet and asks that the original packet be retransmitted.

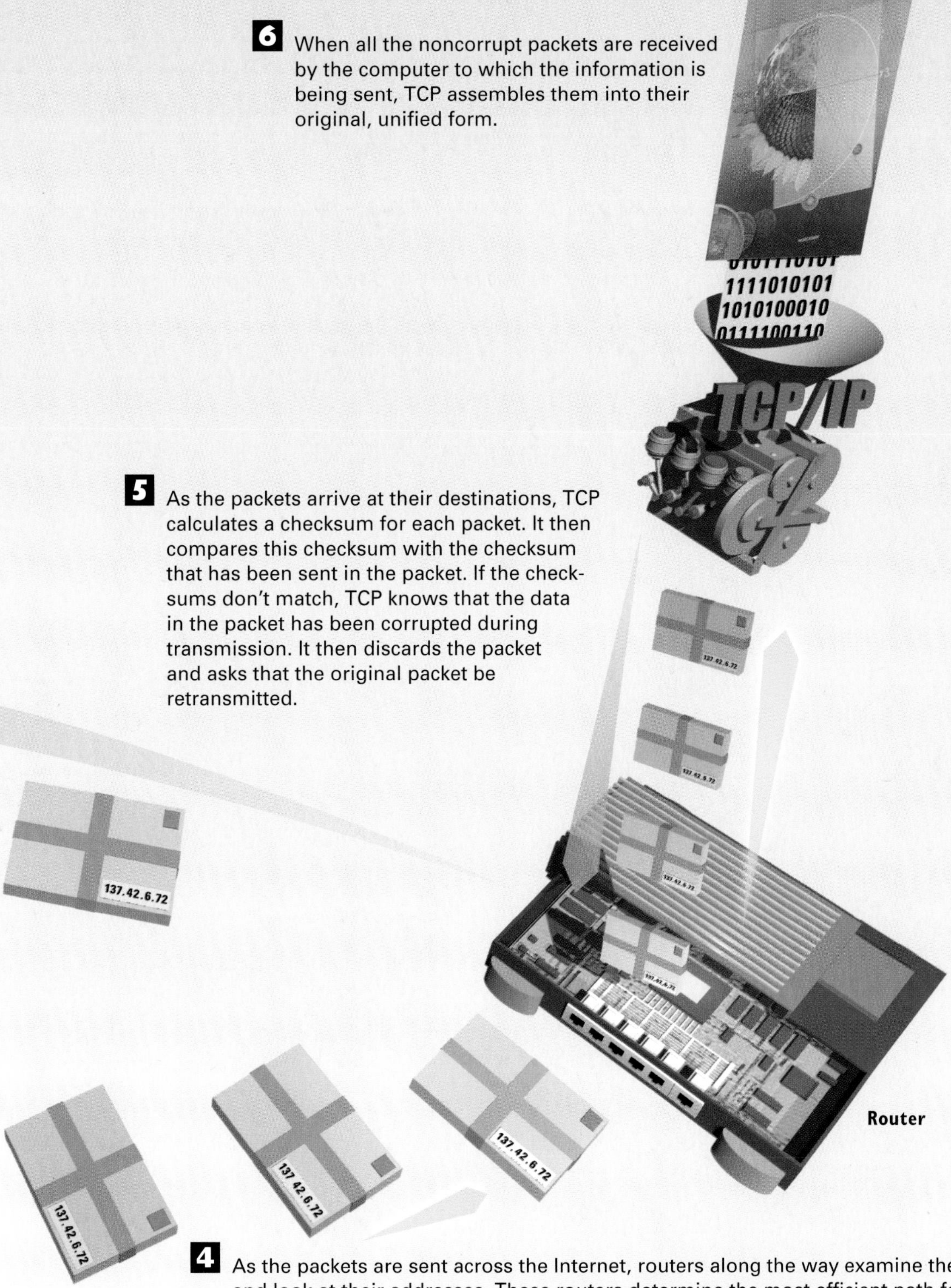

4 As the packets are sent across the Internet, routers along the way examine the IP envelopes and look at their addresses. These routers determine the most efficient path for sending each packet to the next router closest to its final destination. After traveling through a series of routers, the packets arrive. Because the traffic load on the Internet changes constantly, the packets might be sent along different routes and the packets might arrive out of order.

CHAPTER

4

Understanding the Internet's Software Structure

THE Internet works on the client/server model of information delivery. In a client/server model, the client computer connects to a server computer on which information resides; the client depends on the server to deliver information. In effect, the client requests the services of the larger computer. These services can involve searching for information and sending it back to the client, such as when a database on the Web is queried. Other examples of these services are delivering Web pages and handling incoming and outgoing e-mail. Whenever you use the Internet, you're connected to a server computer and requesting the use of that server's resources.

Typically, the *client* is a local personal computer or the software that runs on it, and the *server* (also known as the *host*) is usually a more powerful computer that houses the data. Hosts and clients can be of many makes and manufacturers and run a wide variety of operating systems.

The connection to the server is made in many ways—via a LAN (local area network), via a phone line, via a cable modem or DSL modem, wirelessly, or any one of other countless ways. A primary reason to set up a client/server network is to allow many clients to access the same applications and files that are stored on a server. Also, as previously mentioned, these clients can be any one of many types of computers accessing the Internet in many ways.

In the case of the Internet's World Wide Web, the client is actually the browser on your PC and the server is a host computer located somewhere on the Internet. Typically, the browser sends the server a request for a specific Web page. The server processes that request and sends an answer back to the browser (again, most often in the form of a Web page).

The connection between the client and server is maintained only during the actual exchange of information. Thus, after a Web page is transferred from the host (or server) computer, the HTTP connection between that computer and the client is broken. (HTTP stands for Hypertext Transfer Protocol; it's the protocol used by the World Wide Web.) Even though the HTTP connection is closed, the ISP maintains the TCP/IP connection to the Internet.

The client/server model enables the desktop PC to run the browser software to search the Web, yet still access host servers around the Internet to execute search and retrieval functions. Many of these functions are accomplished through technology called the Common Gateway Interface (CGI). For more information about how CGI works, see Chapter 35, "How CGI Scripting Works." In essence, this architecture enables the Web to be conceived of as a limitless file storage medium and database, distributed among thousands of host computers, all accessible by any individual PC.

The following illustration shows how the Web runs on a client/server architecture. Keep in mind that all other resources on the Internet run on the client/server model as well. For example, in e-mail transactions the client would be the e-mail software on your computer, whereas the server would be the e-mail server to which you connect.

How Client/Server Architecture Works

1 The PC-based browser software controls the client end of the Web application. Using TCP/IP, the browser issues HTTP requests to the host server. The browser can request a specific Web page, or it can ask the host server to perform a database query. In either instance, the request is broken into HTTP packets that are sent across the Internet's TCP/IP communications infrastructure to the host computer.

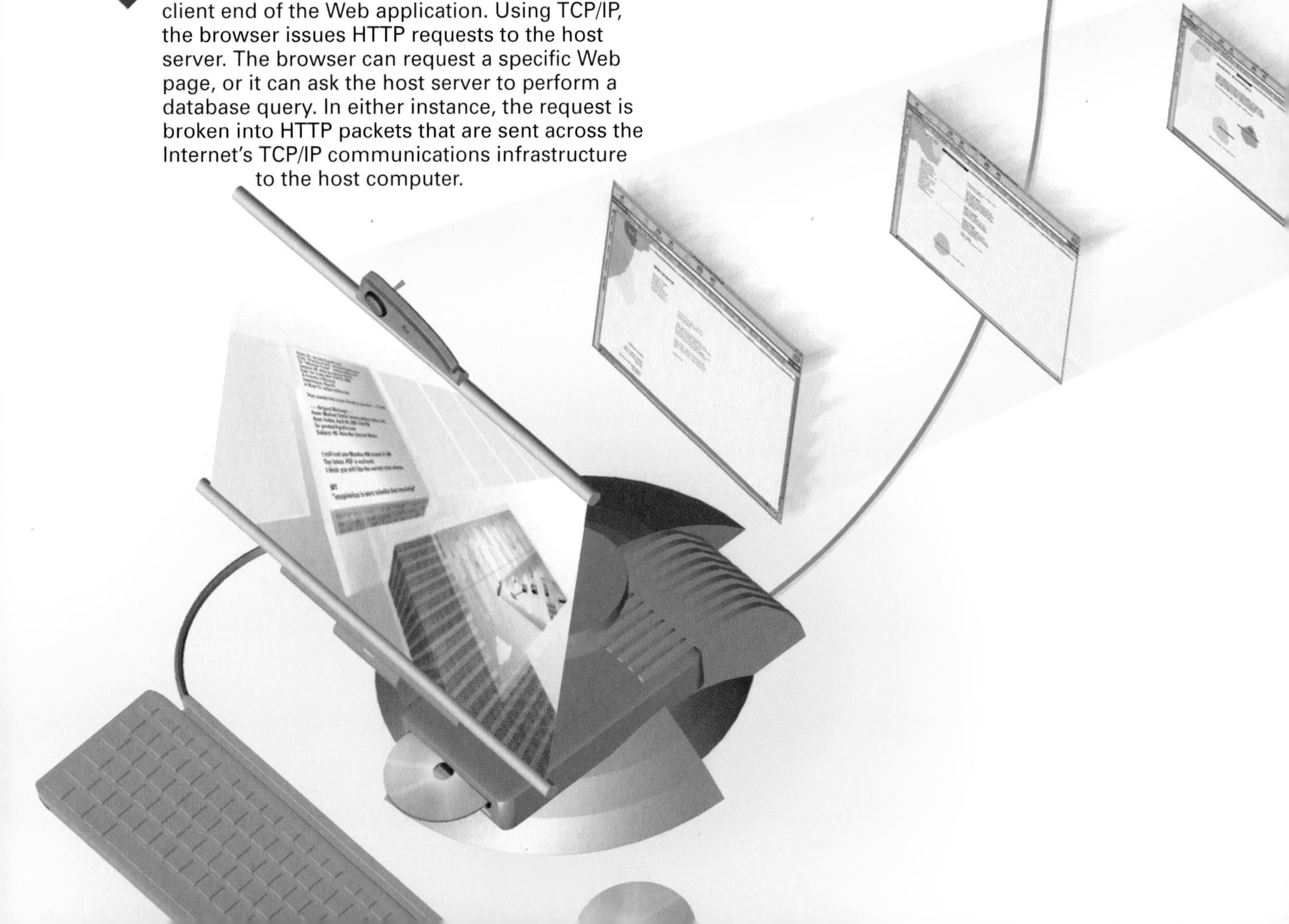

2 The host computer runs the server software that enables the host to separate the actual request from the packets and perform the asked-for services. This will involve either retrieving and sending back to the client PC the specified Web page or executing a database search and sending back to the client the result in the form of a Web page.

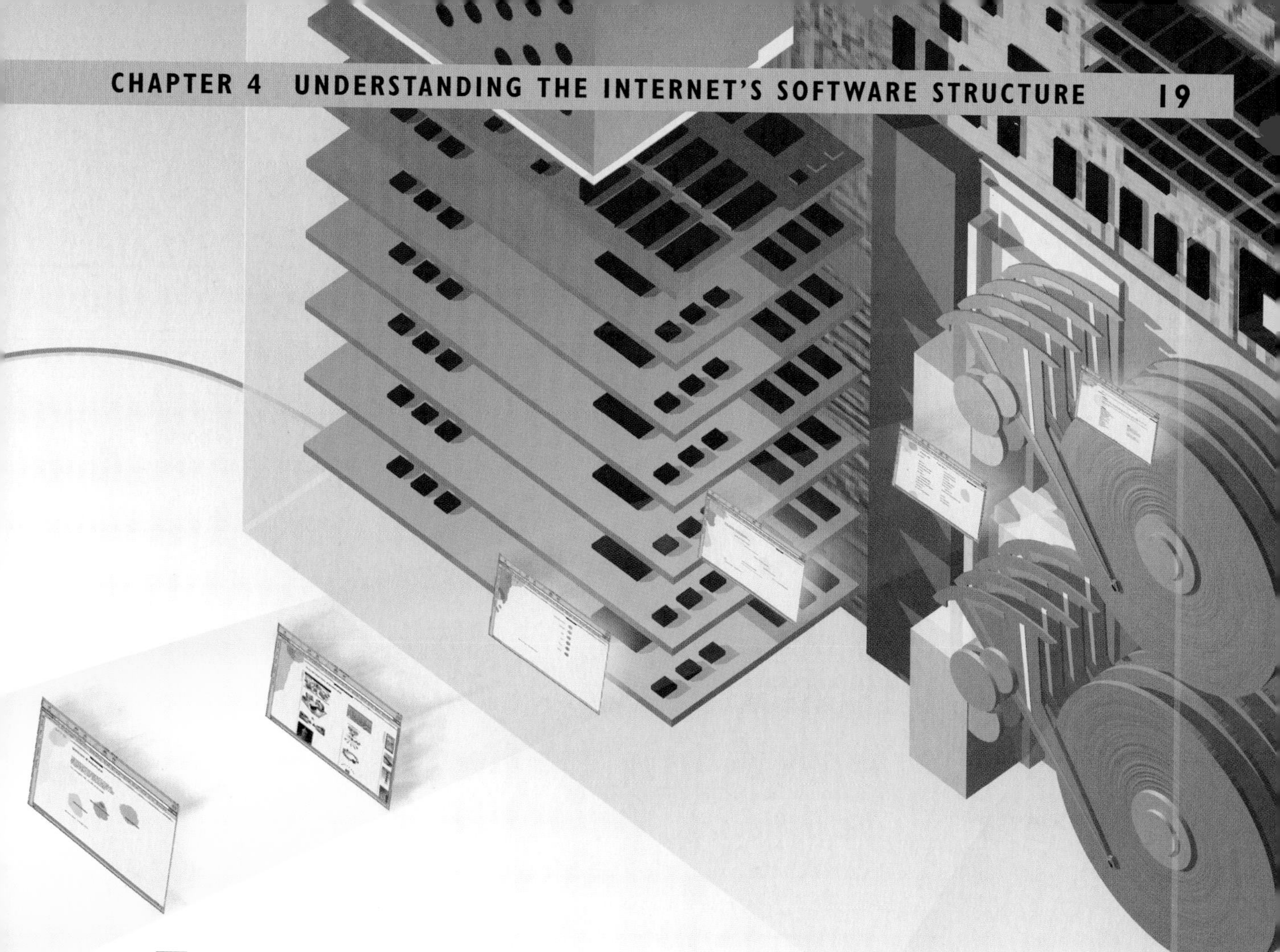

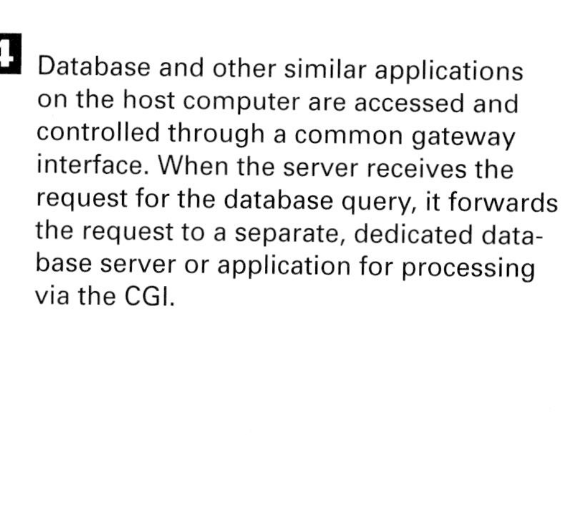

3 The host computer houses the Web site. Web server software enables the host to locate a requested page and return it to the client.

4 Database and other similar applications on the host computer are accessed and controlled through a common gateway interface. When the server receives the request for the database query, it forwards the request to a separate, dedicated database server or application for processing via the CGI.

CHAPTER

5

How Internet Addresses and Domains Work

THE heart of how the Internet works is the Domain Name System (DNS), the way in which computers can contact each other and do things such as exchange e-mail or display Web pages. When someone on the Internet wants to contact a location—for example, to visit a Web site—he types in an address, such as `www.metahouse.com`. (A specific location on the Internet is also referred to as a *uniform resource locator*, or *URL*.) The DNS translates the plain English address, `www.metahouse.com`, into series of numbers called an IP (for Internet Protocol) address. An IP address, such as `123.23.43.121`, marks the location of a computer on the Internet similar to the way a house number and street mark the location of where you live.

In this example, metahouse.com is called a *domain*. To work most efficiently, the Internet has been organized into a number of major domains. Major domains refer to the letters at the end of a plain English address, such as `.com`. A number of common domains are `.com` (commercial), `.edu` (education), `.gov` (government), `.mil` (military), `.net` (Internet service providers and networks—companies and groups concerned with the organization of the Internet), and `.org` (organization).

Domains are organized in a hierarchical manner, so that beneath major domains are many minor domains. As an example of how the DNS and domains work, look at NASA's SPACElink Internet address: `spacelink.nasa.gov`. The top domain is `.gov`, which stands for government. The domain just below that is `.nasa`, which is the NASA domain. Then, `spacelink` identifies the NASA computer that runs the SPACElink program. SPACElink's numeric IP address has changed through the years, but its Internet address has stayed the same.

Computers called *name servers* are responsible for keeping track of such changes and translating them between IP addresses and domain addresses. The Internet can't understand alphanumeric Internet addresses, such as `pgralla@ziffdavis.com`, so name servers translate those addresses into their proper numeric IP addresses, such as `163.52.128.72`. Name servers contain tables that match alphanumeric Internet addresses to numeric IP addresses.

When you connect your computer to the Internet, your computer needs to have an IP address to do common things, such as browsing the Web. Depending on how your computer is set up and your service provider operates, you might have a static address or a dynamic address. A *static* IP address never changes, so if you have one, you will have the same IP address every time you connect to the Internet. However, because the Internet has only a limited number of IP addresses, many ISPs use dynamic addresses. With a *dynamic* IP address, you are given a different IP address every time you connect. In this way, ISPs don't have to have an individual address for every subscriber. Instead, they can share their pool of addresses among all subscribers.

Understanding Internet Addresses and Domains

1 The Internet Protocol (IP) delivers mail based on the specific address of the recipient's e-mail server. This address is expressed as four numbers, separated by periods (called dots), such as 163.52.128.72. However, because it would be difficult to remember such complex addresses, you can instead use Internet addresses made up of words, letters, and numbers. Computers called domain name servers translate the alphabetical address into a numerical address, so e-mail can be sent to the proper location.

2 An Internet address is made up of two major parts separated by an @ (at) sign. The address can tell you a good deal of information about the person who owns the address. The first part of the address (to the left of the @ sign) is the username, which usually refers to the person who holds the Internet account and is often that person's login name or in some way identifies her. The second part of the address (to the right of the @ sign) contains the hostname (which can refer to a specific server on a network), followed by the Internet address, which together identify the specific computer on which the person has an Internet e-mail account.

3 When you send e-mail, it goes to a name server. To deliver the e-mail, the Internet must know the numeric IP address, such as 163.52.128.72. Name servers look up the alphabetical address and substitute the numeric IP address for it so the e-mail can be delivered properly.

4 The Domain Name System (DNS) divides the Internet into understandable groups, or domains. Note the portion of the domain section at the far right of the address. It identifies the largest domain names and type of organization where the person's address resides.

5 To the left of the largest domain is specific information about the organization, which tells routers to which network the e-mail should be sent. It can be a single Internet address, such as `nasa.gov`, or it can be a group of domains and subdomains, such as `spacelink.nasa.gov`.

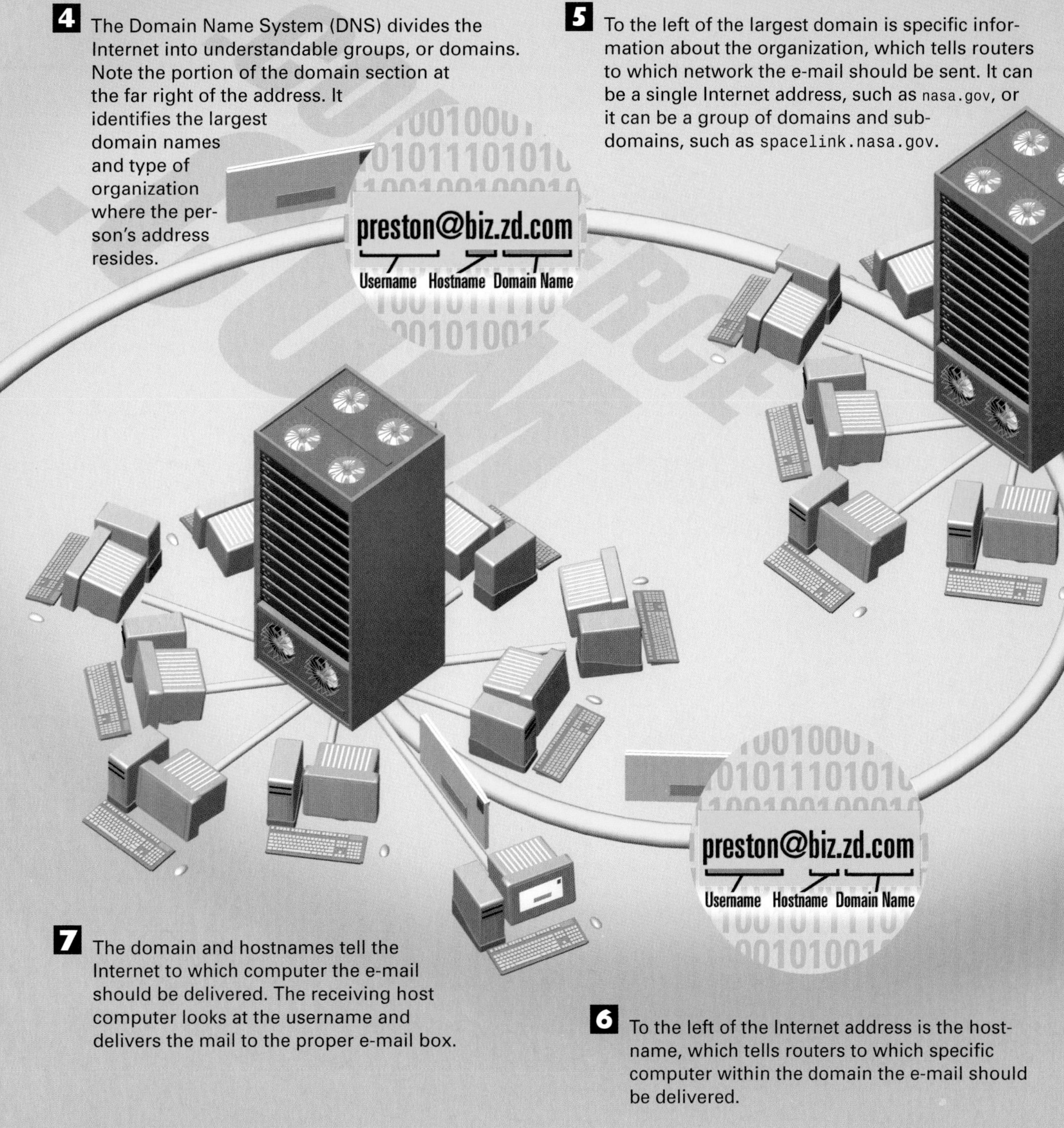

7 The domain and hostnames tell the Internet to which computer the e-mail should be delivered. The receiving host computer looks at the username and delivers the mail to the proper e-mail box.

6 To the left of the Internet address is the hostname, which tells routers to which specific computer within the domain the e-mail should be delivered.

How Domain Name System Servers Work

www.zdp.com

1 When a particular uniform resource locator (URL) needs to be contacted, the address with the URL must be matched to the true IP address. Your Web browser first goes to a local name server maintained by your ISP, online service, or company to get this information. If the IP address is a local one—on the same network as the one you are on—the name server can resolve the URL with the IP address. It will send the true IP address to your computer.

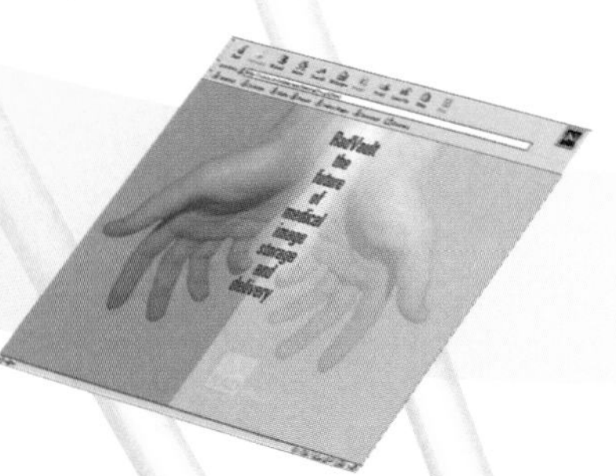

3 If the information you have requested isn't on a local network, the local name server might not have the address you're looking for. In that instance, the local name server must get the information from a name server on the Internet. The local name server contacts the root domain server. The root domain server tells the local server which primary name server and secondary name server have the information about the requested URL.

www.zdp.com

Yes www.zpd.com
123.333.29.8

InterNIC

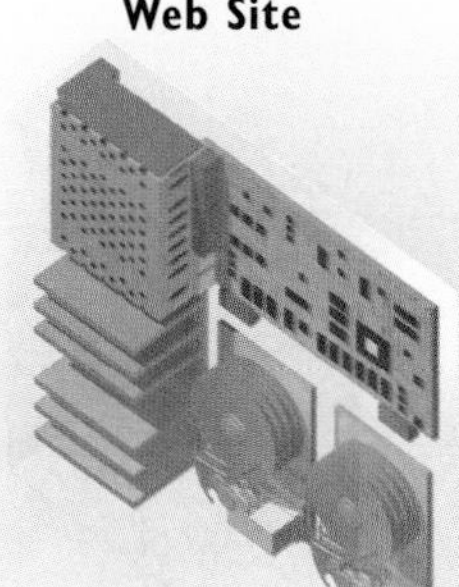

2 Your Web browser now has the true IP address of the place you're trying to locate. It uses that IP address and contacts the site. The site sends you the information you've requested.

www.zpd.com
123.333.29.8

4 The local name server now contacts the primary name server. If the information cannot be found in the primary name server, the local name server contacts the secondary name server. One of those name servers will have the proper information. It then passes the information back to the local name server.

Send it.

www.zpd.com
123.333.29.8

5 The local name server sends the information back to you. Your Web browser now uses the IP address to contact the proper site.

oot

How Static and Dynamic IP Addresses Work

1 When you connect to the Internet, your computer must be identified by a number called an IP address. IP addresses come in two varieties: static and dynamic. When you have a static IP address, your computer keeps the same IP address every time you connect to the Internet. Dynamic addresses, on the other hand, are assigned every time you connect to the Internet.

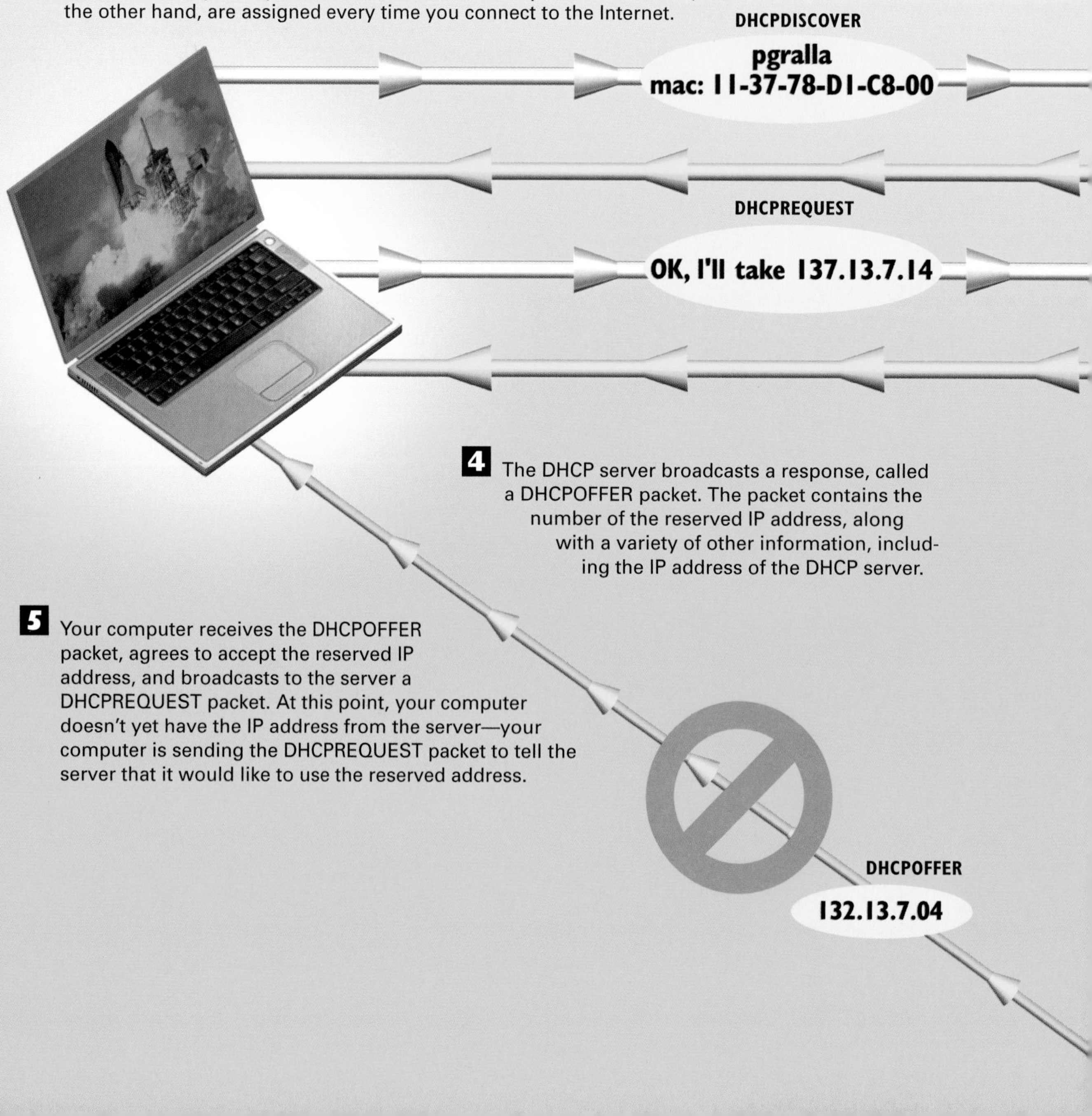

4 The DHCP server broadcasts a response, called a DHCPOFFER packet. The packet contains the number of the reserved IP address, along with a variety of other information, including the IP address of the DHCP server.

5 Your computer receives the DHCPOFFER packet, agrees to accept the reserved IP address, and broadcasts to the server a DHCPREQUEST packet. At this point, your computer doesn't yet have the IP address from the server—your computer is sending the DHCPREQUEST packet to tell the server that it would like to use the reserved address.

2 To obtain a dynamic IP address, your computer sends a broadcast message called a DHCPDISCOVER packet to the network or ISP to which you're connecting. This packet contains identifying information about your computer, including its name.

3 The packet is broadcast throughout the receiving network. It's received by a DHCP server. The DHCP server checks the list of available IP addresses and reserves it for your computer so that no other computer can be assigned that address.

6 If there is more than one DHCP server on the network, your computer might receive more than one DHCPOFFER packet, offering an IP address. Your computer chooses just one DHCPOFFER packet and discards and ignores the rest.

7 The accepted DHCPREQUEST packet is received by the DCHP server. In response, the server sends a DHCPPACK packet to your computer. This packet gives your computer a "lease" on the IP address. Your computer now has full use of that IP address and can use the Internet.

8 The DHCP server and all other DHCP servers note that your computer is using the IP address, so the address is no longer available to be used by other computers. When you disconnect from the Internet, your IP address is released, and DHCP servers can use the address for someone else who connects to the network needing an IP address.

CHAPTER 6 How Routers Work

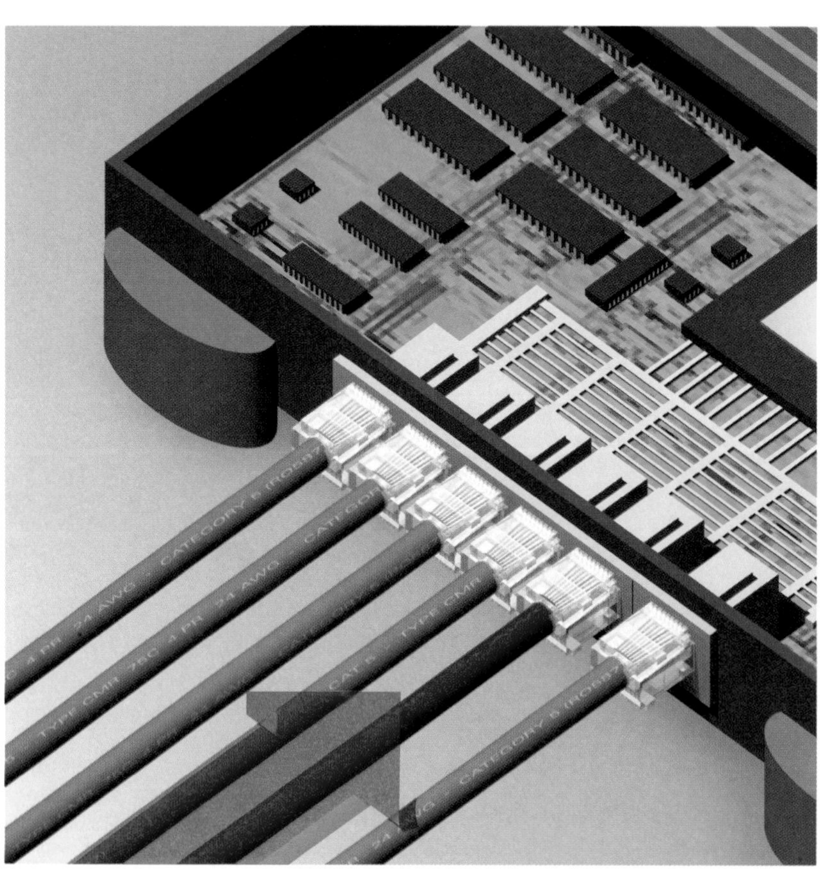

ROUTERS are the traffic cops of the Internet. They ensure all data gets sent to where it's supposed to go via the most efficient route. When you sit down at your computer and connect to the Internet and send or receive data, generally that information first must go through at least one router—and often more than one router—before it reaches its final destination.

Routers open the IP packets of data to read the destination address, calculate the best route, and then send the packet toward its final destination. If the destination is on the same network as the sending computer, such as within a corporation, the router sends the packet directly to the destination computer. If the packet is going to a destination outside the local network, the router instead sends the packet to another router closer to the destination. That router in turn sends the packet to a yet-closer router, and so on, until the packet reaches its final destination.

When routers determine the next router to receive packets, factors such as traffic congestion and the number of *hops* (routers or gateways on any given path) come into play. The IP packet carries a segment that holds the maximum hop counts it can travel, and a router will not use a path that would exceed that predefined number of hops.

Routers have two or more physical ports: receiving (input) ports and sending (output) ports. When an input port receives a packet, a software routine called a *routing process* is run. This process looks inside the header information in the IP packet and finds the address to which the data is being sent. It then compares this address against an internal database called a *routing table*. The routing table has detailed information about the ports to which packets with various IP addresses should be sent. Based on what it finds in the routing table, the router sends the packet to a specific output port. This output port then sends the data to the next router or to the destination itself.

There are two kinds of routing tables: a *static* routing table and a *dynamic* routing table. The static table is simpler and specifies specific paths for packets to use to get to their final destinations. The dynamic table allows packets to have multiple routes to get to their destinations.

At times, packets are sent to a router's input port faster than the port can process them. When this happens, the packets are sent to a special holding area called an *input queue*, which is an area of RAM on the router. That specific input queue is associated with a specific input port. A router can have more than one input queue. Each input port processes packets from the queue in the order in which they were received, so the first packets sent in are the first to get processed and sent out.

If the number of packets received exceeds the capacity of the queue (called the *length* of the queue), packets might be lost. When this occurs, the TCP protocol on the sending and receiving computers have the packets re-sent.

How Routers Send Data to Their Destination

1 A router has input ports for receiving IP packets and output ports for sending those packets toward their destinations. When a packet comes to an input port, the router examines the packet header and checks the destination in it against a routing table—a database that tells the router how to send packets to various destinations.

Dynamic Routing Table

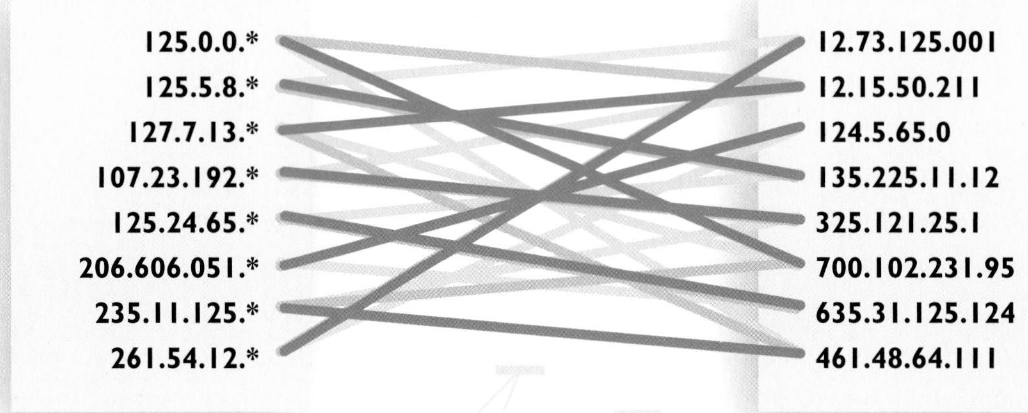

5 Dynamic routing is more useful than static routing. It allows a packet to have multiple routes to reach its final destination. Dynamic routing also enables routers to change the way they route information based on the amount of network traffic on some paths and routers. In dynamic routing, the routing table is called a *dynamic* routing table and changes as network conditions change. The tables are built dynamically by routing protocols, constantly changing according to network traffic and conditions.

6 Two broad types of routing protocols exist: interior and exterior. *Interior* routing protocols are typically used only on routers in a company's intranet, or internal network. These interior routing protocols route traffic bound only for inside the intranet. A common interior routing protocol is the Routing Information Protocol (RIP). *Exterior* protocols typically are used for routers located on the Internet. A common exterior routing protocol is the Exterior Gateway Protocol (EGP).

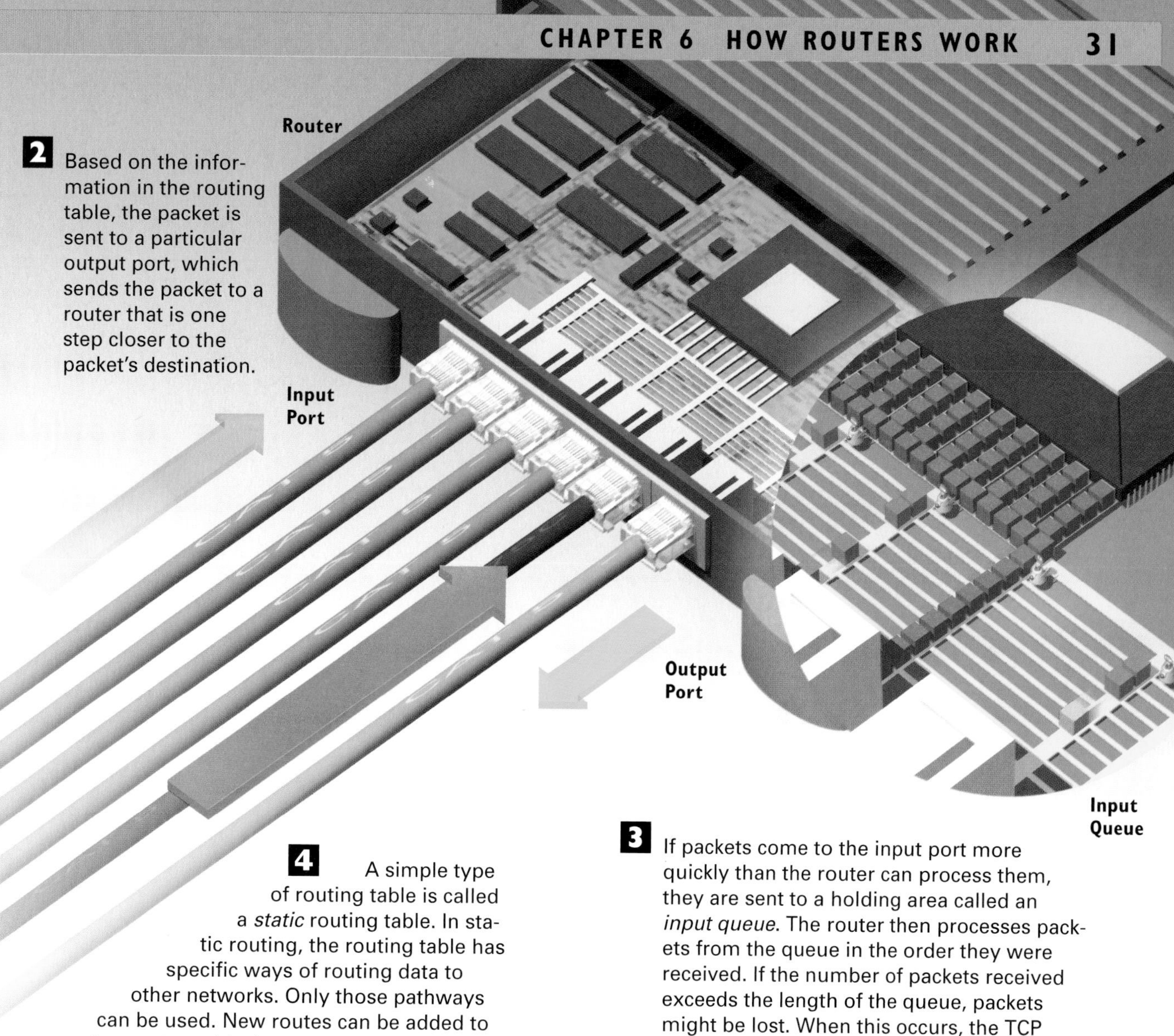

2 Based on the information in the routing table, the packet is sent to a particular output port, which sends the packet to a router that is one step closer to the packet's destination.

3 If packets come to the input port more quickly than the router can process them, they are sent to a holding area called an *input queue*. The router then processes packets from the queue in the order they were received. If the number of packets received exceeds the length of the queue, packets might be lost. When this occurs, the TCP protocol on the sending and receiving computers will have the packets re-sent.

4 A simple type of routing table is called a *static* routing table. In static routing, the routing table has specific ways of routing data to other networks. Only those pathways can be used. New routes can be added to the routing table; however, static routing can't adjust routes as network traffic changes so it isn't an optimal alternative for many routers.

Static Routing Table

125.0.0.*	12.73.125.001
125.5.8.*	12.15.50.211
127.7.13.*	124.5.65.0
107.23.192.*	135.225.11.12
125.24.65.*	325.121.25.1
206.606.051.*	700.102.231.95
235.11.125.*	635.31.125.124
261.54.12.*	461.48.64.111

CHAPTER

7

How Internet File Types Work

THERE are millions of files on the Internet that show you pictures, let you hear music and sounds, let you to watch videos, and let you read articles and run software on your computer. Some of these files can be used on any computer, regardless of whether it is a Macintosh or an IBM-compatible PC. Graphics files, sound files, and video files, for example, can be played on many kinds of computers, as long as those computers have the special software (often called players or plug-ins) required to view, run, or listen to them. Some files require special hardware to work. Other files, such as software programs you download, can run on only a PC or a Mac, or they might require extra memory.

In general, on the Internet you'll find two types of files: ASCII (American Standard Code for Information Interchange) files and binary files. ASCII files are often referred to as *plain text files*, *text files*, or *ASCII text files*. They contain ASCII codes—computer codes that represent the characters on your screen, such as the uppercase letter A or a dollar sign ($). ASCII text files contain nothing but this simple character data. Binary files, by way of contrast, contain special coded data and can be run or read only by specific computers and software.

Interestingly enough, though, Web pages are in fact made up of plain text files. Although they are plain text files, they use special codes in the Hypertext Markup Language (HTML) that instructs your browser how to display the Web page.

In contrast to plain ASCII text files, some files contain sophisticated formatting and graphical information. Files that adhere to the PostScript page description language are of this type. These files are in fact ASCII files, but they contain information about how to format and print the file. HTML pages—the pages that make up the World Wide Web—are also plain ASCII text files that contain coding information that tells your browser how to display a Web page.

Other types of files contain formatting and graphical information, such as those in the Adobe Acrobat PDF format, but many of them are binary files instead of ASCII files. To view or print these types of files, you need special software readers. In the case of PostScript files, you generally need a special PostScript printer that can print files in that language. Files of this type can be viewed in two ways—either when you're online and connected to the Internet or when you're offline and not connected. To view the files when online, you use special plug-in modules or helper applications for your Web browser. To view the files when offline, you need software readers, although in some instances you also can use the same online viewers as well.

Sound, visual image, animation, and video files are also common on the Internet. These files are all binary files, which are made up of bits represented by 0s and 1s. Files of this type are often large, requiring special software readers, players, and sometimes hardware to play and read them. Some of these files can be played or viewed only on a specific type of computer, whereas others can be played or viewed on many types of computers if you have the right software. Some of the files, such as streaming audio files and streaming video files, can be viewed while you're online, connected to the Internet. Other types of files must be viewed with special readers or players when you're offline.

Understanding Internet File Types

File types Many types of files exist on the Internet. Each file has information contained in its header. The header is simply the first line of a file or a specific number of bytes at the beginning of a file. Software that can read or view the files looks into the header of a file to distinguish which kind of file it is and then processes the file accordingly.

Graphics formats You'll find graphics files in many formats, including GIF, JPEG, PNG, PCX, and TIF. GIF and JPEG are two of the most common graphics formats. They enable the exchange of image files between different types of computers and can be downloaded to your computer quickly. A GIF reader or JPEG reader can read binary GIF and JPEG files and display them on your computer. Graphics programs typically read both types of files. A GIF file contains the binary data that displays an image when viewed with the proper reader. Your computer's video card takes information from the reader and displays it on your computer's monitor. Both GIF and JPEG are commonly used graphics formats in Web pages. Your Web browser has the capability to read and display these files on Web pages without needing any added software.

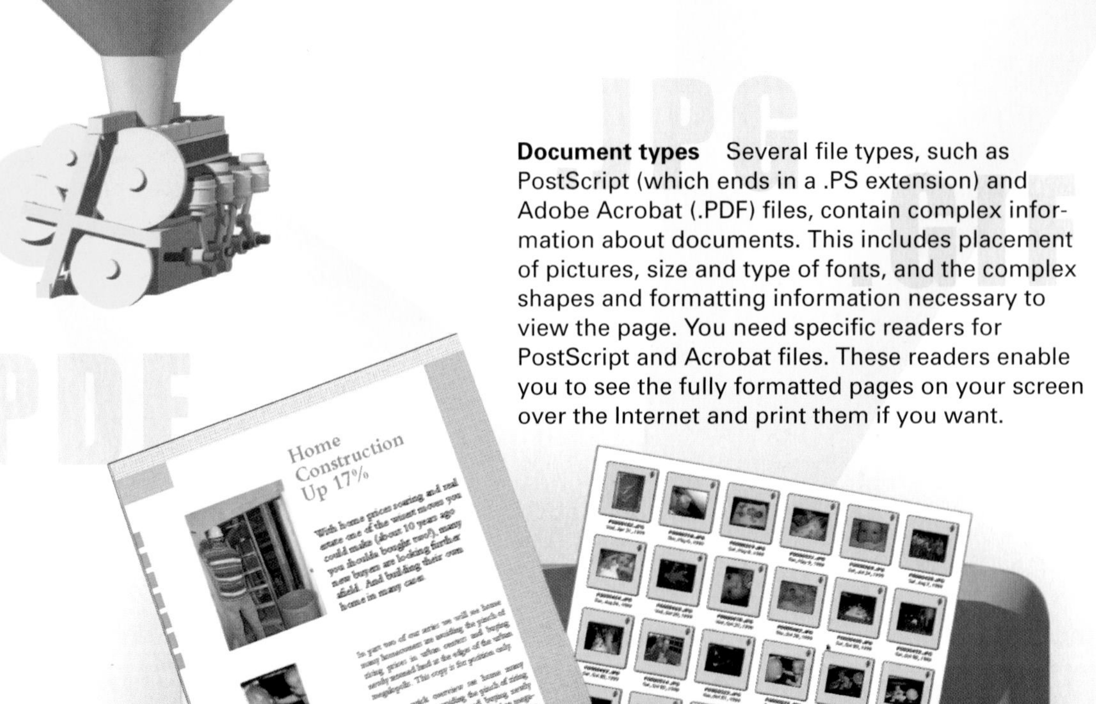

Document types Several file types, such as PostScript (which ends in a .PS extension) and Adobe Acrobat (.PDF) files, contain complex information about documents. This includes placement of pictures, size and type of fonts, and the complex shapes and formatting information necessary to view the page. You need specific readers for PostScript and Acrobat files. These readers enable you to see the fully formatted pages on your screen over the Internet and print them if you want.

Multimedia files You'll find many kinds of binary multimedia files on the Internet that let you listen to or play sounds, music, and videos. Windows sound files (which end in a .WAV extension) and Macintosh sound files are common types of files that you can download to your computer and play with a sound player, as are music files in the MP3 format (these end in an .mp3 extension). Other sound files, such as those created by Real Audio software, enable you to listen to the sounds while the file is downloading. This process is called *streaming audio*. Windows .AVI files are common animation files. Macintosh QuickTime and MPEG files (which end in an .MPG extension) are common video formats. Other animation files enable you to watch the video while the file is downloading. This process is called *streaming video*. You need special software to use all these types of files.

Downloadable software Many executable programs can be found on the Internet that you can download to your computer and use just like any other type of software. Because these software files can be large and take a long time to download, they often are compressed to make them download more quickly. After the file is on your computer, you uncompress it with special decompression software and run it like any other program. Frequently, PC software has been compressed with PKZIP and has a .ZIP extension, whereas Macintosh software can be compressed with a variety of compression software. In general, PC files can be used only with PCs, whereas Macintosh files can be used only with Macintoshes.

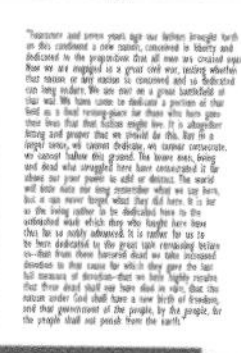

Plain text You'll find many ASCII text files on the Internet that you can read with a text editor or word processor. These can be articles, FAQs (frequently asked questions and their answers), or any other type of informational files.

When creating your own candles, make sure you have all your ingredients ready and at hand before beginning: it is impossible to undo some steps once you start.

You will need:

4 blocks of beeswax (12 to 16 oz)
1 block setting parafin

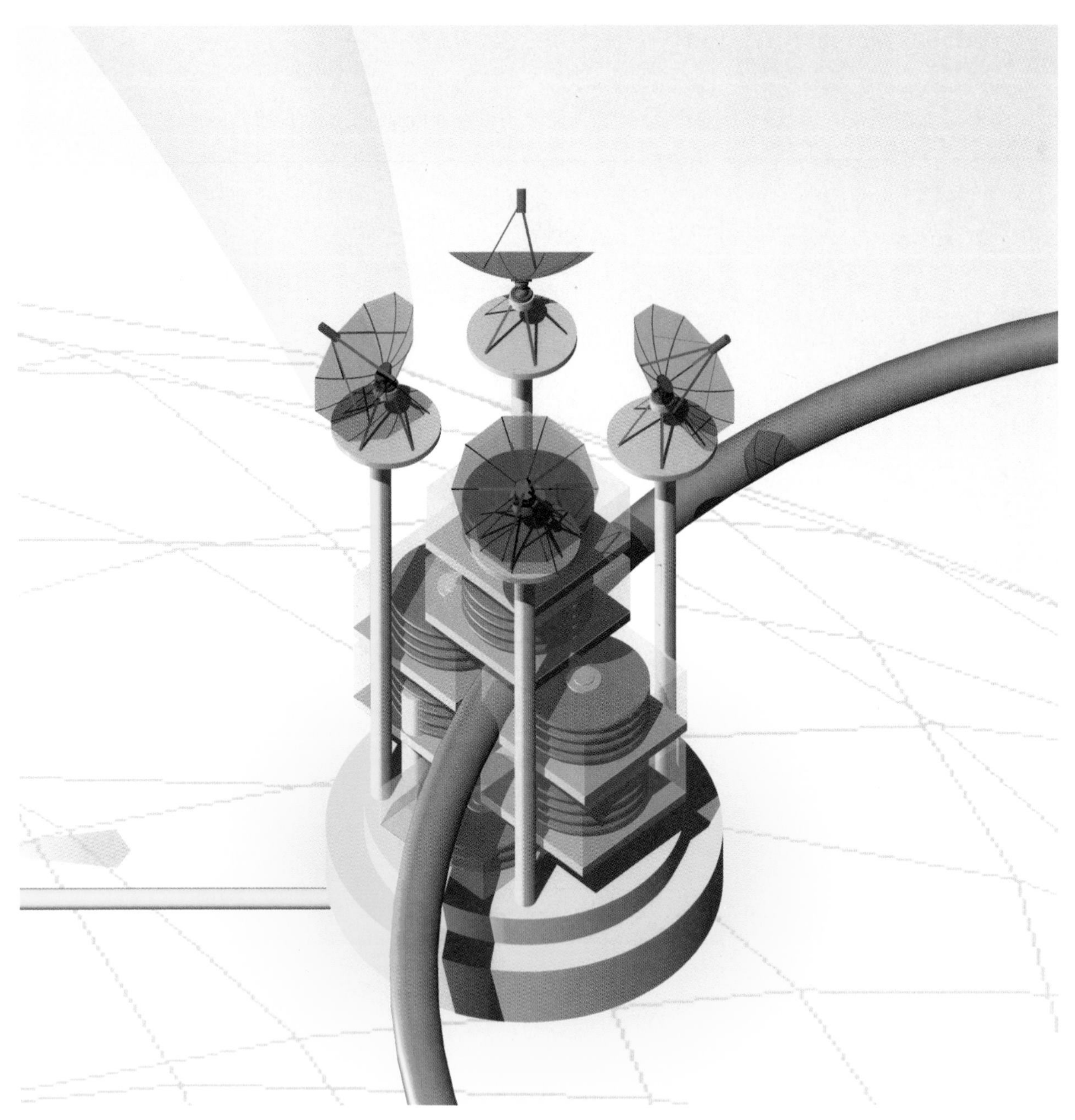

P A R T

CONNECTING TO THE INTERNET

YOU can connect to the Internet in many ways—and many more ways pop up practically every day. They range from simple telephone dial-in connections to high-speed cable and digital subscriber lines (DSL) to satellite connections, TV connections, connections at work and home via local area networks (LANs), and even connections via cellular telephones. This part of the book looks at the myriad ways people and computers gain access to the Internet.

One general rule is true about Internet connections: the faster, the better. People want the fastest connection possible because many pictures, sounds, and videos are available on the Internet. Today, the two most common ways you can connect to the Internet are through a corporate or university LAN or over telephone lines. Direct connections over LANs are generally faster than telephone-line connections—although a connection via new telephone technology called DSL is changing that.

This section looks at all the ways computers can connect to the Internet. Chapter 8, "How Computers Connect to the Internet," provides an overview of the types of Internet connections that are possible. Not only will you examine various kinds of network connections and phone-line connections, but you'll also look at newer, high-speed connections that are becoming available; cable modems and DSL are two such examples.

Chapter 9, "How a Modem Works," examines how the most common way of accessing the Internet works—via a modem. You'll get an inside look at what happens when you dial the phone and make your connection.

Chapter 10, "How Internet/Television Connections Work," looks at what might become one of the primary ways many of us connect to the Internet—through some type of television connection. This chapter looks at using cable television as a way to get onto the Internet and how to use an ordinary television to browse the Internet. It also peers inside a newer technology—Internet-enhanced TV—that adds interactivity to your television set and makes your Internet experience more compelling.

Chapter 11, "How the Digital Subscriber Line (DSL) Works," looks at one of the newer high-speed ways to connect to the Internet—DSLs. These connections enable you to use existing telephone lines to hook up to the Internet at extremely high speeds. To use it, you need a special DSL modem, and your phone company needs special modems as well.

A related technology to DSL is Integrated Services Digital Network (ISDN). ISDN enables you to connect at high speeds to the Internet via normal, existing telephone lines. Not every area in the country has ISDN yet. In some areas it can be an expensive option, but in others it is reasonably priced. It requires a special modem, as well. Chapter 12, "How ISDN Works," explains that technology.

Online services, such as CompuServe, America Online, and The Microsoft Network, at one time competed directly with the Internet for users. Now, instead of competing, those online services have joined the Internet club and provide Internet access to users. An online service can be one of the simplest ways to get an Internet connection. When you connect to an online service, you also get a full connection to the Internet. Chapter 13, "How You Connect to the Internet from Online Services," examines how online services make that Internet connection.

Chapter 14, "How Wireless and Palmtop Connections Work," looks at two of the newest ways to access the Internet. With a satellite connection, you can connect to the Internet using a satellite dish, much like the one now used for satellite TV. In fact, the dish can do double-duty—giving you both satellite TV and a high-speed Internet connection. The connection isn't yet as high speed as a cable modem or DSL connection, but it is much faster than a traditional modem. This chapter also looks at how palmtop devices, such as the Palm from 3COM can access the Web using a traditional modem. More exciting is the ability to connect to the Internet without any wires at all—using cellular technology. So this chapter discusses how cellular palmtops and cellular telephones can get onto the Web. Those connections aren't as high a speed as other ways of getting onto the Internet yet, but one day, they might be faster than normal phone-line connections.

Chapter 15, "How Home Networks Work," examines a fast-growing phenomena—using networks at home to connect to the Internet. Many homes have more than one computer, and users want to be able to share a high-speed connection, such as a cable modem or DSL modem. Home networks make that possible. And increasingly, other devices at home will be connected to the Internet, not just PCs—and this chapter looks at them as well.

As you'll see in this part of the book, connecting to the Internet will become increasingly easy—and at increasingly higher speeds. Not only will you be able to do things more quickly on the Internet, but you will also be able to access entirely new services that will contain video, animation, and other high-bandwidth content. And as satellite connections and the capability to connect wirelessly via small handheld devices and cellular telephones come online, the Internet will eventually be able to be accessed anywhere—not just when you happen to be sitting in front of a PC.

CHAPTER

8

How Computers Connect to the Internet

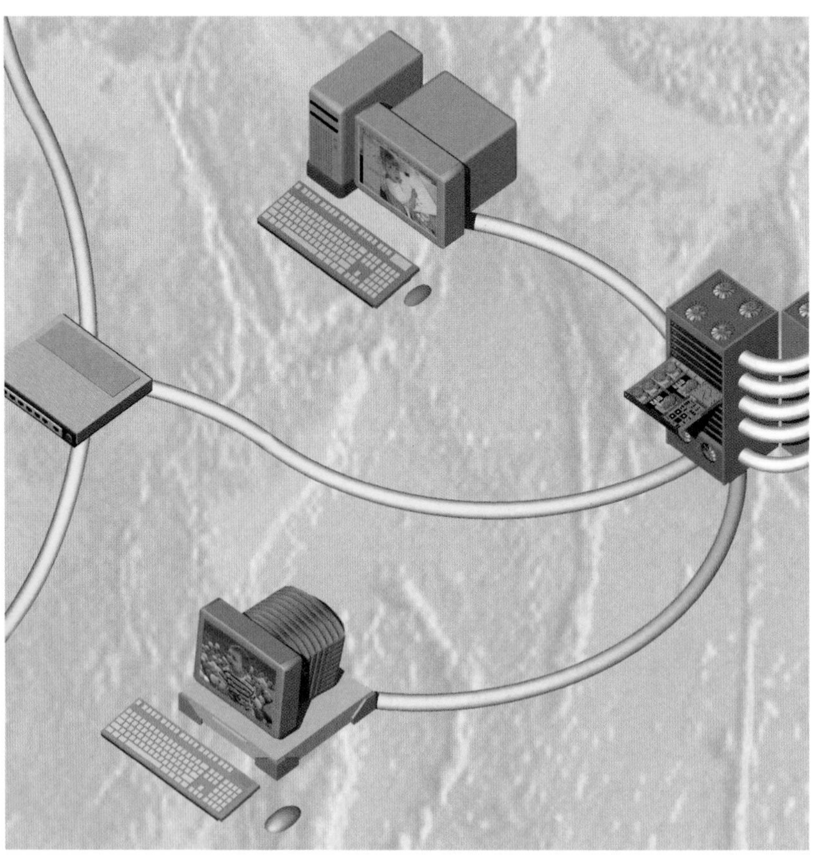

THERE are many different ways your computer can connect to the Internet, ranging from dial-in connections to LANs (local area networks) to wireless connections to connections over cable TV wires. If you are connected to a LAN or campus network at your business or school, you already might be connected to the Internet. If the LAN or campus network you're on is connected to the Internet via a router or bridge, your computer is also connected to the Internet. Often, this offers higher-speed access than when you dial in to the Internet. If you're not connected to the Internet via a network, a variety of options are available for accessing the Internet, and many more appear every day.

The most common option is to find an Internet service provider (ISP) or online service, such as America Online, that lets you dial in to it with your home computer. When you connect this way, you establish a Serial Line Internet Protocol (SLIP) or Point-to-Point Protocol (PPP) connection. (SLIP is an older type of connection, and its use is fading away.) When you dial in to the Internet with these protocols, your computer becomes a part of the Internet and you can access all of its vast resources, such as browsing the Web. PPP is newer and more stable than SLIP and can retransmit packets if they get garbled, which is a fairly common situation you'll encounter when sending information over telephone lines.

Many ways are available to connect to the Internet in addition to dialing in using a traditional modem. Increasingly popular are special cable modems that enable you to use your coaxial television cable to access the Internet. Your local cable company—or another private company—might be able to provide you with this service. Speeds can be up to 100 times faster than regular modem speeds.

Also increasingly popular are Digital Subscriber Line (DSL) connections to the Internet. Similar to cable modems, these offer very high-speed connections to the Internet. The price of DSL will vary according to the connection speed.

Integrated Services Digital Network (ISDN) lines provide relatively high-speed connections to the Internet. Typically, these speeds range from 64Kbps to 128Kbps. You'll need a special ISDN modem and an ISP that offers ISDN access.

The newest type of connections are wireless connections. You can now send and receive e-mail, browse the Web, and access other Internet resources via a cellular phone or cellular palmtop connection. These connections are slower than normal dial-in connections but are becoming popular because you can access the Internet with them wherever you are.

If you're not yet connected and are interested in finding out more about an Internet connection, start at your local college or library. Contact an ISP and find out about their fees. Many national and local service providers exist, so shop around. Lastly, the major online services now include Internet access, so you easily can use them to connect to the Net.

Connecting Your Computer to the Internet

Dumb terminal A terminal that is connected to a mainframe, minicomputer, or other kind of large computer. This type of connection often can be found in libraries or universities, although those institutions are moving toward offering fuller Internet access than dumb terminals provide.

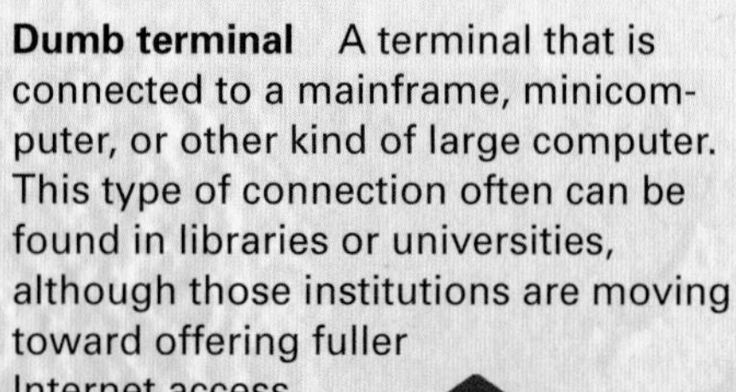

PPP (Point-to-Point Protocol) Similar to SLIP, this is a full Internet connection over telephone lines via modem. It is more reliable than SLIP because it double-checks to ensure that Internet packets arrive intact. It resends any damaged packets.

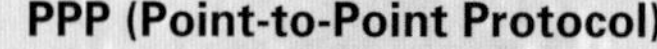

SLIP (Serial Line Internet Protocol) A full Internet connection over telephone lines that sends Internet packets via 9,600bps modems or better.

Direct connection LANs or large computers such as mainframes can be directly connected to the Internet. When a LAN is connected to the Internet, all the computers on the network can have full access to the Net. This type of access is common inside corporations.

Cable modem The Internet can be accessed over some cable TV systems using the coaxial cable that carries television signals. A special cable modem must be used. Cable modems might be capable of sending and receiving data at speeds 20–100 times as fast as conventional modems.

WebTV You also can access the Internet directly on your television set by using a set-top box that dials in to the Internet and then displays Web pages on your television set. The best known of these is the WebTV set-top box and network. You also can use satellite dishes that are similar to television satellite dishes to access the Internet.

Online services All the major online services allow you to tap the full power of the Internet. No special setup is required. When you dial in to the online service, you can use the Internet's resources, including browsing the World Wide Web.

Wireless access Cellular telephones and palmtops can send and receive e-mail and browse the Web. They do this at lower speeds than regular dial-in modems, but the connections are available all the time.

DSL and ISDN lines Special digital telephone connections, called DSL, can be used to connect to the Internet at very high speeds. ISDN lines offer a lower-speed connection—usually from 64Kbps to 128Kbps—but they're still faster than dial-in speeds. ISDN modems must be used with ISDN lines, and DSL modems are required for DSL connections.

CHAPTER 9 How a Modem Works

MOST people connect to the Internet in the most old-fashioned of ways—using a modem. Modems enable your computer to send information to, and receive information from, other computers. In doing so, modems enable you to do things such as hook up to the Internet, browse the World Wide Web, and send and receive e-mail.

Typically, when you use your modem to connect to the Internet, you dial in to an Internet service provider (ISP), for example America Online. When you dial in to and connect to your ISP, you're in fact connecting to a modem attached to a larger computer called a *server*. ISPs typically have banks of hundreds or thousands of modems that accept dial-ins from subscribers trying to connect. If you've ever tried to dial in and been unable to connect (and to be frank about it, who hasn't?), the modems might all be busy, or the receiving computer might be handling too many simultaneous calls.

Modems are controlled by your computer and communications software by a set of command called the *AT command set* (also known as the Hayes command set, named after one of the original modem manufacturers, Hayes). It's a language that instructs the modem on what to do at various points during a communications session, such as opening up a line and sending out tones that the telephone system can understand.

Two types of modems exist—external modems and internal modems. *External* modems are connected to your computer via a serial port, whereas internal modems are attached directly to the computer's motherboard. Typically, external modems cost more, not because they're better, but because they're more expensive to manufacture. External modems need to be put inside a case of some sort and often have lights on them. But however they're attached, they work very much the same.

The lights on an external modem are not there just to look pretty—they have specific purposes. From looking at whether lights are on or off, or are steady or flickering, for example, you'll be able to see things such as when your modem takes control of the phone line, when it has made a connection, when it is sending and receiving data, and whether it's connected at the highest speed possible.

In the modem's earliest days, they could transfer data at only a very slow rate—300 bits per second. Today's modems typically are rated at a much higher speed, 56 kilobits per second. Generally, though, when you dial in to the Internet using your computer, you won't connect at 56 kilobits per second and will usually come in at a lower speed. Things such as line noise force modems to connect at lower speeds, so that data isn't lost during the call. And even in perfect conditions, you can't connect at higher than about 53 kilobits per second.

Increasingly, people use much higher-speed devices, such as cable modems and DSL modems, to connect to the Internet. (Even though these devices are called modems, they aren't true modems and use a different technology to connect to the Internet.) But still, for the foreseeable future the majority of people will continue to connect to the Internet the old-fashioned way—over telephone lines, using a modem.

How a Modem Makes Its Connection

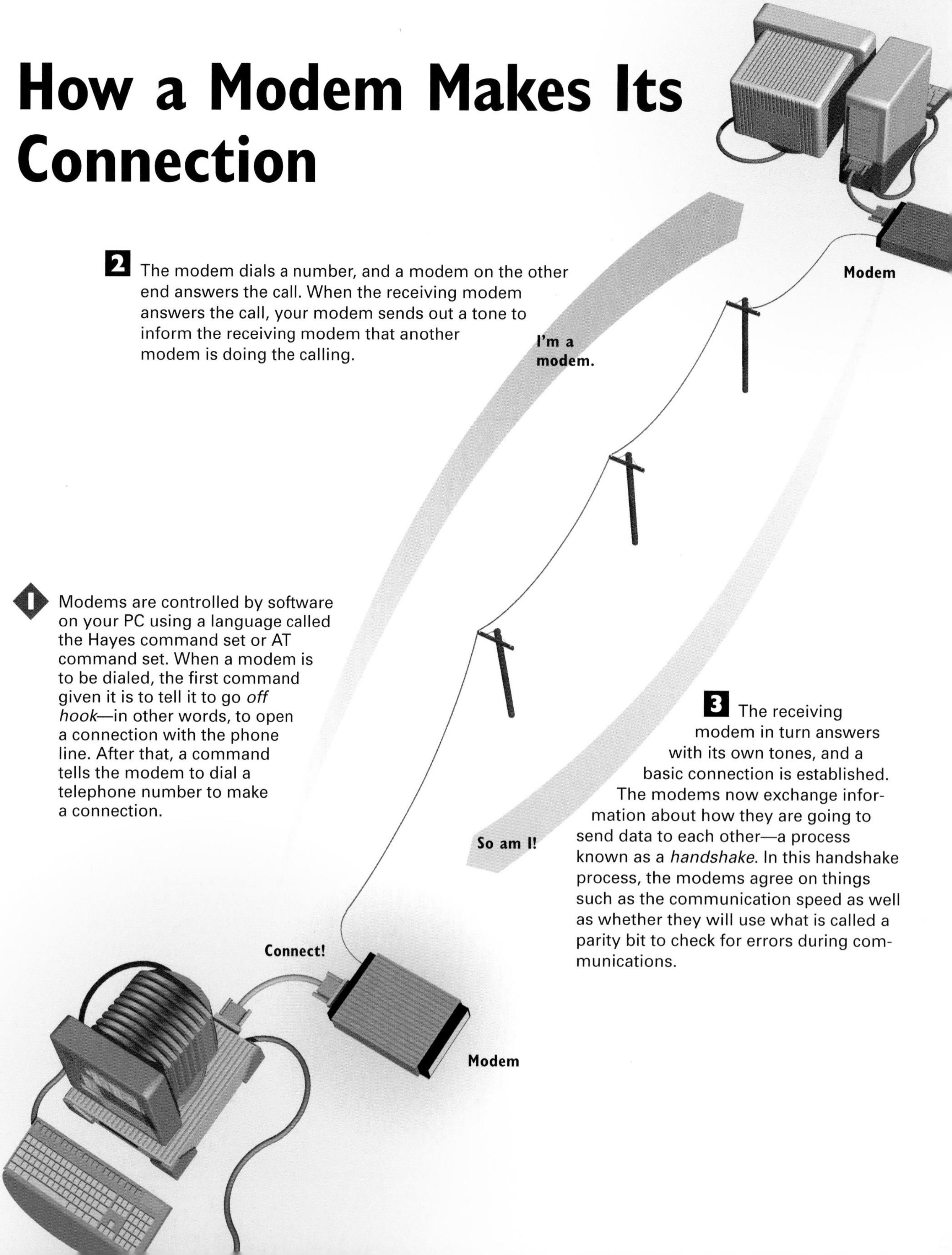

1 Modems are controlled by software on your PC using a language called the Hayes command set or AT command set. When a modem is to be dialed, the first command given it is to tell it to go *off hook*—in other words, to open a connection with the phone line. After that, a command tells the modem to dial a telephone number to make a connection.

2 The modem dials a number, and a modem on the other end answers the call. When the receiving modem answers the call, your modem sends out a tone to inform the receiving modem that another modem is doing the calling.

3 The receiving modem in turn answers with its own tones, and a basic connection is established. The modems now exchange information about how they are going to send data to each other—a process known as a *handshake*. In this handshake process, the modems agree on things such as the communication speed as well as whether they will use what is called a parity bit to check for errors during communications.

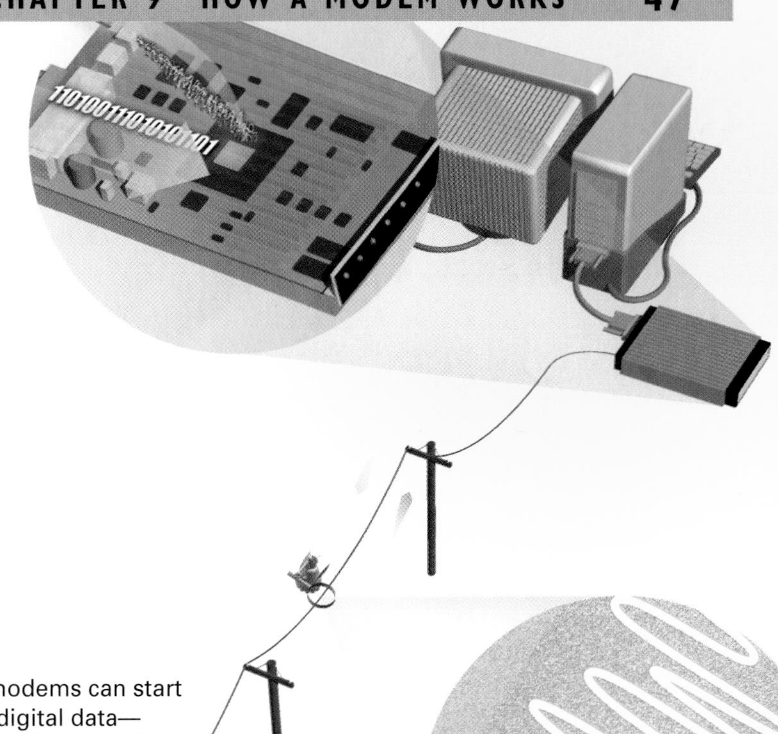

6 The analog signals reach the receiving modem where they are changed by the receiving modem—demodulated—from analog data back to digital data and sent into the computer via the serial port. This modulating and demodulating of data is what gives the modem its name: MOdulating/DEModulating.

4 Now that the connection is established, the modems can start exchanging data. Your computer works with digital data—binary bits of information that are either on or off. Your PC sends this binary data to be communicated to the modem.

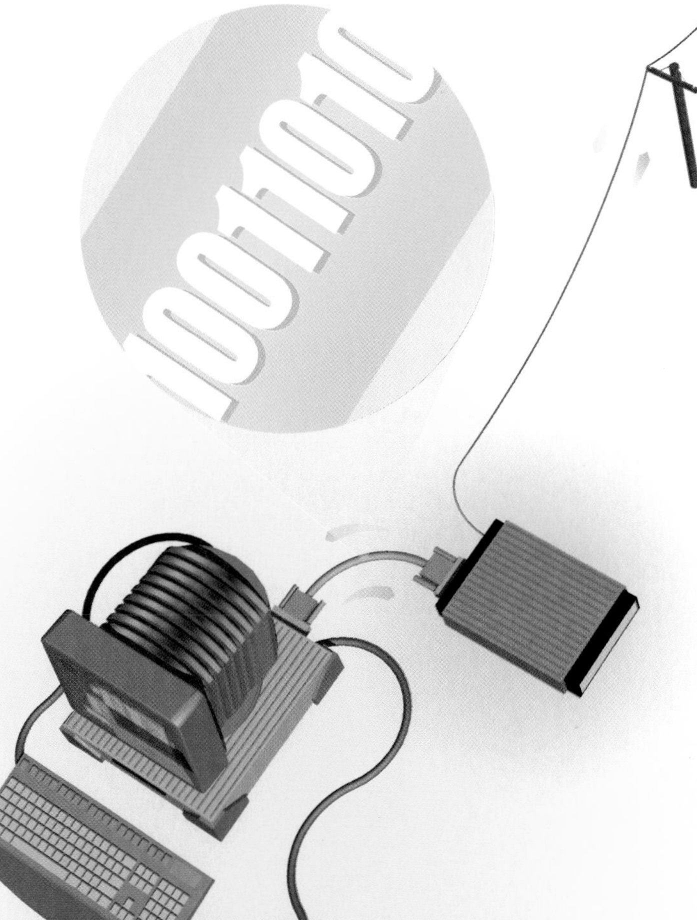

5 The telephone system, unlike a computer, works with analog information—streams of continuous electric current that vary in frequency and strength. The digital data in your computer must be changed to analog information so it can be sent via the telephone system. The modem takes the digital information and changes it—modulates it—into analog signals. The information travels along the telephone system as analog data.

CHAPTER

10

How Internet/ Television Connections Work

WHEN people first began talking about the "information superhighway" several years ago, it wasn't the Internet they were talking about. Instead, it was television—and specifically cable television—that they believed would change the way we lived and worked. There were visions of 500 TV channels, "interactive television," shopping from home, and customized news available whenever you wanted it. This information superhighway was going to hook us all together electronically so we could more easily communicate and get information, services, goods, and entertainment. It didn't pan out that way. Instead, the Internet has become an information superhighway that can do almost everything people imagined could be done by using cable TV.

How much longer the Internet will be the sole driving force behind the information superhighway remains to be seen. Every day, TV and the Internet are drawing closer to each other. The Internet is gaining more TV-like qualities, such as the capability to play videos and music, and even the capability to broadcast live video feeds. Television technology is also developing to be capable of using the Internet to add interactivity to the television experience.

In fact, television and the Internet are already merging. Soon you'll be able to watch a sporting event and simultaneously chat with others while you're watching—all on the same screen. Furthermore, when a batter comes up to bat during a baseball game, you'll be able to use the Net to get detailed statistics about the batter, and even past videos and highlights of his career.

Television and the Internet have already begun to merge in a very real way, primarily through cable modems, TVs that connect to the Net (enabling you to browse the Net through your TV set, such as with WebTV), and interactive TV (which uses the Internet to deliver information to people on their TV screens).

Cable modems offer extremely high-speed access to the Internet. They enable you to access the Net using the existing coaxial TV cable that comes into your house. Cable modems can receive data at up to 1.5 million bits per second and can send data at up to 300,000bps—far faster than normal modems and ISDN lines. They offer T1-like speeds, but at a fraction of the cost of T1 lines. They can deliver these high speeds because they are sent through high-capacity cable lines. Because Internet data and the normal cable signal coexist on the same lines, you can access the Net and watch TV simultaneously. The illustration in this chapter describes how MediaOne provides cable modem access to its customers.

A different technology enables you to browse the Web using your television set. A *set-top box* connects your TV to the Net via a modem, takes the signal from the modems, and sends it to the TV. A remote control–like device enables you to browse the Web while watching TV at the same time. Interactive TV goes a step further and uses a set-top box to enable interactivity with your PC, using Internet technologies. At this point, no single standard exists for how Internet-enhanced TV works, nor even an agreement on which features such a service should have. The illustration in this chapter shows some of the common ways that such a service will work.

How Cable Modems Work

1. The coaxial cable—sometimes called a *broadband wire*—that comes into a home from a pole is divided into two connections by a splitter inside the home. One part of the wire goes to the normal set-top box that provides cable TV access. The other part of the wire goes to a cable modem, sometimes called a *broadband modem*.

2. The cable modem attaches to an ethernet network card inside the computer. The network card is configured the same as any other network card on a computer that is attached to the Internet and has a network address.

3. The signals for sending and receiving data to and from the Internet travel through the coaxial cable, through the cable modem, and into your computer through the network card. The coaxial cable carries television and computer signals simultaneously. The computer signals travel on a 6MHz channel within the broadband spectrum on the coaxial cable.

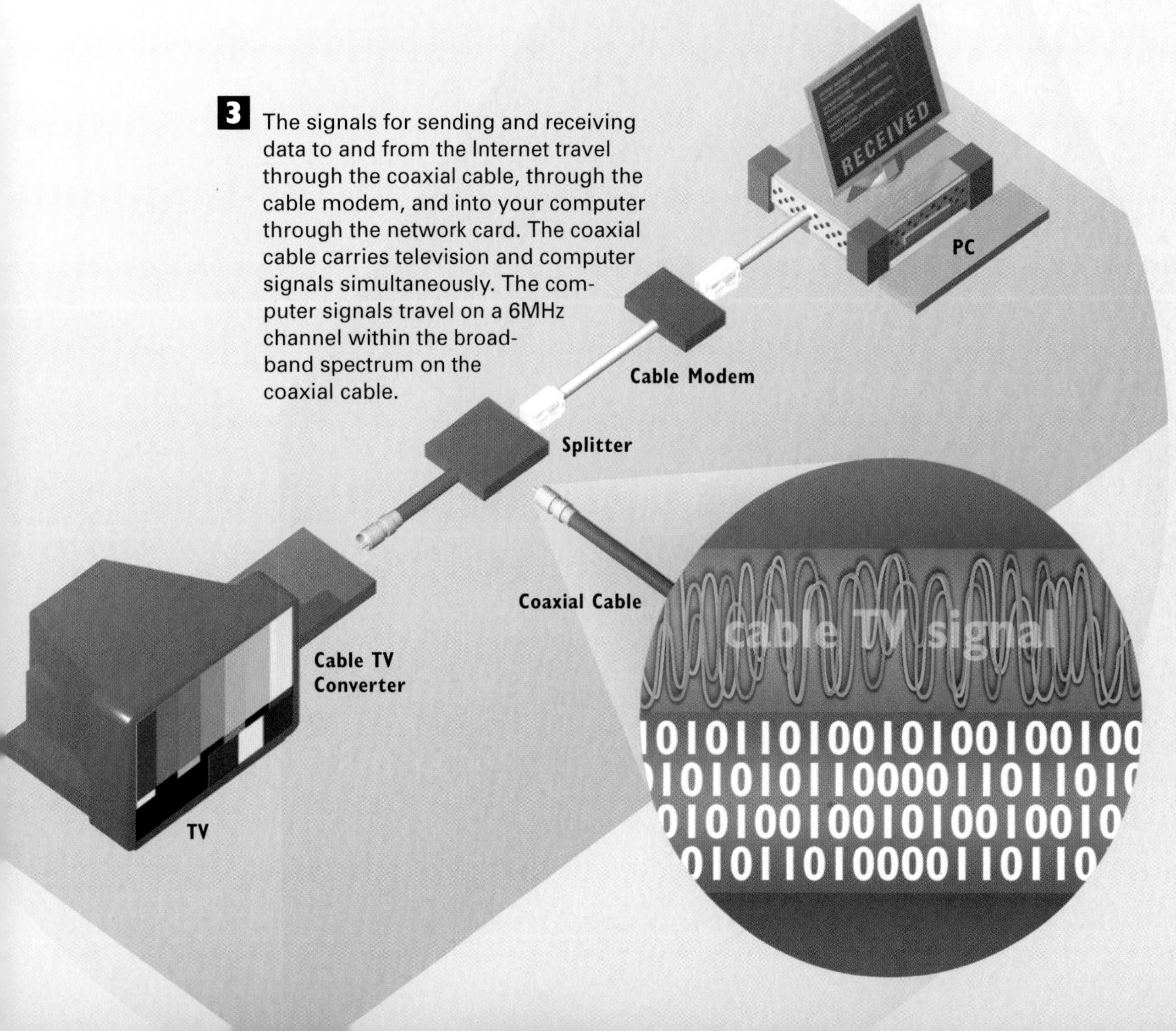

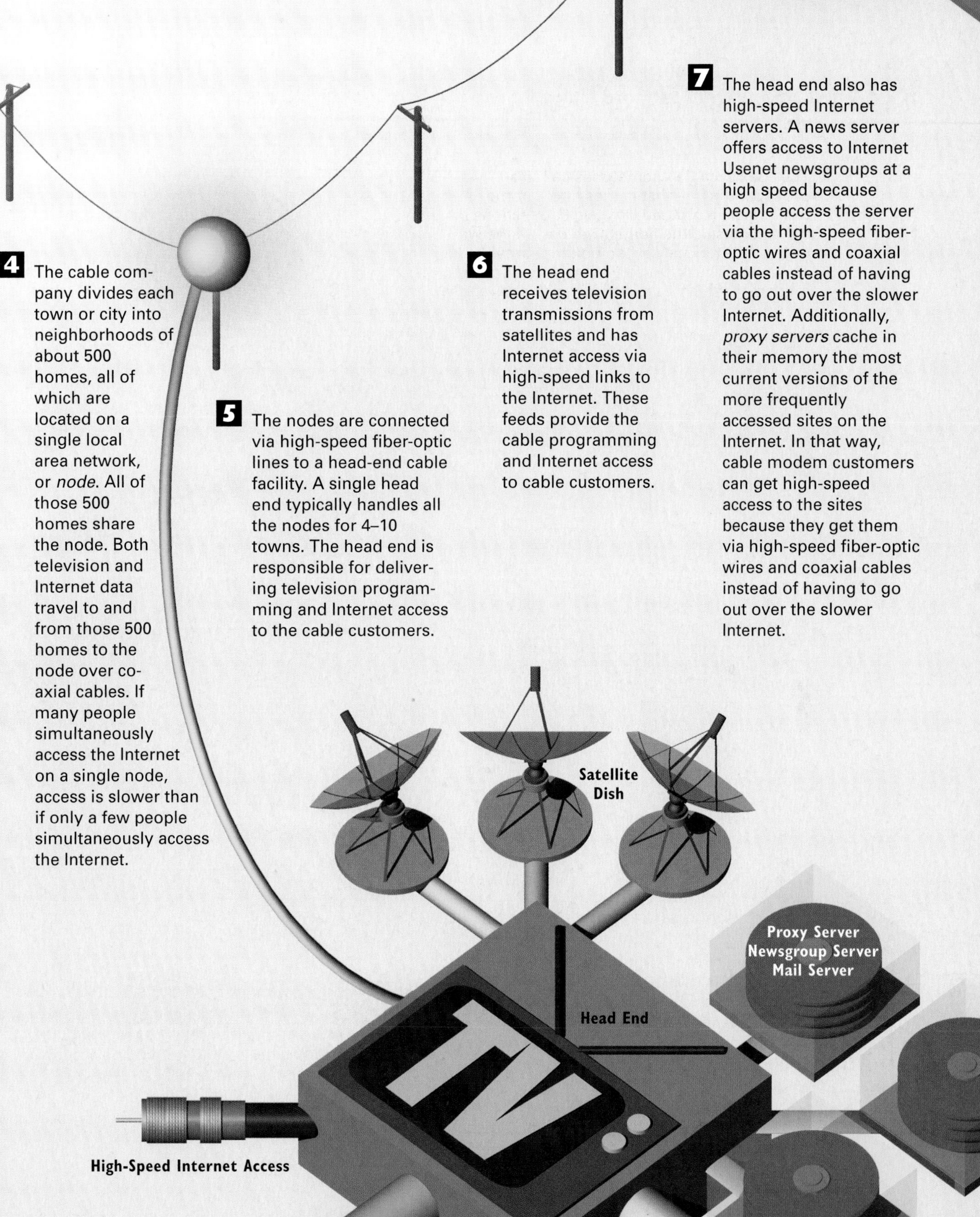

4 The cable company divides each town or city into neighborhoods of about 500 homes, all of which are located on a single local area network, or *node*. All of those 500 homes share the node. Both television and Internet data travel to and from those 500 homes to the node over coaxial cables. If many people simultaneously access the Internet on a single node, access is slower than if only a few people simultaneously access the Internet.

5 The nodes are connected via high-speed fiber-optic lines to a head-end cable facility. A single head end typically handles all the nodes for 4–10 towns. The head end is responsible for delivering television programming and Internet access to the cable customers.

6 The head end receives television transmissions from satellites and has Internet access via high-speed links to the Internet. These feeds provide the cable programming and Internet access to cable customers.

7 The head end also has high-speed Internet servers. A news server offers access to Internet Usenet newsgroups at a high speed because people access the server via the high-speed fiber-optic wires and coaxial cables instead of having to go out over the slower Internet. Additionally, *proxy servers* cache in their memory the most current versions of the more frequently accessed sites on the Internet. In that way, cable modem customers can get high-speed access to the sites because they get them via high-speed fiber-optic wires and coaxial cables instead of having to go out over the slower Internet.

How WebTV Works

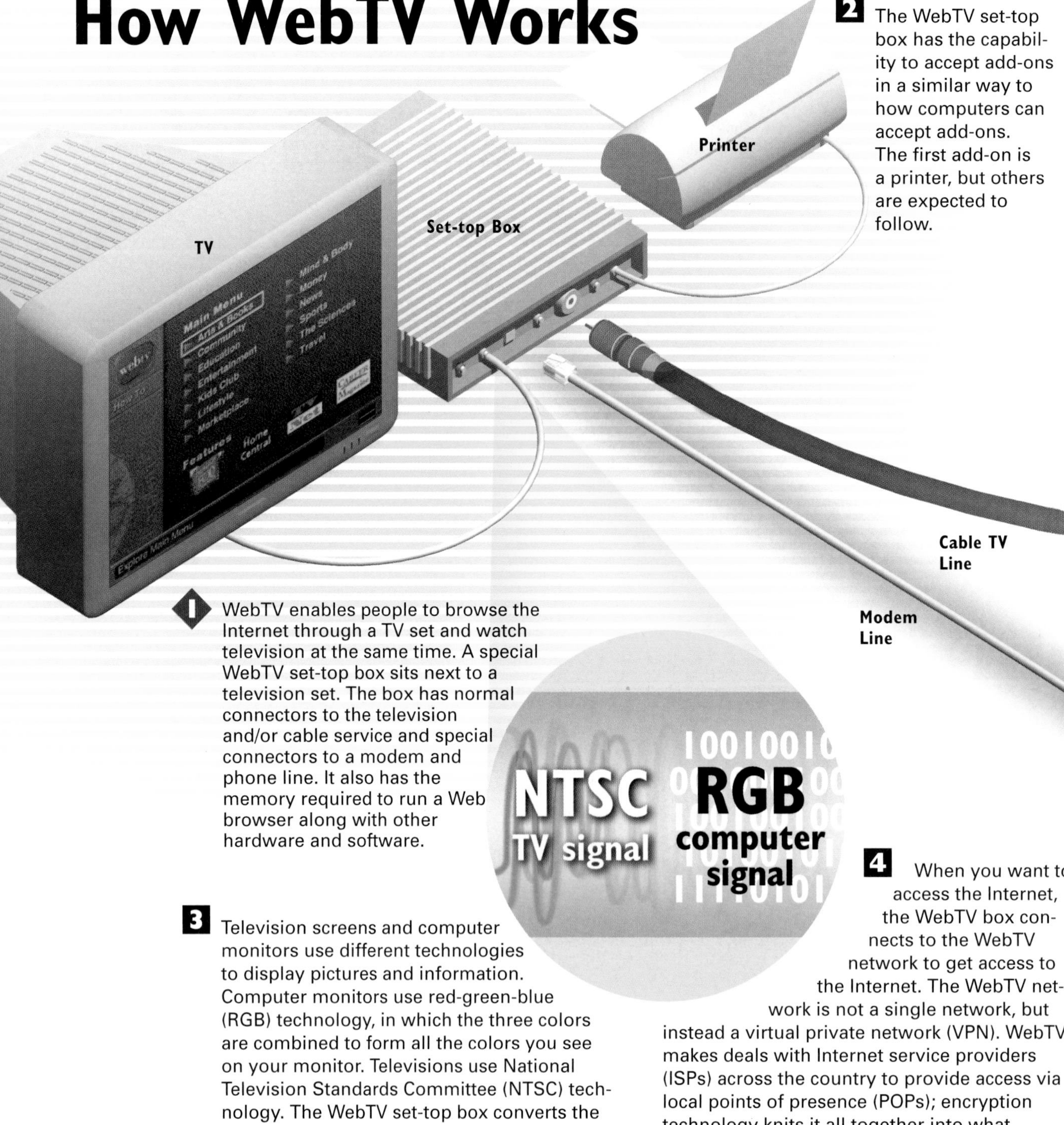

1 WebTV enables people to browse the Internet through a TV set and watch television at the same time. A special WebTV set-top box sits next to a television set. The box has normal connectors to the television and/or cable service and special connectors to a modem and phone line. It also has the memory required to run a Web browser along with other hardware and software.

2 The WebTV set-top box has the capability to accept add-ons in a similar way to how computers can accept add-ons. The first add-on is a printer, but others are expected to follow.

3 Television screens and computer monitors use different technologies to display pictures and information. Computer monitors use red-green-blue (RGB) technology, in which the three colors are combined to form all the colors you see on your monitor. Televisions use National Television Standards Committee (NTSC) technology. The WebTV set-top box converts the signal from the RGB of the Web to the NTSC used by televisions so the signal is as clear as possible.

4 When you want to access the Internet, the WebTV box connects to the WebTV network to get access to the Internet. The WebTV network is not a single network, but instead a virtual private network (VPN). WebTV makes deals with Internet service providers (ISPs) across the country to provide access via local points of presence (POPs); encryption technology knits it all together into what appears to be a single network. This VPN has many Web servers on it to provide capabilities such as e-mail and other services.

Remote

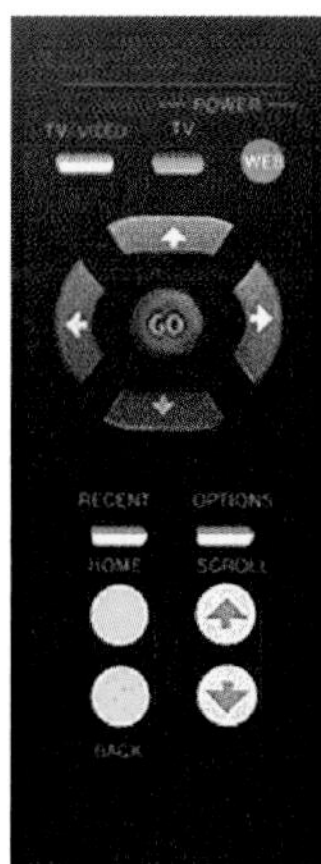

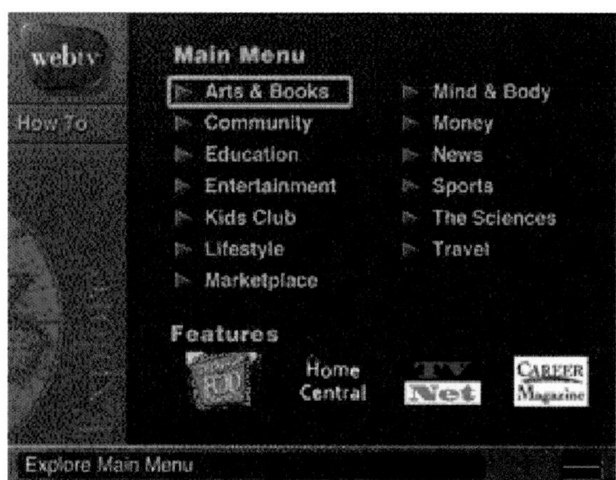

7 The ability to browse the Web is controlled by a simple remote control unit that enables people to scroll, move around the screen, and click objects. The control also allows people to browse the Web, watch television, or view the Web and television simultaneously.

6 WebTV uses its own proprietary Web browser, which adheres to HTML standards and can run common plug-ins. The browser is designed for optimal display on a television set. Some sites, such as *TV Guide*'s, have developed Web sites that make the best use of the browser.

5 To speed up access to Internet sites, the WebTV network runs a series of proxy servers. These proxy servers cache commonly accessed Web pages. When someone who uses WebTV goes to one of those pages, the page is delivered from the proxy server, which delivers the page at a higher speed than if it were accessed from the Internet.

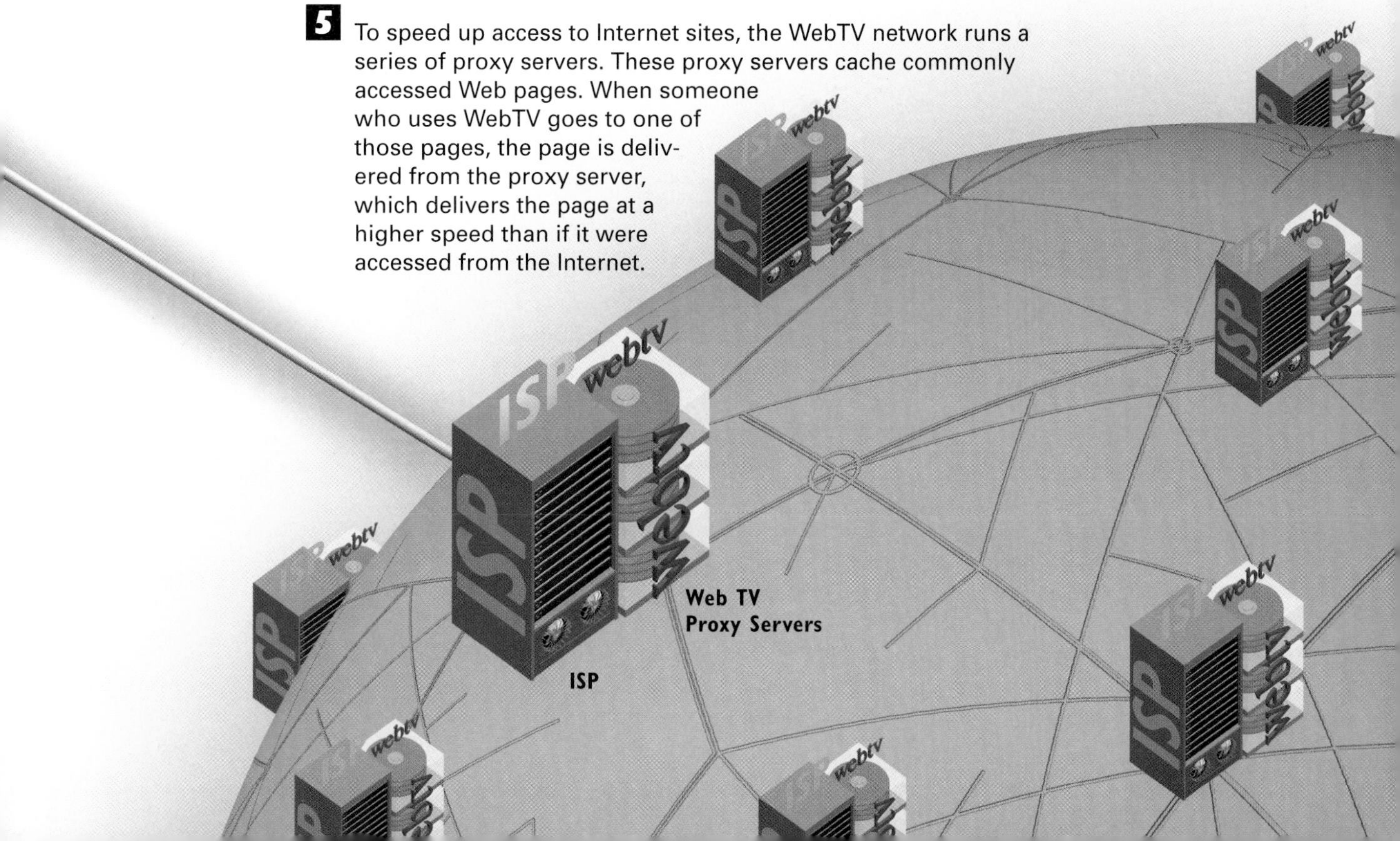

Web TV Proxy Servers

ISP

How Internet-Enhanced TV Works

1 To receive Internet-Enhanced TV, a television set requires a special set-top box that can receive and deliver the Internet-enhanced services. The set-top box has a powerful processor and a hard disk inside it.

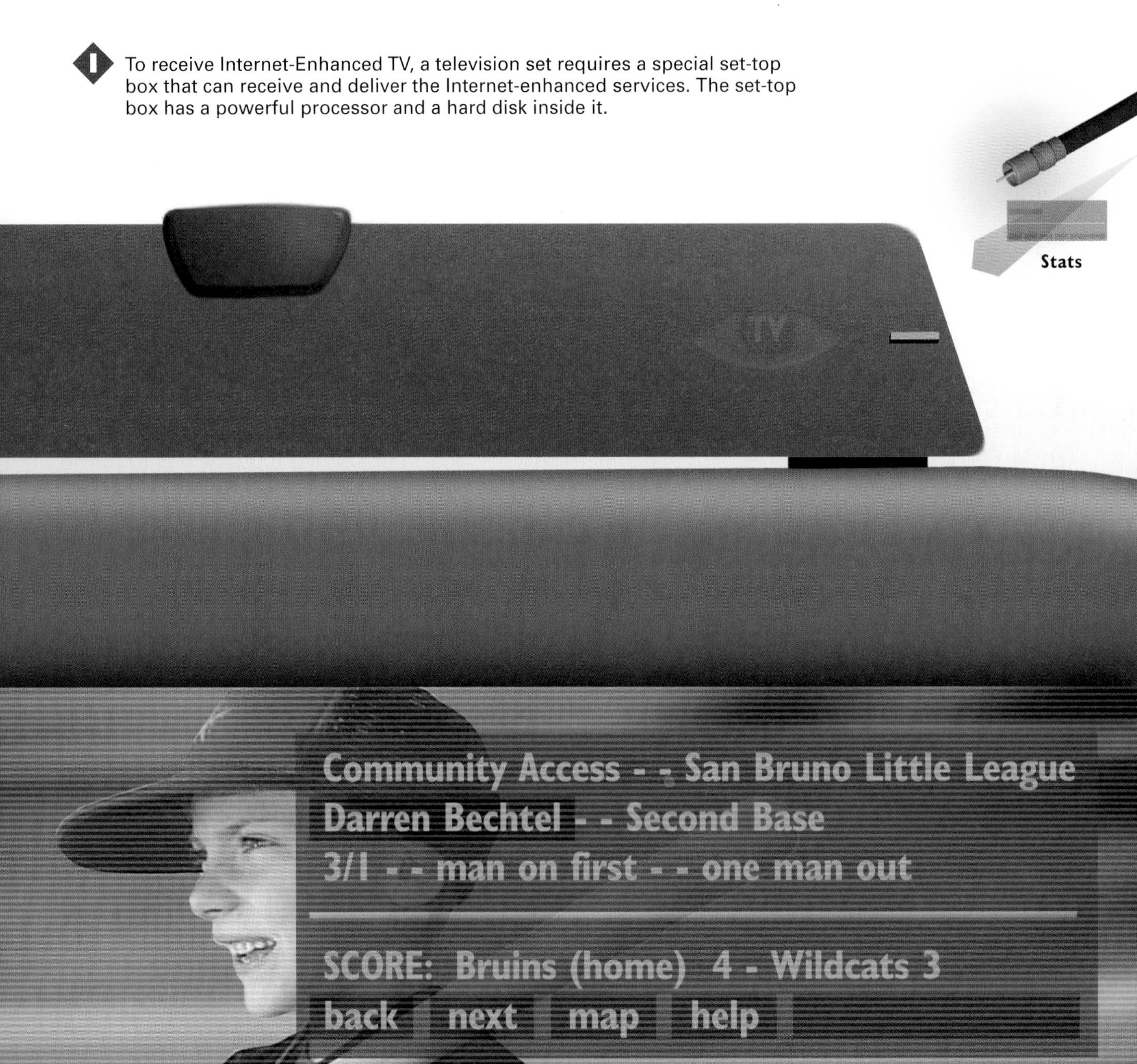

Get Stats

2 Internet-Enhanced TV can work with many types of TV connections, including cable connections, satellite connections, and possibly DSL connections as well. The connection, such as the cable connection shown here, connects directly to the set-top box, not to the television itself.

3 When a TV station sends out a broadcast, it contains the normal TV broadcast, as well as an accompanying enhanced TV signal with Internet-related information. Televisions without the special set-top box display the normal TV broadcast and ignore the enhanced signal.

4 The enhanced signal can contain a variety of extra information, and it can be sent using the Hypertext Markup Language (HTML), the language of the Web. For example, the information might contain statistics about a batter during a baseball broadcast, or it could allow viewers to answer questions during a quiz show. The HTML pages also could contain TV-specific HTML commands that can be displayed only via set-top boxes and not with Web browsers.

5 The set-top box interprets the HTML information and formats it in a way that can be displayed on a TV set. This information can be overlaid on the regular TV show so that you can see the information at the same time that you're watching the show.

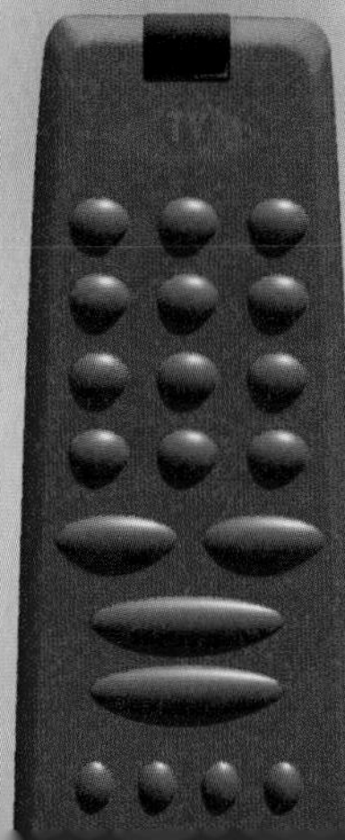

6 Using a special remote control, the viewer can interact with the television—for example, by clicking a link to get baseball statistics or taking a poll during a news show. When a viewer clicks n a link, the link behaves as does any other on a Web page and delivers the information or page requested. The request goes back through the set-top box, is sent to the Web page, and is then delivered via the enhanced TV signal back to the set-top box.

CHAPTER 11

How the Digital Subscriber Line (DSL) Works

IN recent years, a plethora of options could be found for gaining high-speed access to the Internet. Among the newest of those options is the Digital Subscriber Line (DSL), which might eventually prove to be one of the most popular. Several types of DSL technologies are available, but they all work on the same principles. They enable you to use your existing telephone lines to access the Internet at very high speeds—potentially as high as 55 million bits per second (Mbps)—using VDSL (Very high data rate DSL). However, that kind of extremely high-speed connection is used primarily by large corporations because of its cost. Home users will probably get speeds of 1.5Mbps, which is still very fast—about 50 times the speed of a 28,800-bits-per-second (bps) modem. Additionally, DSL technologies enable you to use the Internet at high speeds and simultaneously talk on your telephone, using the same, single phone line.

DSL technologies require that DSL modems be used on each end of the phone line. In fact, the term *DSL* doesn't really refer to a phone line because an ordinary, existing copper phone line can be used for DSL. Instead, it refers to the DSL modems themselves. More confusing still, DSL modems aren't really modems at all. Traditional modems modulate the digital signals from your computer into analog signals so that they can be sent over telephone lines, and then they demodulate them back into digital signals so your computer can understand them—hence the name modem, from the terms MOdulate/DEModulate. DSL modems don't convert signals from digital to analog. Instead, they transmit and receive all data as digital signals. Because the signals don't need to be converted and can be sent as digital data instead of analog data, data can be sent at much higher speeds than data sent via traditional modems.

DSL technology has one drawback; it requires that your house (and DSL modem) be located within a certain distance from the telephone company office and its DSL modem. In cities, this should not be a major problem, but it could be a problem in rural areas. The exact distance required depends on the type and speed of DSL service you use. Higher speeds require that you be closer to the phone company office.

Although many types of DSL service are available, probably the most popular for people at home is standard DSL service. With it, you can receive data at a faster rate than you can send data—for example, you can receive data at 1.5Mbps and send data at 640Kbps.

How DSL Makes Its High-Speed Connection

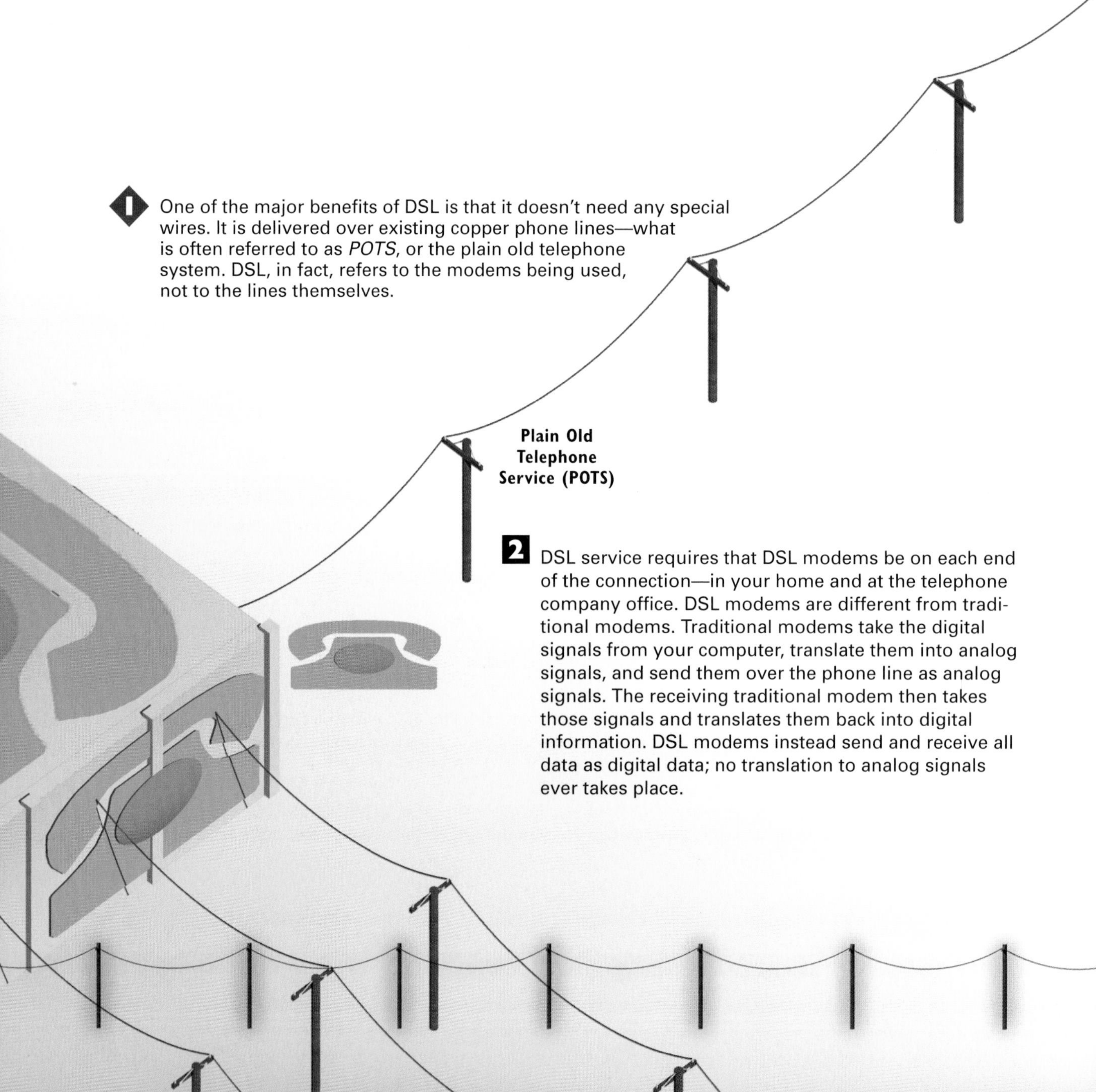

1 One of the major benefits of DSL is that it doesn't need any special wires. It is delivered over existing copper phone lines—what is often referred to as *POTS*, or the plain old telephone system. DSL, in fact, refers to the modems being used, not to the lines themselves.

2 DSL service requires that DSL modems be on each end of the connection—in your home and at the telephone company office. DSL modems are different from traditional modems. Traditional modems take the digital signals from your computer, translate them into analog signals, and send them over the phone line as analog signals. The receiving traditional modem then takes those signals and translates them back into digital information. DSL modems instead send and receive all data as digital data; no translation to analog signals ever takes place.

3 Traditional analog transmissions and voice calls sent over copper telephone wires use only a small portion of the potential bandwidth that can be transmitted over copper telephone wires. DSL enables people to talk on the telephone and use the Internet at high speeds simultaneously—all over a single phone line.

4 DSL divides the phone line into three channels: one for receiving data, one for sending data, and one for talking over the telephone. Therefore, a single phone line can be used for browsing the Internet and talking over the telephone simultaneously. The phone line is not always physically separated into these channels. Rather, modulation techniques can be used to separate the three types of signals: voice, sending, and receiving. The sending and receiving channels can be divided into a variety of speeds. One form of ADSL might be able to receive data at 1.5Mbps, for example, and send it at 640Kbps.

5 To work properly, your DSL modem must be located within a certain distance from the phone company's answering DSL modem. The exact distance varies according to the precise DSL service and speed being offered, and even according to the gauge of the copper telephone wire. For an 8.448Mbps service, for example, the phone company's DSL modem needs to be within 9,000 feet of your modem. At 2.048Mbps, on the other hand, the modem can be located 16,000 feet away.

CHAPTER 12 How ISDN Works

ONE common complaint about the Internet is that ordinary telephone connections are too slow. Even "high-speed" modems that can connect at 28,800Kbps can be too slow to take advantage of the rich graphics now available. The Internet is full of graphics, videos, sounds, and other multimedia files that are very large and take a very long time to be sent across the Internet to your computer.

One affordable way to get a faster Internet connection is to use ISDN (Integrated Services Digital Network). It's a technology that has been around for years, but the advent of the Internet and the need for higher-speed connections has made it more popular.

ISDN enables high-speed connections to the Internet using existing copper cable telephone wires. It isn't available to everyone in the country yet because it requires telephone companies to install special ISDN digital-switching equipment. However, every day more areas of the country offer ISDN service. If ISDN is available in your area, you'll pay extra for the service compared to a normal telephone line. To use ISDN and the Internet, the number you're dialing must be equipped for ISDN access. Many private Internet dial-in providers and online services allow for ISDN access.

ISDN also requires that you have an ISDN modem. Although it looks like a modem, an ISDN modem isn't really a modem at all. Instead, it's a *terminal adapter*, a piece of hardware that lets you send and receive digital signals over ISDN phone lines. Normal modems transform digital signals from your computer into analog signals that can be sent over normal analog telephone lines. Because ISDN is a digital technology, only digital data is sent by the ISDN adapter. Some ISDN devices include the capability to function as a regular modem. This capability is necessary because not every place you can dial into with your computer lets you use ISDN; some services presently allow only regular modem access.

ISDN enables you to use your line for voice calls as well as for sending and receiving data, and in fact, depending on where you get the service, it might support caller ID so you can see the phone number of people who are calling. In some setups, you can even have more than one telephone number sharing a single line. Then, depending on the call, it can be routed to different devices sharing the same ISDN line. For example, you can have a fax number, and all calls to that number automatically will go to your fax machine.

Although ISDN offers higher connection speeds than traditional modems, it is slower than DSL and cable modems. Because of this, and because there have been problems rolling the service out across the country, it hasn't been as popular as its higher-speed DSL and cable modem competitors. Still, when DSL and cable modems aren't available, or in areas where ISDN service is less expensive, it's a good way to get onto the Internet at higher speeds than traditional modems.

How ISDN Makes Its High-Speed Connection

1. To use ISDN service, a computer requires an ISDN modem. In fact, this "modem" isn't really a modem at all and should be called a terminal adapter instead. The ISDN "modem" sends digital information from your computer over ISDN telephone lines and receives digital information from telephone lines.

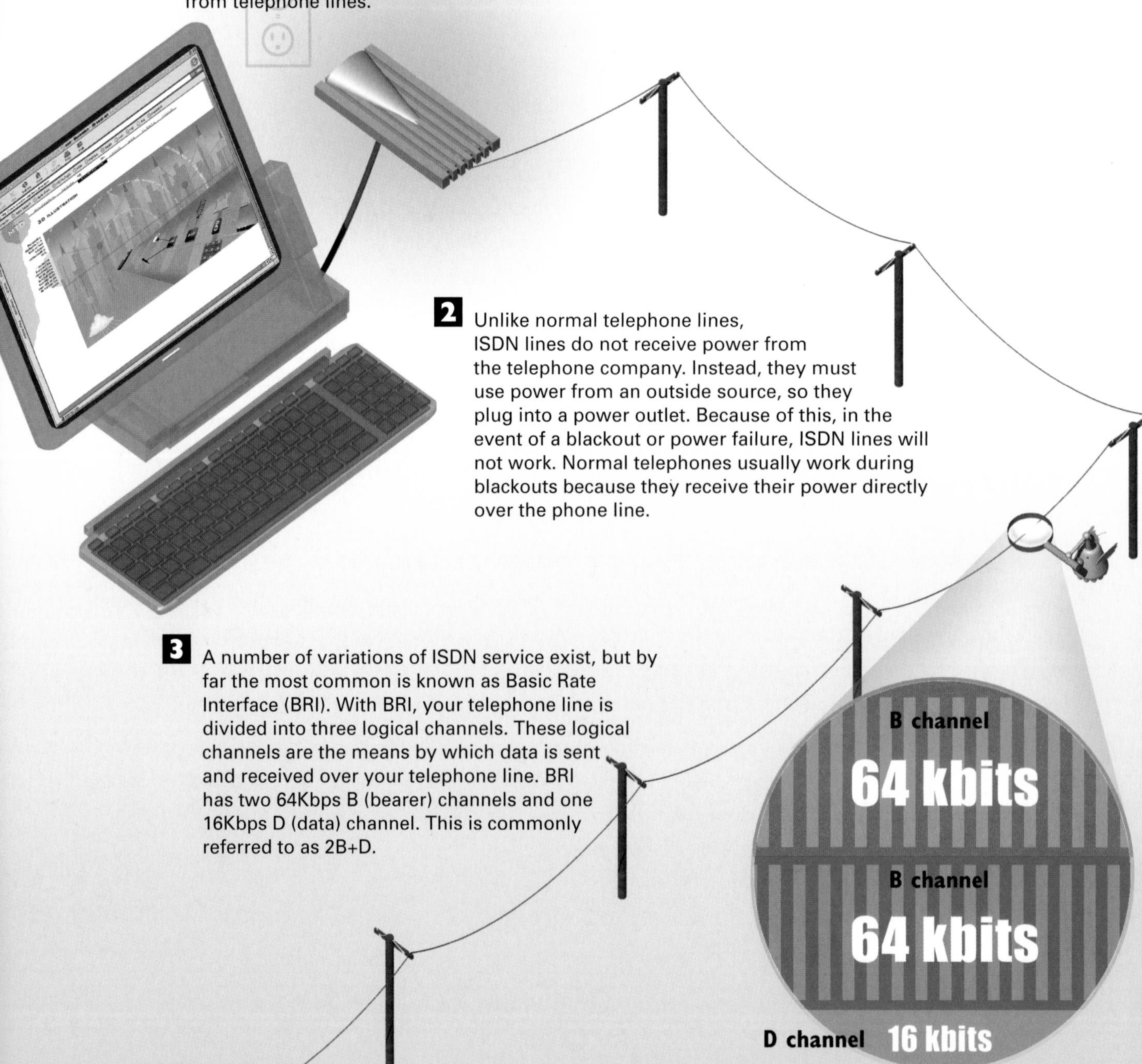

2. Unlike normal telephone lines, ISDN lines do not receive power from the telephone company. Instead, they must use power from an outside source, so they plug into a power outlet. Because of this, in the event of a blackout or power failure, ISDN lines will not work. Normal telephones usually work during blackouts because they receive their power directly over the phone line.

3. A number of variations of ISDN service exist, but by far the most common is known as Basic Rate Interface (BRI). With BRI, your telephone line is divided into three logical channels. These logical channels are the means by which data is sent and received over your telephone line. BRI has two 64Kbps B (bearer) channels and one 16Kbps D (data) channel. This is commonly referred to as 2B+D.

4 The B channels are used to send your data and can be used simultaneously. So, for example, you can be talking on the telephone through one B channel while cruising the Internet on your computer over the other B channel. The D channel is used to send signaling information for routing the data that is being sent over the B channels.

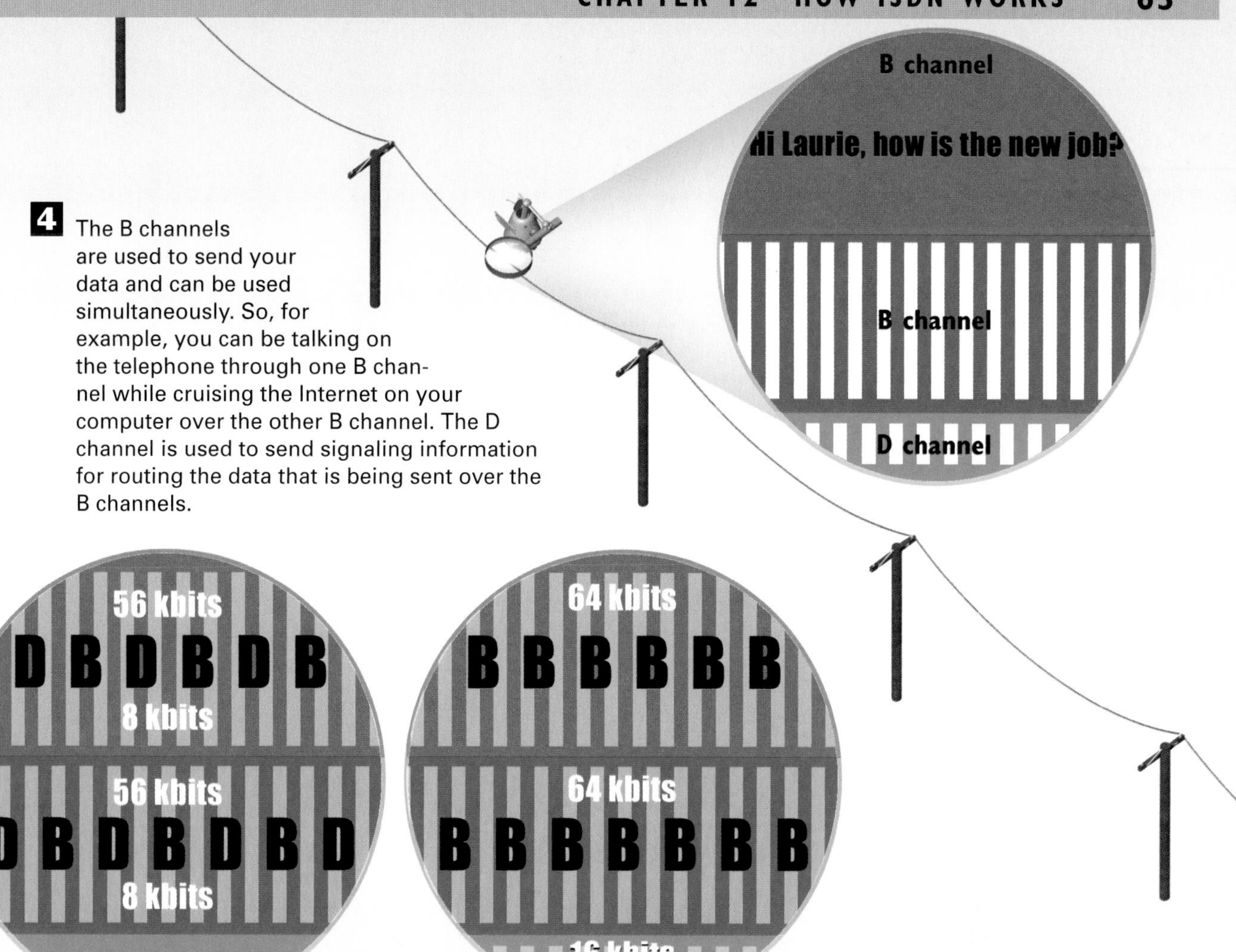

Out-of-band Signaling

In-band Signaling

5 Not all telephone companies have the capability to use the D channel to send signaling information. In cases where the D channel can't be used for signaling information, that information is instead delivered over the B channels. In this instance, each B channel can send and receive data at only 56Kbps because the other 8Kb in each channel is used for signaling information. When the B channels carry signaling information, it is referred to as *out-of-band signaling*. When the D channel carries signaling information, it is referred to as *in-band signaling*.

6 When accessing the Internet, ISDN generally uses the Point-to-Point Protocol (PPP). However, with the Multilink PPP (MP) protocol, the two B channels can be combined into a single channel for a speed of 128Kbps when in-band signaling is used and 112Kbps when out-of-band signaling is used.

Multilink PPP

128 kbits

CHAPTER

13

How You Connect to the Internet from Online Services

THERE are many ways to get access to the Internet; one is by using an online service such as CompuServe or America Online. These online services have long provided their own unique content, special areas, and services available only to their subscribers. They use proprietary software and interfaces to give subscribers access to their resources. Unlike most of the Internet, the content, areas, and services the online companies provide are not always free. To get them, you might have to pay a monthly subscription fee to the online service. These online services are different from Internet service providers (ISPs) that offer only access to the Internet and don't have their own private areas and services.

The services let you access the Internet in a number of ways. To make using the Internet's resources easier, the services often use their own proprietary software or user interface. The user interface requires you to issue a command that is then sent out over a gateway to the Internet. (A *gateway* is a device that sends data from network to network and can translate between the two if they use different kinds of data and protocols.) The information you've asked for is retrieved, sent back over the gateway to your online service, and is displayed for you using the online service's proprietary software.

Most online services also allow you to use your own client software, such as FTP software or newsgroup readers, to use the Internet. To do this, you essentially bypass the online service's proprietary interface. You use the online service as you would a dial-in ISP. First, you dial into the online service to establish a TCP/IP connection. Then, you launch the client software on your computer. It is the TCP/IP connection that gives you access to the Internet's resources.

Online services also let you browse the Web. Some let you use only their own proprietary Web browsers. Others have their own proprietary Web browsers but also allow you to browse the Web using any Web browser of your choice. To use your own Web browser, you first dial into the service to establish a TCP/IP connection. Then, you launch your own Web browser, and you can browse the Web just as you would with any other dial-in ISP.

In addition to letting you browse the Web, online services also let you use other Internet resources, such as Telnet (which lets you gain access to a distant computer on the Internet) and Usenet newsgroups (public Internet discussion areas). In some instances, you gain access to those resources using the online service's proprietary software, whereas in other instances you use normal Internet client software.

Increasingly, the online services are moving toward eliminating their proprietary architecture altogether. The trend is to build the service on the same framework as the Internet, such as the TCP/IP protocol and related technologies. The Microsoft Network, for example, is now based entirely on TCP/IP. America Online and CompuServe are both incorporating elements of Internet technology inside their services and one day might go entirely to an Internet-based model.

How Online Services Connect to the Internet

1. Online services such as CompuServe and America Online provide a very convenient way to use Internet resources. These services have their own software that makes accessing Internet resources such as Telnet and FTP easy. Some also allow you to use your own Telnet, FTP, Gopher, or other software instead of theirs. Using these resources, you can browse the World Wide Web, either with their own proprietary Web browser or by using any other Web browser. Finally, some services let you use special software required to access Internet resources such as Internet Relay Chat (IRC).

2. Each online service has a great deal of resources, content, and special areas that are not available to anyone except people who subscribe to that particular service. These areas use the online service's own proprietary software and interface; they do not work like the Internet. You dial directly into the online service to get at these resources.

3. When you use the resources of an online service, you don't go outside the service to the Internet—instead, you stay behind a firewall. A *firewall* is a security system of accepting or blocking packets as they are transmitted across a network. Individual online services establish firewalls that let only subscribers into the service.

4. Online services use their own proprietary software and interfaces to give you access to many common Internet resources, such as Usenet newsgroups, Telnet, and FTP. You issue a command using the online service's own software. The online service then sends the command out over the Internet via a gateway to retrieve the information. The information is sent back via a gateway, through the online service's own software, and then to your computer.

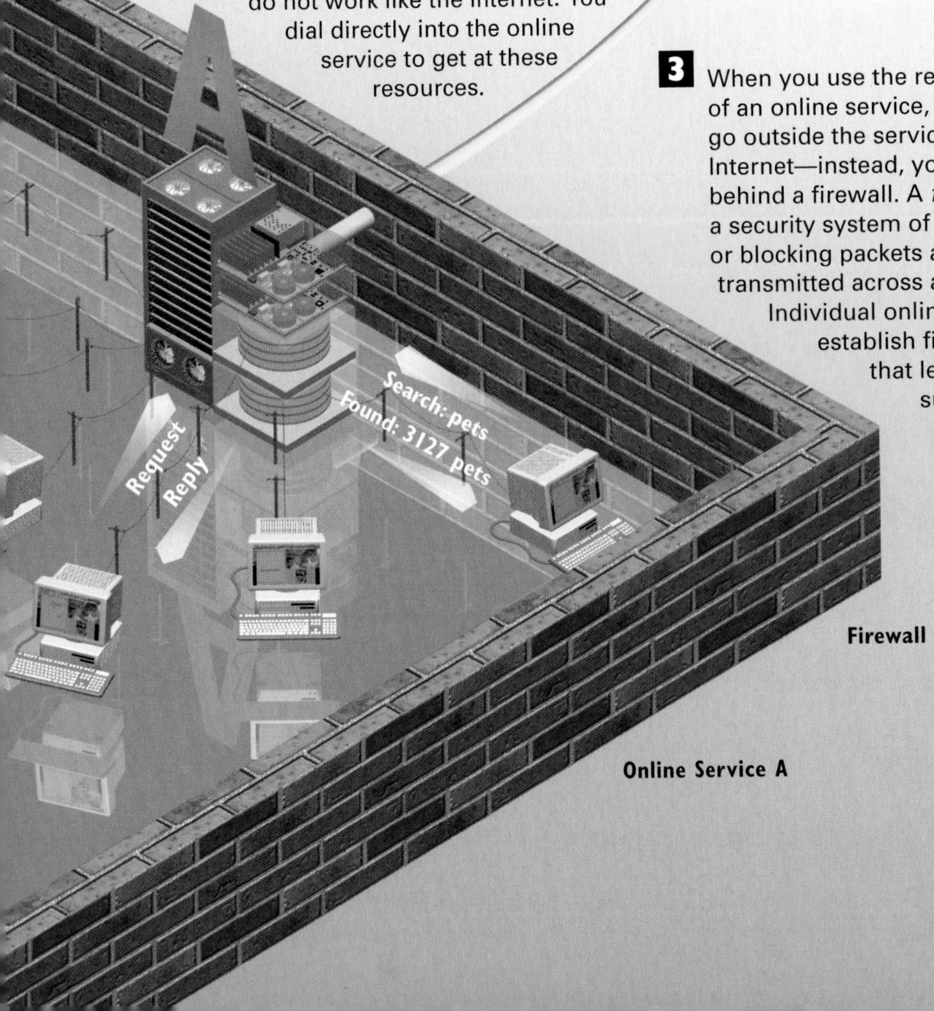

7 Some online services let you use any Web browser you want to browse the World Wide Web. In that instance, you can click an icon on the online service, go into a special area of the online service, or simply launch your Web browser on your own computer, and then begin browsing the Web.

6 Online services also let you browse the World Wide Web. One way to browse the Web is to use the online service's own proprietary Web browser. Typically, you can launch a browser by clicking an icon or going into a special area of the online service.

5 Most services also let you use your own client software to access Internet resources such as Telnet, FTP, and IRC that the services do not have proprietary software for. To do this, you dial into the online service and establish a TCP/IP connection. You can then get directly onto the Internet using your own client software.

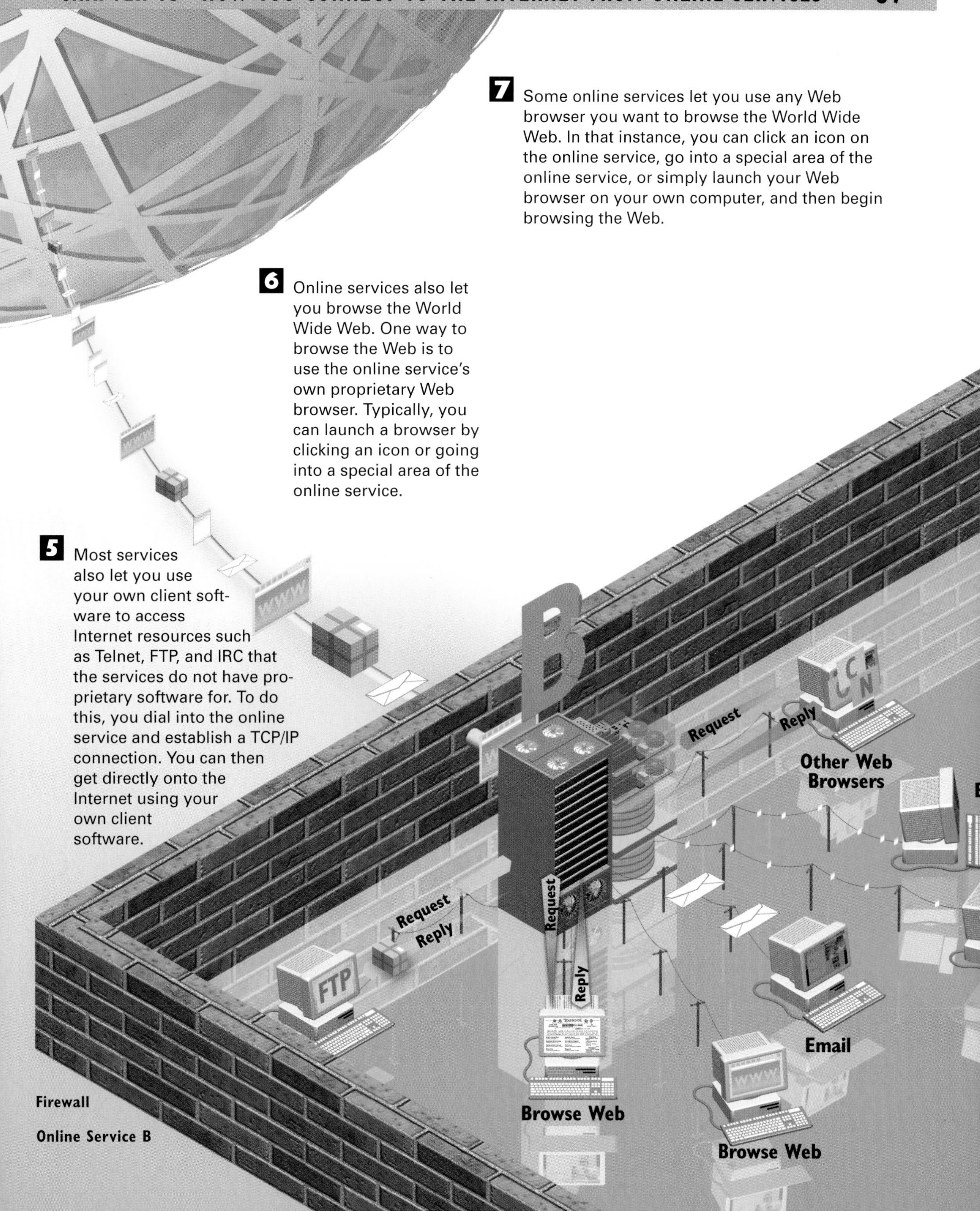

CHAPTER

14

How Wireless and Palmtop Connections Work

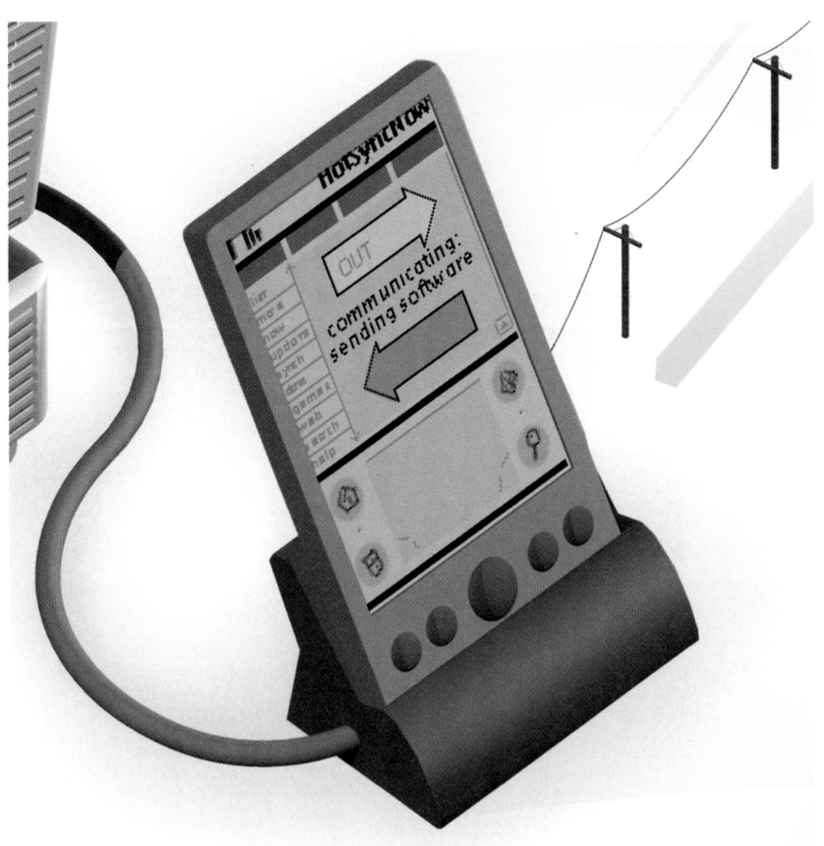

EVERY day, new, unique ways of connecting to the Internet and browsing the Web are being developed. While traditional PCs and modems are still the dominant way people access the Internet, increasingly many other types of devices can access the Web as well—and hardwares other than traditional modems are also becoming more and more popular ways to get onto the Internet, particularly wireless technologies.

Among the newest ways to connect to the Internet and browse the Web are via satellite connections; via Palmtop computers, such as the Palm and Windows CE devices; via cellular telephones; and via a wireless technology called Bluetooth.

When you connect to the Internet using a satellite connection, you can get access at a higher rate than normal 28.8 or 56 kilobits per second modems. You typically get data and Web sites transferred to you at 400 kilobits per second, more than seven times the speed of a 56Kbps modem.

Satellite-access systems are, in a way, odd hybrids. They still require that you use a modem. The modem is used to request information from the Internet, so when you send information through the Internet, it goes at normal modem speeds. However, that requested information is sent back to you at the high satellite transmission speeds, not the slower modem speeds. However, this means that if you're sending e-mail, or transferring a file to someone via FTP, that information is sent at modem speeds, not satellite speeds.

When you access the Internet via satellite, you still use a traditional PC. However, you can also get onto the Web in other ways using new types of digital devices, most notably Palmtop devices. These little computers, sometimes called personal digital assistants (PDAs) can literally put the Web in the palm of your hand. You connect a modem to them and can then get onto the Internet and send and receive e-mail and browse the Web with them.

Some PDAs and cellular telephones can access the Internet without using normal telephone lines (called *landlines*). They use cellular technology to make a connection to the Internet. But because their screens are small and typically can't display graphics, Web pages must be reformatted into a format called Wireless Markup Language (WML) to be viewed properly on them. Some Web pages are built with WML, and those Web pages need not be specially formatted—they can be viewed as is.

How To Access the Internet via a Satellite Connection

1 Accessing the Internet via a satellite connection delivers information to your computer at much higher speeds than do normal modems—at 400 kilobits per second. To use it, you need a satellite dish on your home in the same way that you need a satellite dish to get satellite TV.

6 The satellite in turn sends the information at 400Kbps to the satellite dish in your home.

7 The satellite dish sends the information to your PC via a coaxial cable, the same type of cable used by cable TV systems. Coaxial cable can send data at higher speeds than can normal telephone lines. The coaxial cable sends the data to a network card inside your computer. You now can view the Web page—and you'll have gotten it at 400 kilobits per second rather than at 28.8Kbps or 56Kbps.

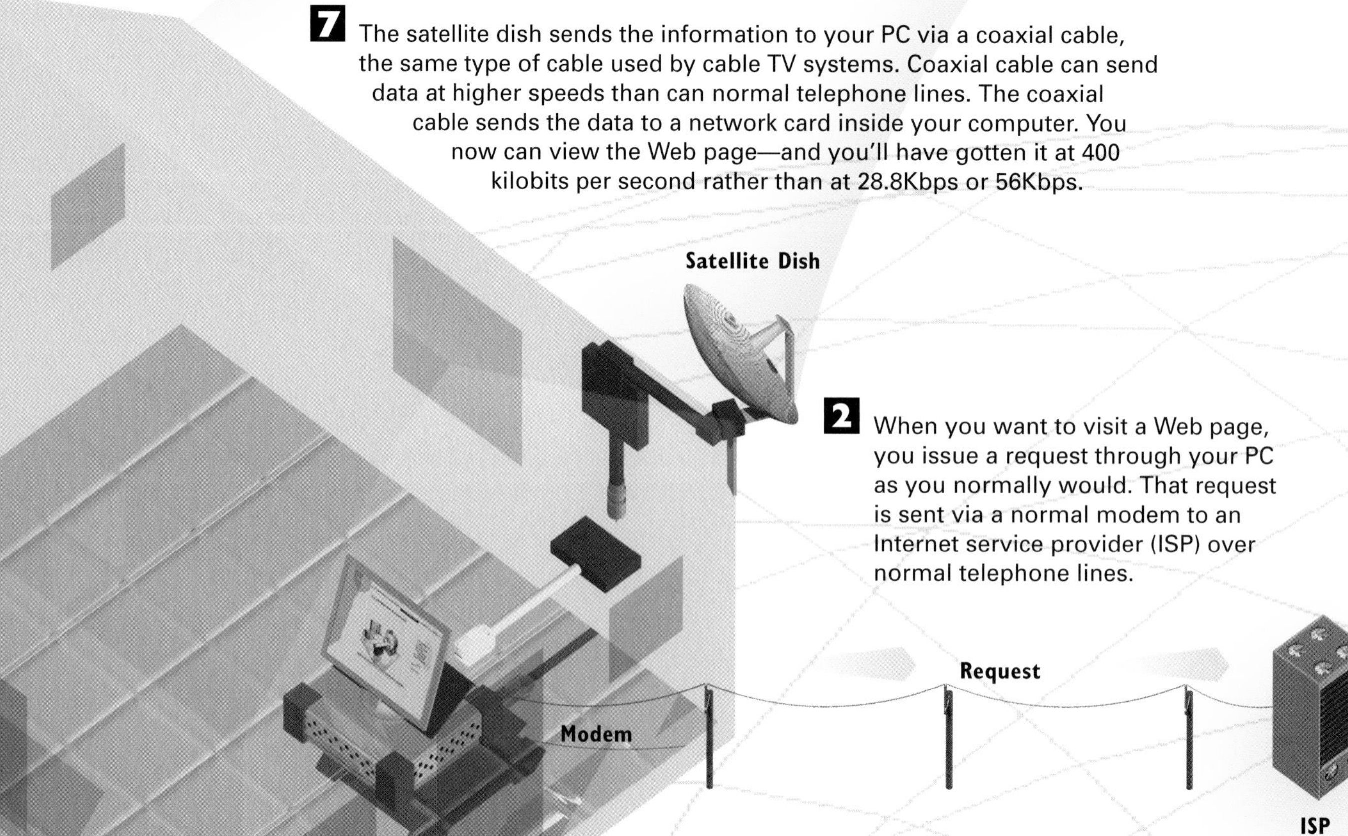

2 When you want to visit a Web page, you issue a request through your PC as you normally would. That request is sent via a normal modem to an Internet service provider (ISP) over normal telephone lines.

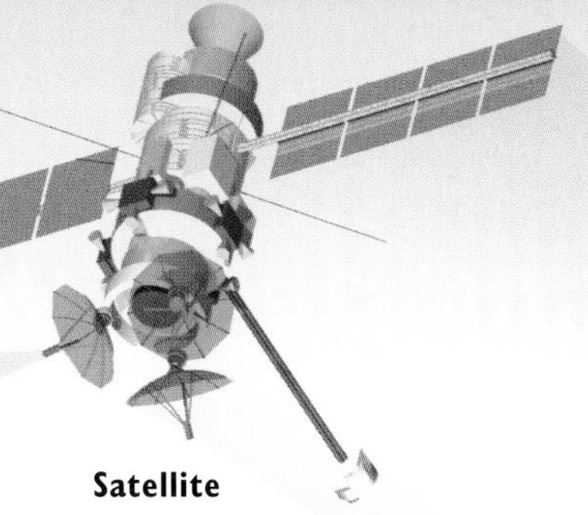

5 The NOC sends the information to a satellite above the earth at 400Kbps.

4 Instead of transferring the information directly back to you over telephone lines, the Web server sends the information to the satellite company's network operations center (NOC) (also called a satellite ground station) via special high-speed links.

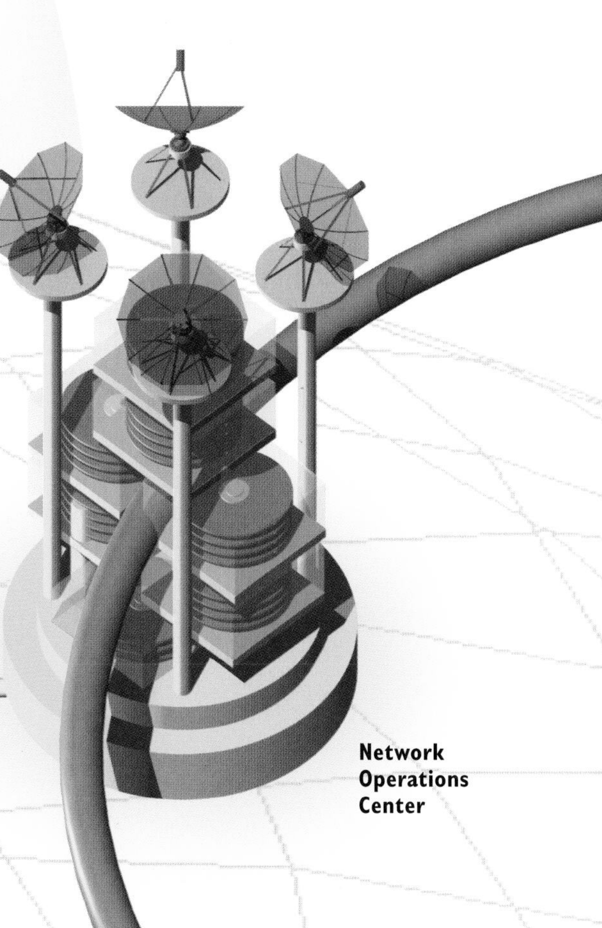

3 Your request to visit the page goes to the Web server that houses the site you want to visit.

How Palmtop Computers Can Browse the Web

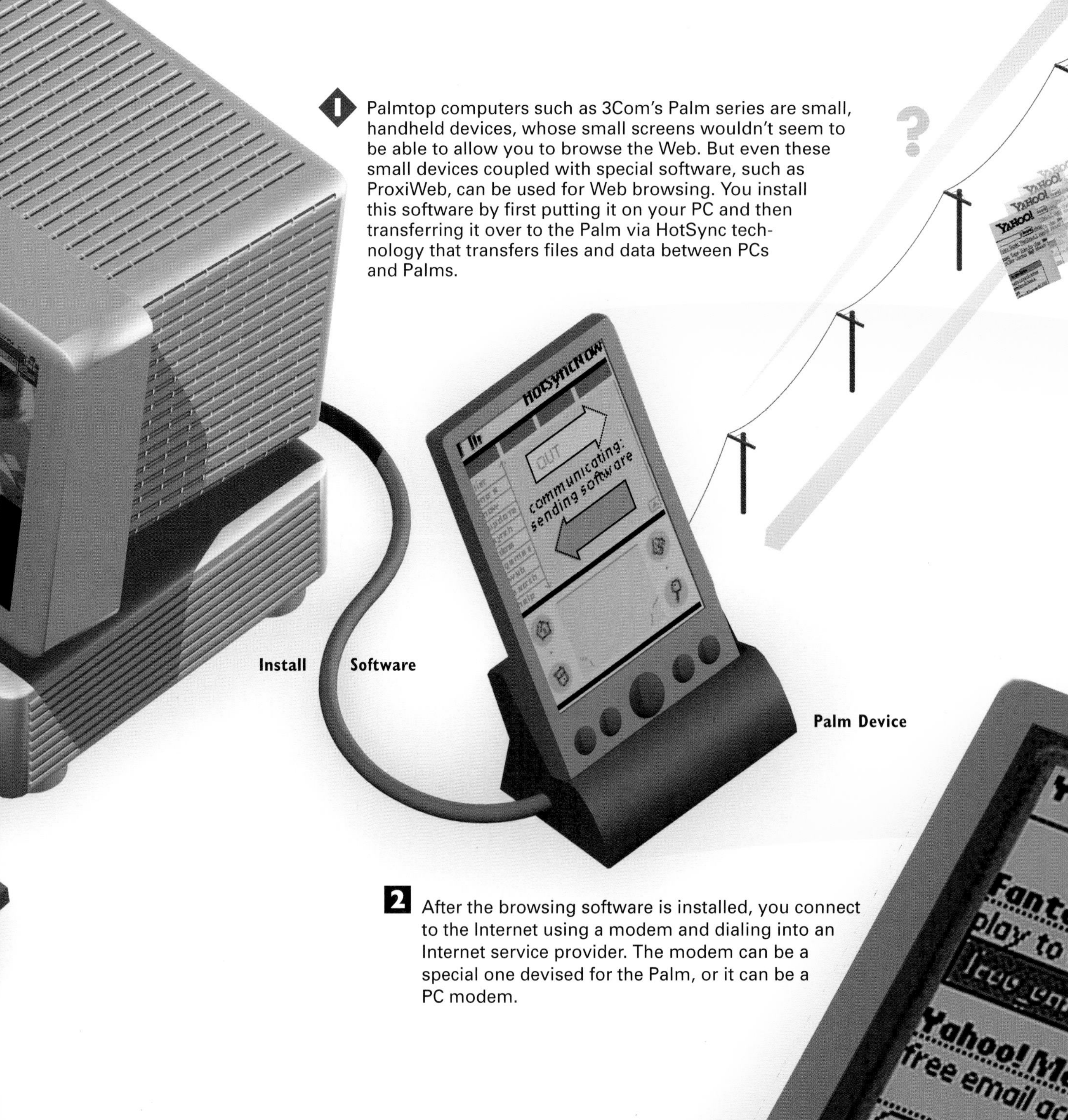

1 Palmtop computers such as 3Com's Palm series are small, handheld devices, whose small screens wouldn't seem to be able to allow you to browse the Web. But even these small devices coupled with special software, such as ProxiWeb, can be used for Web browsing. You install this software by first putting it on your PC and then transferring it over to the Palm via HotSync technology that transfers files and data between PCs and Palms.

2 After the browsing software is installed, you connect to the Internet using a modem and dialing into an Internet service provider. The modem can be a special one devised for the Palm, or it can be a PC modem.

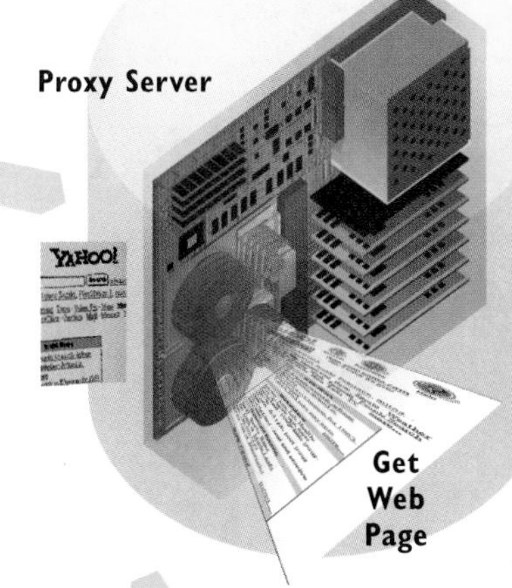

3 After you're connected to the Internet, when you want to visit a Web site you type its location into the browser. Instead of going to the site, though, the ProxiWeb browser contacts a special *proxy server* located on the Internet.

4 The proxy server contacts the Web server that hosts the page you want to visit. The page downloads to the proxy server. As the page is downloaded, the proxy server processes and reformats it, putting into a form that can be easily read by Palm device's small screen. It strips out the HTML coding and changes it into a special format the ProxiWeb browser on the Palm can read, and it changes the graphics into a format that can be read on the Palm as well.

5 After the page is processed and reformatted, it is sent to the Palm device, where it can be read. The links are live just as if it were a normal Web page, so you can click them to view them. When you click a link, you contact the proxy server, which then gets you that page in the same way it sent you the initial page.

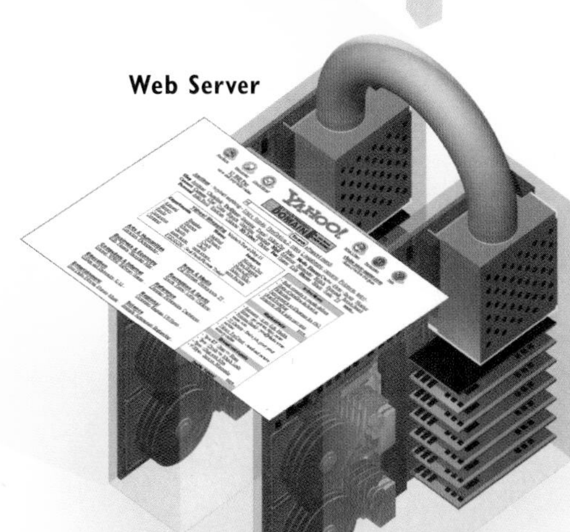

How Cellular Telephones and Palmtops Access the Internet

1 The main way cellular telephones access the Internet is through a protocol called the Wireless Access Protocol (WAP) and its associated markup language, the Wireless Markup Language (WML). To use WAP to access a Web page with a cellular telephone, you first need to make a cellular phone call. When you dial a cell phone, it looks for the nearest cellular antenna, called a *base station*, to transmit the call. The phone scans nearby base stations and locks on one that is either the closest or has the most powerful signal.

MSN 13572
ESN 25817

Who are you?

Get Web Page

WML

2 The phone asks for authorization to make the call. The base station looks at the telephone's mechanical serial number (MSN) and electronic serial number (ESN) to ensure that the phone is allowed to use the cellular network.

3 The base station sends the call to a telephone-wire–based network (also called a landline) and then to a network server and WAP gateway.

8 You can now read the page on your cellular telephone—it has been specially formatted for its display. However, cellular phones have difficulty handling graphics, so not all Web pages will display properly, even after they've been reformatted to WML.

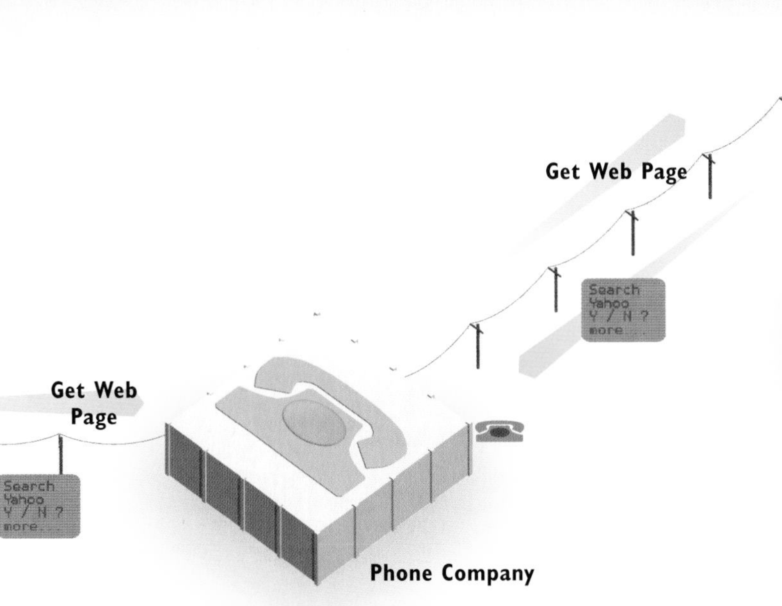

Network Server

7 The WML page is sent back through the landline to a base station. The base station sends the page to your cellular telephone.

6 If the page is in normal HTML format, the gateway reformats the page in WML, so your cell phone can read the page. If the page is already in WML format, the gateway doesn't need to reformat the page.

Get Web Page

WAP Gateway

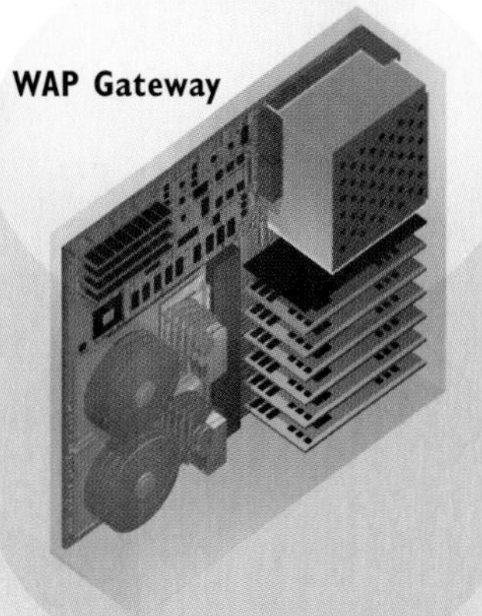

4 The gateway sends the request for the Web page on to the Web server on which the page is located.

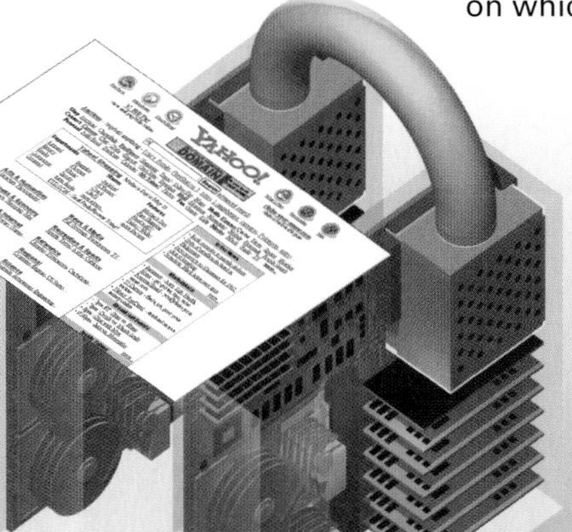

Get Web Page

5 The page is sent back to the WAP gateway.

Router

How Bluetooth Works

3 When a Bluetooth device finds another device, or more than one device, within its range, they go through a series of communications that establish whether they should communicate with one another. Not all devices will communicate—for example, a stereo might not communicate with a telephone. Devices determine whether they should communicate with one another by examining each other's Bluetooth profiles, which are coded into the devices' hardware by the hardware manufacturer. *Profiles* contain information about the device itself, what it is used for, and with which devices it can communicate. If devices determine they should communicate with one another, they establish a connection. The connection of two or more Bluetooth devices is called a *piconet*.

Notebook PC

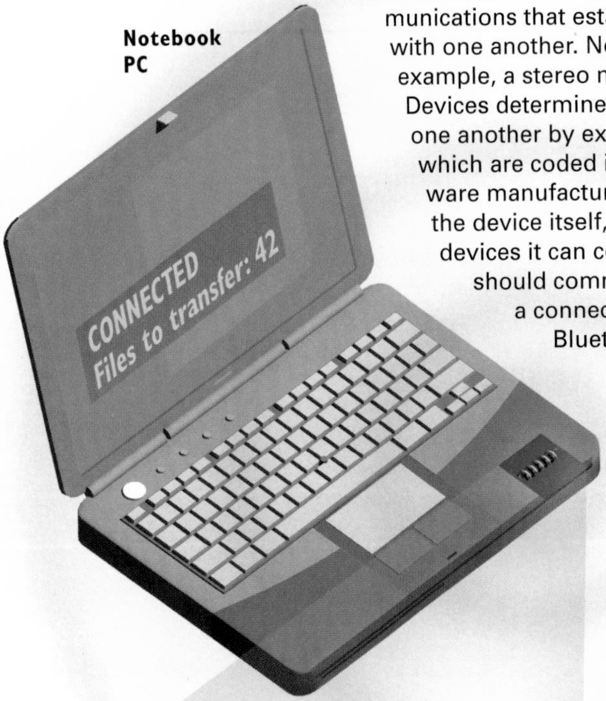

CONNECTED
Files to transfer: 42

2 The Bluetooth device constantly sends out a message, looking for other Bluetooth devices within its range.

1 Bluetooth is a wireless technology that allows computers, telephones, personal data assistants (PDAs), and even home devices such as stereos and TVs to communicate with one another. Each Bluetooth device has a microchip embedded in it that can send and receive radio signals. It can send both data and voice. The radio signals are sent and received in the 2.4GHz radio band, often referred to as the *industrial, scientific, and medical (ISM)* band. Inside the chip is software called a *link controller* that does the actual work of identifying other Bluetooth devices and sending and receiving data.

Bluetooth Chipset

Piconet 1

4 After the connection is established, the devices can communicate with one another. You could use a Bluetooth device to access information from the Internet, if the device it's accessing the data from is connected to the Internet. For example, you could have a home network with Bluetooth capability and connect a palmtop computer to the Internet by connecting through the home network.

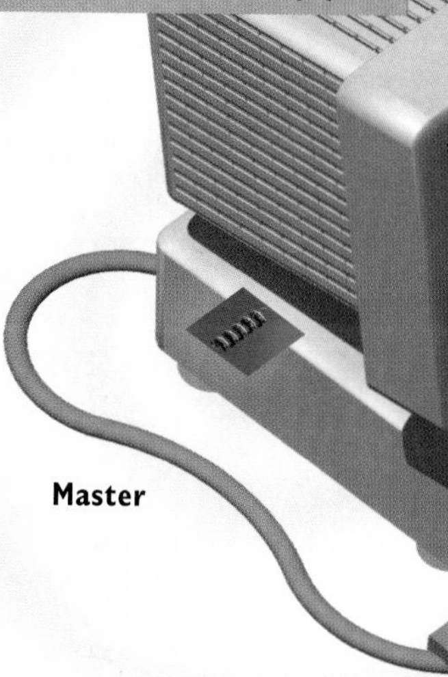

Master

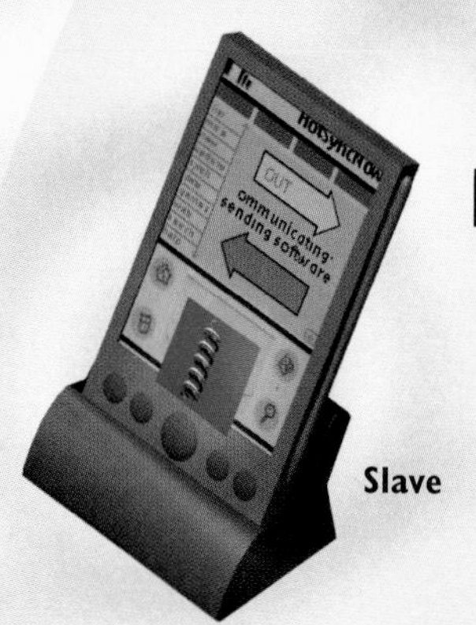

Slave

Handheld

5 If there are many Bluetooth devices or piconets near each other, their radio signals could conceivably interfere with one another. To ensure that doesn't happen, Bluetooth uses *spread-spectrum frequency hopping*. In this technique, the transmitters change their frequencies constantly—1,600 times per second. In this way, the chance of interference is very small—and if interference does occur, it occurs for only a tiny fraction of a second. When two or more devices are connected in a piconet, one device is the master and determines the frequencies to switch among. It instructs all the other devices on which frequencies to switch to, and when.

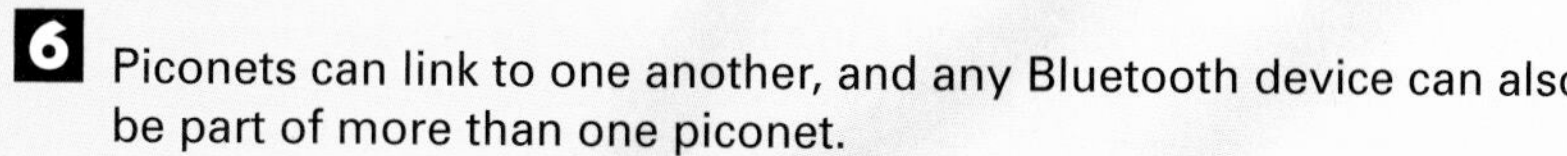

6 Piconets can link to one another, and any Bluetooth device can also be part of more than one piconet.

Slave

Piconet 2

CHAPTER 15 How Home Networks Work

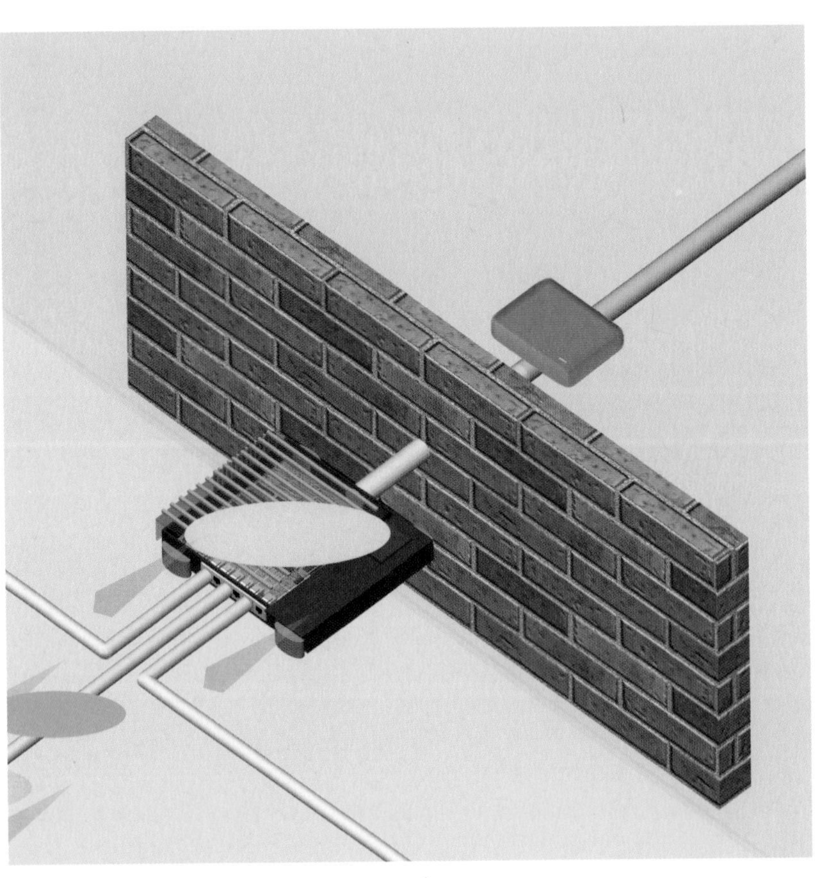

THE more the Internet becomes a pervasive and necessary part of our lives, the more we need access to it—and not just at work, but at home as well.

Internet access at home has become a must-have for most people and families who can afford it. And because people have more than one computer at home, they want to be able to let each computer have Internet access—and they want to be able to share printers and send files back and forth between their computers as well.

This is especially important for people who have high-speed Internet connections, such as cable modems or DSL modems. Typically, these connections cost at least $30 a month or more. Rather than having to pay a separate connection fee for each computer, you can install a home network and allow two or more computers to share the same high-speed connection. That way, you pay for only one connection.

Several types of home networks can be used. By far the most popular right now are those that use a combination hub/router to connect the computers and allow them to share an Internet connection, printers, and files. The *hub* connects all the devices to one another, whereas the *router* does the work of connecting the devices to the Internet. Commonly, individual PCs are connected to the hub/router via the same type of Ethernet cables used in corporate local area networks (LANs). Each PC needs a network card to connect to the network—again, the same kind of network card used in corporate LANs.

Other types of home networks are becoming popular as well. Some home networks connect via the home's telephone wires. Still others connect using wireless technology—and wireless home networks might become the most popular because of the difficulty and expense of stringing Ethernet cable throughout a home. For now, though, the most popular networks are those that use the same Ethernet cables used in corporate LANs.

Increasingly, it's not only computers at home that connect to the Internet. Other types of devices and appliances are being connected as well, such as radio receivers; small, inexpensive e-mail devices that only send and receive e-mail; and even traditional home appliances such as refrigerators, microwave ovens, and alarm clocks.

Connecting these types of devices and appliances will make life more convenient—you'll be able to use your refrigerator to automatically generate shopping lists, for example, and send orders directly to grocery stores. And you'll have an alarm clock that can change the time it awakens you based on traffic reports it garners from the Internet. These kinds of devices aren't mere fantasy—they are already being sold or tested and will soon be sold in a department store near you.

How Home Networks Let You Share Your Internet Connection

1 The main reason people set up home networks is to share high-speed Internet access, such as via a cable modem or DSL modem, among several computers. To give the home network access to the Internet, an Ethernet cable runs from the cable modem or DSL modem to the networking device, called a *hub/router*.

3 The hub/router does two primary jobs: It connects all the PCs to each other so they can share files and devices such as printers, and it connects all the PCs to the Internet so they can each have a high-speed Internet connection. For the hub/router to do its job, it needs an IP address, which it's given by a server run by the Internet service provider (ISP) that runs the cable or DSL service.

7 In addition to gaining Internet access through the hub/router, the PCs also can share resources such as printers. So, any computer on the network can print to a printer attached to any other computer, as long as the computes are set up to share resources.

192.168.1.100

Check Mail

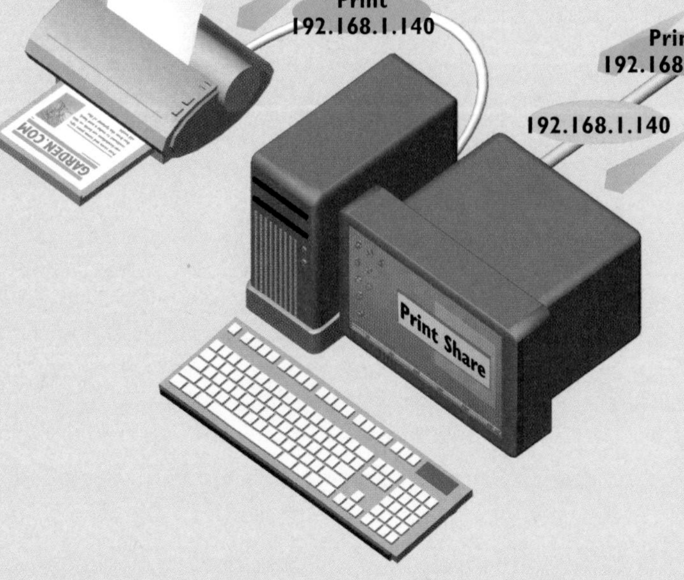

6 When a second PC is turned on, it does the same thing the first PC does: It contacts the hub/router and gets an internal IP address. This internal IP address will be different from the first—for example, it might be 192.168.1.148. But to the outside world, the IP address looks like the IP address of the router. The PC now has full access to the Internet. Other computers on the home network can get internal IP addresses and access to the Internet in the same way using the home router.

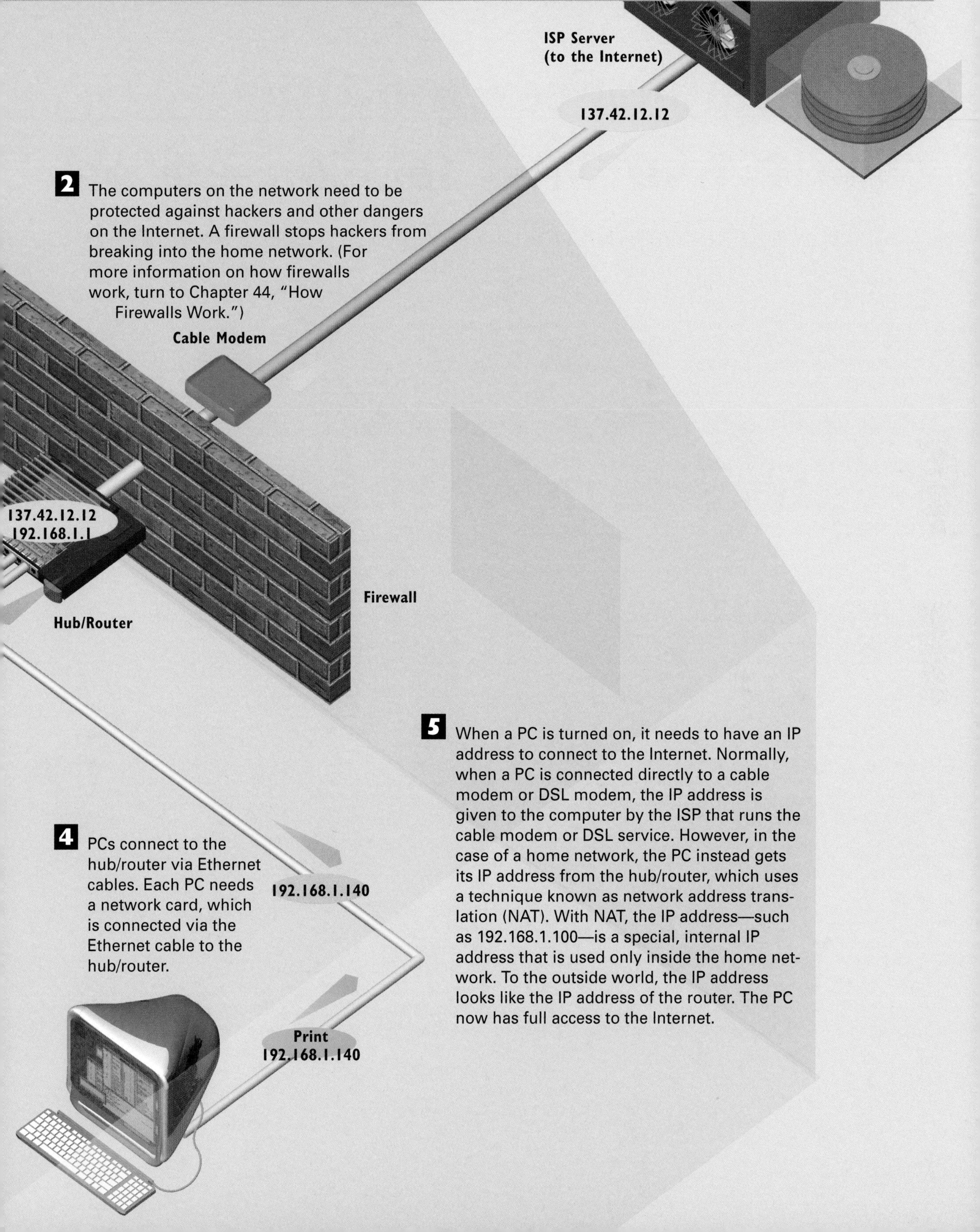

ISP Server
(to the Internet)

137.42.12.12

2 The computers on the network need to be protected against hackers and other dangers on the Internet. A firewall stops hackers from breaking into the home network. (For more information on how firewalls work, turn to Chapter 44, "How Firewalls Work.")

Cable Modem

137.42.12.12
192.168.1.1

Firewall

Hub/Router

5 When a PC is turned on, it needs to have an IP address to connect to the Internet. Normally, when a PC is connected directly to a cable modem or DSL modem, the IP address is given to the computer by the ISP that runs the cable modem or DSL service. However, in the case of a home network, the PC instead gets its IP address from the hub/router, which uses a technique known as network address translation (NAT). With NAT, the IP address—such as 192.168.1.100—is a special, internal IP address that is used only inside the home network. To the outside world, the IP address looks like the IP address of the router. The PC now has full access to the Internet.

4 PCs connect to the hub/router via Ethernet cables. Each PC needs a network card, which is connected via the Ethernet cable to the hub/router.

192.168.1.140

Print
192.168.1.140

How Appliances and Other Devices Connect to the Internet

Wireless connections In theory, any type of device or appliance—from your television to your heating system to your refrigerator—connects to the Internet, either by wires or wirelessly. This illustration shows how devices other than computers can connect to the Internet. None of what you see in this illustration is science-fiction—every example shown here is either already being tested or already being sold. It is often not realistic to expect Ethernet cable to be easily strung all over the house to connect devices to a home network that in turn can connect those devices to the Internet. So, homes wanting to connect devices to the Internet either can use an entirely wireless network or can use a wireless network access point that can hook into a wired network and connect wireless devices to the Internet.

Wireless Hub/Router

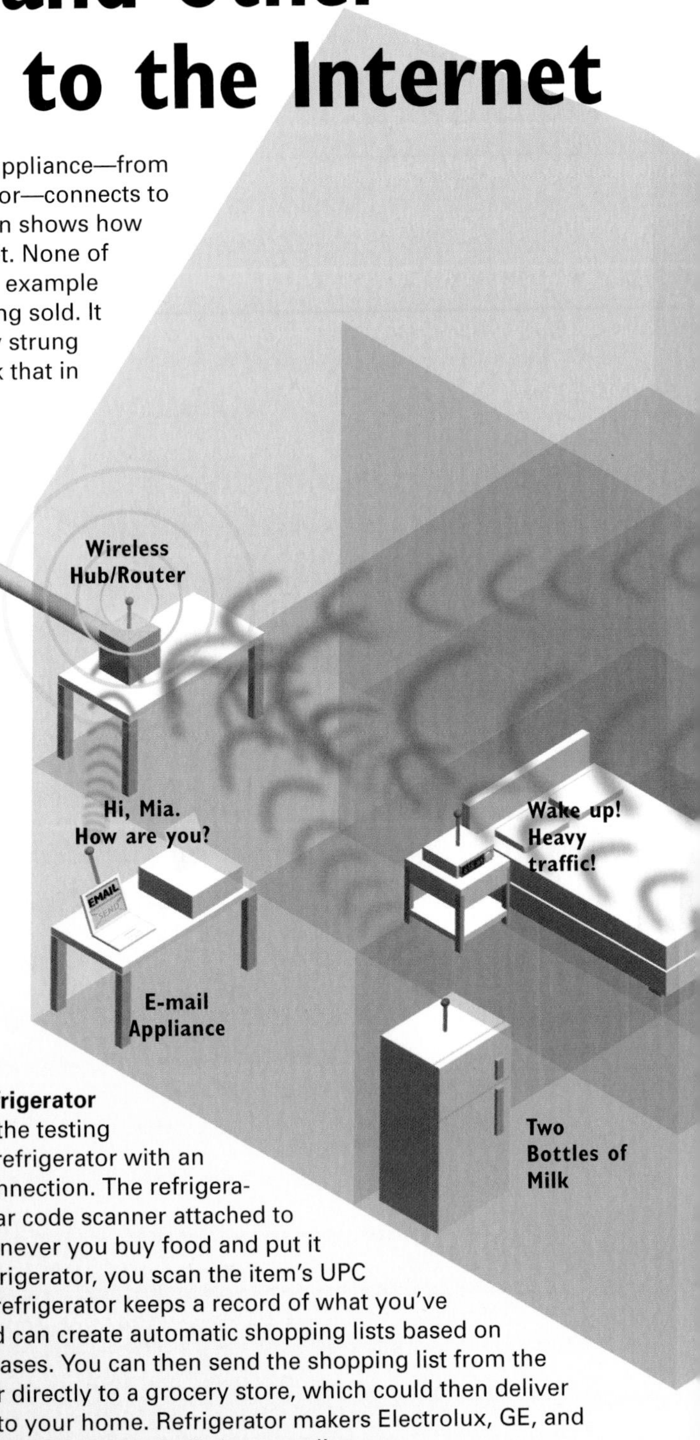

E-mail terminal For people who want access to e-mail throughout the house but can't afford a PC in every room, inexpensive e-mail terminals can be used. These terminals are use primarily for sending and receiving e-mail, although some have basic Web-browsing capabilities as well. They are already being sold. These terminals can be connected to the Internet via telephone wires, Ethernet cable, or in the future, wirelessly.

Hi, Mia. How are you?

Wake up! Heavy traffic!

E-mail Appliance

Internet refrigerator Already in the testing phase is a refrigerator with an Internet connection. The refrigerator has a bar code scanner attached to it, and whenever you buy food and put it into the refrigerator, you scan the item's UPC code. The refrigerator keeps a record of what you've bought and can create automatic shopping lists based on your purchases. You can then send the shopping list from the refrigerator directly to a grocery store, which could then deliver the goods to your home. Refrigerator makers Electrolux, GE, and Whirlpool are planning to sell these appliances.

Two Bottles of Milk

Security and monitoring system Security systems can be connected to the Internet so that you can, for example, look through security cameras when you're far away and make sure your house is OK. You can also put a Webcam in your young children's rooms and be able to monitor them when you're in another room or away from home.

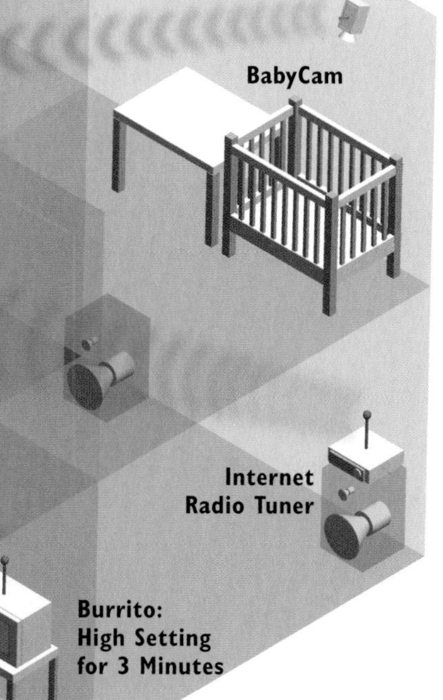

Internet home control Ultimately, every part of your home will be able to be monitored and controlled via the Internet, from the lights to the heating system, security system, and beyond. You'll be able to monitor and control your home either through a central keypad and monitor at home, via a PC at home, or via a PC or some other Internet-connected device when you're away from home. Sunbeam, which makes the Mr. Coffee coffee maker, has announced that it will be selling a set of nine Internet-connected home devices, including a smart, Internet-connected alarm clock called the TimeHelper. The device can beep a warning when the Internet-connected Smart Coffeemaker runs low on water, check Internet traffic reports to see what traffic is like, set your alarm to the best time for getting into work, and even turn off or on your electric blanket based on weather reports. The Internet alarm clock is expected to sell for $40–$80.

Internet radio tuner One of the newest home devices that uses an Internet connection is a radio tuner. These tuners connect to the Internet and play Internet radio stations. They are already being sold. (For information about how Internet radio stations work, turn to Chapter 36, "How Music and Audio Work on the Internet.") They connect in a variety of ways, either through a PC or by themselves through an Ethernet connection. (In the future, they might connect wirelessly.) They can play the music in speakers throughout the house. Those speakers can be wired directly to the tuner in the traditional way, connected wirelessly, or connected via a home's telephone wires.

Internet microwave oven Also in the testing phase is an Internet-connected microwave oven. When you want to cook something, you put it into the microwave and pass a bar code scanner over the product's UPC code. Directions for cooking the item are sent directly to the microwave oven, which then cooks the item according to the directions. Samsung is planning on selling an Internet microwave oven. Some day, regular ovens might have this same capability as well.

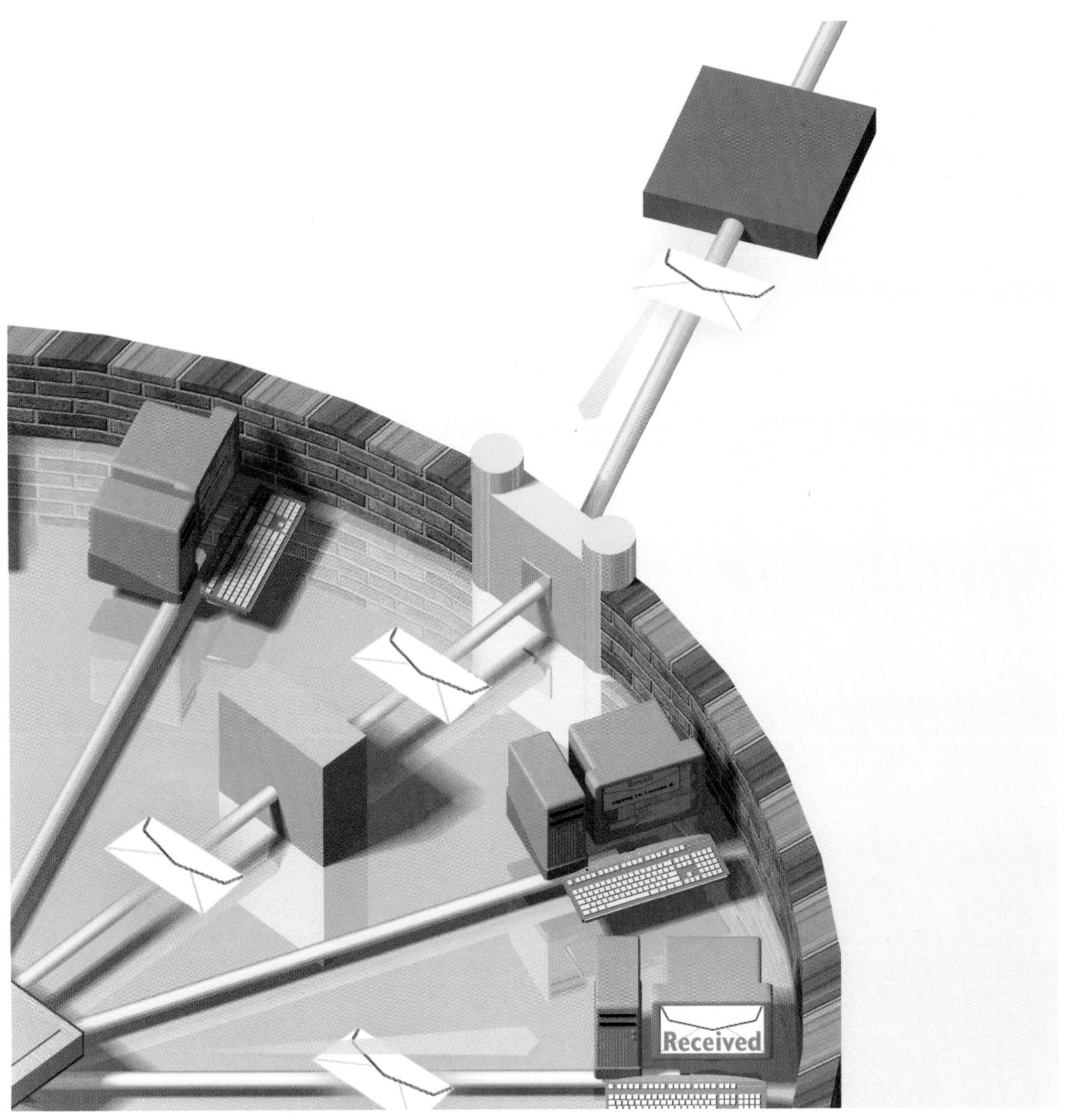
Received

PART

COMMUNICATING ON THE INTERNET

SINCE its very earliest days, the Internet has been concerned primarily with one task—making it easier for people to communicate with one another using computers. The Internet was created to enable university researchers to share their thoughts, work, and resources, and for military people to communicate with each other in case of war and even, theoretically, a nuclear attack.

Today, more than two decades after the inception of the first networks that grew into the Internet, it is still primarily a communications medium. Millions of people from all over the world share their thoughts, hopes, work, gossip, and comments on the wires and computers that make up the Internet. Many of the means of communication, such as electronic mail, have changed very little in the past 20 years. Yet other, entirely new ways of communicating have been devised, such as enabling you to use the Internet as your telephone, completely cutting out long-distance charges, even if you're calling to the other side of the world. Technologies enable people to communicate privately, one on one; others allow for vast discussion groups that span the globe, and still others enable both private communication with one person and public communication with large groups.

This section of the book looks at the main ways people communicate on the Internet.

Chapter 16, "How E-mail Works," takes a long look at what continues to be the most popular way for people to communicate on the Internet—electronic mail, or e-mail. E-mail remains possibly the greatest use of the Internet and is used for business and personal communication. You'll see how e-mail gets routed from your computer through the maze of wires that makes up the Internet and then ends up in the proper recipient's inbox. You'll look at all the elements of a mail message and learn how you can send binary files, such as pictures and sounds, through e-mail. You'll also explore mailing lists, where you can subscribe to any one of thousands of public discussions via e-mail or receive what are essentially electronic newsletters delivered to your e-mail inbox. You'll also look at how you can look up anyone's e-mail address using white page directories that use a technology called the Lightweight Access Directory Protocol (LADP). Finally in this chapter, you'll take a look at how e-mail can be encrypted so that snoopers and hackers can't read it as it makes its way across the Internet.

Chapter 17, "How E-mail Spam Works," covers one of the most controversial modes of communication on the Internet—the use of spam, the equivalent of junk mail via e-mail, that is sent to millions of people each day. Although spam is a problem on newsgroups as well as e-mail, e-mail is the greatest area of controversy. Spam annoys people and wastes their time while they clean out their mailboxes; it clogs the Internet so that other messages might be delivered late (or not at all); and it can be delivered by piggybacking onto other people's e-mail servers, costing them money. The chapter looks at how spam is sent, as well as ways that it can be blocked.

Chapter 18, "How Newsgroups Work," explores Usenet newsgroups—public discussion groups in which anyone can participate. Many thousands of these groups focus on every subject conceivable. You'll see how newsgroups work and how you can decipher their often arcane names.

Chapter 19, "How Internet Chat and Instant Messaging Work," covers the various ways people can *chat* on the Internet. When people chat on the Internet, they don't actually speak but type comments on their keyboards instead, and then people all over the world can read and respond to them. This chapter closely examines how instant messaging works—a way in which people can chat one on one with others. Two of the most popular pieces of software for communicating on the Internet—America Online Instant Messenger (AIM) and ICQ—are chat software. This chapter also discusses the first type of Internet chat, called Internet Relay Chat (IRC). Although not as popular as it used to be, it's still a way many people chat with each other online.

Finally, Chapter 20, "How Internet Phone Calls Work," details one of the more intriguing new uses of the Internet—using it as your telephone. Today you can dial into your local Internet provider with your computer, and if you have the right hardware and software, you can talk with anyone similarly connected to the Internet anywhere in the world, all without paying long-distance telephone charges. This chapter also covers a new type of low-cost telephone service that has sprung up: IP Telephony. In IP Telephony, you talk over your telephone as you would normally—the phone call appears no different to you. But the Internet, rather than the normal phone system, is used to make the connection to the person you're calling.

CHAPTER 16 How E-mail Works

ELECTRONIC mail, or e-mail, might be the most heavily used feature of the Internet. You can use it to send messages to anyone who is connected to the Internet or connected to a computer network that has a connection to the Internet, such as an online service. Millions of people send and receive e-mail every day. E-mail is a great way to keep up with far-flung relatives, friends, co-workers in different branches of your company, and colleagues in your field.

E-mail messages are sent in the same way as most Internet data. The TCP protocol breaks your messages into packets, the IP protocol delivers the packets to the proper location, and then the TCP reassembles the message on the receiving mail server so it can be read.

You can also attach binary files, such as pictures, videos, sounds, and executable files to your e-mail messages. Because the Internet isn't capable of directly handling binary files in e-mail, the file first must be encoded in one of a variety of encoding schemes. Popular schemes are MIME and uuencode. The person who receives the attached binary file (called an *attachment*) must decode the file with the same scheme that was used to encode the file. Many e-mail software packages do this automatically.

When you send e-mail to someone on the Internet, that message often has to travel through a series of networks before it reaches the recipient—networks that might use different e-mail formats. Gateways perform the job of translating e-mail formats from one network to another so that the messages can make their way through all the networks of the Internet.

A mailing list is one of the most intriguing uses of e-mail. It connects a group of people who are interested in the same topic, such as Japanese cartoons or home schooling. When one person sends e-mail to the mailing list, that message is automatically sent to everyone on the list. You can meet others and talk to them on a regular basis about your shared interests, hobbies, or professions. To get onto a mailing list, you send an e-mail note to the mailing list administrator and include your e-mail address.

Mailing lists can be moderated or unmoderated. A *moderated* mailing list is screened by the list administrator, who might kill duplicate messages or messages not related to the list's theme. An *unmoderated* mailing list is wide open; all mail sent to it is automatically sent to everyone on the list.

Often, when you want to subscribe to a mailing list, you send a message to a computer instead of a person. That computer, known as a *list server* (also called a *listserv*), reads your e-mail and automatically subscribes you to the list. You can unsubscribe from the list in the same way.

In the past, finding the e-mail address of someone was very difficult if you knew only her name. These days, it's not so hard. A variety of "white page" directories have sprung up on the Internet that enable you to easily look up people's e-mail addresses. These sites mainly use a standard called the Lightweight Directory Access Protocol (LDAP), which enables you to find people's e-mail addresses without even having to visit a Web site. Using the protocol, you can search for e-mail addresses on the Internet from directly within your e-mail program.

One problem with e-mail is that it's not secure—snoopers and hackers can read it as it gets sent along the public wires that make up the Internet. To ensure that no one except the sender and receiver can read it, encryption can be used—software that scrambles the mail so only those with the proper encryption keys can read it.

How E-mail Is Delivered over the Internet

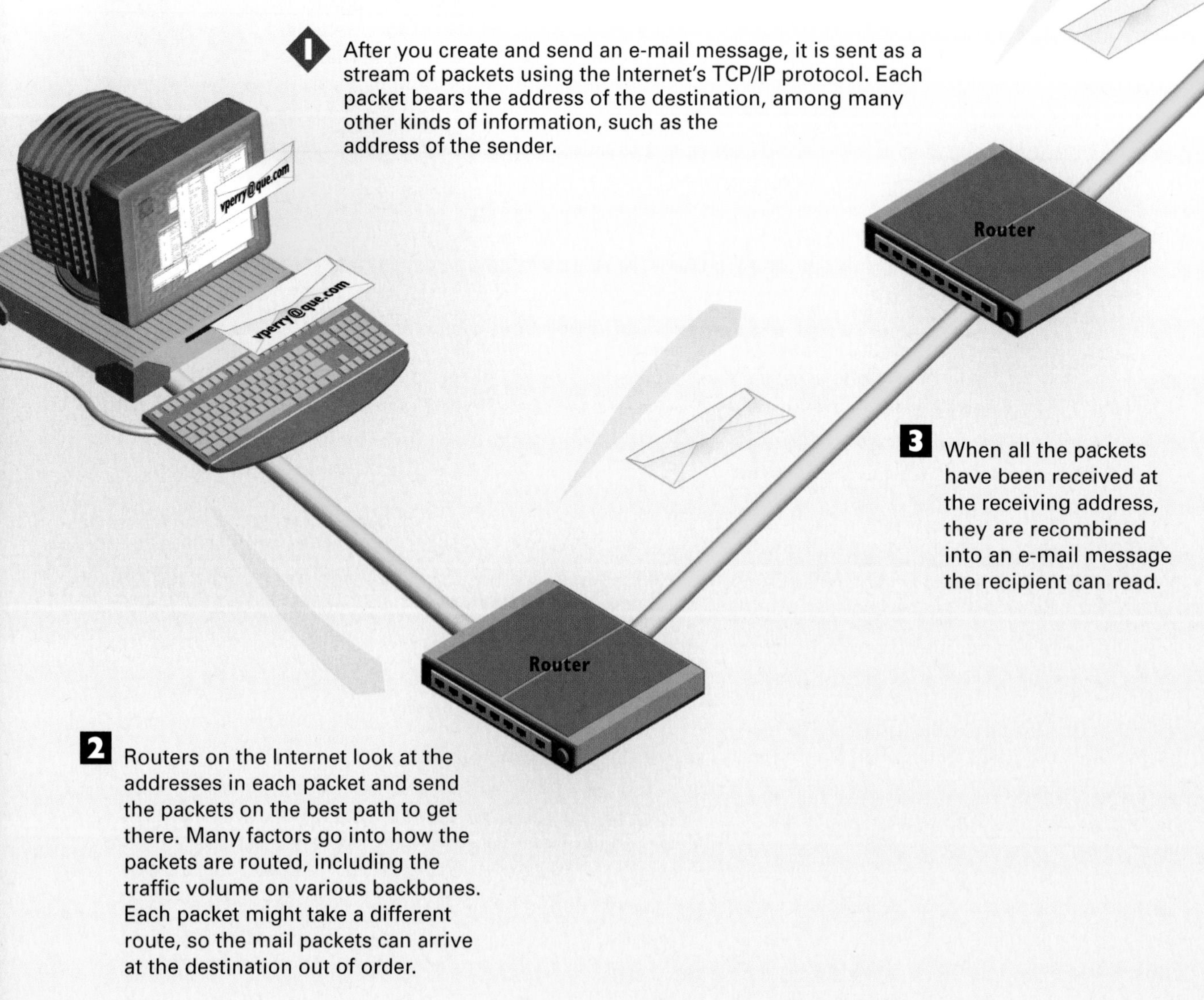

1 After you create and send an e-mail message, it is sent as a stream of packets using the Internet's TCP/IP protocol. Each packet bears the address of the destination, among many other kinds of information, such as the address of the sender.

2 Routers on the Internet look at the addresses in each packet and send the packets on the best path to get there. Many factors go into how the packets are routed, including the traffic volume on various backbones. Each packet might take a different route, so the mail packets can arrive at the destination out of order.

3 When all the packets have been received at the receiving address, they are recombined into an e-mail message the recipient can read.

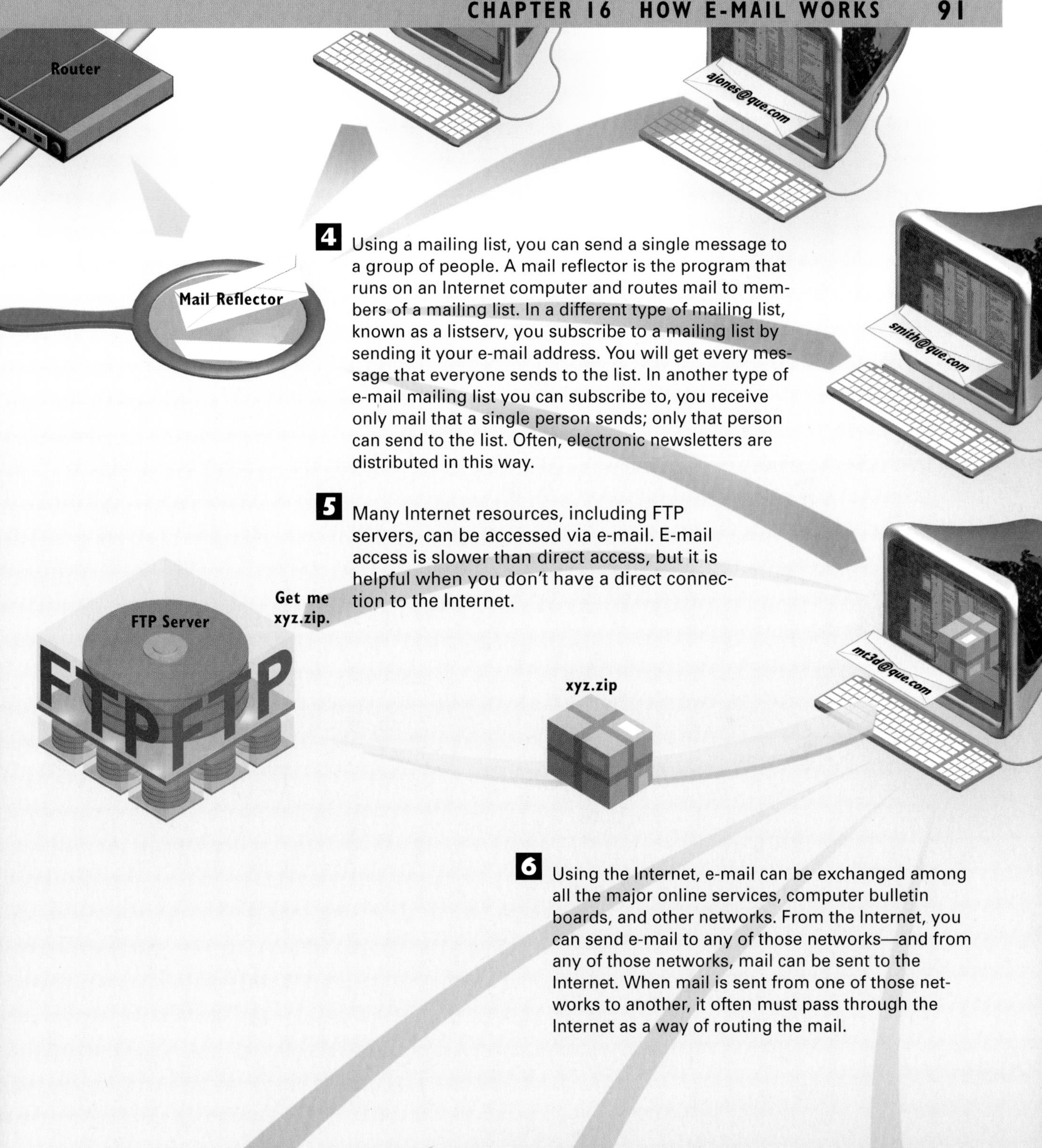

4 Using a mailing list, you can send a single message to a group of people. A mail reflector is the program that runs on an Internet computer and routes mail to members of a mailing list. In a different type of mailing list, known as a listserv, you subscribe to a mailing list by sending it your e-mail address. You will get every message that everyone sends to the list. In another type of e-mail mailing list you can subscribe to, you receive only mail that a single person sends; only that person can send to the list. Often, electronic newsletters are distributed in this way.

5 Many Internet resources, including FTP servers, can be accessed via e-mail. E-mail access is slower than direct access, but it is helpful when you don't have a direct connection to the Internet.

6 Using the Internet, e-mail can be exchanged among all the major online services, computer bulletin boards, and other networks. From the Internet, you can send e-mail to any of those networks—and from any of those networks, mail can be sent to the Internet. When mail is sent from one of those networks to another, it often must pass through the Internet as a way of routing the mail.

How E-mail Software Works

1 After the Internet delivers mail to your e-mail box, you need some way to read the mail, compose new mail, and respond to your messages. To do all this, you use e-mail software, sometimes called *mailers* or *readers*.

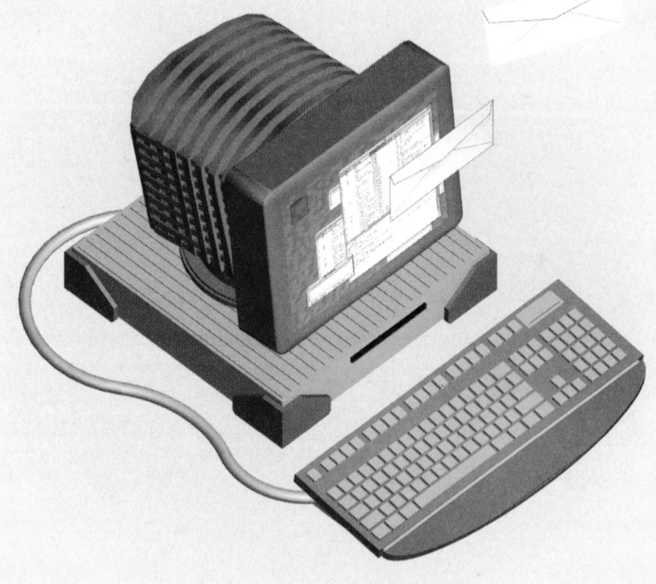

2 When someone sends you an Internet e-mail message, the message isn't delivered straight to your computer. Instead, it gets sent to a mail server. Your e-mail software logs in to the mail server and checks to see whether you have mail.

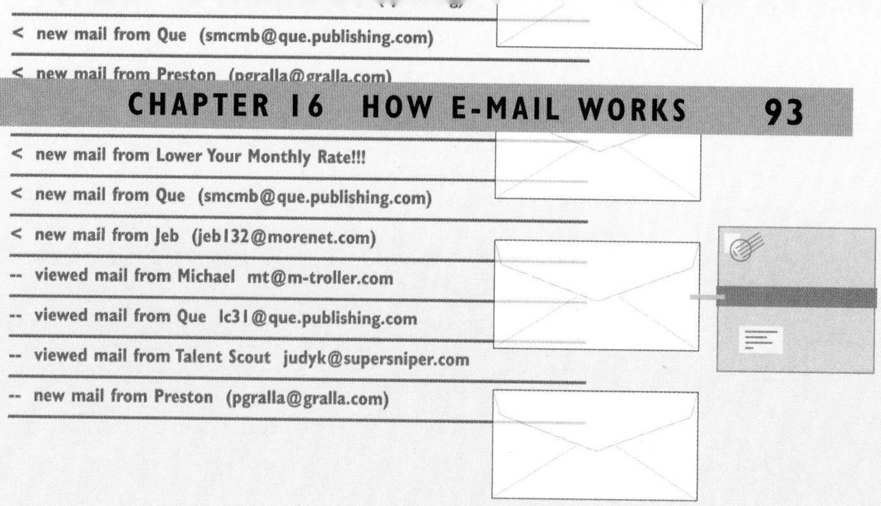

< new mail from Que (smcmb@que.publishing.com)
< new mail from Preston (pgralla@gralla.com)
< new mail from Lower Your Monthly Rate!!!
< new mail from Que (smcmb@que.publishing.com)
< new mail from Jeb (jeb132@morenet.com)
-- viewed mail from Michael mt@m-troller.com
-- viewed mail from Que lc31@que.publishing.com
-- viewed mail from Talent Scout judyk@supersniper.com
-- new mail from Preston (pgralla@gralla.com)

3 If you have new mail, you'll see a list of your new mail messages when you log in to the server. You'll often see the name of the sender, the subject of the message, and the date and time the message was sent.

4 When you want to read a mail message, you tell your software to download it to your own computer. There, you read the message using your mail reader, and then you can file it, delete it, or respond to it.

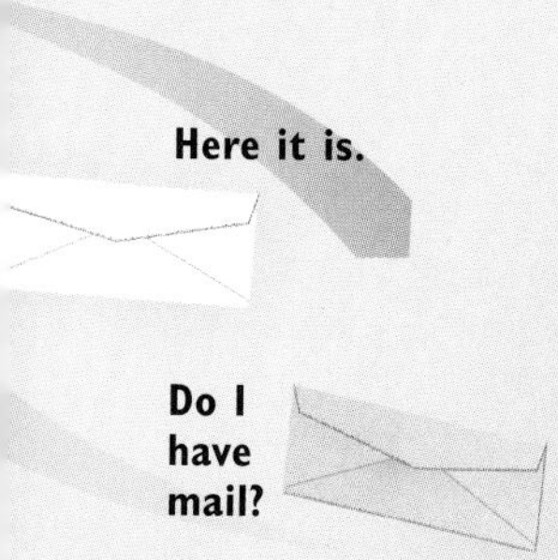

Here it is.
Do I have mail?

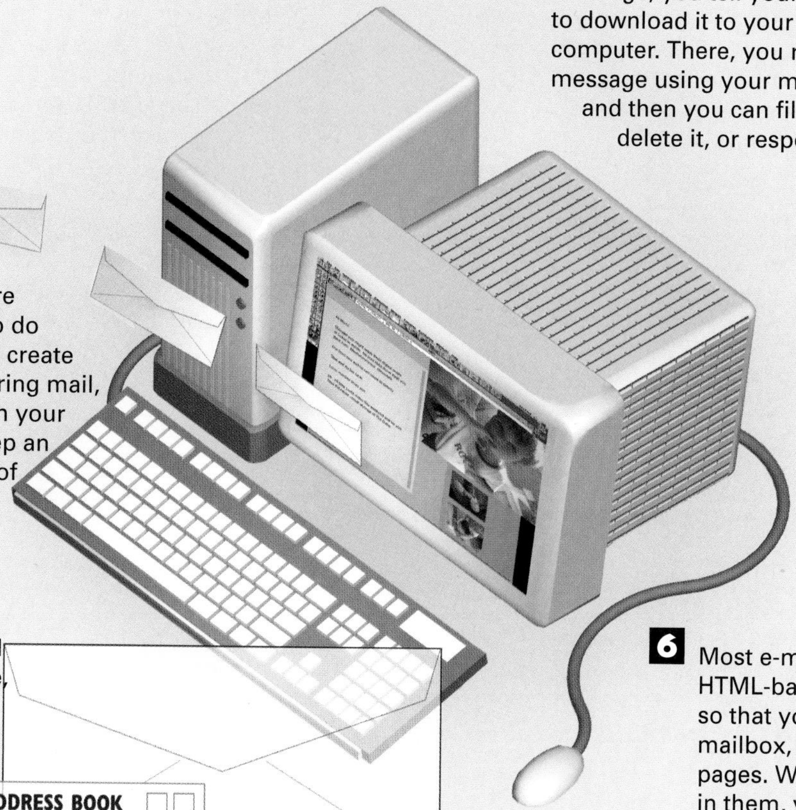

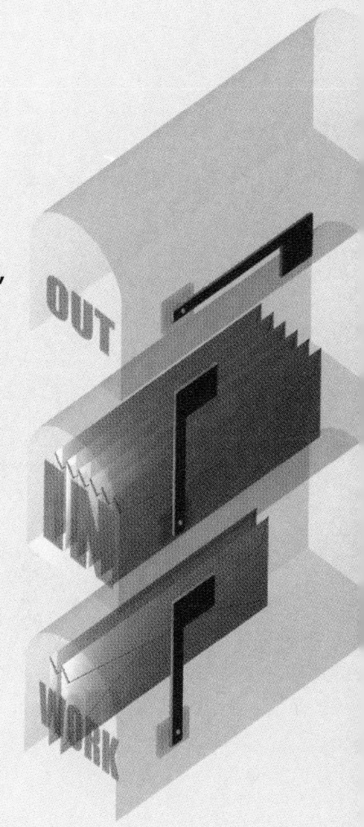

OUT
IN
WORK

5 E-mail software enables you to do things such as create folders for storing mail, search through your messages, keep an address book of people to whom you send mail, create group mailing lists, create and add a signature file, and more.

6 Most e-mail software reads HTML-based pages sent to you so that you can receive, in your mailbox, fully formatted Web pages. When you click the links in them, your browser launches and visits the page to which it is linked.

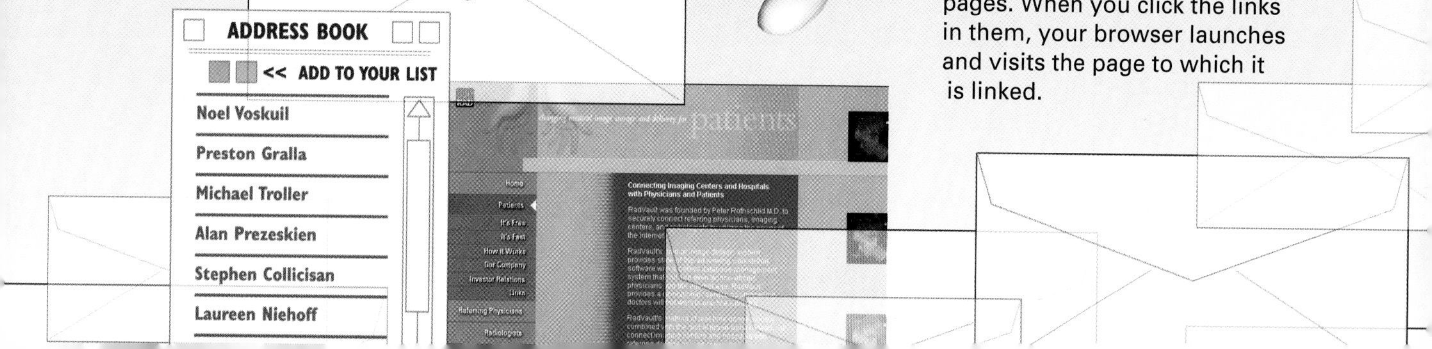

ADDRESS BOOK
<< ADD TO YOUR LIST
Noel Voskuil
Preston Gralla
Michael Troller
Alan Prezeskien
Stephen Collicisan
Laureen Niehoff
patients
Connecting Imaging Centers and Hospitals with Physicians and Patients

How a Mailing List Works

johnp@aoll.com
miagralla@prodigy.com
billybob@sun.com
jqpublic@usa.gov
asmith@jupiter.com
fredg@tozikal.net
janeq@aoll.com

ADMIN

1 Mailing lists are a way for groups of people to have public discussions via e-mail. After you join a mailing list, every message you write to the list can be read by everyone on the list.

Join request from:
gabegralla@zdnet.com

2 To join a mailing list, you must subscribe to it. You subscribe by sending an e-mail message to the mailing list administrator and asking to join the list. To cancel a subscription to the list, you send a cancellation request to the list administrator.

3 The mailing list itself is a database of the e-mail addresses of people who have subscribed to it. When you ask to subscribe, you are added to the database.

4 When the computer on which the database resides receives a message to be sent to the mailing list, it automatically mails the message to every address in the mailing list database. Some mailing lists are very active, and people on them can get dozens of messages every day. Because of that, it's a good idea to check your mail frequently and clean out your mailbox. Otherwise, you can bog down your mail server, which can make it difficult for you to read your mail because you'll have so much of it.

ADMIN

You are now part of the soccer mailing list.

Ready for soccer season?

Send Message

johnjames@neti.com
billybob@sun.com
gabegralla@zdnet.com
jqpublic@usa.gov
asmith@jupiter.com
fredg@tozikal.net
janeq@aoll.com
sallyr@goto.com

Send Message

Send Message

Send Message

Send Message

Send Message

How E-mail Is Sent Between Networks

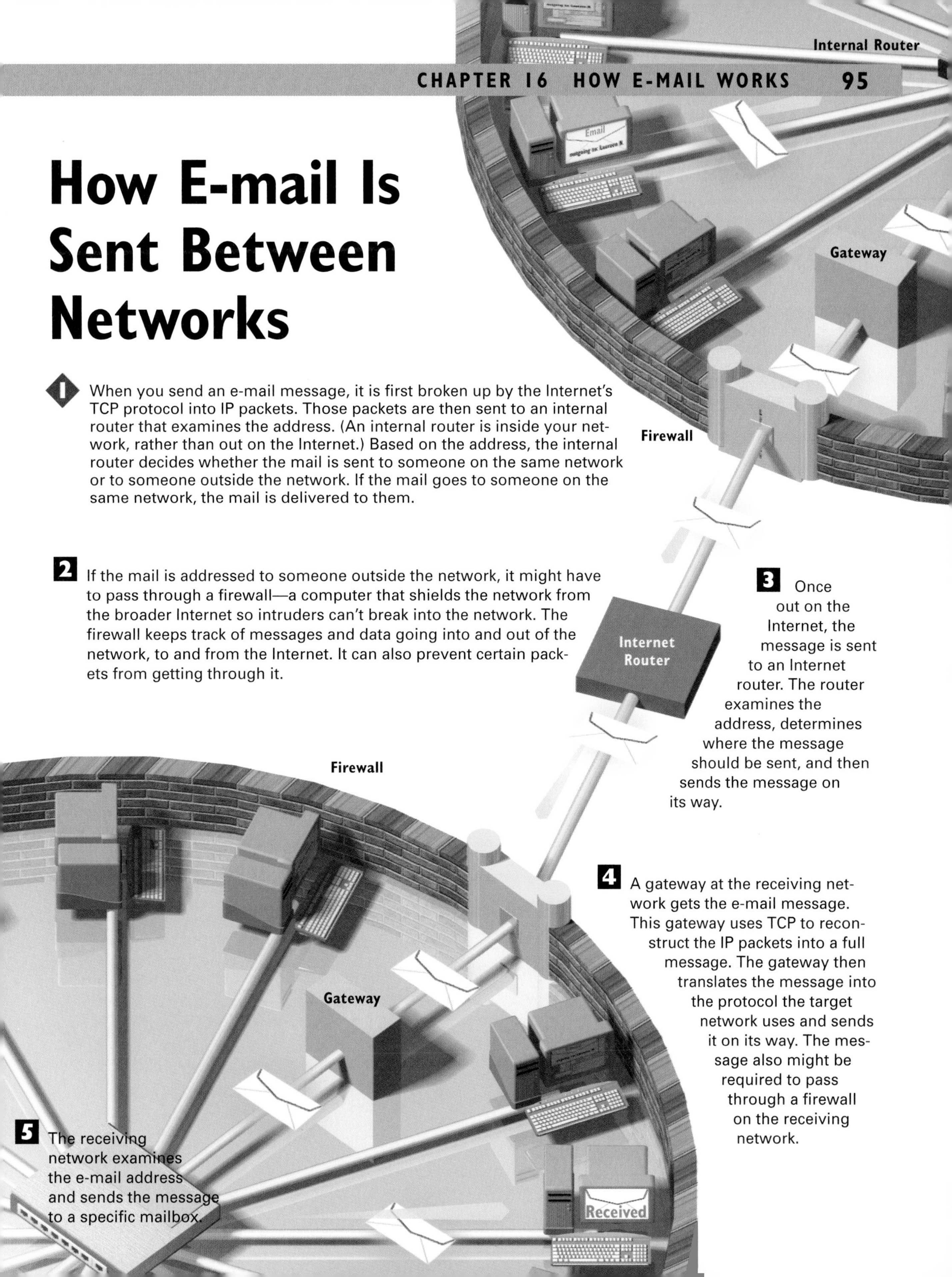

1. When you send an e-mail message, it is first broken up by the Internet's TCP protocol into IP packets. Those packets are then sent to an internal router that examines the address. (An internal router is inside your network, rather than out on the Internet.) Based on the address, the internal router decides whether the mail is sent to someone on the same network or to someone outside the network. If the mail goes to someone on the same network, the mail is delivered to them.

2. If the mail is addressed to someone outside the network, it might have to pass through a firewall—a computer that shields the network from the broader Internet so intruders can't break into the network. The firewall keeps track of messages and data going into and out of the network, to and from the Internet. It can also prevent certain packets from getting through it.

3. Once out on the Internet, the message is sent to an Internet router. The router examines the address, determines where the message should be sent, and then sends the message on its way.

4. A gateway at the receiving network gets the e-mail message. This gateway uses TCP to reconstruct the IP packets into a full message. The gateway then translates the message into the protocol the target network uses and sends it on its way. The message also might be required to pass through a firewall on the receiving network.

5. The receiving network examines the e-mail address and sends the message to a specific mailbox.

Internal Router
Gateway
Firewall
Internet Router
Firewall
Gateway
Received

How White Page Directories (LDAP) Work

1 Millions of people have e-mail addresses on the Internet, but finding an e-mail address has always been difficult if you know only a person's name. The Lightweight Directory Access Protocol (LDAP) makes creating white page–style directories easier, so you now can look up people's addresses if you know only their names. An LDAP directory is a database that follows LDAP rules and protocols for organizing its information. It is located on an Internet server. A company or business maintains the server and is responsible for keeping the information on it up-to-date by adding new names, deleting old names, and updating existing names.

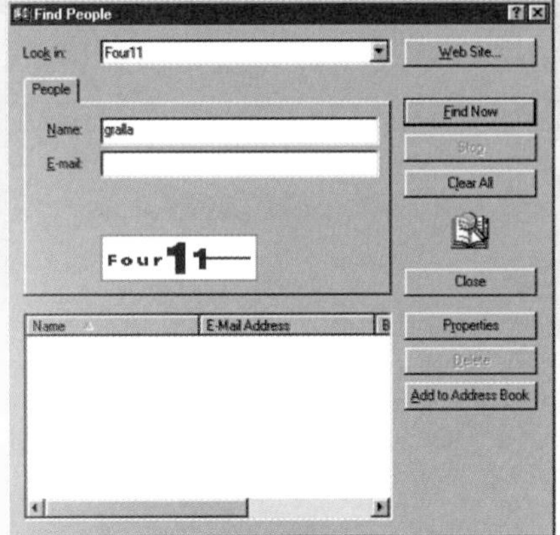

BINDRESPONSE

2 Like much other Internet technology, LDAP works on a client/server model. The client runs on a local computer. Many types of clients are available for many types of computers. To find someone's e-mail address, you run the client on your computer and type in the name of the person whose e-mail address you want to find.

Add Name to Address Book

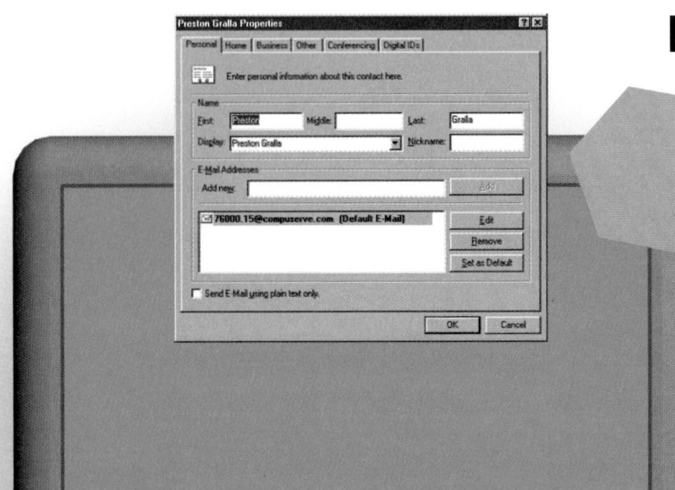

8 Depending on the software you're using, you can now add the name and e-mail address to your local address book, or you can immediately send an e-mail to the person.

3 Before sending the request itself, the client sends an LDAP command, called the `BindRequest`, to the server. Basically, this is a command telling the server the client wants to make a request.

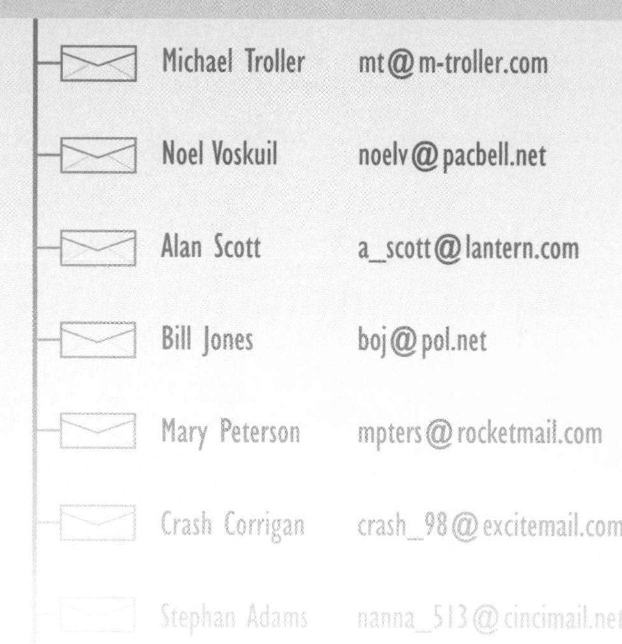

BINDREQUEST

4 The server answers with a command called the `BindResponse`, telling the client it can go ahead and make a request.

FIND "GRALLA"

5 The client then sends the request to the server, sending a person's name and asking for his e-mail address.

7 The client receives the results and displays them on the local computer.

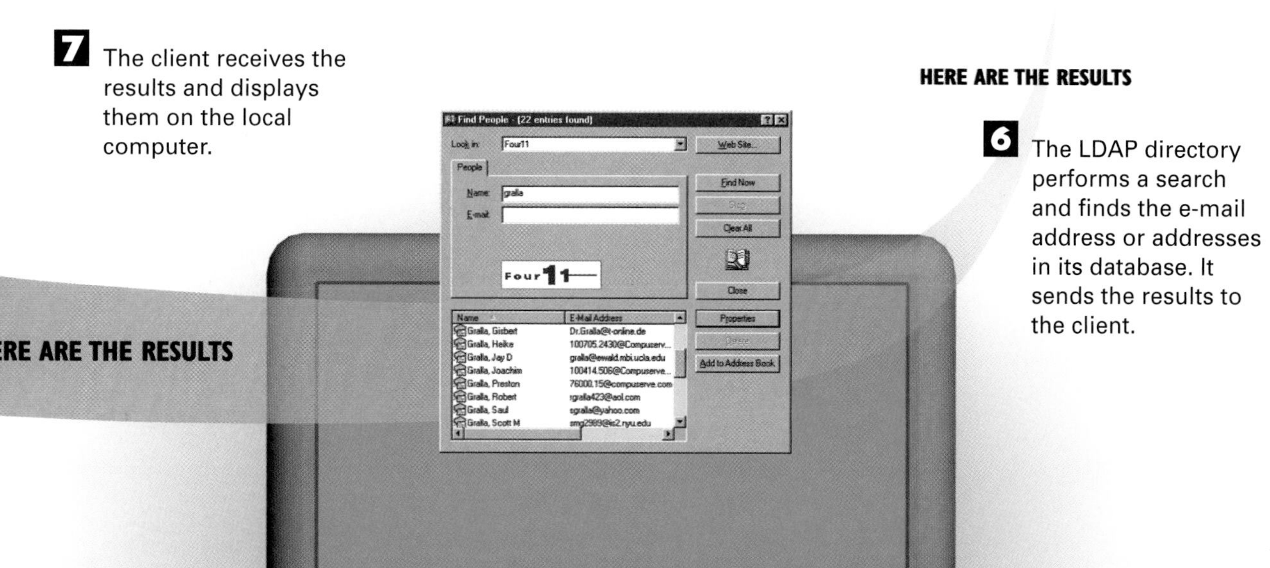

HERE ARE THE RESULTS

6 The LDAP directory performs a search and finds the e-mail address or addresses in its database. It sends the results to the client.

How Encryption Can Keep E-mail Private

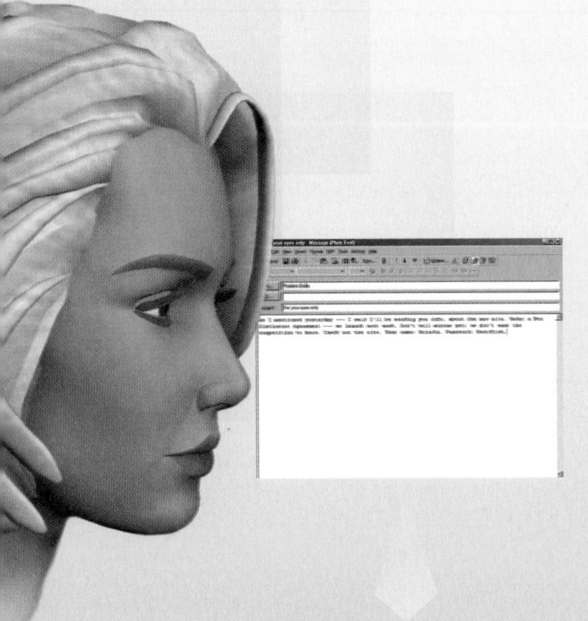

1 Encryption can be used to hide e-mail messages so snoopers and hackers can't read them as they are sent across the Internet. Many types of encryption exist, but in the most common one, keys are used. Everyone gets a public and private key. The *public key* is available for anyone to use to encrypt mail; the *private key* is used only by the recipient to decrypt it. This illustration shows how to encrypt e-mail with the popular encryption program Pretty Good Privacy (PGP). To start using PGP, someone uses her normal e-mail program to compose a piece of mail. After she composes the mail, she decides whether she wants to encrypt the message.

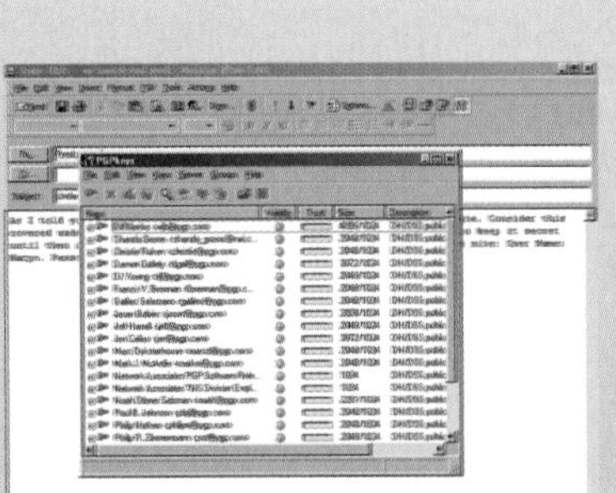

2 When someone decides to encrypt a piece of e-mail, she has to have a copy of the public key of the person to whom she is going to send the message. That key can be obtained a number of ways—from a public Internet site, or the recipient can send it via e-mail. After the person has the key, she stores it in a key ring on her computer and can call it up at any time.

3 After choosing the key of the person who will receive the message, the message is encrypted using that person's public key.

4 The encrypted e-mail is sent in the same way that any normal e-mail is. The difference is that the e-mail is encrypted so that anyone who reads the mail as it makes its way across the Internet won't be able to understand it—he'll see only random characters.

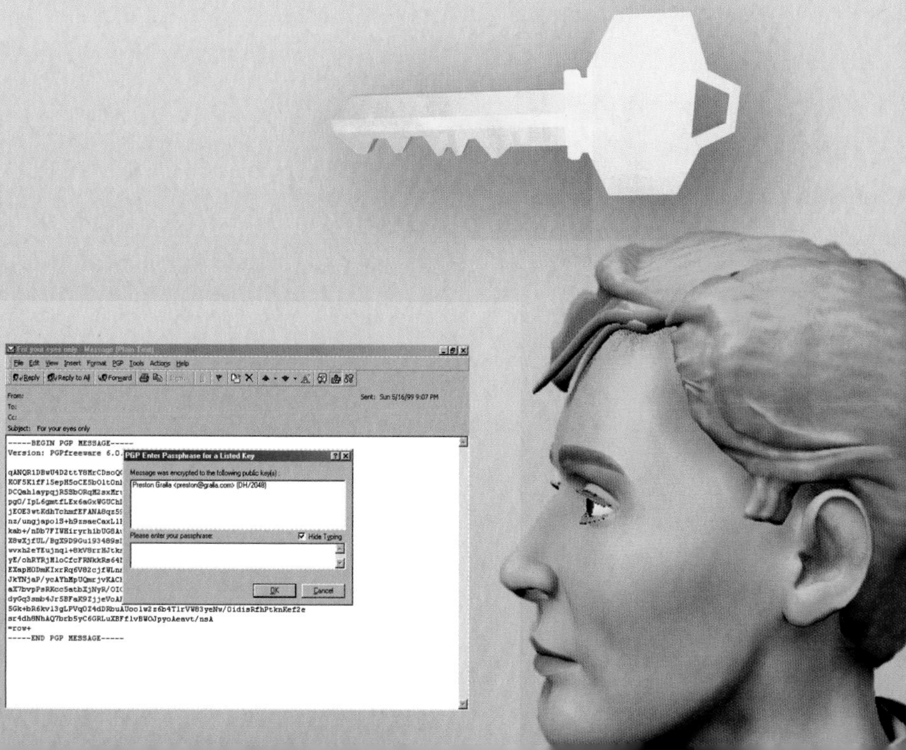

5 The person receives the e-mail as he does any normal piece of e-mail. However, the e-mail is encrypted, and so can't yet be read. So, the person uses his private key to decrypt the message. Before the message can be decrypted, a password for the private key typically must be typed in. However, some e-mail programs and encryption software can be set so that the message is decrypted automatically, as soon as it's received.

6 The private key decrypts the message, and the person can read it and use it like any other piece of e-mail.

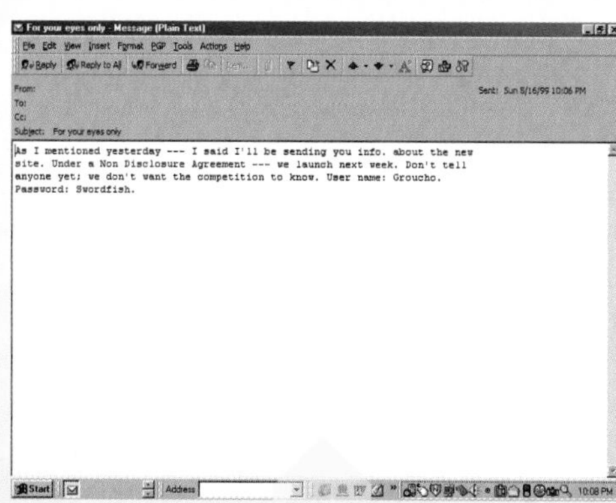

CHAPTER 17 How E-mail Spam Works

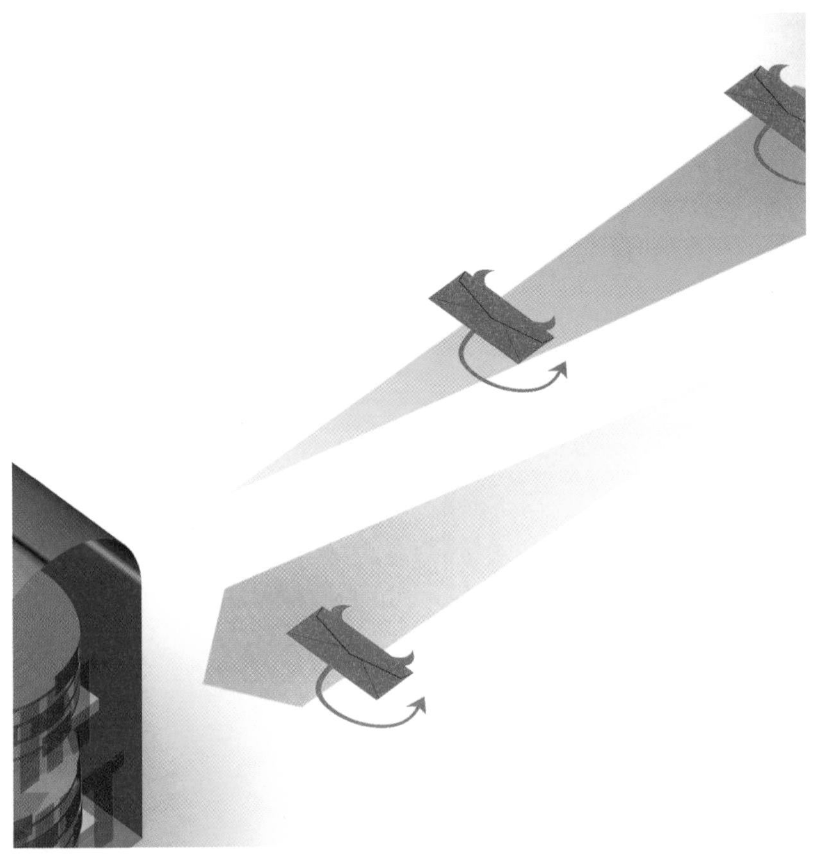

ONE of the most contentious issues to surface on the Internet in the last few years has to do with what Internet users call *spam*. Spam is unsolicited junk e-mail that commercial companies send out, asking you to buy their goods and services. At times it might contain inducements to visit the seller's site. The e-mail usually contains a phone number to call, an address to send money to, or a Web site to visit to buy the goods and services.

The term *spam* comes from a Monty Python skit in which every item on a menu contained Spam luncheon meat. It was originally used to refer to unsolicited postings for commercial products or services on Usenet, especially when they were cross-posted to several newsgroups.

Spam might seem like a minor annoyance, but the truth is, it can cause major problems. Spam floods the Internet with unwanted mail, which can lead to delayed or lost mail. It clogs the Internet pipeline, making other information slower to send. It wastes time for those who have to go through their e-mail boxes deleting unsolicited mail, especially when they pay for their e-mail service by the hour. Additionally, it's fairly common for spammers to hide their real e-mail addresses by forging other people's names onto the From or Sender header of an e-mail message. So, those people whose names were forged might be the target of angry mail. This makes it difficult for Webmasters and mail administrators to filter spam messages by From address or domain name. Sometimes spammers even use other people's servers to deliver their bulk e-mail; in essence, forcing someone else to pay the costs of the spammer's mail delivery.

In some ways, spam is not very different from traditional junk mail. Spammers buy or compile massive lists of e-mail addresses, in the same way that junk mailers buy or compile U.S. Postal addresses. The spammer then uses special software to send a solicitation to every person on the list—not uncommonly, tens of thousands of pieces of e-mail in a single spam mailing. To hide their true identities, spammers forge names onto the headers of e-mail messages and even "relay" their spam to another mail server on the Internet, so that finding out where the mail comes from is impossible. Often, a user will request to be taken off the list by replying to e-mail addresses the spammers provide. However, this verifies the user's address and he will get even more spam.

A variety of ways have been devised to block spam, including having e-mail filters on e-mail software ignore any mail from known spammers. This doesn't always work well, however, because spammers often change or forge their e-mail addresses. There are also calls for the courts or Congress to take action. Congress has considered several laws, including one that would ban spam entirely, in the same way that junk faxes were banned several years ago. Until then, try doing an Internet search for Web sites that will help you download and install software to help filter your e-mail and stop spam.

How E-mail Spam Is Sent

05/21	CONTINENTAL.COM	URGENT MESSAGE
05/21	Cf@mailaol.co	Classmeister 5.0 + Special Offer (com/msg)
05/21	OIL.PATCH.MARKET	E-MAIL LIST FOR SALE GETS RESULTS QUICKLY
05/22	4063986@us.net	~~~ Cable Television Descrambler - Easy To Make !!!
05/22	seanpage@infocom	Business Offer!!!
05/25	TheCreditMan@big	You Are Guaranteed Credit!
05/25	Jill the coy one	4 Million Email Addresses For Sale
05/26	dospub@www.usa.c	publish at home
05/27	Unknown@unknown	This is awesome!
05/27	56369130@swbell.	WANT REVENGE - Get It Right Here - FREE SAMPLES !!!
05/28	To Embrace	A Surprise Birthday Party And Gift For YOU :-)))))
05/29	kat@hol.gr	adults only
05/29	connect@internet	Qualify For Survey Sweepstakes Win $25

1 *Spam* is a term used to describe unsolicited e-mail sent to you, often by commercial firms that attempt to sell you goods and services. Spam is sent out as bulk e-mail, often to lists of 10,000 or more people at once. It's inexpensive to send, so its use has exploded on the Internet to the point where it is common for someone to get several dozen of these messages in a single day. Spam has become enough of an annoyance to warrant calls to ban it outright.

2 To send out unsolicited bulk e-mail, a spammer first needs to get a list of e-mail addresses. Often, spammers buy the lists from companies that compile them. These companies use automated software robots to get the e-mail addresses. The robots get the lists from a number of sources. One way is to go into Usenet newsgroups and harvest e-mail addresses by looking inside every message, which usually has in it the e-mail address of the person who posted it.

Anawave Gravity - [news.admin.net-abuse.email]

File Edit Bookmarks View Go Directory Window Options Help

Newsgroups: news.admin.net-abuse.email

From	Status	Subject	Lines	Date
ORAC		Re: AGN postmaster likes to get complaints.	27	5/23
ORAC		Re: UCE from Cyberpromo via cts.com	56	5/25
Peter Kolding		Re: UCE from Cyberpromo via cts.com	54	5/28
Bruce Harper		Re: ml.org	38	5/26
Michael Kohne		Re: ml.org	27	5/27

Subject: Re: I just talked to AGIS about the IEMMC
From: aiken@unity.ncsu.edu (Wayne Aiken)
Newsgroups: news.admin.net-abuse.email,alt.stop.spamming,news.admin.net-abuse.misc

Torbjörn Andersson (d91tan@oxe.docs.uu.se) wrote:
: Majestic7@NOSPAMcryogen.com (JOWazzoo) wrote:
: > Quantum is going to run the databse for these guys. I presume you are
: > referring to Walt Rines.

Rules: Decode Binary Rule Run Outbox 0 Waiting 0 Errors

Document: Done

Get e-mail address.

ADD: all addresses

3 E-mail addresses also can be harvested from e-mail directories on the Web sites that allow people to look up others' e-mail addresses. Software robots can go into the directory and grab every address in the directory. Robots also can go into chat areas, such as those on America Online, and gather e-mail addresses.

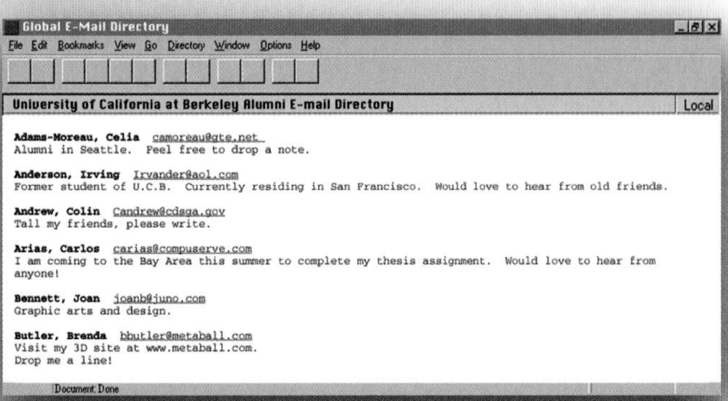
Global E-Mail Directory

File Edit Bookmarks View Go Directory Window Options Help

University of California at Berkeley Alumni E-mail Directory

Adams-Moreau, Celia camoreau@gte.net
Alumni in Seattle. Feel free to drop a note.

Anderson, Irving Irvander@aol.com
Former student of U.C.B. Currently residing in San Francisco. Would love to hear from old friends.

Andrew, Colin Candrew@cdsga.gov
Tall my friends, please write.

Arias, Carlos carias@compuserve.com
I am coming to the Bay Area this summer to complete my thesis assignment. Would love to hear from anyone!

Bennett, Joan joanb@juno.com
Graphic arts and design.

Butler, Brenda bbutler@metaball.com
Visit my 3D site at www.metaball.com.
Drop me a line!

Document: Done

Get e-mail address.

ADD: all addresses

Bulk Mail List

salmon@earthlink.com
welt@well.com
vegrebski@excite.com
ncsof@webtv.net
straxy@vets.org
johns1739@aol1.com
stevej@apple.com
johnh@liberty.net
alxop1@webtv.net
corpflak@msn.com
sillysam7@kidstoys.net
morm@cheerybar.com
johnqp@prodigy.com
eatright3@heath.com
qwertz@yahoo.com
aiken@unity.net
triweb@li.com
zgooby@znakz.com
joanh@juno.com
hotrod99@fastcar.com
richir@kerbanko.com
morefun@home.com
rebar@builder.org
freddie592@aol1.com
strand@femtonet.com
xtheria@fast.com
george@whths.gov
bigboat@nautilus.com
travelr@trips.fun.com
boffo@snafu.com
yabbadabba@aol1.com
morepower@scottie.com
bigdaddy@lukas.com

4 Some spammers include in the e-mail a return address to which someone who no longer wants to receive spam can send a message and be taken off the spam list. When the remove message is received, a robot automatically takes the person off the list. However, spammers rarely do this because most people would opt not to be on the spam lists.

5 The spammer either buys the resulting e-mail list or compiles one of her own. The spammer uses the list, along with bulk mailing software, and sends a spam message to every person on the list. In the message might be a return address, Web site, or phone number where the receiver can get more information about the goods and services being sold.

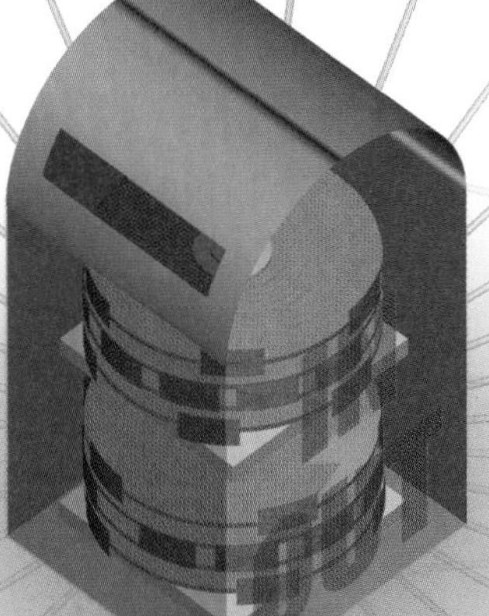

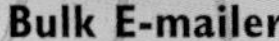

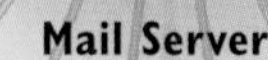

6 Spammers realize that spam offends most people, so the spammers go to great lengths to hide their true e-mail addresses. As one way of hiding their real e-mail addresses, they "forge" parts of the message header in the e-mail address, such as the From, Sender, and Reply fields so it appears that the e-mail has come from someone other than the spammer. Doing this is sometimes called *spamouflage*.

7 As a further way of hiding their true addresses, spammers relay their bulk spam to a server that is not associated with them and then have that server send out the bulk spam. Sometimes spammers have the bulk spam relayed among several different servers to make tracing who really sent the mail even more difficult.

How E-mail Spam Is Blocked

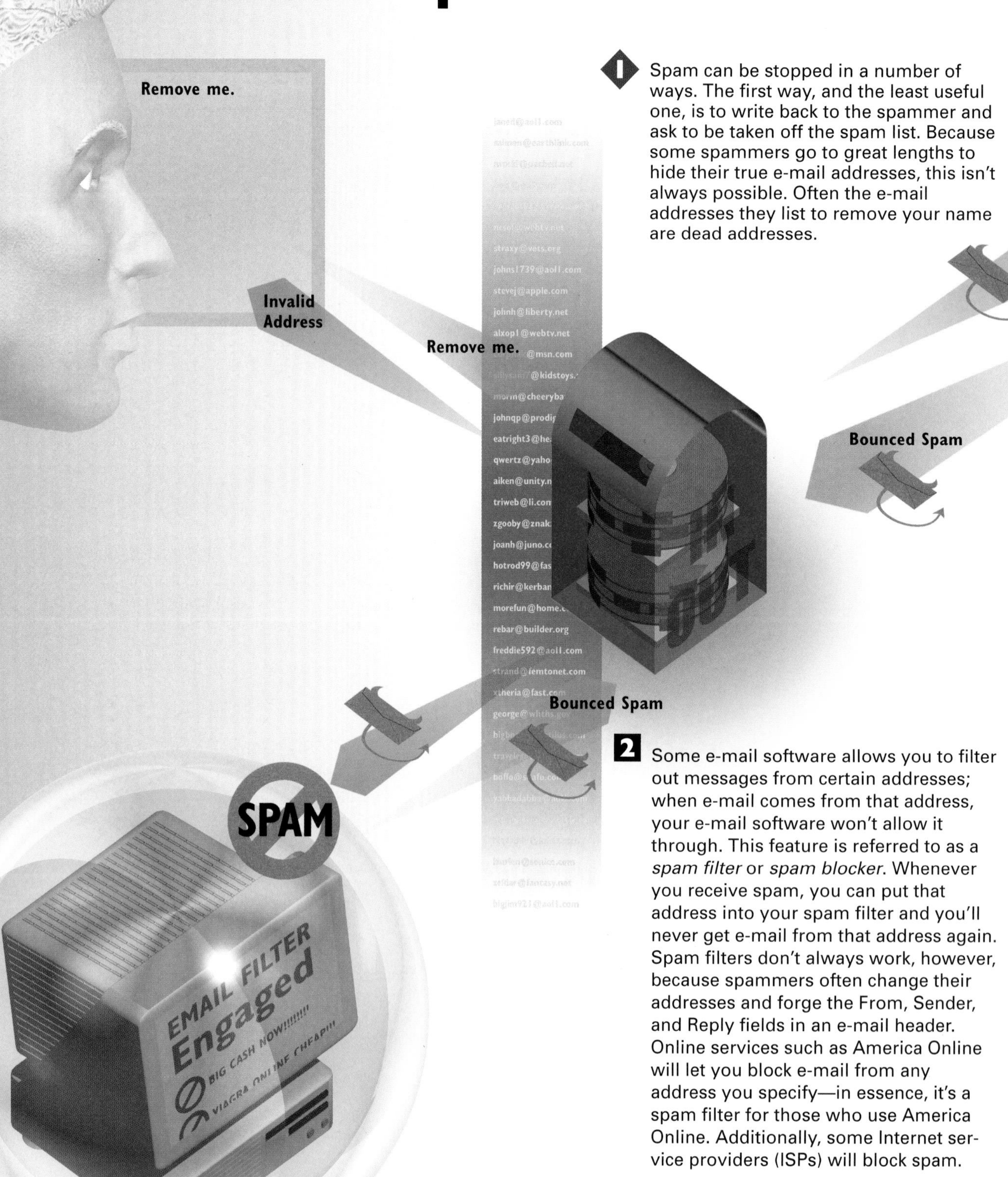

1 Spam can be stopped in a number of ways. The first way, and the least useful one, is to write back to the spammer and ask to be taken off the spam list. Because some spammers go to great lengths to hide their true e-mail addresses, this isn't always possible. Often the e-mail addresses they list to remove your name are dead addresses.

2 Some e-mail software allows you to filter out messages from certain addresses; when e-mail comes from that address, your e-mail software won't allow it through. This feature is referred to as a *spam filter* or *spam blocker*. Whenever you receive spam, you can put that address into your spam filter and you'll never get e-mail from that address again. Spam filters don't always work, however, because spammers often change their addresses and forge the From, Sender, and Reply fields in an e-mail header. Online services such as America Online will let you block e-mail from any address you specify—in essence, it's a spam filter for those who use America Online. Additionally, some Internet service providers (ISPs) will block spam.

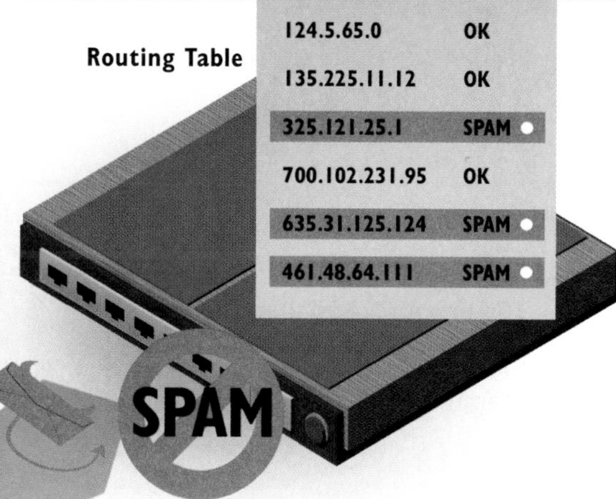

3 ISPs and online service such as America Online can block spammers from sending bulk mail to their subscribers. A router examines all incoming mail to the ISP or online service. The router has been told that when e-mail comes from certain addresses, to block mail from getting into the network. These addresses are put in a routing table that can be changed whenever new spammers are found. ISPs have a variety of other ways for detecting spam as well.

4 Because spammers often change their addresses, using routing tables doesn't always work. Online services and ISPs have gone to court to ban spammers from sending e-mail to their customers. Although the law remains murky, in a number of instances, the courts have decided in favor of online services and the ISPs and have banned spammers from sending mail through them.

5 A number of laws and schemes have been proposed to regulate or outlaw spam. In one plan, every piece of spam would have to contain a specific piece of information in the message header, identifying it as unsolicited e-mail. In this way, people could set their spam filters to block every single piece of spam, filtering out that piece of information. Some laws have been proposed that would outlaw spam entirely, in the same way that junk faxes were banned.

6 One way to prevent being spammed is to be sure that your e-mail address isn't added to spam lists. To do this, when posting to Usenet newsgroups, edit your header so that it doesn't contain your e-mail address. You should also notify e-mail directories that you'd like to be taken off their lists. In this way, your e-mail address won't be harvested by robots, and you should get less spam.

CHAPTER 18 How Newsgroups Work

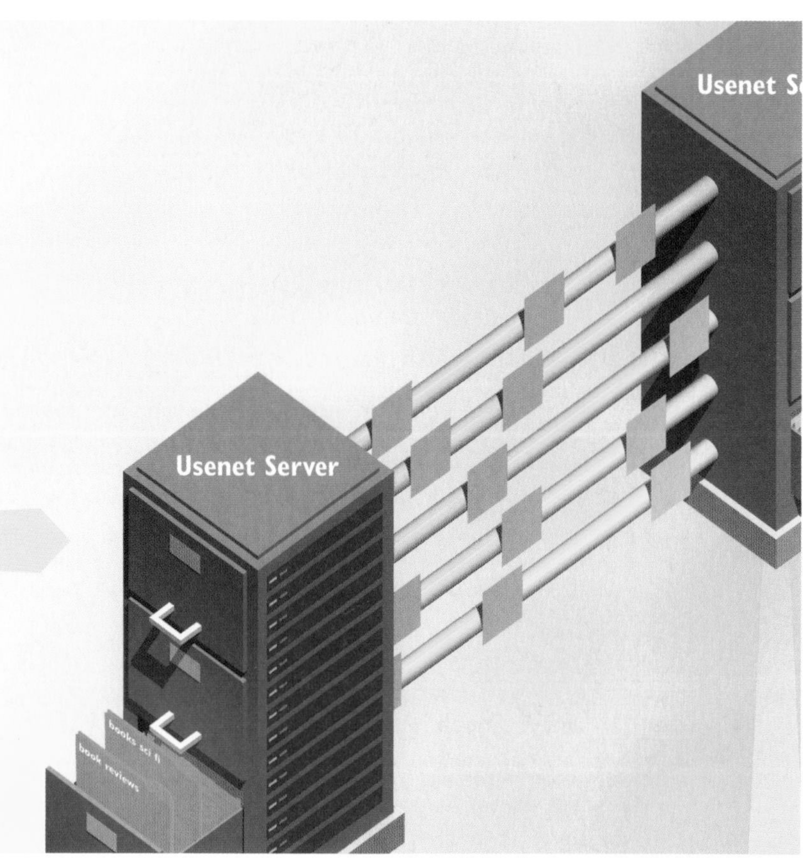

USENET, the world's biggest electronic discussion forum, provides a way for messages to be sent among computers across the entire Internet. People from all over the world participate in discussions on thousands of topics in specific areas of interest called *newsgroups*.

Hundreds of different major hierarchies of newsgroups exist, such as recreation (identified by the letters "rec") and computers (identified by the letters "comp"). Within these major hierarchies are subcategories (such as rec.arts) and further subcategories (such as rec.arts.books). Individual newsgroups can cover anything from movies to parenting, ecology, sports teams, clip art, and news about Usenet itself. Not all Internet sites carry all newsgroups. An administrator at each site decides which newsgroups to carry.

To participate in newsgroups, you need special software to read and respond to them. Readers are available for PC, Macintosh, and Unix computers. Online services such as CompuServe and America Online have their own proprietary software that lets you participate in newsgroups.

A good newsgroup reader lets you view the ongoing discussions as threads. *Threads* are ongoing conversations grouped by topic. So, for example, the rec.arts.books newsgroup might have many different threads going on at one time, each discussing a different book.

Many newsgroups have a list of Frequently Asked Questions, or FAQs (pronounced "facks"), associated with them. These FAQs answer common questions about the newsgroup. It's a good idea to read the FAQ before submitting questions to the newsgroup as a whole.

You participate in newsgroups by reading the messages and responding to them. There are moderated and unmoderated newsgroups. In a *moderated newsgroup*, each message goes to a human moderator. The moderator looks at the messages, ensuring they're appropriate for the group. If they are appropriate, the messages are posted. All messages sent to an *unmoderated newsgroup* are automatically posted.

When messages are posted, Usenet servers distribute them to other sites that carry the newsgroup. A site usually carries only the most current messages; otherwise, they would soon run out of storage space. Some sites *archive*, or store, old discussions.

A convenient way to check newsgroups is to subscribe to those that interest you. That way, whenever you check the Usenet server, new messages in your subscribed newsgroup will be delivered to you. You can also cancel your subscription to a newsgroup if you are no longer interested in it. You can read newsgroups without subscribing to them; in that case, you must manually ask to read specific newsgroups instead of having it done automatically for you.

Binary files such as pictures and multimedia can be posted in newsgroups. These files must be specially encoded for them to be posted. To view them, you must transfer them to your computer and then unencode them with special software. A common encoding scheme used on newsgroups is called uuencode. Most Usenet software readers have unencoding built in.

How Usenet Works

1 Usenet is a global bulletin board and discussion area. It collects messages about many thousands of topics into newsgroups, which are freewheeling discussion areas in which anyone can participate. Newsgroups can be found on many host computers across the Internet. Thousands of newsgroups exist that cover just about every topic you've ever imagined and many you probably haven't thought of.

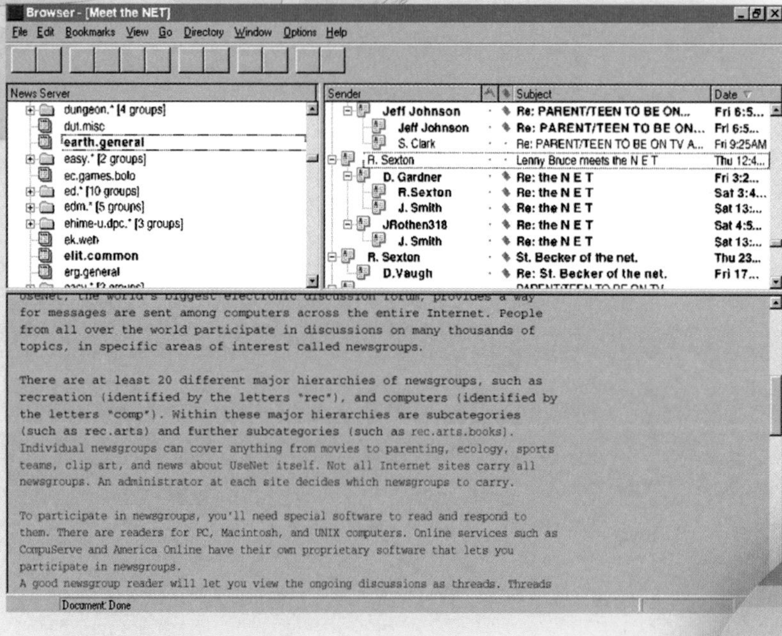

2 To participate, people send and read messages that are posted to the newsgroup. Two kinds of newsgroups exist: moderated newsgroups and unmoderated newsgroups.

3 In a *moderated* newsgroup, a human moderator receives and reads all the messages for the newsgroup. The moderator then decides which messages should be posted. The messages to be posted are put on a newsgroup server. The other messages are discarded. In *unmoderated* newsgroups, all messages are put directly on the server. Newsgroups and all their messages are stored on a Usenet server. They are organized by broad categories and then broken down into specific topics.

USENET.REC.ARTS.BOOKS

POST MESSAGE?

YES NO

Has anyone here read "Player of Games"? An awesome read IMHO! The Culture universe sounds like a fun place!

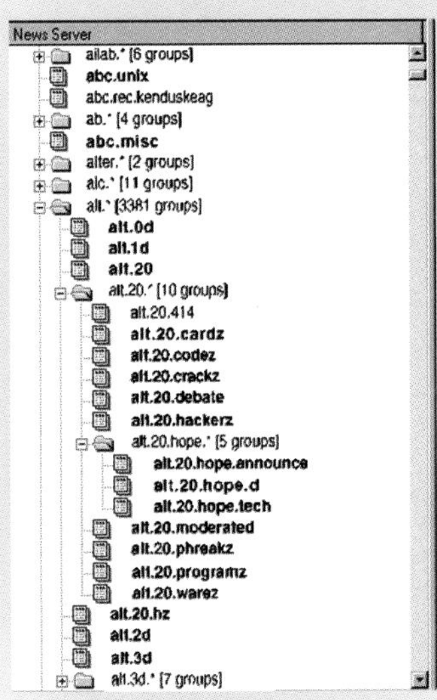

6 Newsgroup reader software lets you read messages and respond to newsgroups. The software gives you ways to manage your newsgroups by also allowing you to subscribe to newsgroups, which means new messages will automatically be delivered to you when you check the server. You'll also be able to cancel your subscription.

5 Pictures, multimedia files, and even executable programs can be posted in newsgroups for other people to see and use. However, because of the technology used in newsgroups, those files must be specially encoded to be posted. To view, play, or use the files, you first must transfer them to your own computer and then unencode them with special software. A common encoding scheme used on newsgroups is called uuencode. Versions of this encoding and decoding program are available that work on PC, Macintosh, and Unix computers. MIME is another encoding scheme.

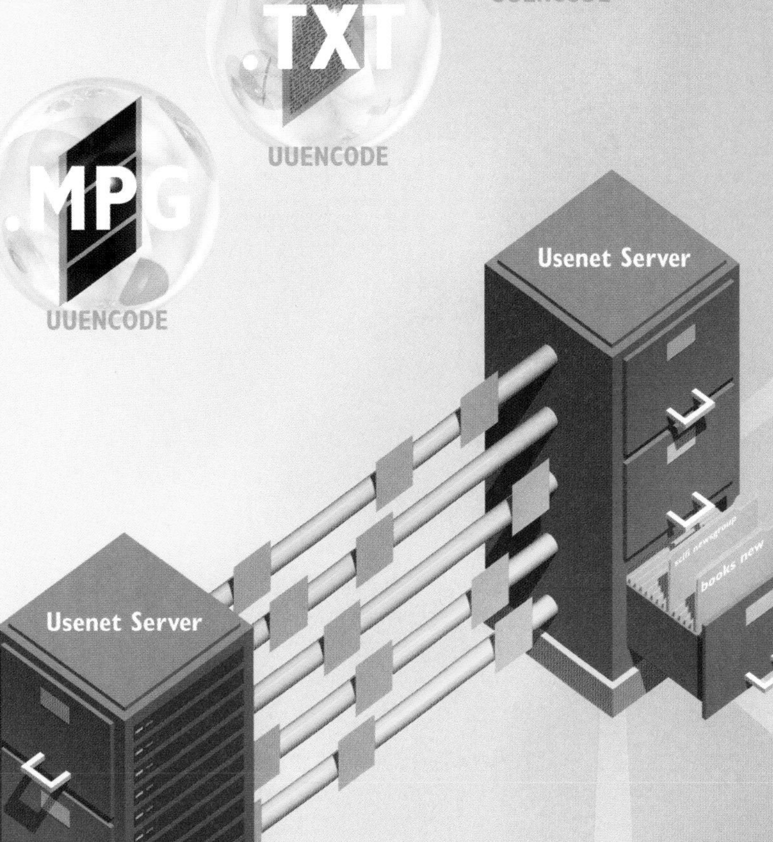

4 Usenet servers communicate with one another so that all messages posted on one server are duplicated on the other servers. Although there are many Usenet servers, not all servers carry all newsgroups. Each site decides which newsgroups to carry.

CHAPTER 19

How Internet Chat and Instant Messaging Work

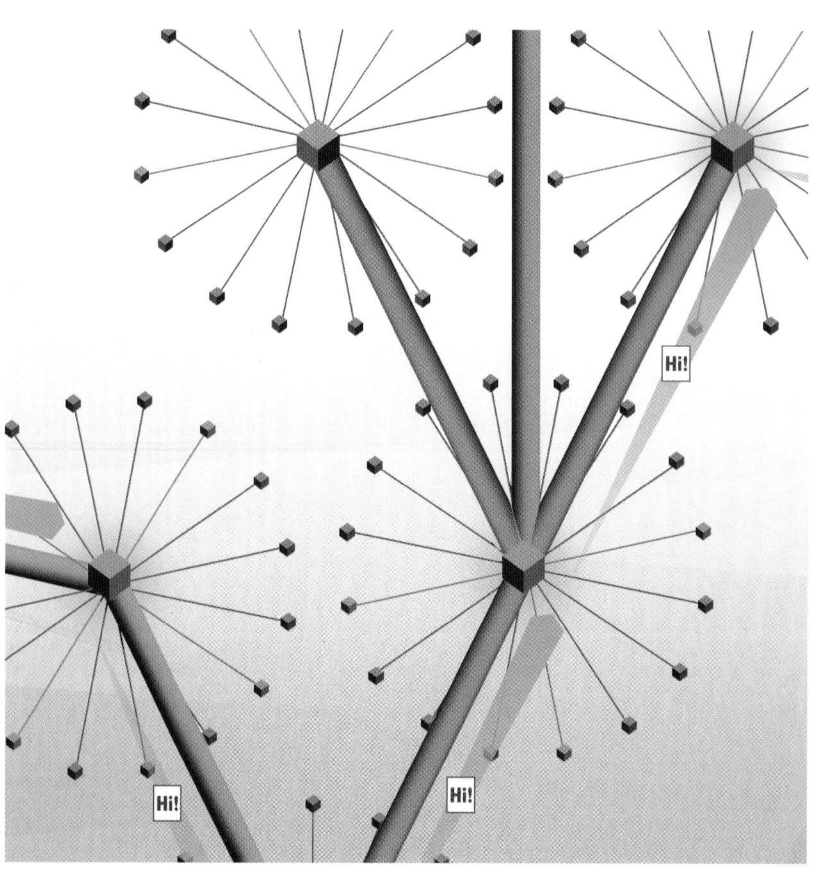

ONE of the most immediate ways to communicate with others via the Internet is to participate in live chat. Chat doesn't refer to people actually talking to each other and hearing each other's voices. Instead, it means that you hold live keyboard "conversations" with other people on the Internet—that is, you type words on your computer and other people on the Internet can see those words on their computers immediately, and vice versa. You can hold chats with many people simultaneously all over the world.

A number of ways are available to chat on the Internet, but one of the most popular ones is called *Internet relay chat (IRC)*. Every day, thousands of people all over the world hold conversations on many topics via IRC. Each topic is called a *channel*. When you join a channel, you can see what other people on the channel type on their keyboards. In turn, everyone in the channel can see whatever you type on your keyboard. You can also hold individual side conversations with someone. Channels live on various servers around the world. Some servers have only a few channels, and others have many of them.

IRC has facilitated communications during natural disasters, wars, and other crises. In 1993, for example, during the attempted Communist coup in Russia when Russian legislators barricaded themselves inside the Parliament building, an IRC "news channel" was set up for relaying real-time, first-person accounts of the events taking place.

IRC follows a client/server model, which means that both client and server software are required to use it. Many IRC clients are available for many types of computers, so whether you have a PC, Macintosh, or Unix workstation, you can use IRC.

Your IRC client communicates with an IRC server on the Internet. You log on to a server using the client and select a channel on which you want to chat. When you type words on your keyboard, they are sent to the server. The server is part of a global IRC server network. The server sends your message to other servers, which, in turn, send your messages to people who are part of your channel. They can then see and respond to your message.

You can chat on the Internet in other ways, as well. Many Web sites, for example, use proprietary chat software that doesn't use the IRC protocol but enables you to chat when you're on the site.

Another type of chat is called *instant messaging*. In instant messaging, you communicate privately, one on one, with another person. You can create special lists so you're informed when your "buddies" come online ready to chat, and they're informed when you come online.

How IRC Works

1. Internet relay chat (IRC) is a way for people all over the world to "chat" with one another by using their keyboards. The typed words are instantly relayed to computers all over the world, where recipients can read them. This process occurs in real-time, so everyone sees the words as people type them.

2. IRC runs on a client/server model; therefore, to use it, you need client software on your computer. Many IRC clients are available for PCs, Macintoshes, Unix workstations, and other kinds of computers.

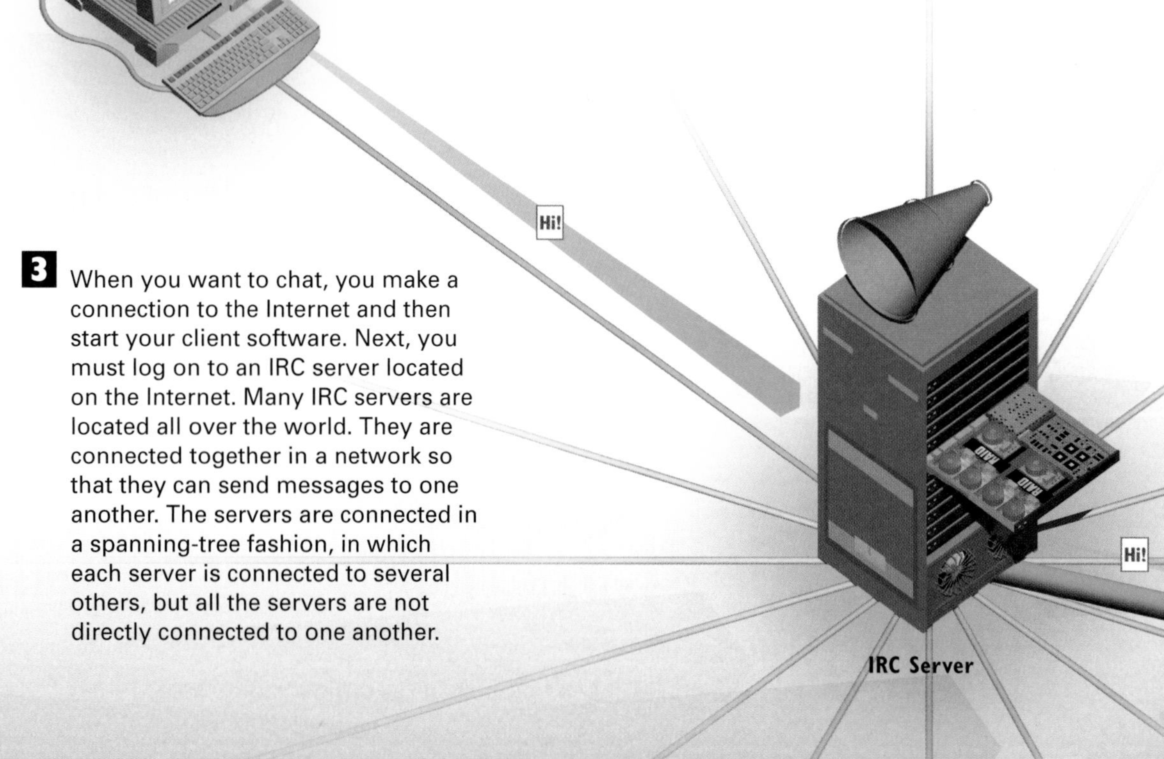

3. When you want to chat, you make a connection to the Internet and then start your client software. Next, you must log on to an IRC server located on the Internet. Many IRC servers are located all over the world. They are connected together in a network so that they can send messages to one another. The servers are connected in a spanning-tree fashion, in which each server is connected to several others, but all the servers are not directly connected to one another.

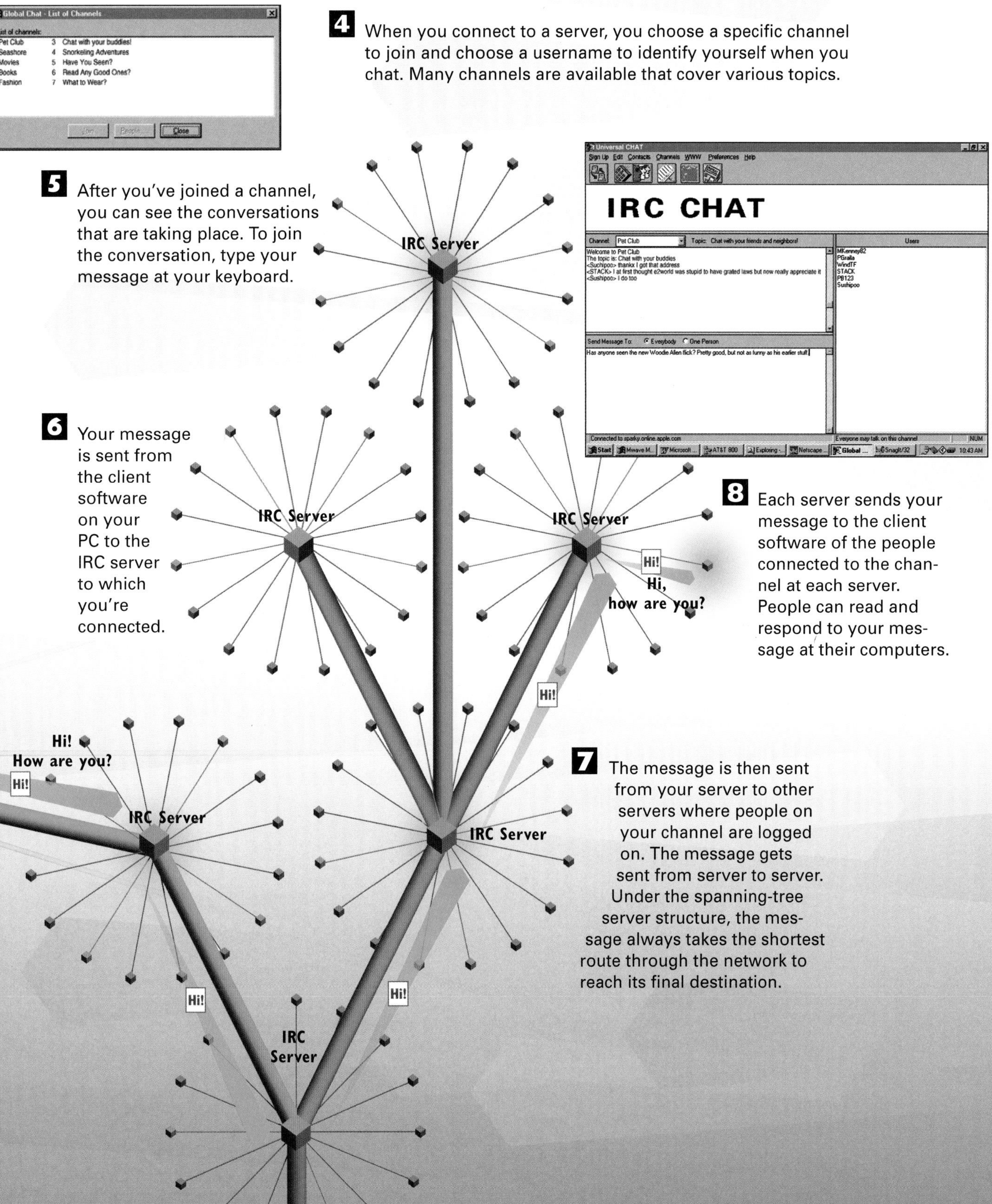

4 When you connect to a server, you choose a specific channel to join and choose a username to identify yourself when you chat. Many channels are available that cover various topics.

5 After you've joined a channel, you can see the conversations that are taking place. To join the conversation, type your message at your keyboard.

6 Your message is sent from the client software on your PC to the IRC server to which you're connected.

7 The message is then sent from your server to other servers where people on your channel are logged on. The message gets sent from server to server. Under the spanning-tree server structure, the message always takes the shortest route through the network to reach its final destination.

8 Each server sends your message to the client software of the people connected to the channel at each server. People can read and respond to your message at their computers.

How Instant Messaging Works

1 The Internet version of America Online's Instant Messenger (AIM), one of the most popular instant messaging systems, runs as a piece of client software on your computer. To use it, you must be connected to the Internet. When you run the software, it opens up a TCP connection to an Instant Messenger login server. The software sends your screen name and password over the connection to log you into the server.

4 When you establish a connection with the AIM server, your client software sends a list of your buddies to the server. The server checks to see whether any of the buddies are online—and it continues to do that for as long as you run the software on your computer. If you change the list of buddies during your session, that information is sent to the server as well so it can keep track of new buddies or ignore buddies you've deleted from your list.

3 Instant message software includes buddy list capabilities. That means you keep a list of people you want send instant messages to, and when they come online, you are notified so you can send instant messages to and receive instant messages from them. You create a buddy list in your AIM software by adding your buddies' screen names to it.

Cool Lizard is online.

"Hi Mia. Are you interested in getting together next week?"

"Sure. Monday would be best for me. Let's chat later to confirm it."

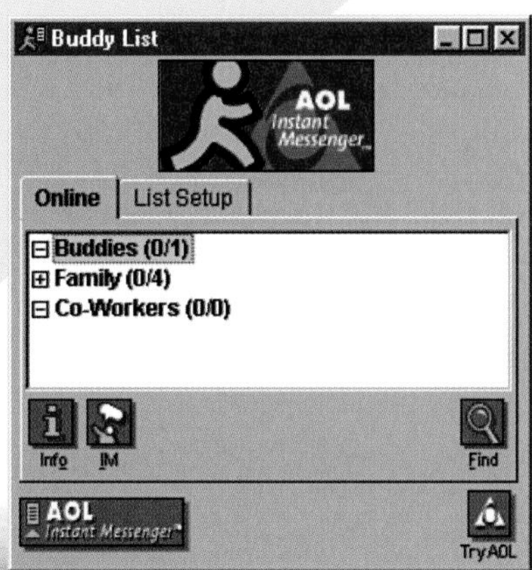

5 When any of your buddies runs AIM and logs in, your client software is told that he's online, and you get a notice that he's online. You can now send messages to and receive instant messages from him.

2 The server checks the screen name and password. If they're correct, the login server instructs the Instant Messenger software to close the connection to the login server and to open up a new connection to a different AIM server—the one that will handle your instant message session. This connection uses a special communications protocol that allows for AIM functionality.

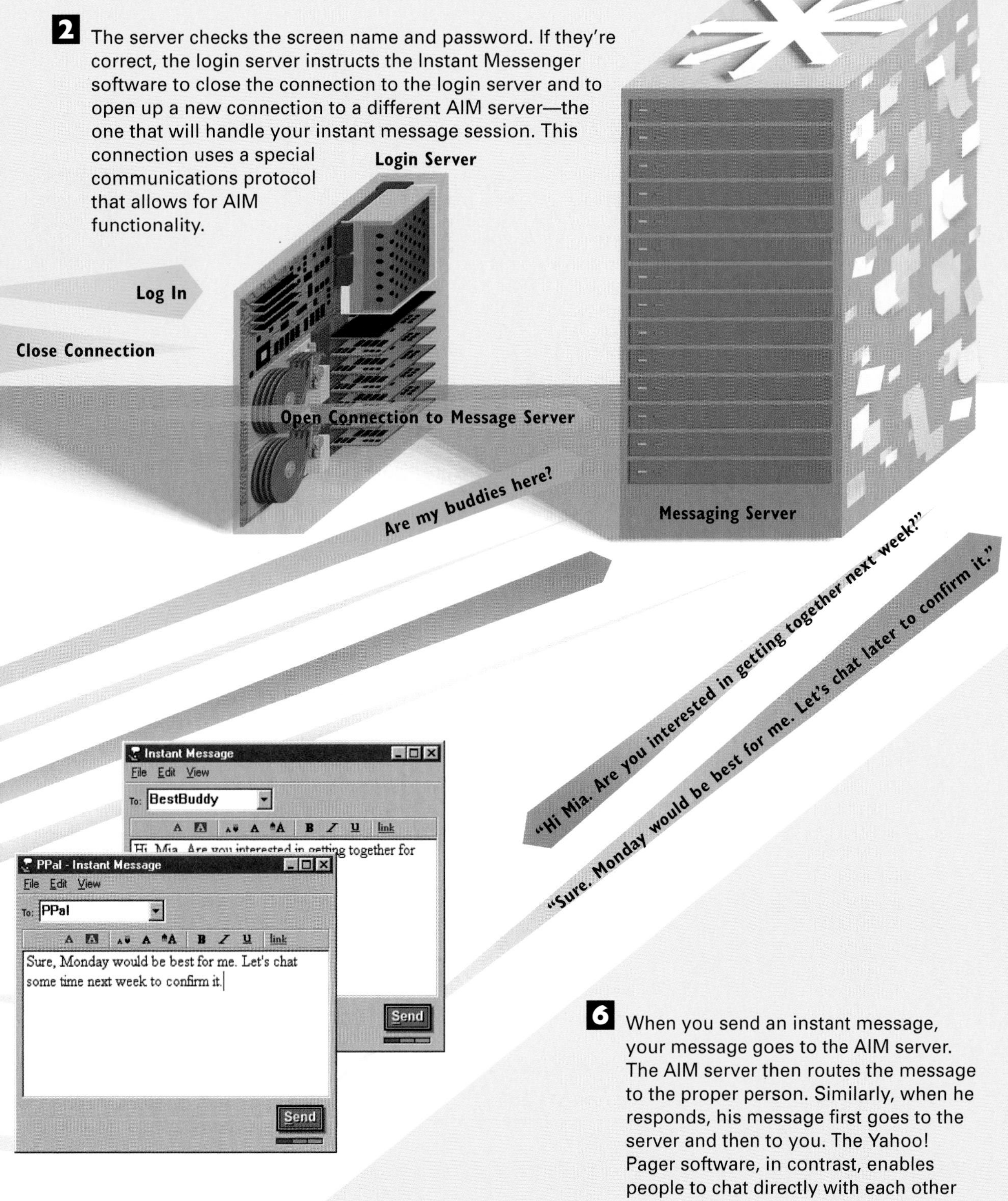

6 When you send an instant message, your message goes to the AIM server. The AIM server then routes the message to the proper person. Similarly, when he responds, his message first goes to the server and then to you. The Yahoo! Pager software, in contrast, enables people to chat directly with each other without having to go through a server.

CHAPTER

20

How Internet Phone Calls Work

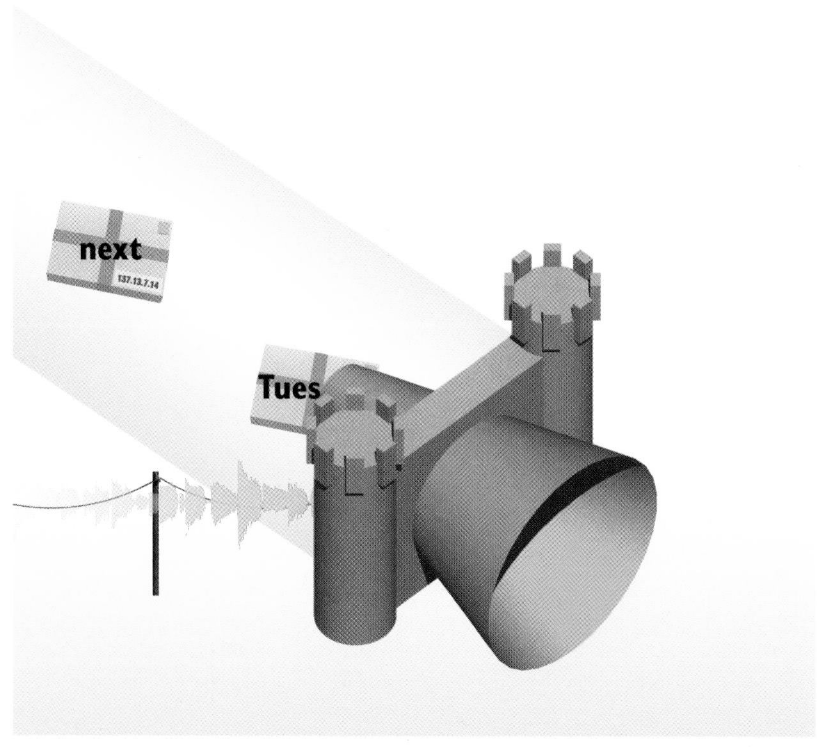

THE Internet has pioneered many new ways to communicate, such as e-mail, live chat, and newsgroups. But it can be used to enable some old-fashioned communications as well: You can make telephone calls using the Internet. When you do so, the sound of your voice and that of the person you're talking to are broken down into packets. Those packets are delivered using the Internet's TCP/IP protocol.

You can make telephone calls over the Internet in two ways. In the first way, you use your computer and special hardware and software to make calls, so you communicate through your PC. In the second way, often referred to as *Internet telephony*, or *voice over IP*, you make a phone call as you normally do on your telephone, except your call is routed over the Internet rather than through the normal phone service. This usually cuts the cost of making long-distance phone calls.

The revolutionary part of using the Internet to make phone calls from your PC is the price: It's free. You pay only for your Internet connection, as if you were browsing the Web or sending e-mail. You don't actually have to pay for the phone call itself. In addition, you can make calls anywhere in the world. However, you will be able to make telephone calls to and receive calls only from someone who has an Internet address, so you won't be able to replace your telephone by using the Internet. A number of competing products enable you to talk over the Internet, but as yet, they don't communicate with one another. No standard way of making Internet telephone calls exists, so you can talk only to people who use the exact same software you do for making and receiving phone calls.

Many schemes and software packages enable you to make phone calls from your PC over the Internet. You don't actually use your telephone with any of them. Instead, you speak into a microphone attached to your computer and listen through speakers and a sound card.

Although each company's software works somewhat differently, in general, they use similar ways of enabling people to make phone calls over the Internet. To make a phone call, first you must know someone's IP address. (You can consult directories that function as telephone books to get this information.) After you find the person's Internet address, you can connect to him by running special software and then double-clicking his name. (The person on the other end must be running the same software you are using.) A message goes out to him over the Internet to see whether he's available to talk.

When you make phone calls over the Internet using your normal phone, things work differently. You make the call as you would any other phone call. After you make the call, however, your voice is digitized and converted into IP packets, and then it's delivered using the same TCP/IP technology the rest of the Internet uses. On the other end of the call, the digitized voice data is converted and can be listened to over the phone.

How PC Phone Calls on the Internet Work

1 When you connect to the Internet and want to send or receive telephone calls with special phone software, you connect to a special directory. The directory contains a list of all the people who can connect to the Internet using that particular phone software.

2 You can look up someone's name in the directory. The directory matches a person's name (such as Gabe Gralla) with his Internet IP address (such as 192.168.1.1). It's important that the directory match a name with an IP address because someone potentially can have a different IP address every time he logs on to the Internet. The directory matches names to the most current IP addresses.

3 When you find someone in the directory you want to call, the directory looks up the IP address and then routes your call directly to that computer. The phone "rings" at the person's computer, and he picks up the receiver. The two of you can now talk, using the sound cards and microphones attached to your computers.

Hi Gabe, how have you been?

4 When you talk into the microphone, software turns your voice into binary data files that computers can read. It also compresses the voice data to make it smaller and capable of being sent over the Internet more quickly. Normally, voice files are very large, and without compression, they would be too large to quickly send over the Internet.

5 The software also determines the speed of the Internet connection. If the connection is a high-speed connection, it creates voice files of high quality. If it's a lower-speed connection, it creates files of a lesser sound quality because at lower speeds it would take too long to send voice files, even after they had been compressed.

6 The software breaks up the voice files into a series of packets to be sent over the Internet using the Internet's TCP/IP protocol.

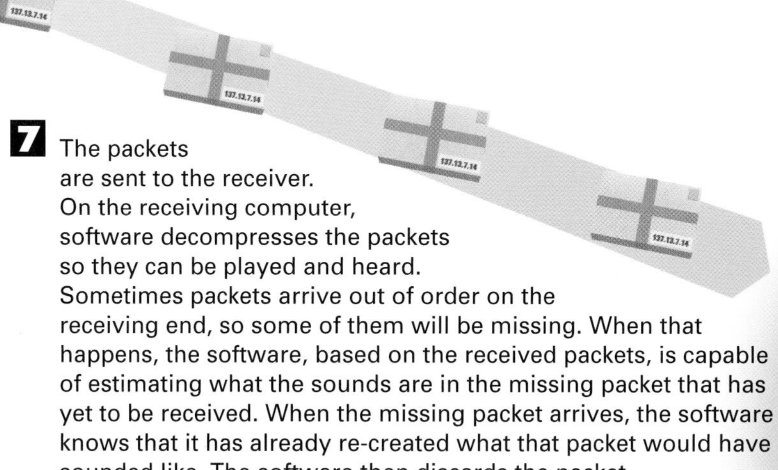

7 The packets are sent to the receiver. On the receiving computer, software decompresses the packets so they can be played and heard. Sometimes packets arrive out of order on the receiving end, so some of them will be missing. When that happens, the software, based on the received packets, is capable of estimating what the sounds are in the missing packet that has yet to be received. When the missing packet arrives, the software knows that it has already re-created what that packet would have sounded like. The software then discards the packet.

How Internet Telephony Works

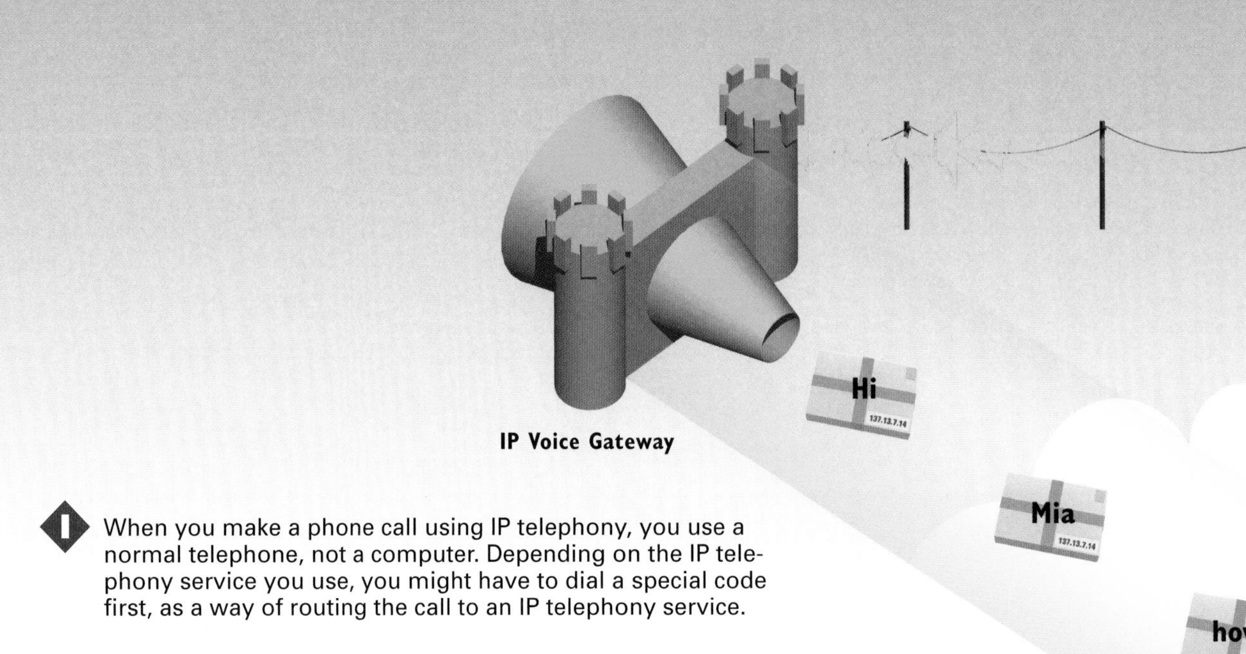

1. When you make a phone call using IP telephony, you use a normal telephone, not a computer. Depending on the IP telephony service you use, you might have to dial a special code first, as a way of routing the call to an IP telephony service.

2. The first part of the call goes over the normal Public Switched Telephone Network (PSTN), as does any other call; at this point, it is no different in any way.

6 The call travels on the PSTN the same as any other telephone call. The person receiving the call picks up the phone and talks, the same as with any other telephone conversation. When the receiving person speaks into the phone, the voice is sent back through the PSTN to the IP voice gateway and across the Internet in the same way that the call was initially made.

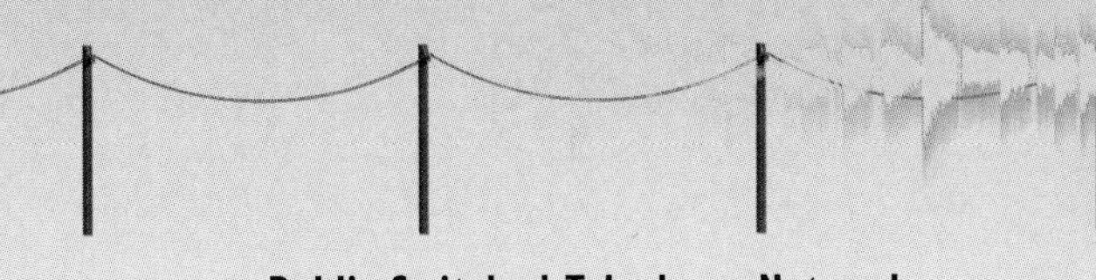

Public Switched Telephone Network

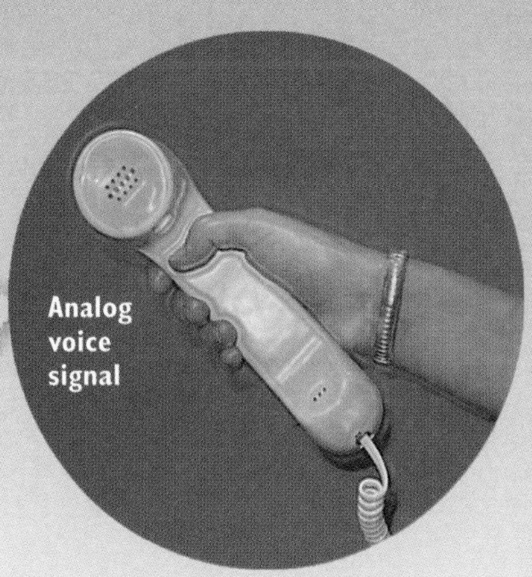

5 The voice packets are sent to the IP voice gateway nearest to the phone call's destination. The receiving IP voice gateway takes the voice packets, uncompresses them, converts them back into their original form, and then sends them through the PSTN.

4 The gateway breaks up the compressed, digitized voice signal into IP packets. These packets are sent out across the Internet the same as any other IP packets, using the Internet's TCP/IP protocol.

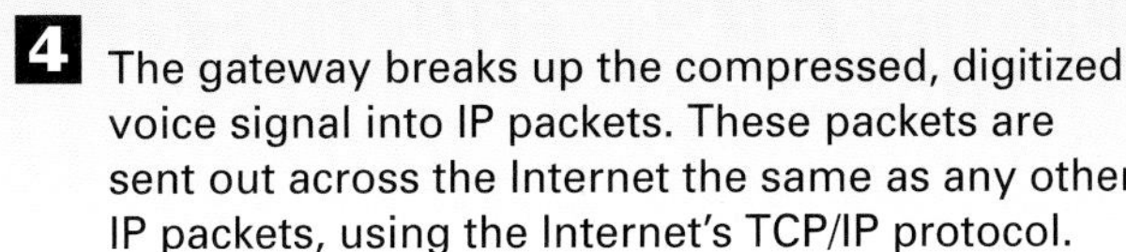

3 The call is sent to a special IP voice gateway. This gateway—a server and server software—might be located at the branch of the telephone company or might instead be in a different location. The gateway converts the voice signal to digital data and compresses it. It compresses it because the data files of an uncompressed voice call could be too large to deliver in a timely fashion across the Internet.

out

lunch

next

IP Packets

IP Voice Gateway

IP (Internet Protocol) Telephony refers to telephone calls that are made over normal telephones but are delivered, in part, through the Internet instead of solely through a voice network, commonly called the Public Switched Telephone Network, or PSTN. Because the calls are routed through the Internet, they can be delivered at less cost than normal phone calls. But the voice quality might not be as good as calls delivered over the normal phone network.

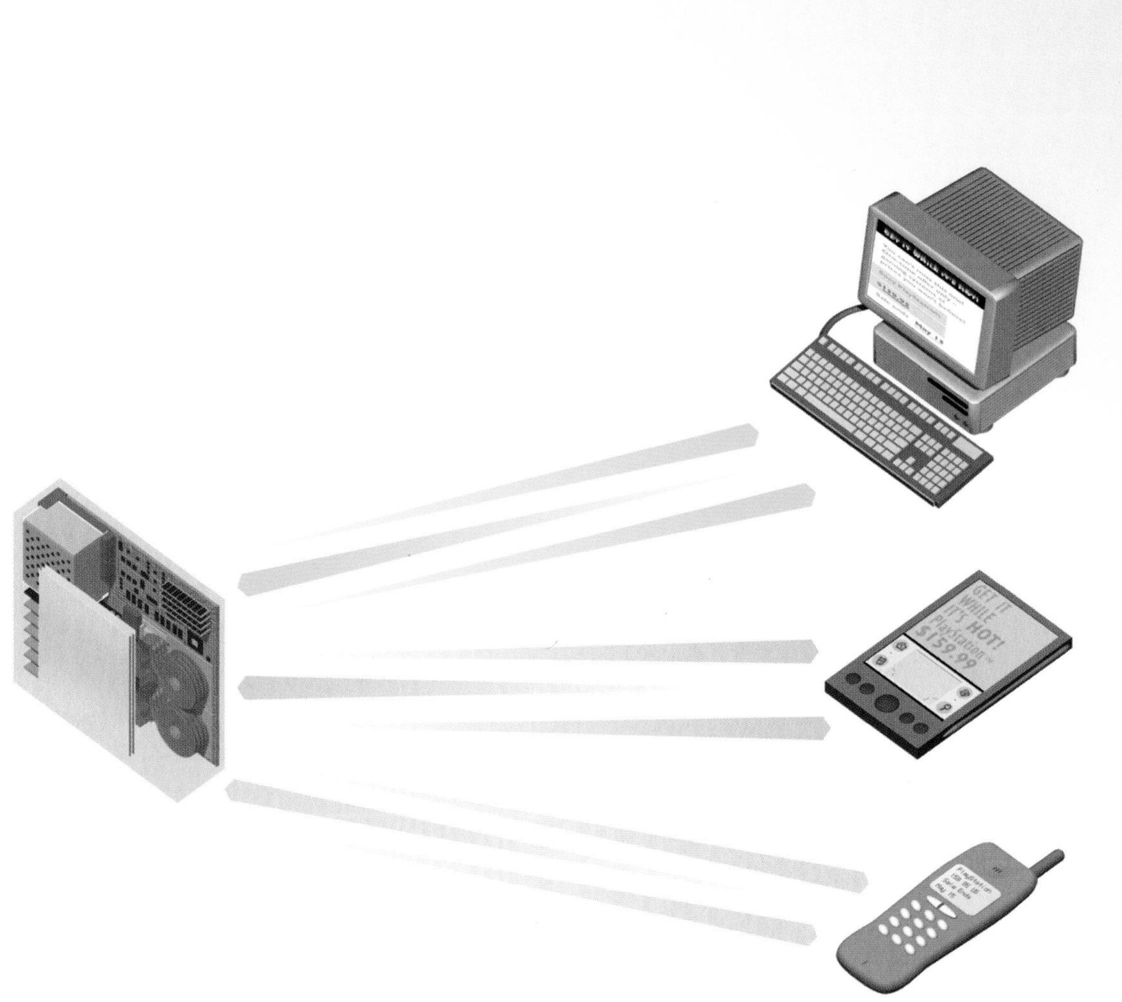

GET IT WHILE IT'S HOT!

You can't miss this one!
One-time offer only –
gaming systems at
prices you won't believe!

Sony PlayStations

P A R T

USING THE WORLD WIDE WEB

WHEN many people use the word "Internet," they are really talking about the World Wide Web. The Web is the most interesting, most innovative, most visible, and fastest growing part of the Internet. To a great degree, the explosive growth of the Web has been what has fueled the enormous amount of interest in the Internet in the past several years. When people refer to "surfing the Net," they're usually talking about using the World Wide Web.

This section of the book looks in great detail at how the World Wide Web works, from such basic technologies as how Web pages work to more advanced features, such as imagemaps and the way the Web is becoming increasingly integrated directly into your computer. You'll learn what the Web comprises and how a Web browser works and thoroughly investigate URLs (uniform resource locators), as well as many other aspects of the Web and Web browsers.

Chapter 21, "How Web Pages Work," examines the most basic part of the Web. It starts by covering the general technology of the Web and describes how the Web works. Web pages are, in essence, multimedia publications that can include music, audio, video, and animation, as well as graphics and text. Web pages are connected via hypertext that enables you to jump from any page to any other page, and to graphics, binary files, multimedia files, and other Internet resources. To jump from one page to another, or to another resource, you merely click a hypertext link.

The chapter details how all that works and looks at the client/server model of the Web. It shows what happens behind the scenes when you type a URL into your browser—how that information gets routed properly so you visit the Web site that interests you. The chapter also delves into how Web pages are organized on a site and how an entire Web site works as a unit to deliver its information to you.

Chapter 22, "How Web Browsers Work," examines browsers. Web browsers are pieces of software that interpret the language of the Web, Hypertext Markup Language (HTML), and then display those results on your computer. The chapter begins by delving into how browsers do that job.

Browsers, however, now go far beyond merely allowing you to visit the Web. Both Netscape Communicator and Internet Explorer have grown to become full-blown application suites. Communicator, for example, includes the Navigator browser along with many other programs for communicating with others on the Internet. It includes a news reader, an e-mail package, conferencing and whiteboard software, and even a powerful editing tool that enables you to create and publish your own Web pages.

This chapter discusses one of the most common, and annoying, facts about the Web—the sometimes incomprehensible error messages you receive when you can't get to a Web site or Web page. You'll see what those messages mean and understand why you can't visit a Web page or site when you get one of them.

As mentioned earlier, HTML is the language of the Web. Chapter 23, "How Markup Languages Work," explains how HTML forms the building blocks for creating Web pages. The language is an essential set of directions that tells your browser how to display and manage a Web document. The chapter shows in detail how all that works.

Chapter 24, "How Hypertext Works," looks at hyperlinks, which set the Web apart from most other portions of the Internet. This chapter describes the various ways documents can link to each other on the Web and explains concepts such as relative links and absolute links.

Chapter 25, "How URLs Work," looks in great detail at URLs, the addresses you type into your browser to visit a Web site. You'll look at the underlying structure of a URL and gain a better understanding of how a URL is put together and what it can tell you about the site you're visiting. You'll also see precisely how URLs help retrieve documents from the Web.

Chapter 26, "How Image Maps and Interactive Forms Work," looks at two technologies you use every day on the Web without realizing it: imagemaps and interactive forms. Image maps aren't maps in a traditional sense. Instead, they're graphics with URLs embedded inside them. When you click one part of the graphic, you're sent to one site, and when you click another, you're sent to a different site. An imagemap might be a picture of a house, for example, and when you click the living room, you're sent to an entertainment site; when you click a home office, you're sent to a business site.

Interactive forms are the forms you fill out on the Web for doing things such as registering at a site or sending information about yourself before you're allowed to download a particular piece of software free of charge.

Chapter 27, "How Web Host Servers Work," looks at Web server software. As mentioned before, the Web works on a client/server model. Your Web browser (the client) contacts the Web server. This chapter explains how Web server software interacts with your browser to deliver Web content to you.

Chapter 28, "How Web Sites Work with Databases," looks at databases. Databases are used on the Web for many things. Web indexes and search sites such as Yahoo! are, in essence, databases that interact with the Web.

Finally, Chapter 29, "How Internet-Based Software Works," shows you how Web-based software (called ASPs for Application Service Providers) works. This is one of the more intriguing uses of the Internet because it enables you to run software not from your own computer, but instead from a distant computer on the Internet. That way, you never need to upgrade—every time you connect to that software, you always get the newest version.

CHAPTER

21

How Web Pages Work

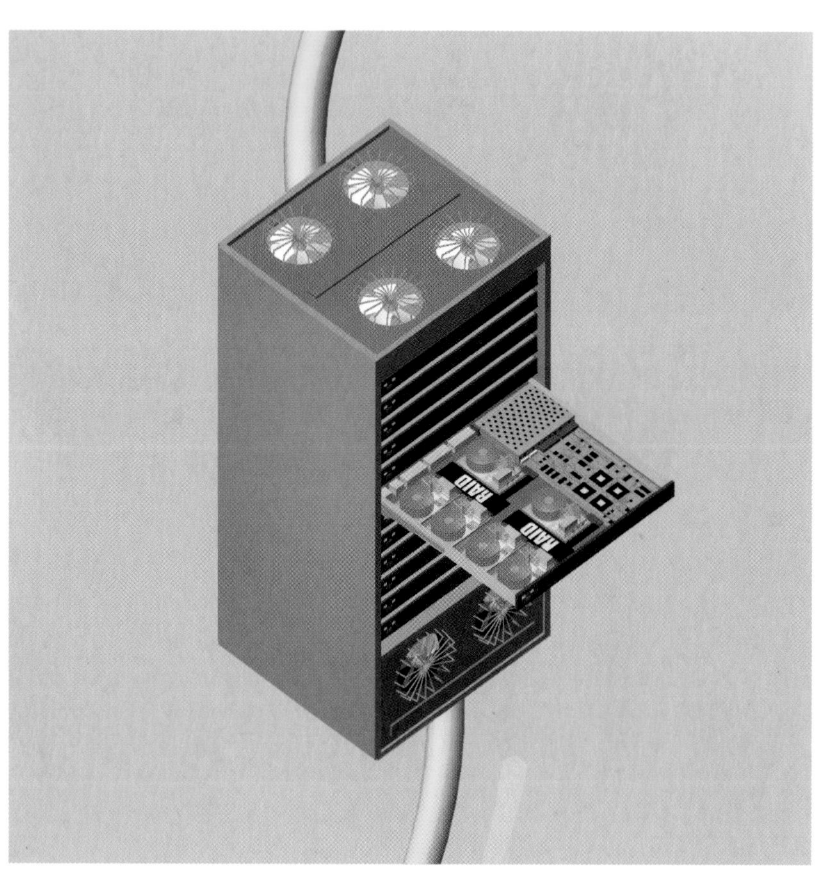

THE World Wide Web is the fastest growing and, in many ways, the most exciting and intriguing part of the Internet. When people refer to "surfing the Net," more often than not they're talking about using the World Wide Web.

As its name implies, the World Wide Web is a globally connected network. The Web contains many things, but what makes it so fascinating to so many are the Web "pages" that incorporate text, graphics, sound, animation, and other multimedia elements. In essence, each page is an interactive multimedia publication that can include videos and music as well as graphics and text.

Pages are connected to one another using *hypertext* that allows you to move from any page to any other page, and to graphics, binary files, multimedia files, as well as any Internet resource. To jump from one page to another, you click a hypertext link—a link that connects Web pages and resources.

The Web operates on a client/server model. You run Web *client* browser software, such as Netscape Navigator or Microsoft's Internet Explorer, on your computer. That client contacts a Web *server* and requests information or resources. The Web server locates and then sends the information to the Web browser, which displays the results.

Pages on the Web are built using a markup language called Hypertext Markup Language (HTML). The language contains commands that tell your browser how to display text, graphics, and multimedia files. It also contains commands for linking the page to other pages and to other Internet resources.

The term *home page* often is used to refer to the first, or top, page in a collection of pages that make up a Web site. This is to distinguish it from the many pages collected together as a single "package" of sorts that often make up Web sites. The home page is similar to a magazine cover or the front page of a newspaper. Usually, it acts as an introduction to the site, explaining its purpose and describing the information found on other pages throughout the site. In this way, the home page often acts as the table of contents for the rest of the site.

In general, Web sites use three types of organizational structures to organize their pages. In a *tree structure*, a pyramid or an outline format enables users to easily navigate through the site and find the information they want. In a *linear structure*, one page leads to the next, which then leads to the next, and so on, in a straight line. Finally, in a *random structure*, pages are connected to one another seemingly at random.

The last illustration in this chapter shows how someone might build her own pages using an HTML editor. After you create your pages, you use FTP software to post them onto a small portion of a Web server. You can either rent the server space from a local Internet service provider (ISP) or set up your own Web server. (Some sites also let you build Web pages by using the site's built-in tools. In that case, you wouldn't build a page from scratch and send it via FTP—instead, you'd build the page using online tools provided by the site.

How the World Wide Web Works

1 The World Wide Web is the fastest growing and most innovative part of the Internet. When you browse the Web, you view multimedia pages composed of text, graphics, sound, and video. The Web uses hypertext links that allow you to jump from one place to another on the Web. The language that enables you to use hypertext links and to view Web pages is called Hypertext Markup Language, more commonly known as HTML.

2 The Web works on a client/server model in which client software—known as a *Web browser*—runs on a local computer. The server software runs on a Web host. To use the Web, you first make an Internet connection and then launch your Web browser.

3 In a Web browser, you type the URL for a location you want to visit or click a link that sends you to the desired location. The names for Web locations are uniform resource locators (URLs). Your Web browser sends the URL request using Hypertext Transfer Protocol (HTTP), which defines the way the Web browser and Web server communicate with each other.

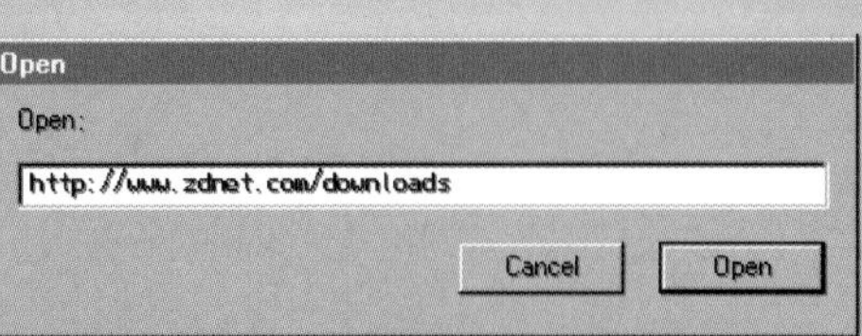

4 When the server finds the requested home page, document, or object, it sends that home page, document, or object back to the Web browser client. The information is then displayed on the computer screen in the Web browser. When the page is sent from the server, the HTTP connection is closed and can be reopened.

http://www.zdnet.com/downloads

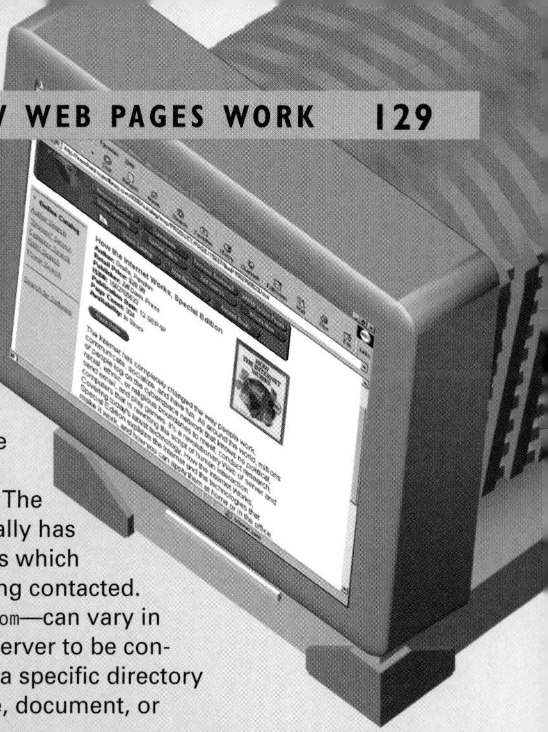

http://www.zdnet.com/downloads

7 URLs contain several parts. The first part—the `http://`—details which Internet protocol to use. The second part—the part that usually has a `www` in it—sometimes indicates which type of Internet resource is being contacted. The third part—such as `zdnet.com`—can vary in length and identifies the Web server to be contacted. The final part identifies a specific directory on the server and a home page, document, or other Internet object.

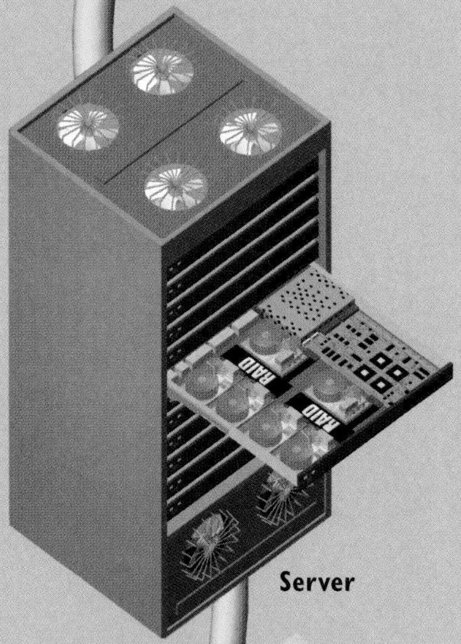

6 The request is sent to the Internet. Internet routers examine the request to determine to which server to send the request. The information just to the right of the `http://` in the URL tells the Internet on which Web server the requested information can be found. Routers send the request to that Web server.

Server

http://www.zdnet.com/downloads

Router

5 The Web server receives the request using the HTTP protocol. The request tells the server which specific document is being requested and where that document is located.

How Web Pages Are Organized on a Web Site

1 The *home page* is the first or top page of any Web site. A site can be just one page or can comprise dozens or even hundreds of pages. In the latter case, the home page acts as a table of contents to organize the site and help users find information available on the site.

2 Underlined or highlighted hyperlink text is often embedded in the home page. The hyperlinks serve to connect the top page with other pages throughout the site.

3 Related documents residing together on a Web host computer make up a Web site. However, a single server can host multiple Web sites, each contained in a separate area or directory, much like a hard drive can accommodate multiple directories. Some Web sites are so large and heavily trafficked that they can't fit on a single server and require multiple servers.

4 Good Web design principles suggest that pages throughout a site link back to the home page. This approach enables users to always find their way back to the top of a site to navigate in other directions.

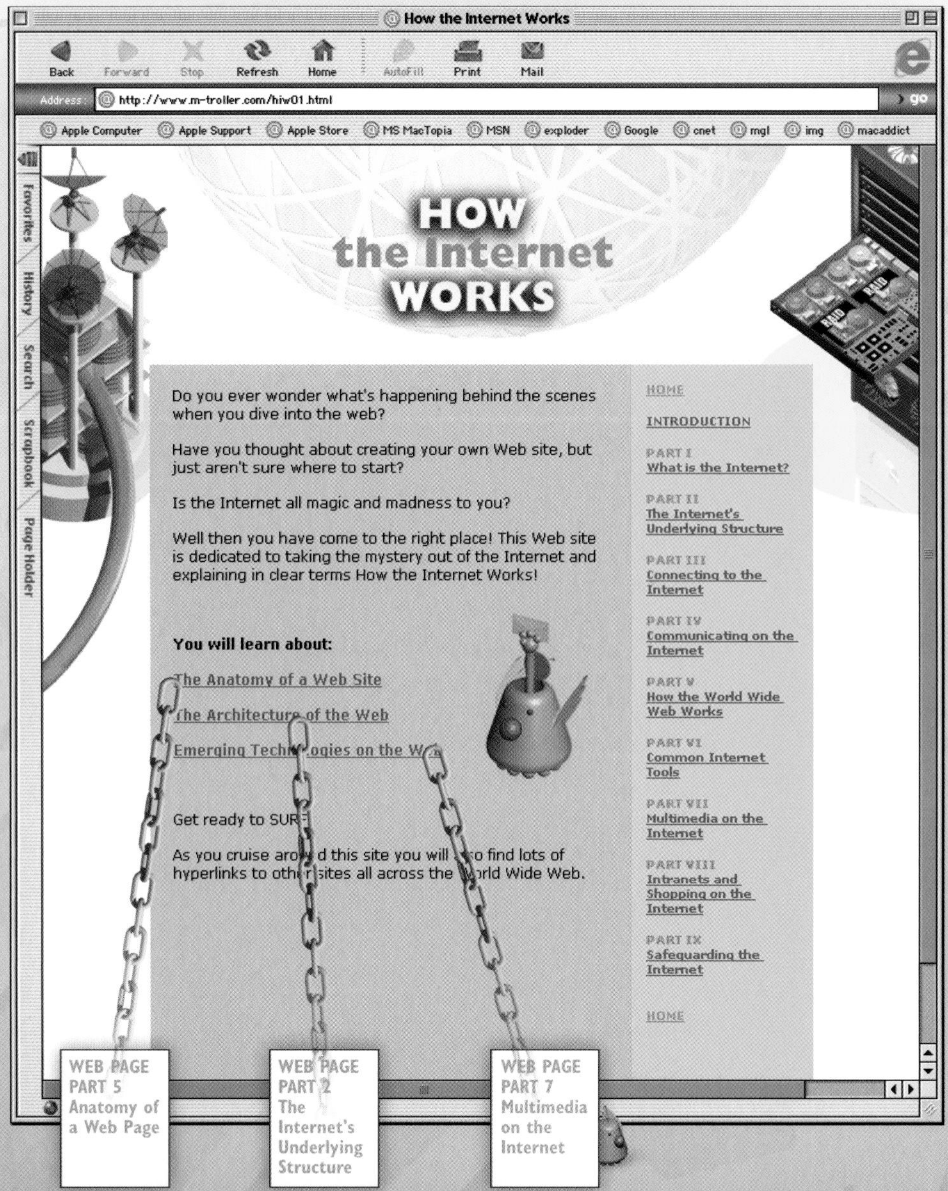

5 Documents within a site can be linked to any other document in the site—and even to documents on other sites. Most Web sites, however, are designed in a pyramid or an outline structure that gives users a visual model to understand how information is arranged and indicates how to find and navigate through the site's documents.

Linear

6 Web sites typically are organized in one of three ways. The first is an outline or a tree structure, which arranges information hierarchically, moving from general information to more specific data.

Tree

7 The second organizational method is linear, in which one page leads to the next, which leads to the next one, and so on.

Random

8 The third organizational structure is really a lack of structure, in which pages are connected to one another seemingly at random. (It's this last structure, though, that makes it clear why the Web is called the Web.)

How Web Sites Are Constructed

1 First, the raw materials are collected for the Web page. Content can be any number of things: family photos, poems, personal opinions, text of any kind, and even sound clips and movies. Text can easily be compiled with any word processor, such as Microsoft Word.

Text

Graphics

Multimedia

HTML Page

2 A page can come to life with a few well-chosen images. In designing a family home page, for example, a scanned photo might work well on the Web page. Icons or colored bullets spruce up a text list, and navigational icons, such as arrows or pointers, let a user move logically around the site. A whole range of shareware image editors is available on the Internet. *Shareware* is software you can try out for free, and for which you must pay only if you use it after a certain length of time.

3 Software is available that facilitates the arrangement of text, images, and other media without requiring a single line of HTML to be typed; one such program is Adobe's PageMill. However, if the pages need to be tweaked, there is no substitute for knowing a little HTML. Before posting new pages, they should be previewed from the hard disk using a Web browser. If any changes are necessary, it is easier to make them at this stage. It's best to preview the page with both Internet Explorer and Netscape Navigator because the same page can look different in each browser.

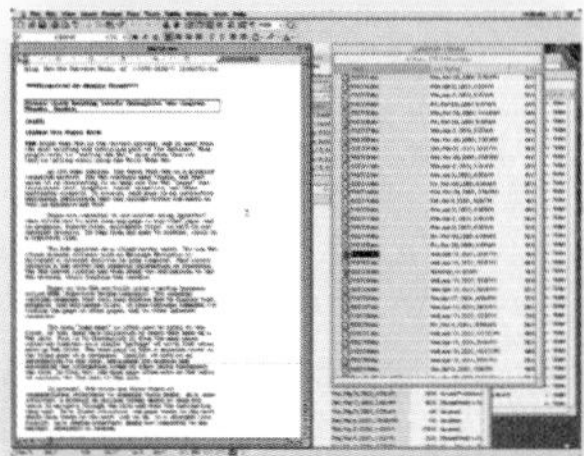

Text Editor

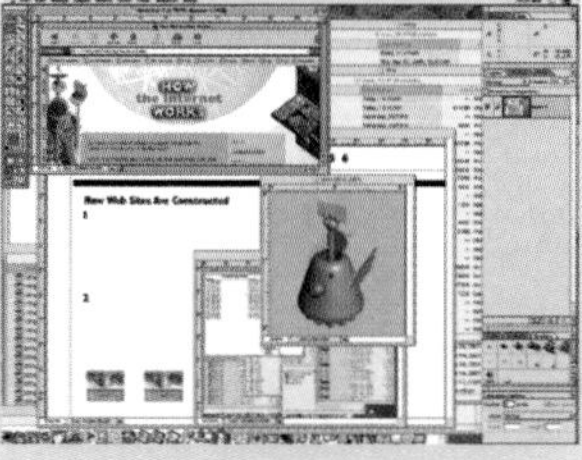

Image Editor

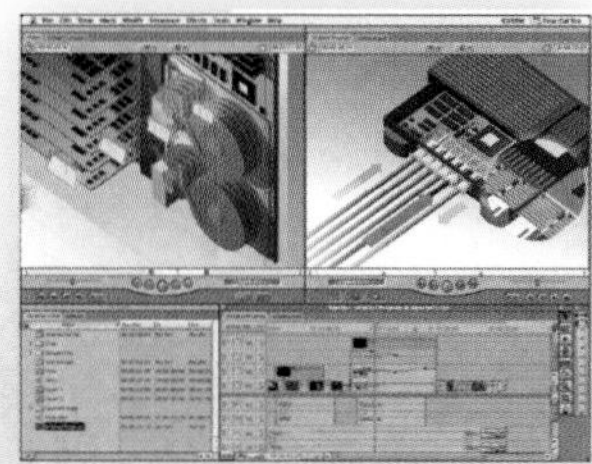

Media Editor

6 An FTP program is used to log on to the ISP's Web server; many good ones are available as shareware on the Internet. The ISP issues a username and password at sign-up time, which are used to log on to the directory where the HTML page, graphics, and other media will be placed. After the various elements are put in the correct folder, the "live" pages can be checked on the Web using the URL provided by the ISP.

5 The Web page can typically be posted by means of a dial-up connection to the Internet (via a local ISP). Many ISPs provide the space for doing this free of charge as part of their monthly fee.

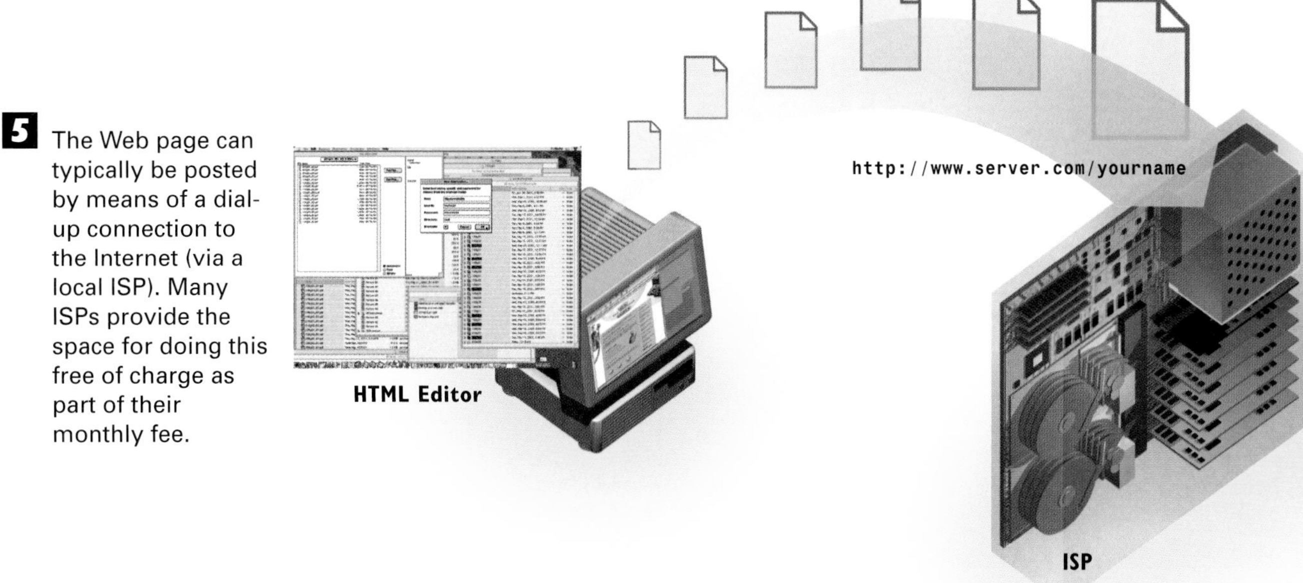

4 If you want to add other media to your pages, such as digitized sound, music, or video, you need access to the digital files, or you can digitize them yourself with additional computer hardware. When you are dealing with media with large file sizes—such as a 4MB movie—it will take users a very long time to download the file. During editing, try to trim all the fat out of video and audio clips. Also try to scale back the length and resolution of audio and video to decrease file size.

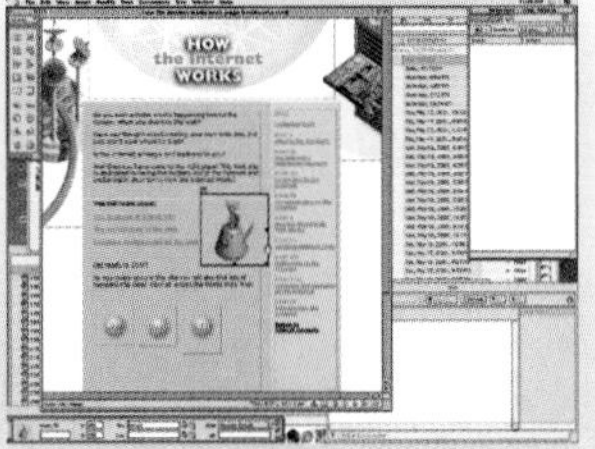

HTML Editor

CHAPTER 22 How Web Browsers Work

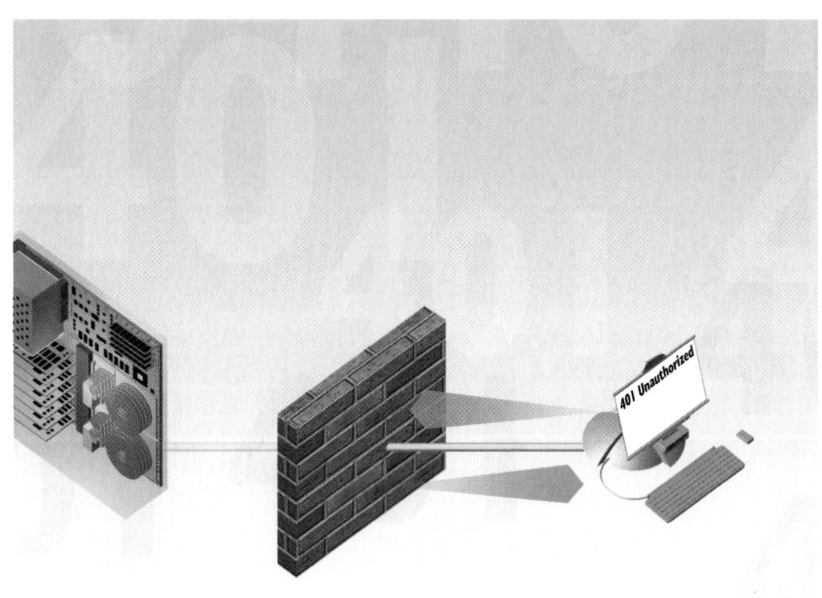

LIKE much of the Internet, the World Wide Web operates on a client/server model. You run a Web client on your computer—called a Web browser—such as Netscape Communicator or Microsoft's Internet Explorer. That client contacts a Web server and requests information or resources. The Web server locates and then sends the information to the Web browser, which displays the results.

When Web browsers contact servers, they're asking to be sent pages built with Hypertext Markup Language (HTML). They interpret those pages and display them on your computer. They also can display applications, programs, animations, and similar material created with programming languages such as Java and ActiveX, and scripting languages such as JavaScript.

Sometimes, home pages contain links to files the Web browser can't play or display, such as sound or animation files. In that case, you need a plug-in or a helper application. You configure your Web browser or operating system to use the helper application or plug-in whenever it encounters a sound or animation file the browser can't run or play.

Over the years, Web browsers have become increasingly sophisticated. Browsers have now become full-blown software suites that can do everything from videoconferencing to letting you create and publish HTML pages. They have also begun to blur the line between your local computer and the Internet—in essence, they can make your computer and the Internet function as a single computer system.

Toward this end of bringing the Internet more directly into computers, Microsoft has integrated Web browsing and the Internet directly into the operating system. For example, with Internet Explorer 4.0 and above, and with Windows 98 and above, the Windows desktop can be HTML-based. This means Web links can be directly embedded into the desktop. So, for example, you can have links to your favorite Web pages right on the desktop. And even applications such as word processors now have Web capabilities built into them, such as being capable of browsing the Web or building home pages. Even more significantly, using technology that Microsoft calls Active Desktop, Internet-based *desktop components* can live on the desktop. These components can be things such as stock tickers, which deliver live Web content directly to the desktop. You don't need to go fire up your Web browser to get the information; it's delivered straight to your Windows desktop without your having to do anything.

Both Microsoft and Netscape have also built entire suites of software around their browsers. Netscape, for example, calls its suite Netscape Communicator. Communicator includes modules for reading newsgroups; for reading, sending, and managing Internet mail; for audio conferencing; for collaborative work on *whiteboard applications* in which people can view and mark up the same documents simultaneously; and more. These enhancements will help usher in an era of collaborative computing. Not only will the Internet be used to transmit and receive information, but it will also alter the way we do business and help us communicate more effectively.

When browsing the Internet, one of the most frustrating experiences is the error messages browsers display when they're having trouble contacting a Web site. Depending on which browser you use, and which version of the browser you're using, those messages might differ. Version 5.0 and above of Internet Explorer, for example, sometimes displays error messages in plain English. But most browser don't. The final spread in this chapter lists the most common browser error messages—and what they mean.

How a Web Browser Works

1 Web browsers consist of client software that runs on your computer and displays home pages on the Web. There are clients for PC, Macintosh, and Unix computers.

2 A Web browser displays information on your computer by interpreting the Hypertext Markup Language (HTML) that is used to build home pages on the Web. Home pages usually display graphics, sound, and multimedia files, as well as links to other pages, files that can be downloaded, and other Internet resources.

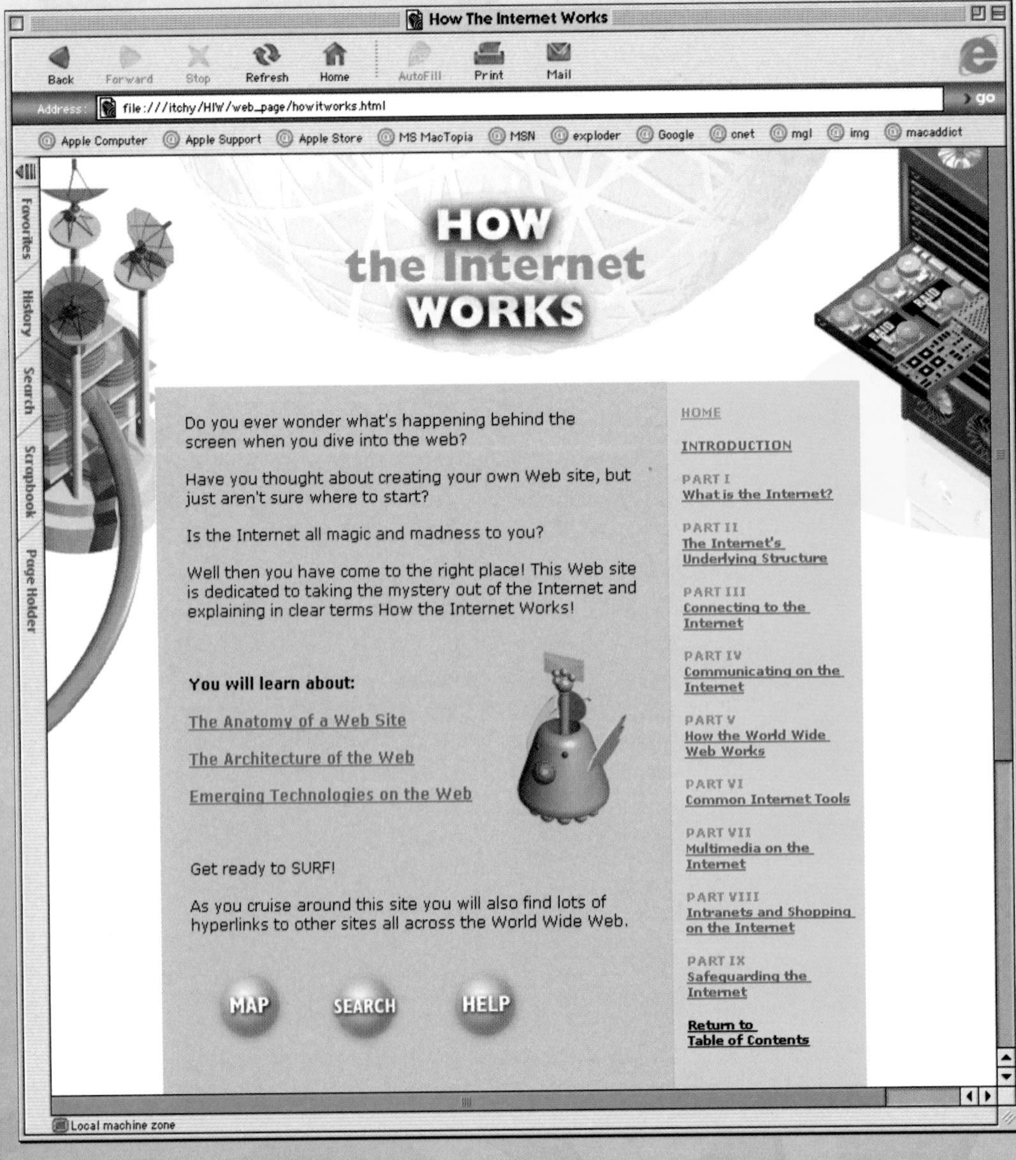

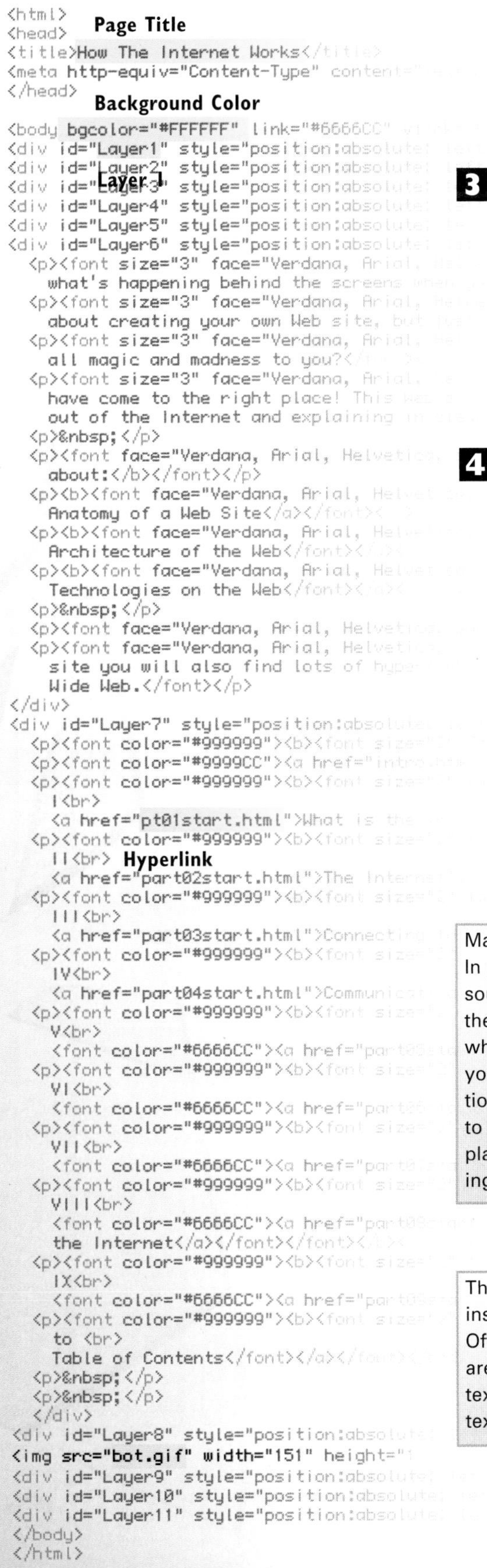

Page Title

Background Color

Layer 1

Hyperlink

```
<html>
<head>
<title>How The Internet Works</title>
<meta http-equiv="Content-Type" content=
</head>
<body bgcolor="#FFFFFF" link="#6666CC"
<div id="Layer1" style="position:absolute;
<div id="Layer2" style="position:absolute;
<div id="Layer3" style="position:absolute;
<div id="Layer4" style="position:absolute;
<div id="Layer5" style="position:absolute;
<div id="Layer6" style="position:absolute;
  <p><font size="3" face="Verdana, Arial,
    what's happening behind the screens
  <p><font size="3" face="Verdana, Arial,
    about creating your own Web site, but
  <p><font size="3" face="Verdana, Arial,
    all magic and madness to you?</
  <p><font size="3" face="Verdana, Arial,
    have come to the right place! This
    out of the Internet and explaining
  <p> </p>
  <p><font face="Verdana, Arial, Helvetica,
    about:</b></font></p>
  <p><b><font face="Verdana, Arial, Helvet
    Anatomy of a Web Site</a></font><
  <p><b><font face="Verdana, Arial, Hel
    Architecture of the Web</font></
  <p><b><font face="Verdana, Arial, Hel
    Technologies on the Web</font></a><
  <p> </p>
  <p><font face="Verdana, Arial, Helvetica,
  <p><font face="Verdana, Arial, Helvetica,
    site you will also find lots of hyper
    Wide Web.</font></p>
</div>
<div id="Layer7" style="position:absolute;
  <p><font color="#999999"><b><font size="
  <p><font color="#9999CC"><a href="intro.htm
  <p><font color="#999999"><b><font size="
    I<br>
    <a href="pt01start.html">What is the
  <p><font color="#999999"><b><font size=
    II<br>
    <a href="part02start.html">The Interne
  <p><font color="#999999"><b><font size=
    III<br>
    <a href="part03start.html">Connecting
  <p><font color="#999999"><b><font size=
    IV<br>
    <a href="part04start.html">Communicat
  <p><font color="#999999"><b><font size=
    V<br>
    <font color="#6666CC"><a href="part05
  <p><font color="#999999"><b><font size=
    VI<br>
    <font color="#6666CC"><a href="part06
  <p><font color="#999999"><b><font size=
    VII<br>
    <font color="#6666CC"><a href="part07
  <p><font color="#999999"><b><font size=
    VIII<br>
    <font color="#6666CC"><a href="part08
    the Internet</a></font></font></b>
  <p><font color="#999999"><b><font size=
    IX<br>
    <font color="#6666CC"><a href="part09
  <p><font color="#999999"><b><font size=
    to <br>
    Table of Contents</font></a></font>
  <p> </p>
  <p> </p>
  </div>
<div id="Layer8" style="position:absolute;
<img src="bot.gif" width="151" height="
<div id="Layer9" style="position:absolute;
<div id="Layer10" style="position:absolute;
<div id="Layer11" style="position:absolute;
</body>
</html>
```

3 The coding in the HTML files tells your browser how to display the text, graphics, links, and multimedia files on the home page. The HTML file your browser loads to display the home page doesn't actually have the graphics, sound, multimedia files, and other resources on it. Instead, it contains HTML references to those graphics and files. Your browser uses those references to find the files on the server and then display them on the home page.

4 The Web browser also interprets HTML tags as links to other Web sites, or to other Web resources, such as graphics, multimedia files, newsgroups, or files to download. Depending on the link, it performs different actions. For example, if the HTML code specifies the link as another home page, the browser retrieves the URL specified in the HTML file when the user clicks the underlined link on the page. If the HTML code specifies a file to be downloaded, the browser downloads the file to your computer.

Many types of files exist on the Internet that Web browsers can't display. In particular, this pertains to many kinds of multimedia files, such as sound, video, and animation files. Still, there are often references to these types of files on Web pages. To view or play these files, you need what are called helper applications and plug-ins. You must configure your Web browser or operating system to launch these helper applications and plug-ins whenever you click an object that needs them in order to be viewed. Helper applications and plug-ins also can be used for displaying virtual reality pages, for chatting on the Internet, and for performing other Internet tasks.

The meanings of tags are easily decipherable. Every HTML tag, or instruction, is surrounded by a less-than and a greater-than sign—<P>. Often tags appear in pairs, the beginning tag and the ending tag. They are identical except for a simple slash in the end tag. So, a paragraph of text frequently is surrounded by tags such as this: <P> Paragraph of text.</P>. Also, tags are not case sensitive. <P> equals <p>.

What Common Browser Error Messages Mean

Server Does Not Have a DNS Entry When you type a URL in your browser to visit a site, your computer contacts a server called a Domain Name System (DNS) server. The DNS server translates the URL into the IP number that computers can understand—and after it does that, your browser can go to the site. (For more information about DNS servers, see Chapter 5, "How Internet Addresses and Domains Work.") If you get an error message telling you the server doesn't have a DNS entry, it means that the server doesn't have a listing for the URL you typed. This usually means either you typed the URL incorrectly or something is wrong with the DNS server. Check the URL and retype it.

503 Service Unavailable This is a catch-all error message for a variety of problems, but all of them mean that the Web site has been incapable of being contacted by your browser. The problem might be that the site's server has crashed because of too much traffic or that there's network congestion.

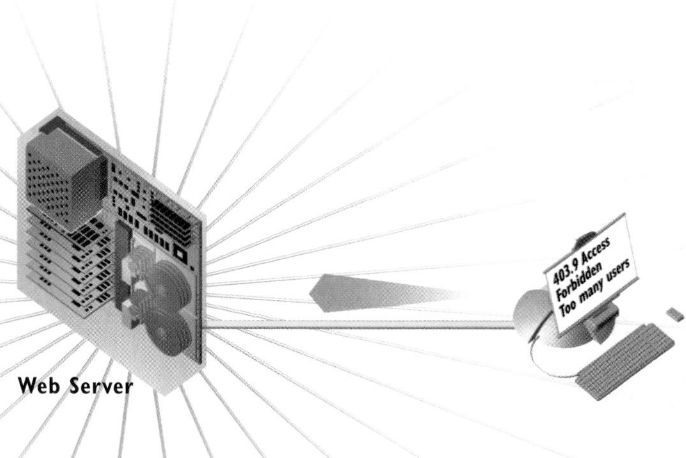

403.9 Access Forbidden. Too Many Users Are Connected. Some Web sites recognize that if they get too much traffic at once, the entire site can be brought down and no one will be able to visit. Those sites put a limit on the number of people who can come to the site at once—that way, the site is always available, even if everyone who wants to visit can't get in. If you get this "Too Many Users Are Connected" message, it usually means that the Web site is up and running, but you can't get in because the maximum number of people are already on the site. Keep trying—when one person leaves, another can come in, and it might be you.

Spinning hourglass This isn't an error message your browser displays—instead, your Windows cursor turns into a spinning hourglass. The spinning hourglass tells you that your browser is trying to make a connection to a Web site. If it keeps spinning and a connection is never made, it can mean that an Internet router someplace between where you are and where you're trying to visit has crashed and you can't make the connection. It can also mean that you've lost your local Internet connection for some reason.

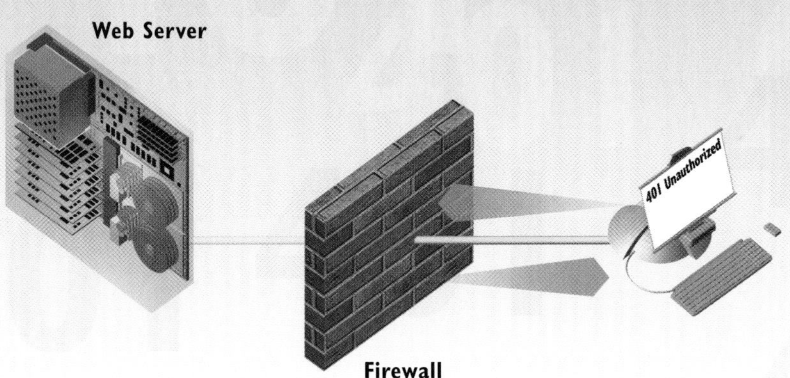

401 Unauthorized and 403 Forbidden If you get either of these error messages, you're trying to enter a Web site that allows only certain people in—and it's not allowing you to enter. Typically, these types of Web sites are password protected and also might allow only visitors who are from certain domains, such as zd.com. If you've entered a password, you might have entered it improperly, or you might not be in a domain that's allowed to enter the Web site.

404 Not Found When you get this message, you've arrived at the correct Web site, but the specific page you're looking for can't be found. That specific page might have been deleted from the site or moved—or you might have typed the location incorrectly.

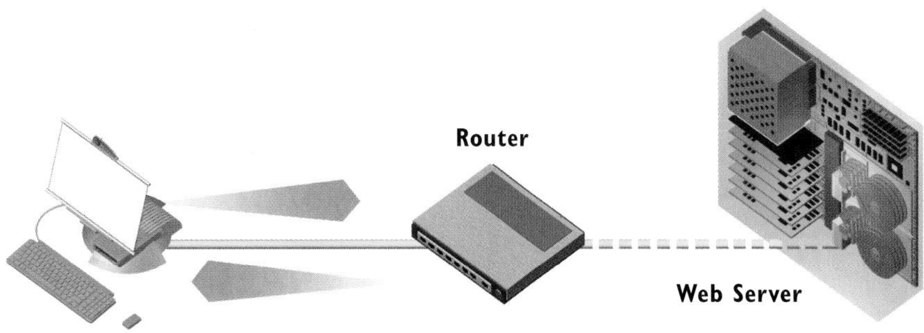

CHAPTER 23

How Markup Languages Work

MARKUP languages are the road signs of a Web page. They are sets of directions that tell the browser software how to display and manage a Web document, much like written music scores are instructions that tell a musician how to play a particular song. These instructions (called tags or markups) are embedded in the source document that creates the Web page.

Tags reference graphic images located in separate files, and they instruct the browser to retrieve and display these images within the page. Tags can also tell a browser to connect a user to another file or URL when he clicks an active hyperlink. So each Web page has everything it needs to be displayed on any computer with a browser that can interpret the markup language.

Your original text will probably have headings, multiple paragraphs, and some simple formatting. A Web browser will not understand all these layout instructions because the original text isn't formatted with HTML, the language of the Web (discussed later in this chapter). Paragraphs, carriage returns, indents, and multiple spaces will be shown instead as a single space if no HTML markup is added.

Markup languages should not be confused with programming languages, such as C+ or Pascal. Programming languages are used to write complex applications, such as word processors or spreadsheets. Markup languages, in contrast, are much simpler and describe the way information should be displayed—for example, by defining when text should be boldface. In markup languages, tags are embedded within documents to describe how the documents should be formatted and displayed.

Hypertext Markup Language (HTML) is the markup language of the Web. It defines the format of a Web document and enables hypertext links to be embedded in the document. You can use any text editor or word processor to add HTML tags to an ASCII text document, although a number of shareware and commercially available HTML editors can assist Web page authors as well.

The Web evolves daily, and HTML also expands and changes along with it. The newest changes to HTML are a group of technologies that together are termed *Dynamic HTML (DHTML)*. These technologies allow HTML to be more than a static language, and they enable HTML to perform animations and become more interactive and flexible.

The eXtended Markup Language (XML) promises to bring even more significant changes to the Web. It's dramatically different from other markup languages because it separates the content of a page from its presentation. Rather than doing things such as giving instructions on text size, it tags different types of content and then has other technologies such as templates and style sheets determine how that content should look. For example, if a book were to be presented on the Web, it would tag chapter titles, chapter numbers, chapter text, and so on. It could then use style sheets to define how chapter titles, chapter numbers, and chapter text should look. Doing this means you can build the content of a page once and present it to many different devices, and in many different ways, without doing much extra work.

How HTML Works

1 To display Web pages in any browser, you must add HTML tags to your original text. This process is called *tagging*.

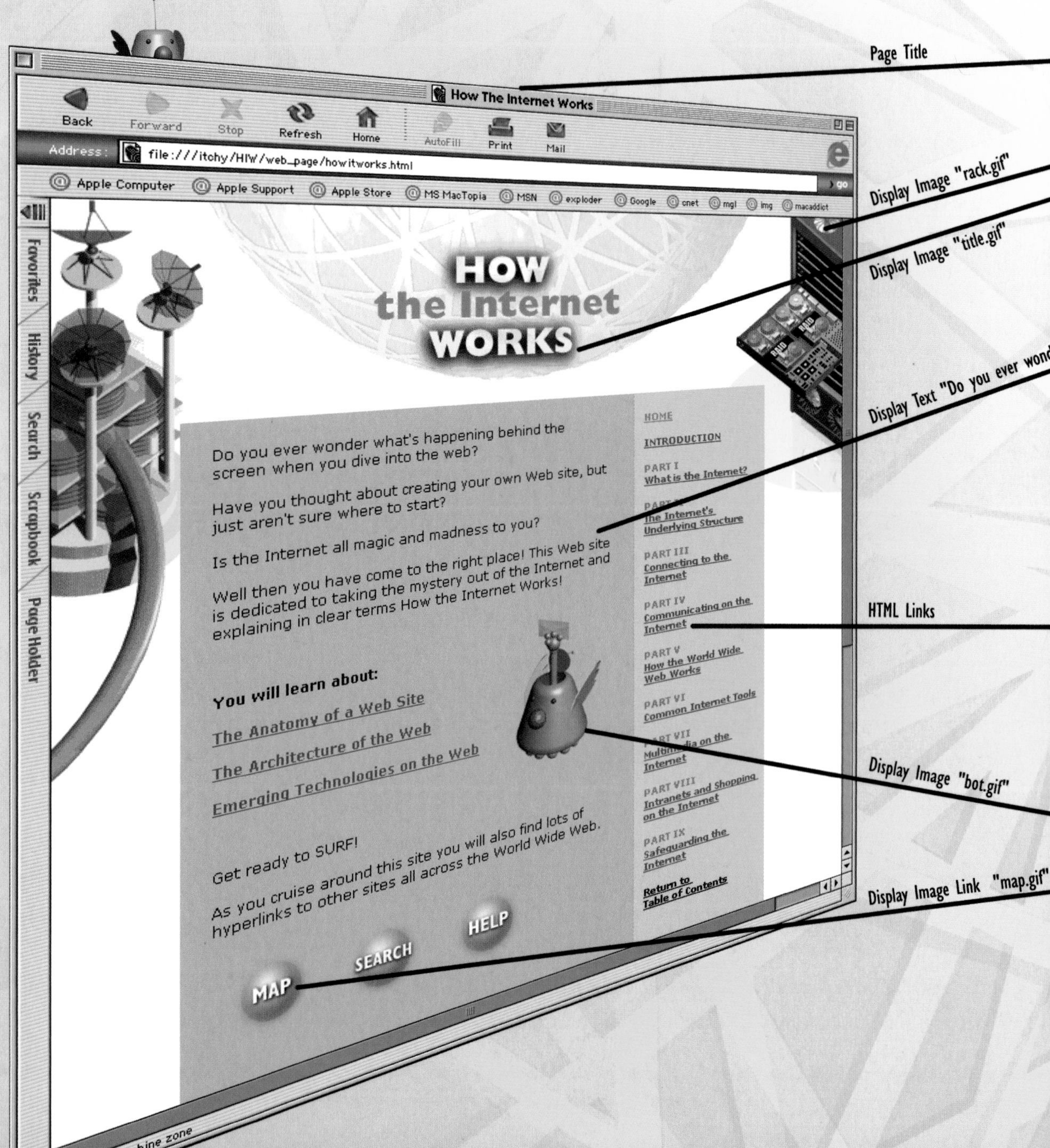

2 Use HTML to give your text structure. All HTML files begin and end with the HTML tags. Headings are marked as such, as are paragraphs, line breaks, block quotes, and special character emphasis. Any carriage returns or indentations within the source text do not affect the browser's display of the page. HTML tags need to be put in if they are to be displayed in a browser.

3 The finished HTML document will be the source page for any browser on any computer. This simplicity of HTML makes cross-platform compatibility easy and reliable. The more complex and specialized the HTML tagging, the longer it will take to download and display the document.

Title

Graphic

Graphic

Text

Text

Hyperlinks

Graphic

Graphic Hyperlink

```
<html>
<head>
<title>How The Internet Works</title>
<meta http-equiv="Content-Type" content="text/html; charset=iso-8859-1">
</head>

<body bgcolor="#FFFFFF" link="#6666CC" vlink="#666666">
<div id="Layer1" style="position:absolute; left:601px; top:-66px; width:180px; height:320px; z-index:1"><img src="rack.gif" width="217" height="372"></div>
<div id="Layer2" style="position:absolute; left:0; top:0; width:203px; height:352px; z-index:2"><img src="rtside.gif" width="125" height="450"></div>
<div id="Layer3" style="position:absolute; left:106px; top:0px; width:494px; height:162px; z-index:3"><img src="title.gif" width="545" height="173"></div>
<div id="Layer4" style="position:absolute; left:91px; top:180px; width:502px; height:875px; z-index:4; background-color: #CCCCCC; layer-background-color: #CCCCCC; border: 1px none #0000
<div id="Layer5" style="position:absolute; left:506px; top:180px; width:156; height:877px; z-index:5; background-color: #FFCC99; layer-background-color: #FFCC99; border: 1px none #00000
<div id="Layer6" style="position:absolute; left:115px; top:201px; width:369px; height:604px; z-index:6">
  <p><font size="3" face="Verdana, Arial, Helvetica, sans-serif">Do you ever wonder
   what's happening behind the screen when you dive into the web?</font></p>
  <p><font size="3" face="Verdana, Arial, Helvetica, sans-serif">Have you thought
   about creating your own Web site, but just aren't sure where to start?</font></p>
  <p><font size="3" face="Verdana, Arial, Helvetica, sans-serif">Is the Internet
   all magic and madness to you?</font></p>
  <p><font size="3" face="Verdana, Arial, Helvetica, sans-serif">Well then you
   have come to the right place! This Web site is dedicated to taking the mystery
   out of the Internet and explaining in clear terms How the Internet Works!</font></p>
  <p> </p>
  <p><font face="Verdana, Arial, Helvetica, sans-serif" size="3"><b>You will learn
   about:</b></font></p>
  <p><b><font face="Verdana, Arial, Helvetica, sans-serif" size="3"><a href="pt05_ch2102.html">The
   Anatomy of a Web Site</a></font></b></p>
  <p><b><font face="Verdana, Arial, Helvetica, sans-serif"><a href="pt01_ch0101.html"><font size="3">The
   Architecture of the Web</font></a></font></b></p>
  <p><b><font face="Verdana, Arial, Helvetica, sans-serif"><a href="pt07_ch3205.html"><font size="3">Emerging
   Technologies on the Web</font></a></font></b></p>
  <p> </p>
  <p><font face="Verdana, Arial, Helvetica, sans-serif">Get ready to SURF!</font></p>
  <p><font face="Verdana, Arial, Helvetica, sans-serif">As you cruise around this
   site you will also find lots of hyperlinks to other sites all across the World
   Wide Web.</font></p>
</div>
<div id="Layer7" style="position:absolute; left:517px; top:198px; width:139px; height:631px; z-index:7">
  <p><font color="#999999"><b><font size="2" face="Verdana, Arial, Helvetica, sans-serif"><a href="index.html"><font color="#9999CC">HOME</font></a></font></b></font></p>
  <p><font color="#9999CC"><a href="intro.html"><b><font size="2" face="Verdana, Arial, Helvetica, sans-serif">INTRODUCTION</font></b></a></font></p>
  <p><font color="#999999"><b><font size="2" face="Verdana, Arial, Helvetica, sans-serif">PART
   I<br>
   <a href="pt01start.html">What is the Internet?</a></font></b></font></p>
  <p><font color="#999999"><b><font size="2" face="Verdana, Arial, Helvetica, sans-serif">PART
   II<br>
   <a href="part02start.html">The Internet's Underlying Structure</a></font></b></font></p>
  <p><font color="#999999"><b><font size="2" face="Verdana, Arial, Helvetica, sans-serif">PART
   III<br>
   <a href="part03start.html">Connecting to the Internet</a></font></b></font></p>
  <p><font color="#999999"><b><font size="2" face="Verdana, Arial, Helvetica, sans-serif">PART
   IV<br>
   <a href="part04start.html">Communicating on the Internet</a></font></b></font></p>
  <p><font color="#999999"><b><font size="2" face="Verdana, Arial, Helvetica, sans-serif">PART
   V<br>
   <font color="#6666CC"><a href="part05start.html">How the World Wide Web Works</a></font></font></b></font></p>
  <p><font color="#999999"><b><font size="2" face="Verdana, Arial, Helvetica, sans-serif">PART
   VI<br>
   <font color="#6666CC"><a href="part06start.html">Common Internet Tools</a></font></font></b></font></p>
  <p><font color="#999999"><b><font size="2" face="Verdana, Arial, Helvetica, sans-serif">PART
   VII<br>
   <font color="#6666CC"><a href="part07start.html">Multimedia on the Internet</a></font></font></b></font></p>
  <p><font color="#999999"><b><font size="2" face="Verdana, Arial, Helvetica, sans-serif">PART
   VIII<br>
   <font color="#6666CC"><a href="part08start.html">Intranets and Shopping on
   the Internet</a></font></font></b></font></p>
  <p><font color="#999999"><b><font size="2" face="Verdana, Arial, Helvetica, sans-serif">PART
   IX<br>
   <font color="#6666CC"><a href="part09start.html">Safeguarding the Internet</a></font></font></b></font></p>
  <p><font color="#999999"><b><font size="2" face="Verdana, Arial, Helvetica, sans-serif"><a href="index.html"><font color="#000000">Return
   to <br>
   Table of Contents</font></a></font></b></font></p>
  <p> </p>
  <p> </p>
  </div>
<div id="Layer8" style="position:absolute; left:351px; top:380px; width:129px; height:132px; z-index:8"><img src="bot.gif" width="151" height="154"></div>
<div id="Layer9" style="position:absolute; left:120px; top:622px; width:77px; height:68px; z-index:9"><a href="map.html"><img src="map.gif" width="83" height="83" border="0"></a></div>
<div id="Layer10" style="position:absolute; left:215px; top:623px; width:65px; height:76px; z-index:10"><a href="searchHIW.html"><img src="search.gif" width="83" height="83" border="0"
<div id="Layer11" style="position:absolute; left:312px; top:622px; width:67px; height:101px; z-index:11"><a href="helpme.html"><img src="help.gif" width="83" height="83" border="0"></a>
</body>
</html>
```

4 Most Web browsers enable your document to retain its structural integrity when you display, or *parse*, it. Headings will appear in a larger font size than text within paragraphs, for example, and block quotes will be uniformly indented. However, the look might vary from browser to browser. Note that browsers determine the exact font, size, and color. Also be aware that the relative importance of the elements is always kept intact.

How Dynamic HTML Works

1 Dynamic HTML (DHTML) differs from traditional HTML in that it enables Web pages to be changed on-the-fly, after they've been downloaded. In plain HTML, after a page is downloaded, it is static and can be changed only when a user takes an action of some kind. But DHTML, for example, could cause an animation of a rocket to fly across your browser window several seconds after the page has been downloaded—without your doing anything.

2 DHTML does its work without having to contact the server after the page downloads, so it can perform some interactive functions more quickly than other technologies that have to contact the server. The instructions for performing the commands are in the HTML commands that are in the page itself.

3 Although DHTML is often referred to as if it were a single technology, it is, in fact, a general term used for a group of technologies that can work together or by themselves to change a Web page after the page has been downloaded to your computer. These technologies are the Document Object Model (DOM), Cascading Style Sheets (CSS), and client-side scripting languages, such as JavaScript.

Elements of DHTML

Plain HTML | **Dynamic HTML**

Document Object Model (DOM)

How DHTML Works

HOW DHTML Works

4 The DOM defines every object and element on a Web page and enables those objects to be manipulated or accessed. This includes fonts, graphics, tables, and visual elements, as well as elements you can't necessarily see, such as the browser's version number and the current date and time. Without DOM, all the elements on a page are static. So on the simplest level, DHTML could use the DOM to change the font of every letter, individually, on a Web page.

5 Cascading Style Sheets are, in essence, templates that apply formatting and style information to the elements of a Web page. They're called *cascading* because any single page can have more than one style sheet associated with it. Additionally, Cascading Style Sheets enable images to overlap one another. This enables animations to be created easily on a page.

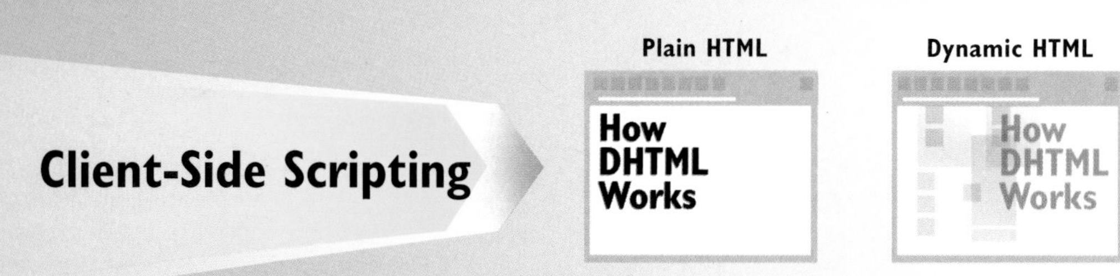

6 Client-side scripting languages perform much of the work of DHTML. These languages access the DOM and manipulate its elements, and they do the same to Cascading Style Sheets. They perform the actions of DHTML. So a script, for example, could turn a word a different color when a mouse moves across it, or it could create easy-to-use collapsible navigation on every page on a Web site.

How XML Works

1 XML solves several a major problems for Web developers. Without it, to deliver Web pages to different devices such as computers, cell phones, and wireless Palm devices, a developer must create and maintain three separate Web sites, with special coding for each device—HTML for the computer, WAP for the cell phone, and what's called Web clipping for the wireless Palm devices. It's an expensive, difficult, and time-consuming proposition. And even if a developer is building a site only for computers, every time the design changes, all the pages must be recoded—again, an expensive and time-consuming proposition.

HTML

PC

Web Clipping

Handheld

WAP

Cellular Telephone

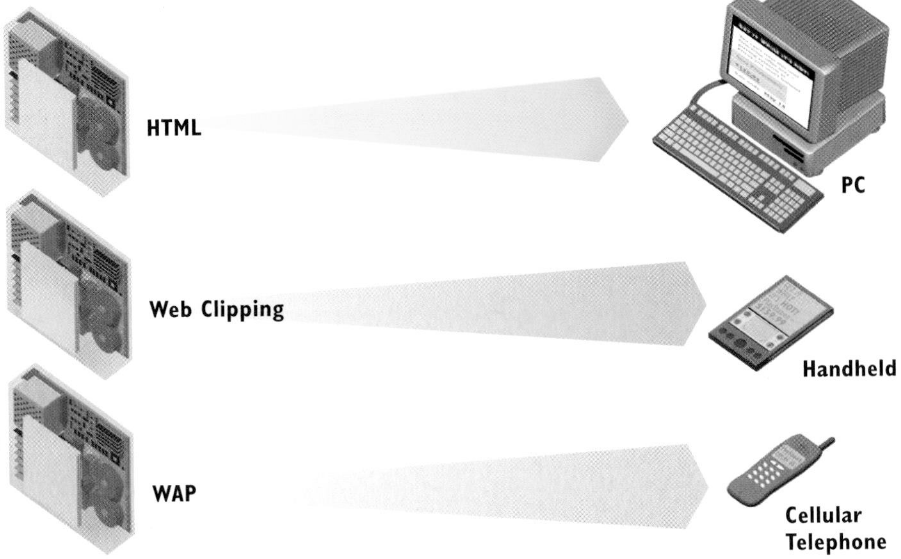

2 With XML, a developer can create the Web site just once. Then it can be automatically formatted to several types of devices, such as Internet-connected computers, wireless Palm devices, and cell phones using WAP. And even if the site is being built for only computers, when there is a redesign, with XML, all the pages need not be rebuilt.

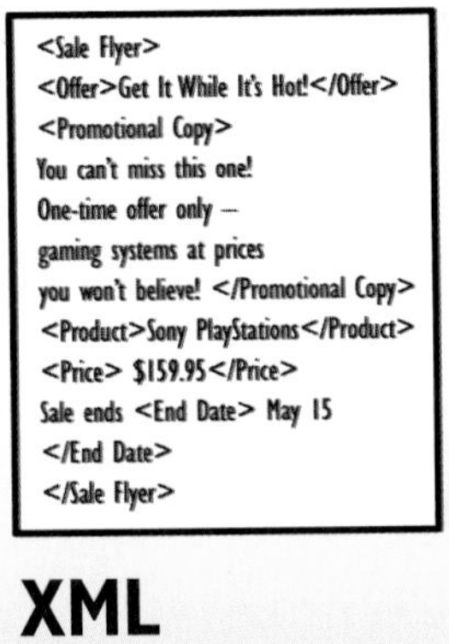

```
<Sale Flyer>
<Offer>Get It While It's Hot!</Offer>
<Promotional Copy>
You can't miss this one!
One-time offer only –
gaming systems at prices
you won't believe! </Promotional Copy>
<Product>Sony PlayStations</Product>
<Price> $159.95</Price>
Sale ends <End Date> May 15
</End Date>
</Sale Flyer>
```

XML

XSLT

3 The most important concept to understand about XML is that the language is used only to convey information about content, not about the presentation of the content. So, for example, it doesn't give instructions on what size text should be. But it uses tags to define the type of content on the page. Then it uses other techniques, as you'll see in the next steps, to display those pages. In that way, a single page can be displayed many different ways, without having to go back and alter the original page—only the designs, which are separate from the content, need to be changed.

6 After the site knows what kind of device is visiting, it takes the XML, and using XSLT, changes it into the proper format—for example, a WAP document that the cell phone can view with its WAP microbrowser or an HTML document for a computer.

I'm a PC.

Who are you?

I'm a Handheld.

Here is your clipped Web page.

I'm a cellular phone.

5 When a device visits a site built with XML, there needs to be some way for site to know what type of device it is— a computer, for example, or a cell phone. Common Gateway Interface (CGI) scripts can detect which device is contacting the site.

GET IT WHILE IT'S HOT!

You can't miss this one! One-time offer only -- gaming systems at prices you won't believe!

Sony PlayStations

$159.95

Sale ends May 15

HTML

PlayStation
159.95 US
Sale Ends
May 15

WAP

4 When XML content is posted on a Web site, different designs need to be applied to that content so that it can be viewable by devices connecting to it—for example, cell phones. eXtensible Style Language Transformations (XSLT) can be applied to the XML. XSLT can take XML and apply different designs to it or change it to other forms of XML—for example, it can take the XML and turn it into a WAP page that can be viewed by a cell phone and take the same XML and turn it into a HTML document with a different design.

CHAPTER 24 How Hypertext Works

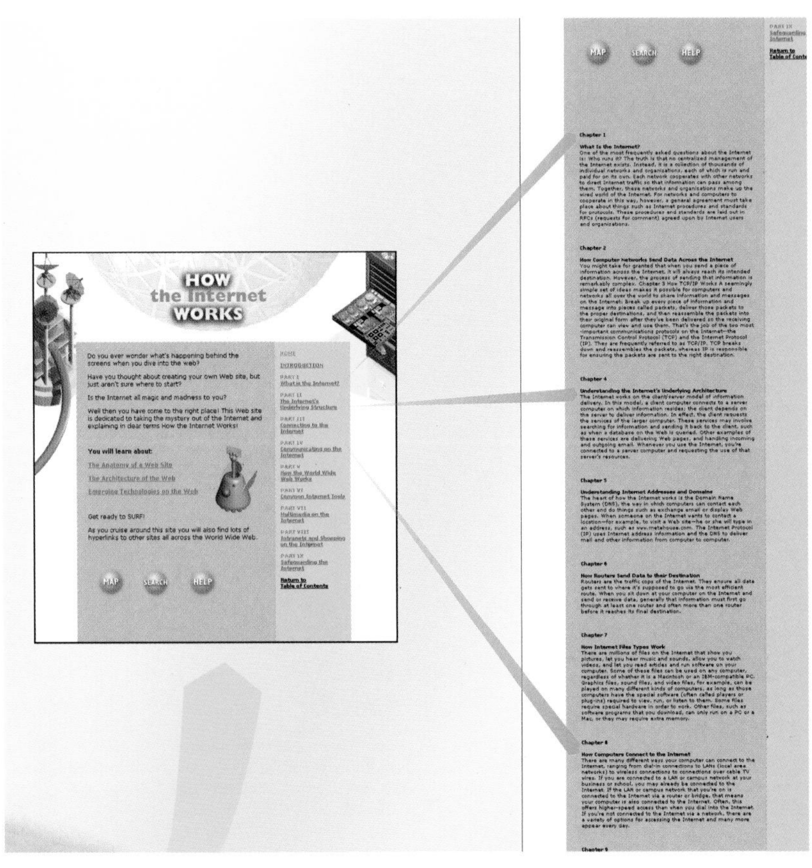

IN the late 1960s, a computer scientist named Ted Nelson introduced hypertext, a concept that lays the foundation for the World Wide Web and its connections between documents, or pages.

Nelson wanted to create a new way of exploring information. He wanted to provide the reader with a spontaneous means of accessing more and more in-depth information about something that sparked the reader's interest when reading text on the page. Rather than reading a document from beginning to end, digesting the material in a sequential order, the reader could highlight a word and receive more information on the meaning of that word, for example.

Nelson imagined that you could read the United States Constitution, come across the term "electoral college," and then open another document that explains how the electoral college works. From that document, you might open another document that lists the votes of the electoral college from its founding to the present. From there, you might choose to open a document about William Jefferson Clinton, then another about the First Cat, Socks, then another about the care and feeding of felines, and so forth. Ultimately, you could find a subject that wasn't even remotely connected to the Constitution, but which you would find interesting or entertaining.

This hypertext concept was obviously on Tim Berners-Lee's mind when he began thinking about how researchers could share their work across the Internet. He envisioned a system in which a document could be linked to other documents, enabling researchers to easily find more and related information simply by following a link from one document on the network to another.

Typically, hypertext consists of a hyperlink that appears onscreen as a highlighted word, icon, or graphic. By moving a mouse cursor over the item, or object, and clicking it, you easily navigate to additional information. On the Web, that information can be located at any other place on the Web, be it on the same host server or one across the globe. A linked object can be various media, such as text (linking from one character to a whole document, for example), a graphical button (such as direction arrows that move from page to page), or still images (photos, icons, or a comic strip), for example. The documents and objects that are being linked to can be on the same site as the original document or on an entirely different site.

Hypertext links are embedded into a Web document using Hypertext Markup Language (HTML). A text link usually appears onscreen as an underlined word or phrase and is sometimes rendered in a different color from other text, depending on how your Web browser interprets the HTML codes. When you place the mouse cursor on this underlined text and click the mouse button, you initiate a request by the browser for a new Web page or—if the text references an internal link to information in the same document—direct your browser to scroll to another, specific point within the same document.

Images or icons can also act as hyperlinks. When you move the mouse cursor over the icon or graphic and click the mouse button, you launch the request to retrieve the linked information.

How Hyperlinks Work

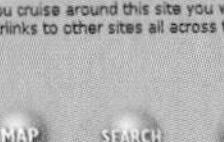

1. The "hyperlinking" begins when you first retrieve a Web page from a remote Web server. Target links within the page move you quickly from one part of the page to the next.

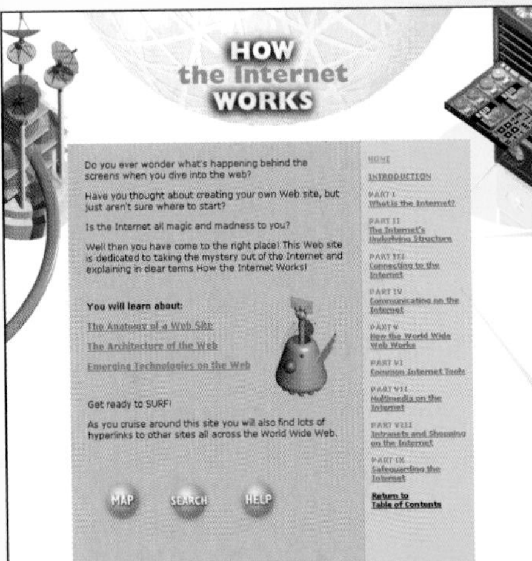

<a href="#target">Part 1</a>

<a href="#target">Part 2</a>

<a href="#target">Part 3</a>

2 A *relative* link is used to initiate a request by your Web browser to retrieve a page located on the same Web server as the page from which you are linking. Web developers use relative links when they're pointing to a page under their control because this enables the to more easily maintain their HTML coding if their server locations change.

<a href="/oursite/relative/chapter_4.html">Chapter 4</a>

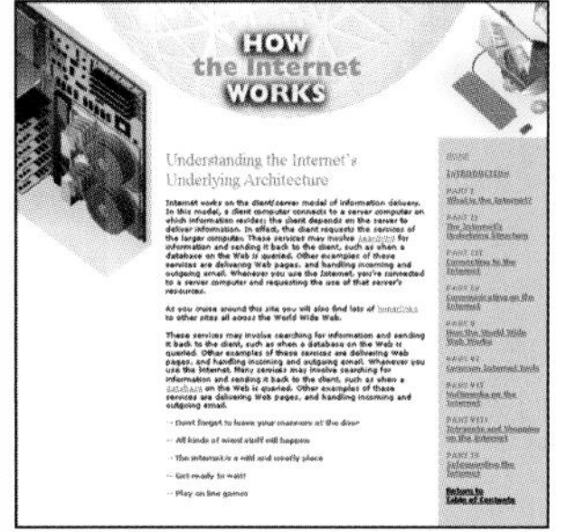

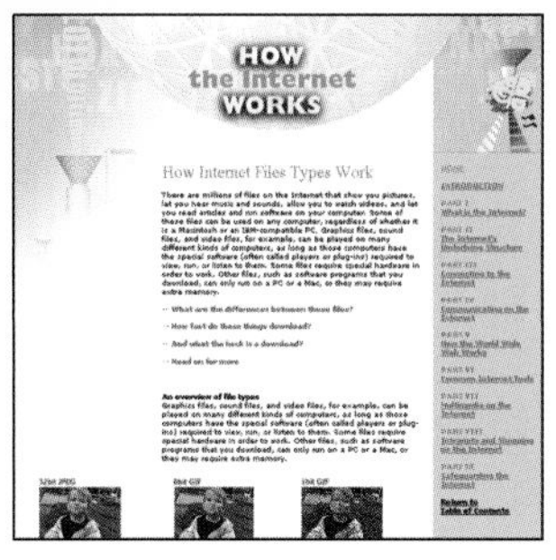

<a href="/oursite/relative/chapter_7.html">Chapter 7</a>

3 A hyperlink that leads to a completely different Web server uses an *absolute* link. Because these links might not be under the control of the Web developer who created the page, there is a chance that this will be a "dead link"—the page will have been moved without the Web developer knowing about it.

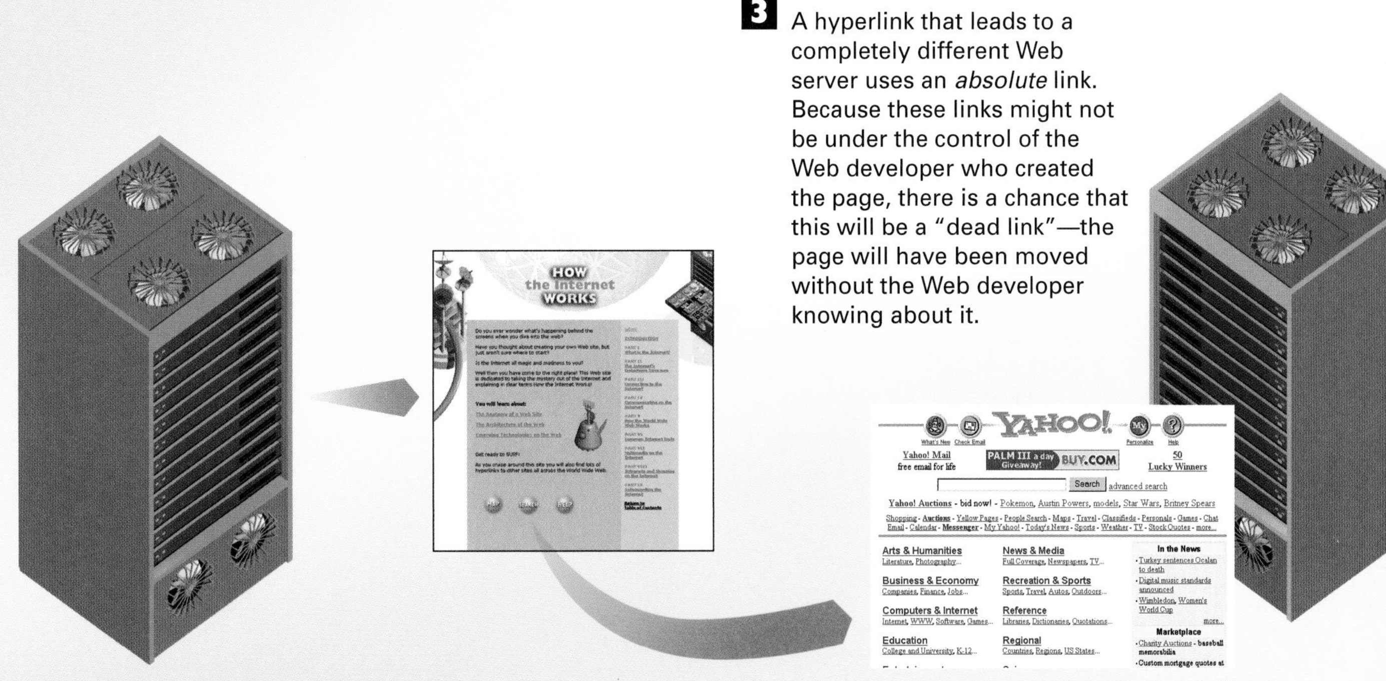

<a href=www.yahoo.com><img src="searchyahoo.gif"></a>

CHAPTER 25 How URLs Work

THE Web pages and the hosts that make up the World Wide Web must have unique locations so that your computer can locate and retrieve the pages. The unique identifier for a host is called the Internet Protocol (IP) address, and the unique identifier for a page is called the uniform resource locator (URL). A URL functions much like a postal or e-mail address. Just as postal and e-mail addresses list a name and specific location, a URL, or Web address, indicates where the host computer is located, the location of the Web site on the host, and the name of the Web page and the file type of each document, among other information.

A typical URL looks like this:

`http://www.zdpress.com/internetworks/index.html/`

If you were to interpret the instructions in this URL from left to right, it would translate to: "Go to the host computer called `zdpress` (a commercial business), in a directory called `internetworks`, and retrieve a hypertext document with the filename `index.html`." The URL, or address, tells the browser which document to fetch and exactly where to find it on a specific remote host computer somewhere on the Internet.

The first part of the URL indicates what type of transfer protocol will be used to retrieve the specified document. The most common request is for a hypertext document that uses Hypertext Transfer Protocol (HTTP).

The second portion of the URL refers to the specific host computer on which the document resides, which is to be contacted by the browser software. This part of the address is also called the *domain name*. See Chapter 5, "How Internet Addresses and Domains Work," for more information about domains.

The third part of the URL is the directory on the host computer that contains a specific Web site or multiple Web sites. This is always located after the first single slash in the URL and is essentially the subdirectory on the hard disk that houses the Web site. Subdirectories might also be indicated in this part of the address. For example, if the previous URL were changed to `http://www.zdpress.com/internetworks/partone/chapters/chapte.html` there would be two subdirectories—`part one` and `chapters`.

In the preceding example, the filename is `chapte.html`. This is always the last portion of the URL. If you see an address without a filename, it is assumed that the filename `index.html` contains the requested Web page. Therefore, the default document a Web server will deliver to the client when no other filename is listed is `index.html`. (Note that sometimes the last portion of the URL might not be a filename—it could be other types of information required by a Web server, such as codes required to log on to the Web server.)

The illustration in this chapter shows the process necessary to request and retrieve a Web document. When a request for a document occurs for the first time in a Web-browsing session, the host computer must first be located to find the file. After that, the specific subdirectory and document are retrieved.

How URLs Are Structured

1 The first part of the URL indicates which type of transfer protocol will be used to retrieve the specified document. The most common request is for a hypertext document that uses the HTTP protocol.

3 The third part of the URL is the directory on the host computer that contains a specific Web site. A host computer can house multiple Web sites. This third segment of the address is essentially the root directory that houses the HTML document, CGI, image, and so on that is being requested. Subdirectories might also be indicated in this part of the address.

http://www.sample.com/samples/sample.html

2 The second portion of the URL is the specific host computer on which the document resides, which is to be contacted by the browser software. This part of the address is also called the *domain*. Domain names end in a suffix that indicates which type of organization the domain is. For example, `.com` indicates a commercial business, `.edu` indicates a college or university, `.gov` indicates a government office, `.mil` indicates a military facility, and `.org` indicates a not-for-profit organization. The suffix also can indicate the country in which the host computer is located. For example, `.ca` is in Canada, and `.au` is in Australia.

4 The last segment of the URL is the filename of the specific Web page you are requesting. If no filename is indicated, the browser assumes a default page, usually called `index.html`.

How URLs Help Retrieve Web Documents

1 The Web browser installed on your local computer sends your TCP/IP software a signal that it is ready to request a document. TCP/IP makes a connection with the host TCP/IP software. After the connection is established, your browser makes a request for a document by sending its URL through the two-way connection maintained by TCP/IP to the server.

2 The HTTP server is the portion of the host computer that runs HTTP server software. TCP/IP makes and maintains the connection this way. The browser can use HTTP to send requests and receive pages through the host's Web server software. This software enables the host to communicate with the client browser, in HTTP, over TCP/IP.

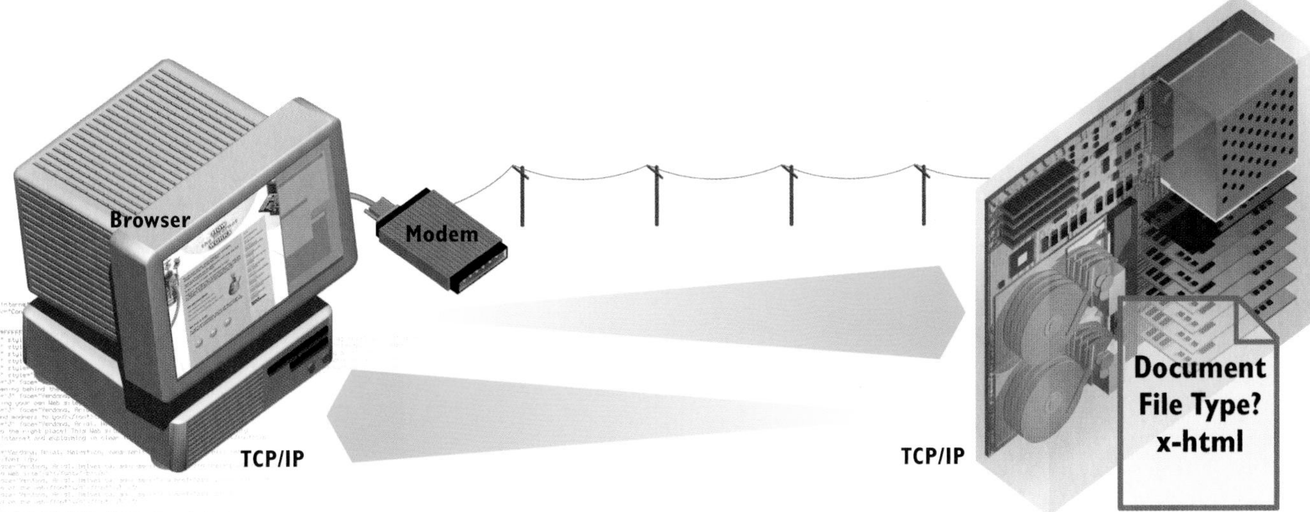

3 The server then receives the transmitted URL and responds in one of three ways. It follows the directory path given in the URL; the server finds the file on its local hard disk and opens it; the server runs a CGI script or detects an error (such as `file not found`) and generates an error document to be sent back to the client.

4 If the document is found, the host checks its file type (usually either x-html or x-text) and sends this information to the client with the requested page. When the client receives the page, it first checks the file type. If the type is one it can display, it does so; otherwise, it prompts the user to see whether she wants to save it to disk or open it using a helper application. The x-html file type is by far the most common one used when transmitting Web pages.

5 The browser on your local computer reads the file type. If it is an HTML document, the browser examines the content, breaking it down into meaningful parts. Two general parts include text, which is displayed by the browser word for word. The other part consists of HTML markup information called *tags*, which are not displayed but display formatting information, such as normal text, bold headers, or colored hypertext. The results are displayed on your monitor.

CHAPTER 26 How Image Maps and Interactive Forms Work

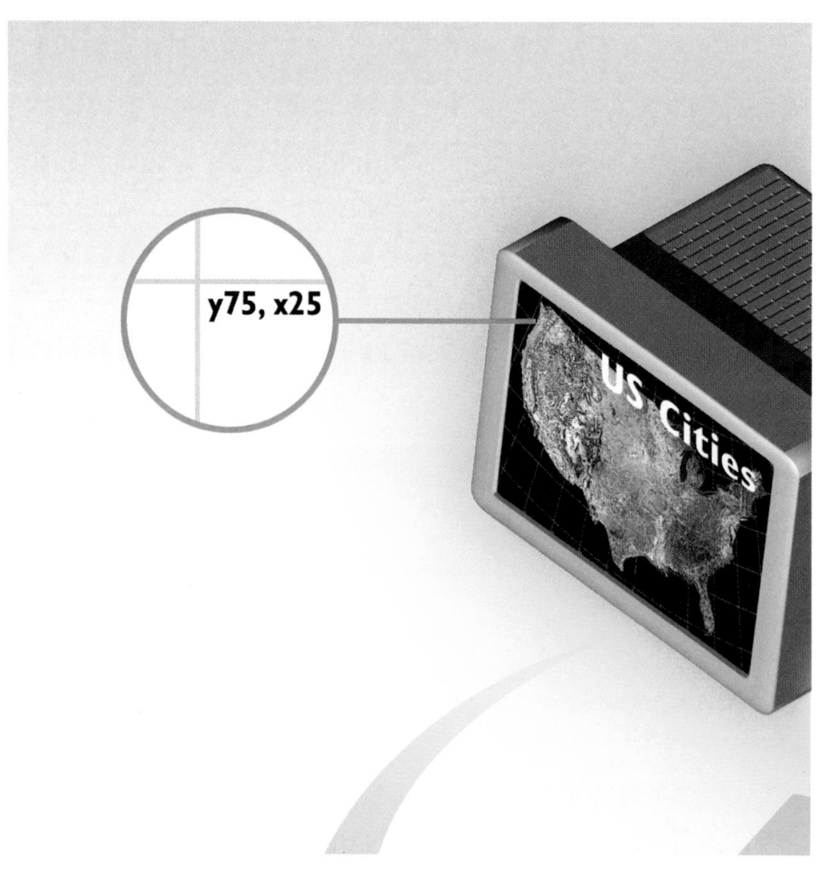

GRAPHICS called image maps and functions called interactive forms demonstrate two of the more common and helpful uses of HTML. *Image maps* are static images that have been turned into clickable images with various clickable parts. *Interactive forms* are HTML-based pages you fill out by providing information such as your name, e-mail address, and similar information. Both image maps and interactive forms are created using Common Gateway Interface (CGI), a communications protocol by which a Web server can communicate with other applications. (For more information about how CGI works, turn to Chapter 35, "How CGI Scripting Works.")

Image maps can be thought of as fancy hyperlinks. However, instead of a word, an entire icon, or an image linking to another page, an image is divided into different segments, or coordinates, that link to different HTML pages. That is, image maps link to another document through a predefined *hot* area within an image. As soon as you click your mouse on a hot spot, a CGI script and special image map coordinates file with the suffix .map go to work. A CGI application reads the map file to match coordinates of a mouse click with a corresponding URL. For instance, imagine an electronic map of the United States in which you click Washington, D.C. In the HTML code for that page, the electronic map is surrounded by a tag and an attribute called `ISMAP`. The code looks something like this:

```
<A HREF="some.server/maps/clickable.map>
<IMG SRC+"clickable.map" ISMAP>
</A>
```

The x,y coordinate of your mouse click is sent to the server. The coordinates are received by the server and then redirected to a CGI application. The CGI application scans the file for matching coordinates and then forwards the corresponding URL to the server. Lastly, if the Web page resides on the same server, it delivers that Web page to the client browser. If not, the server returns the URL to the client browser, which in turn sends a request to the correct server for the page. You then see the page about Washington, D.C. begin to load on your browser. Behind the scenes, the server passed your mouse click coordinates to a CGI application via the CGI. Then, the CGI application matched those coordinates to its URL in a .map file. Finally, the URL sent the URL back to the server, which redirected the client browser to the new Web page.

Forms work differently, although they also use CGI. In a form, when you fill in information on a Web page, that information goes to the server for processing. Next, the server redirects the information to a CGI application that is called by the form *submit*. (CGI scripts are activated by the server in response to an HTTP request from the client.) Lastly, a CGI application might send form data to another computer program, such as a database; save it to a file; or even generate a unique HTML document in response to the user's request.

How Image Maps Work

1 In this map example, the user clicks Seattle. The x,y grid coordinate is 75, 25. In the HTML code, the browser recognizes the ISMAP image tag attribute. The mouse click activates the browser to send the x,y coordinate of the click to the server. The location of the `National.map` file is also sent to the server.

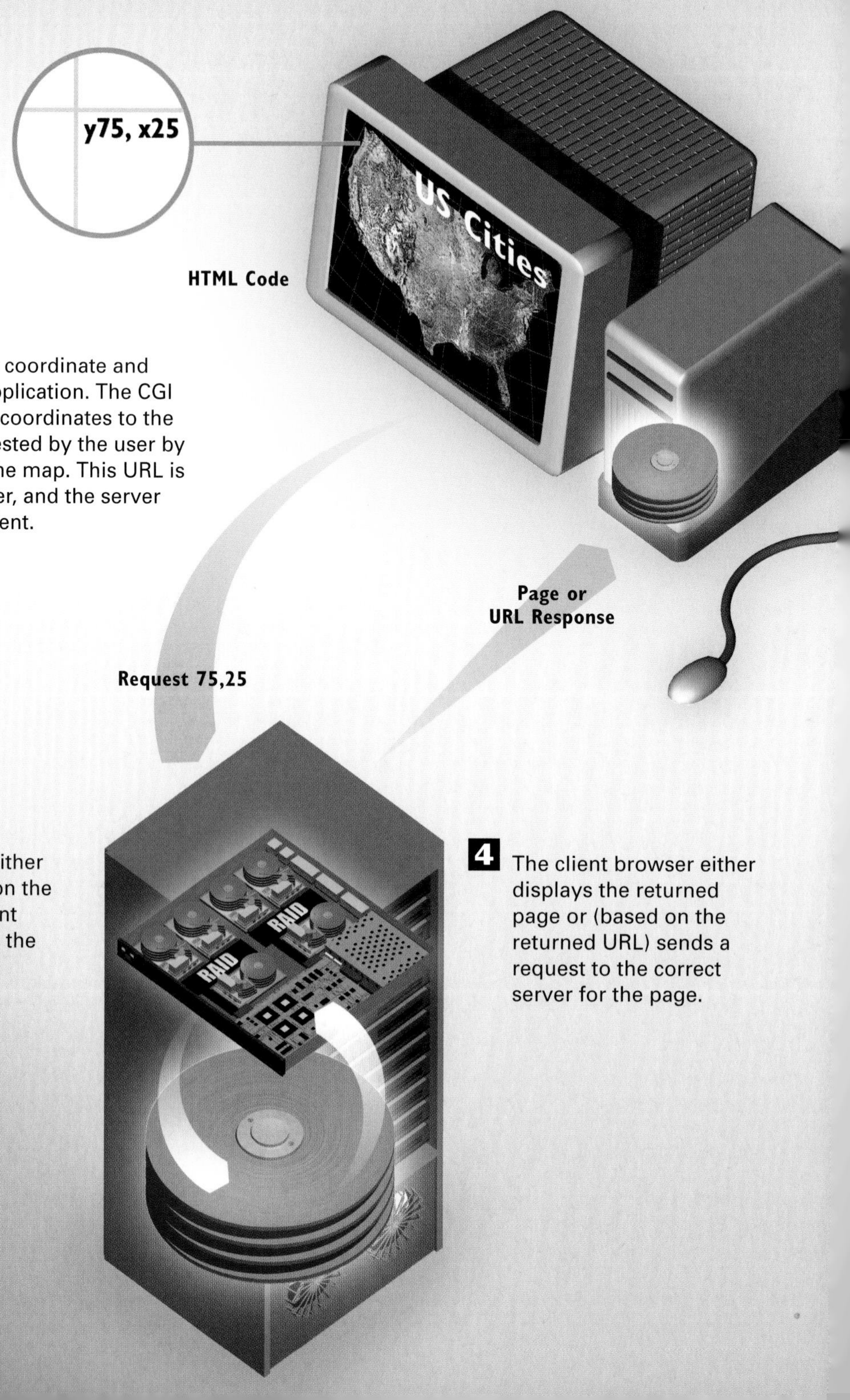

2 The server hands off the coordinate and map file data to a CGI application. The CGI application matches the coordinates to the URL that has been requested by the user by clicking that portion of the map. This URL is handed back to the server, and the server sends the page to the client.

3 The Web document is either served up (if it resides on the same server) or the client browser if forwarded to the new URL.

4 The client browser either displays the returned page or (based on the returned URL) sends a request to the correct server for the page.

How Interactive Forms Work

1. In working with an interactive form, the user clicks a data-entry submit button. The data in the data fields is sent to the server with the request.

Home> Products> Windows: <

Login to Download

Login to Download

Name

Email

Postal Code

Notify me of updates

Platform of product you are downloading:

WINDOWS

Are you using for:

SELECT

Do you own another product?

SELECT

Do you own a Palm OS device?

SELECT

GO!

Submit Form Data

2. When a form submission is received by the server, it activates a CGI application, a program, or a script that interacts with a Web server; it then passes the resulting information to a Web form. (The application could add the form data to a database or compare it to a password list of eligible users, among other tasks.) The program's output goes either to another program, such as a database, or into a unique HTML document, or both.

CHAPTER 27 How Web Host Servers Work

TO serve up pages, Web sites need a *host*—a computer—and server software that runs on the host. The host manages the communications protocols and houses the pages and the related software required to create a Web site on the Internet. The host machine often uses the Unix, Windows NT, Linux, or Macintosh operating systems, which have the TCP/IP protocols built in.

The server software resides on the host and serves up the pages and otherwise acts on the requests sent from the client browser software. The server is not responsible for TCP/IP communications—the host operating system does that—but instead the server handles the HTTP requests and communications with the host operating system.

Different types of server software (database servers or network servers, for example) exist that perform various types of services for various types of clients. Specifically, a *Web server* is an HTTP server, and its function is to send information to the client software (typically a browser) using the Hypertext Transfer Protocol (HTTP).

Usually, the client browser requests that the server return an HTML document. The server receives this request and sends back a response. The top portion of the response includes transmission information, and the rest of the response is the HTML file.

A Web server does more than send pages to the browser, however. It passes requests to run Common Gateway Interface (CGI) scripts to CGI applications. These scripts run external mini-programs, such as a database lookup or interactive forms processing. The server sends the script to the application via CGI and communicates the results of the script back to the browser, if appropriate. Moreover, the server software includes configuration files and utilities to secure and manage the Web site in a variety of ways.

How Web Server Software Works

1. Client (browser) software sends its request for data to the host, where the Web server software processes the request.

2. Included in the browser's request are the desired information and the file formats the browser can accept.

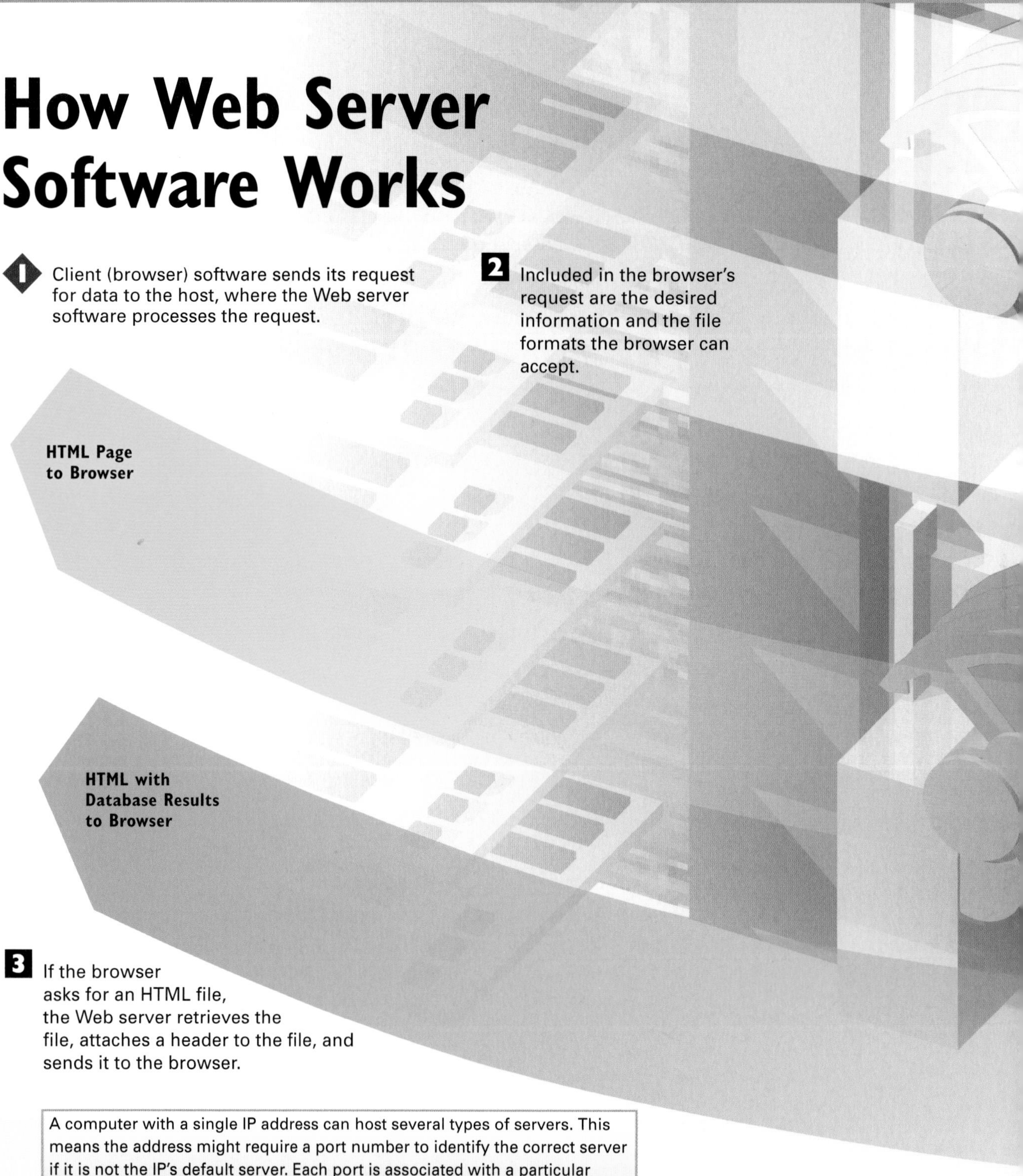

HTML Page to Browser

HTML with Database Results to Browser

3. If the browser asks for an HTML file, the Web server retrieves the file, attaches a header to the file, and sends it to the browser.

A computer with a single IP address can host several types of servers. This means the address might require a port number to identify the correct server if it is not the IP's default server. Each port is associated with a particular server. Ports are identified by a number from 0 to 65,535, but common server types, such as FTP servers, are given the same number by convention.

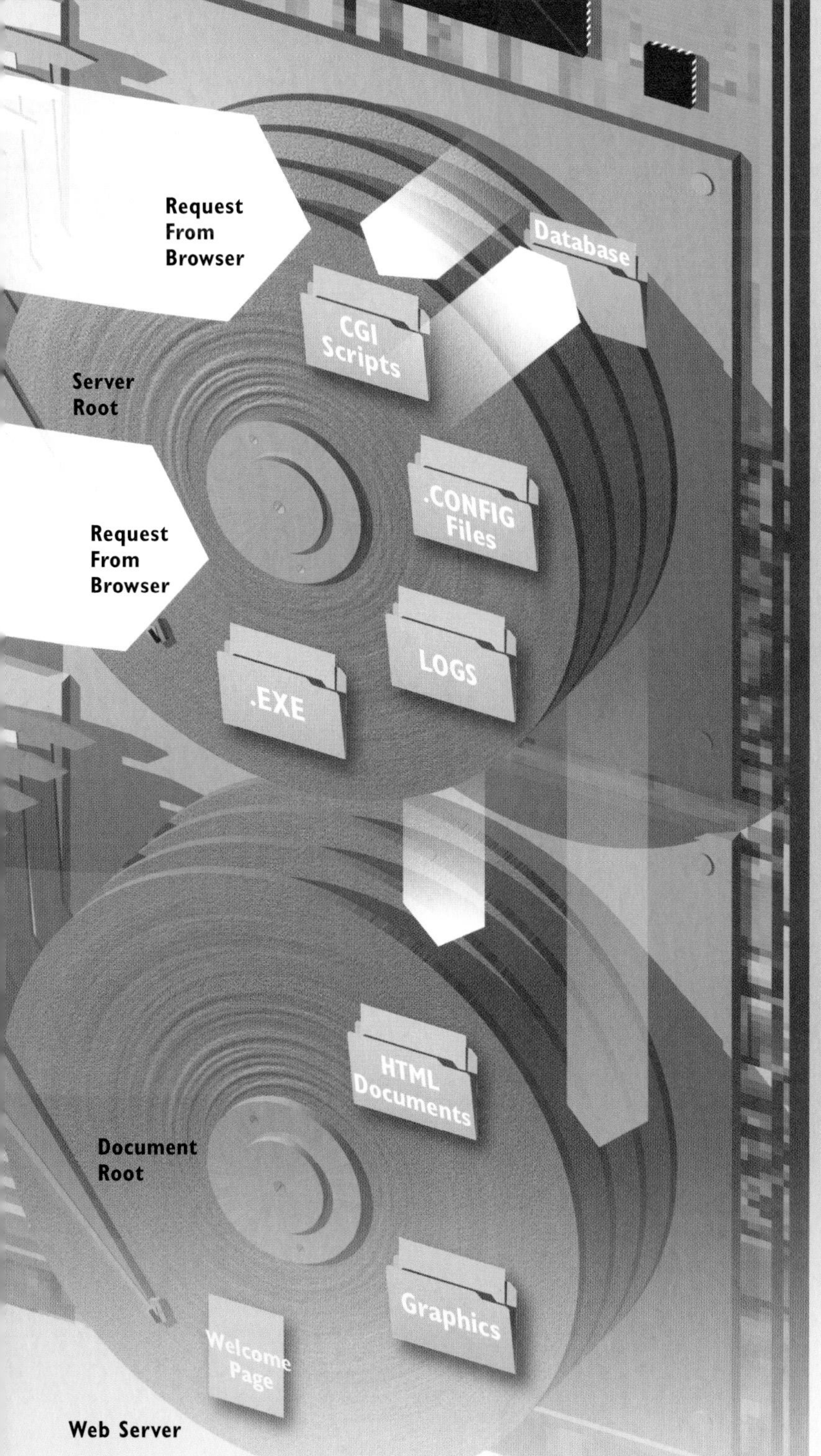

Request From Browser

Database

CGI Scripts

Server Root

.CONFIG Files

Request From Browser

LOGS

.EXE

HTML Documents

Document Root

Graphics

Welcome Page

Web Server

4 If the browser has asked for specific database information, the Web server passes a request through CGI to the application, which performs a database lookup, for example. The CGI script returns the results to the Web server, which in turn attaches a header to the data and sends it to the browser.

The host computer must have a unique IP address to send and receive information across the Internet. Because raw IP addresses are very intimidating, they are assigned a unique domain name, which is less daunting. The domain name is part of a hierarchical lookup system called the Domain Name System (DNS).

IP Address	=	Domain Name
83.382.1.838		books.que.com

CHAPTER

28 How Web Sites Work with Databases

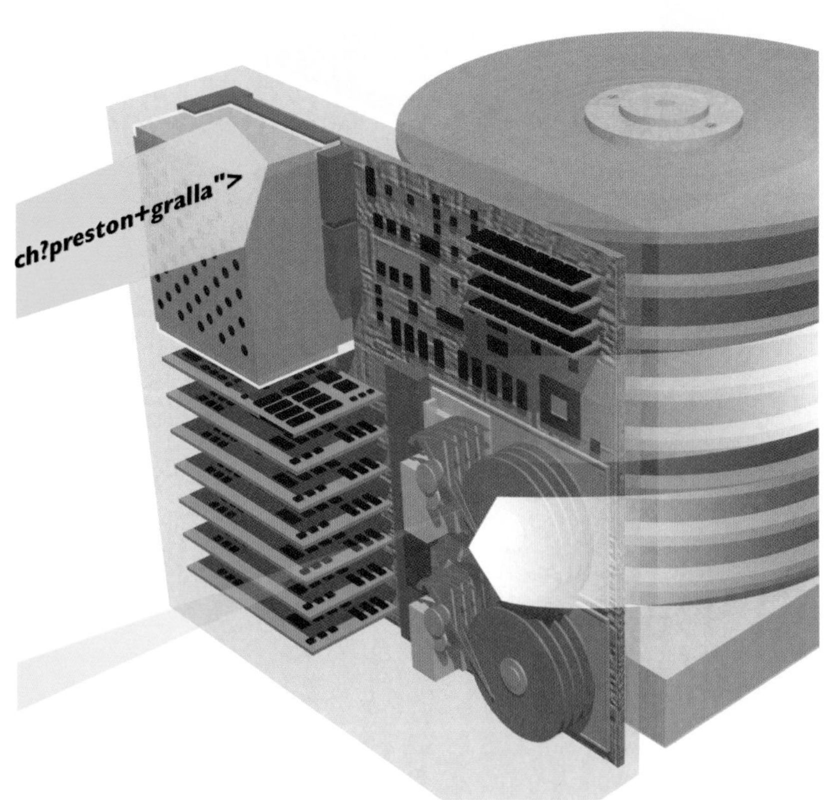

ONE of the most useful applications of the Web is its capability to link a Web site with a database so Web surfers can search for information. In essence, the Web page becomes the front-end for database applications, enabling you to select search criteria and execute even complex searches of a database that resides on the host computer.

A well-known and widely used example of this type of linking between Web sites and databases is the popular Yahoo! Web site (`www.yahoo.com`). The Yahoo! site serves as a front-end to an extensive database of Web site descriptions, which can be searched according to keywords. The Welcome page includes a search dialog box in which you enter a keyword that represents the subject matter you are looking for. Clicking the Search button sends a request from the browser to the Web server to bring back a list of all Web sites that contain your keyword.

Furthermore, not only can the Web serve up data, it can also collect it. For example, many Web sites ask users to "register" their names, addresses, and other demographic information that is captured and stored in a database.

But how does this all work? You don't have to be a corporate giant—or for that matter even an able programmer—to link your Web site to a database. In fact, linking a Web site to a database can be relatively simple. The database can take just about any form and can be as simple as a FileMaker Pro database or as complex as an Oracle SQL database. The bridge that brings together Web sites and databases is the Common Gateway Interface (CGI).

On the client side of the database, you see a Web page that includes a form in which you enter your search terms. When you execute the search, the Web server passes your search information to a CGI script, which then searches the database. So a search on the Yahoo! site for public relations firms looks like this:
`http://search.yahoo.com/bin/search?p=public+relations`

When the Web server receives this URL, it identifies the URL as a trigger for a CGI script (called *script* in this example) and passes it along with the search criteria ("public relations," in this example) to the miniprogram using CGI. The CGI script then sends the search to the database, receives the results of the query, and passes it on to the Web server to be sent back to the client. That's a lot of handing off of requests and data, but typically even a search of a large database is very fast because the majority of Unix and Windows NT databases—the types most often used—can perform these tasks simultaneously. All of this happens behind the scenes, of course—you won't need to do any kind of database work or scripting yourself. Instead, the Web sites you visit have easy-to-use interfaces that take care of interacting with databases; you'll have to type only what you're looking for.

How the Web Works with Databases

1 The search begins on a Web page that includes a form field to accept search terms and HTML codes to execute a CGI script. The browser might pass the data to the Web server in a query string. The *query string* contains the name of the CGI script in a directory called `cgi-bin`. This directory is followed by a subdirectory that includes the search terms, often separated by a question mark or slashes. The HTML code might look like this: `<a href="cgi-bin/search?preston+gralla/">`.

<a href="cgi-bin/search?gralla">

HTTP Response

4 The database returns the data to the Web server via CGI in the form of a new HTML page. The server then sends the page back to the client browser as a new HTML page.

2 When the Web server receives the URL with the embedded search terms, it sends the information through the CGI program to the database. Typically, the program is stored in a unique directory that contains all the CGI scripts serviced by the Web server.

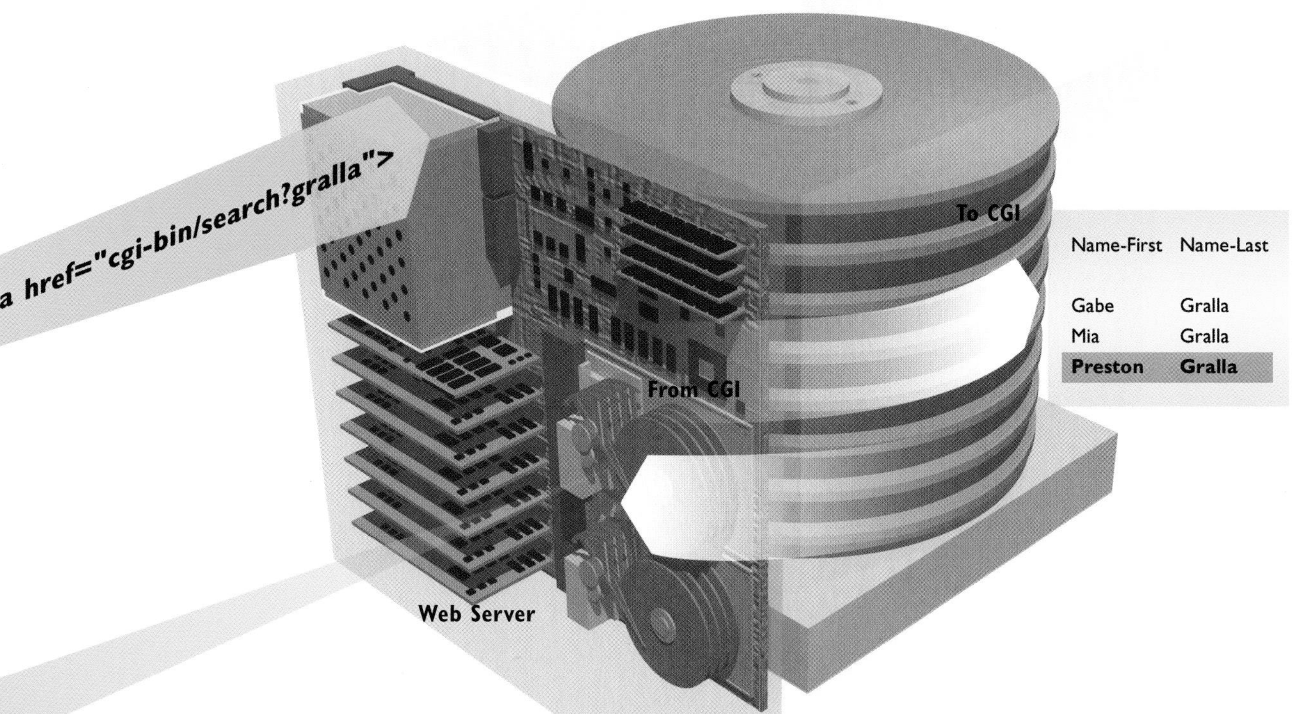

3 The database retrieves the record or records that match the search criteria. The database record might contain text and numeric data as well as references to graphics or other data types.

CHAPTER
29
How Internet-Based Software Works

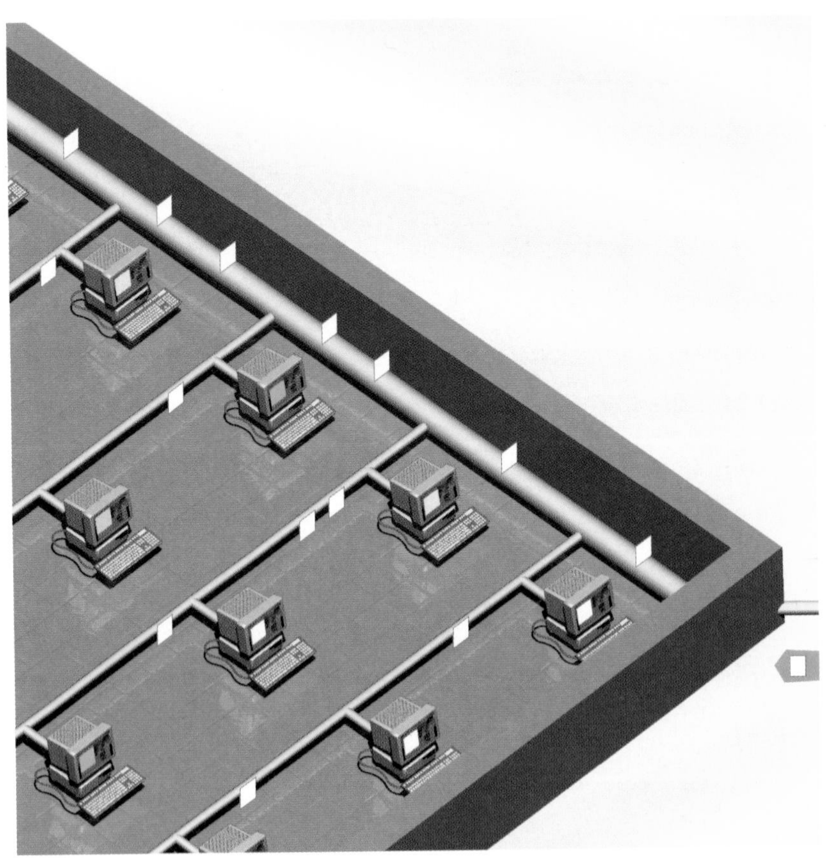

SOME people believe that in the not-too-distant future, much of the software you run won't physically be found on your computer. Instead, it will be located, at least in part, on an Internet server somewhere. You'll turn on your computer, it will have instant, high-speed access to the Internet, you'll choose software to run from a server, and it will always be up-to-date because the company in charge will continually update it.

To a certain extent, this type of Internet-based computing has a *Back to the Future* kind of feel to it. In the days before the advent of the personal computer, all software was run on a mainframe or large minicomputer, and people accessed it via a dumb terminal that had no processing power itself. In some ways, Internet-based software goes back to that model. The difference is that instead of dumb terminals, people have powerful computers that can still do a lot on their own. And not many people expect that all software will be run this way.

No matter what the future holds, today some software is already being run that way. The software is being provided by application service providers (ASPs), which have a variety of ways of letting you run software over the Internet. The most common way is one in which you visit a Web site, and the software runs inside your browser. But there are variations as well, such as services that run Web servers, while you or your business runs client software that requires the use of those servers.

You might already be using an ASP without realizing it. For example, Web-based e-mail services, such as HotMail, in fact are forms of ASPs—in essence they allow you to run an e-mail program from within your browser.

Corporations turn to ASPs because they enable them to do business more cheaply. Rather than having to build a large infrastructure of internal servers or have a large support staff for installing and troubleshooting software and hardware, they contract with an ASP and let the ASP bear all those costs.

It's not only corporations, though, that eventually might turn more to ASPs. Microsoft has announced its vision for the future of software in its .Net plan, and that plan includes ASP-like features. At this point, the details of .Net are quite hazy. But what's come out so far indicates that a good part of it will include a far tighter relationship between the software on your computer and servers on the Internet, and it might even include software running similarly to ASPs.

How Application Service Providers Work

1 There is no single, standard way that ASPs enable people and companies to run software over the Internet; many variations exist. In one common way, however, a corporation contracts with an ASP to provide servers for the entire corporation for client/server software that the corporation uses—for example, the Lotus Notes workgroup and e-mail program.

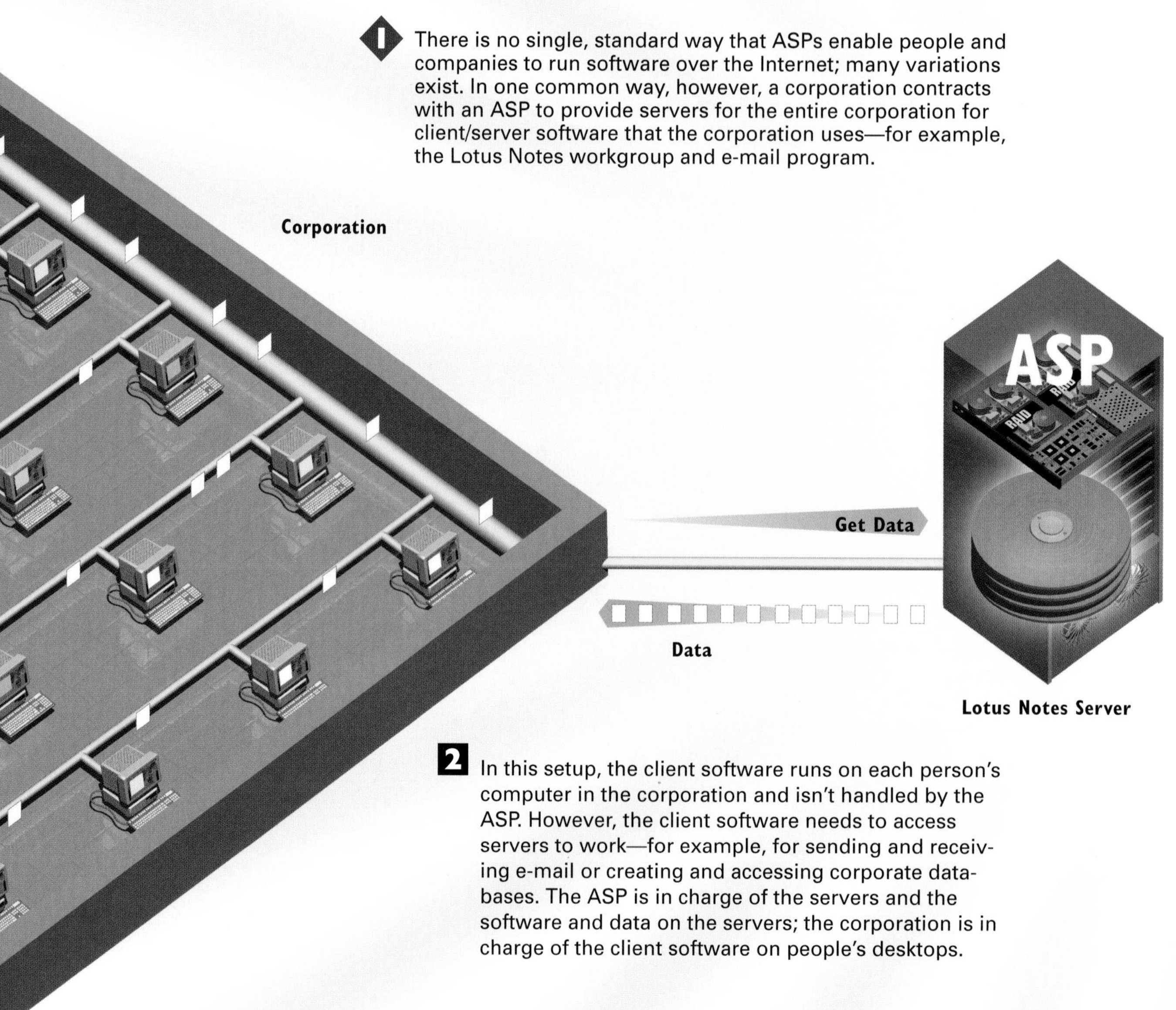

2 In this setup, the client software runs on each person's computer in the corporation and isn't handled by the ASP. However, the client software needs to access servers to work—for example, for sending and receiving e-mail or creating and accessing corporate databases. The ASP is in charge of the servers and the software and data on the servers; the corporation is in charge of the client software on people's desktops.

3 Another type of ASP is completely Web based and can be used by individuals as well as corporations. It's a way for people to run software directly in their Web browsers, so they don't have to have any software on their own computers. In this instance, we'll look at how individuals use ASPs. To use the software, someone visits a Web site that allow her to run an application—for example, a piece of personal finance software or an e-mail program.

Get my finance data.

ActiveX

Personal Finance ASP Server

4 The Web site delivers the software to the person's Web browser. The software can be created using many kinds of tools, such as ActiveX or Java.

5 The software runs inside the person's browser. Depending on the software, it might allow the person to save data to her own PC, or she might be required to save it to the Web site. When the person leaves the Web site, the software stops running, and it leaves no traces behind on the person's computer.

6 Another type of ASP requires someone to download a small piece of software to her computer. It's a kind of "helper" software—it's not the application itself, but instead helps the application run.

Connect

Helper

7 After the person downloads the helper, she chooses the actual application she wants to run—a graphics program, for example, or a piece of personal finance software. The helper application goes out to a Web site and downloads a core part of the application to the person's hard disk.

Get application.

Here it is.

Lotus Notes Server

8 The person now runs the application on her own computer. If she needs other elements of the application other than the core that was downloaded to her computer, the helper application goes out and gets it. When the person stops running the application, the helper program deletes it from the hard disk, leaving behind no trace.

Application

Application downloads and then launches.

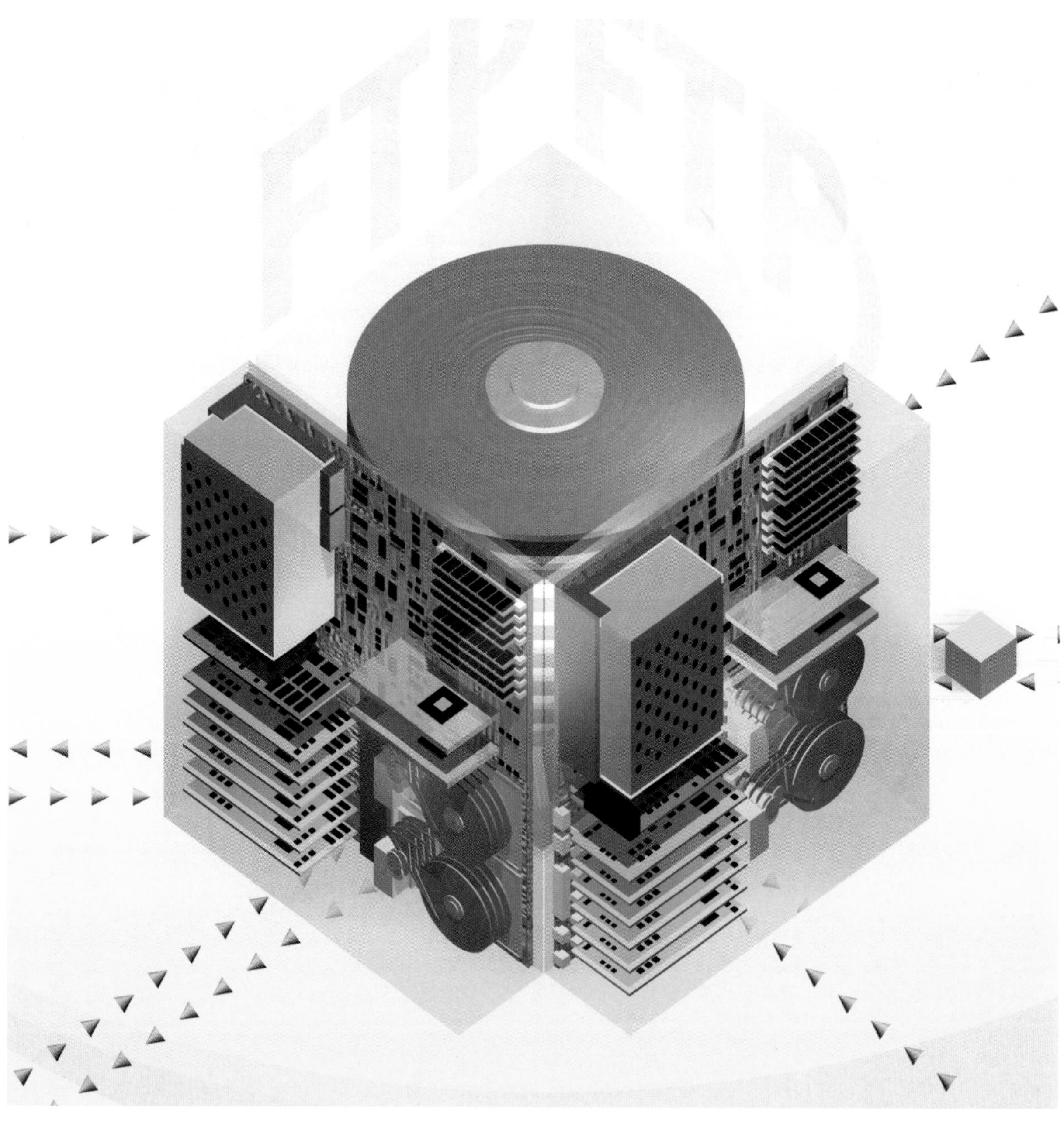

PART

USING COMMON INTERNET TOOLS

AN enormous amount of information and entertainment is available on the Internet, but how do you access it? Although using the Internet gets easier every day, it's still not quite as simple as turning on your television or reading your daily newspaper.

The solution is to use a variety of Internet tools. These tools enable you to tap into the colossal resources of the Internet. Some of these resources, such as the World Wide Web, are quite well known. Others, such as FTP (file transfer protocol) are used quite often—and sometimes people use them without even knowing it. Still others, such as Telnet, are not nearly as popular, although they are still useful. Many of these Internet tools predate the Web, but they are still useful today.

For many people, the term "Internet" really means the World Wide Web, but as this section of the book shows, a world exists well beyond the Web. (Turn to Part 4, "Using World Wide Web," for information about the Web—the fastest growing and most visible part of the Internet.) And this section of the book also shows you some of the advanced underlying technologies that make the Internet and the World Wide Web a richer, more interactive, more entertaining, and more productive medium. Many of these technologies have changed the very nature of the Internet and have turned it into a truly interactive medium—one that people can navigate efficiently. The technologies also enable Web publishers and Internet developers to more effectively present information to people.

This section looks at how the most common and useful Internet tools work.

Chapter 30, "How Telnet Works," covers one of the older Internet technologies, and one that is still in widespread use—Telnet. Telnet enables you to take over the resources of a distant computer while sitting at your own computer. What you type on your keyboard is sent across the Internet to the distant computer, the commands are carried out by the distant computer, and the results of your commands are sent to your own computer screen. It appears as if you're sitting at the distant computer's keyboard. Telnet is used in many ways, notably by libraries making their catalogs available over the Internet. When you log in to a distant computer using Telnet, you often use a menuing system.

Chapter 31, "How FTP Downloading Works," covers one of the most popular uses of the Internet—downloading files. Generally, files are downloaded from the Internet using FTP, the Internet protocol. Not only will you look at how FTP works, but you'll also look at how files are compressed and decompressed on the Internet. A compressed file takes less time to be sent over the Internet to your computer. You might not know it, but many times when you're on a Web site and download a file, you're actually using the FTP protocol.

Chapter 32, "How Internet Searching Works," examines Internet search engines. The Internet contains such a vast amount of information that it's often impossible to find exactly what you want. Search engines look through the entire Internet—not only Web pages, but other sites such as newsgroups—and find information you're looking for, based on keywords you type.

Chapter 33, "How Agents Work," looks at agents on the Internet. *Agents* are programs that do your bidding across the Internet automatically, without you doing anything. They can find the latest news and download it to your computer; they can find you the best deal on the

CD you want to buy; they can perform important Web maintenance tasks; and more. They are becoming so complex that systems are being developed to enable agents to interact with one another so they can perform jobs cooperatively.

Chapter 34, "How Java, ActiveX, and JavaScript Work," examines three other types of technologies that are transforming the Internet—Java, JavaScript, and ActiveX. These three technologies might do more to transform the Internet than almost any other technologies currently available. These technologies add multimedia and interactivity, but more importantly, they begin to treat the Internet as if it were an extension of your computer. In essence, they enable your computer and the Internet to interact as if they were one large computer system. This enables things such as news tickers, interactive games you can play with others, multimedia presentations combining animations, sounds, music, graphics, and much more.

Java, a computer language developed by Sun Microsystems, enables applications to be run from the Internet. The programs run inside your Web browser. One benefit of Java applications is that they can be run on any computer, such as a PC, a Macintosh, or a Unix workstation.

ActiveX, a competing technology from Microsoft, can also essentially turn the Internet into an extension of your computer. Similar to Java applets, ActiveX controls are downloaded to your computer and run there. They can do anything a normal application can do and can also interact with the Web, the Internet, and other computers connected to the Internet. To run them, a browser that supports ActiveX, such as Internet Explorer, is necessary.

JavaScript, which despite its name is not really related to Java, is simpler than Java and ActiveX and can be written by people who don't have substantial programming experience. JavaScript is commonly used to create interactive forms, site navigation, and similar features.

Finally, Chapter 35, "How CGI Scripting Works," examines CGI (Common Gateway Interface) scripting. This might appear as one of the more mundane Internet technologies, but without it, very little Web interactivity would take place. CGI is a standard way in which the Web interacts with outside resources—most commonly, databases. You've probably run CGI scripts many times without knowing it. If you've filled out a form on a Web page to register to use a site and then later received an e-mail notification with a password for you to use, you've probably run a CGI script. CGI enables programmers to write code that can access information servers (such as Web servers) on the Internet and then send the information to users.

CHAPTER 30 How Telnet Works

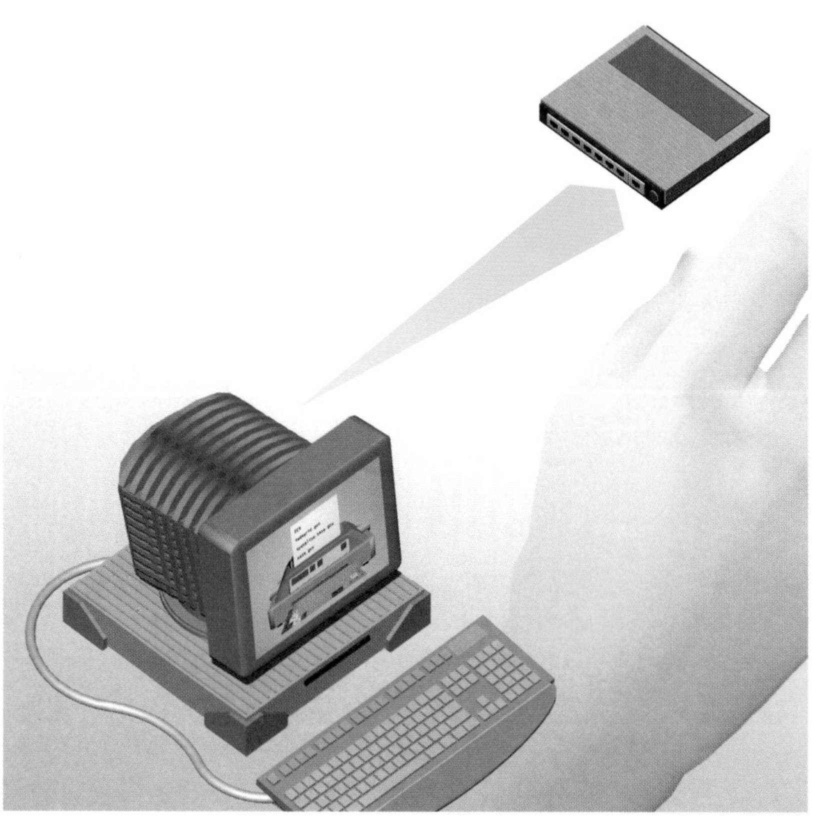

ONE of the more remarkable features of the Internet is the way it lets you use the resources of a distant computer somewhere else in the world. From your own home or office, you can log onto another computer, issue commands just as if you were at that computer's keyboard, and then gain access to all the computer's resources. You do this with an Internet resource called Telnet. Telnet follows a *client/server model*, which means that you run a piece of software on your own PC (the client) to use the resources of a distant server computer. This distant computer is called the *host*.

The host allows many clients to access its resources at the same time; it isn't devoted to a single user. To use Telnet and the host's resources, you must know the address of the Internet host whose resources you want to access.

When you use Telnet, before you can take over the resources of a host computer you typically have to log onto the host. Often, you can use the name "guest" to log on. Some systems require that you also give information about yourself, such as your name and address. And some might require that you choose a username and a password that you will use the next time you log in.

You can access many hosts on the Internet by using Telnet. They are all different computers, so many of them don't work or look alike. For example, some might be Unix-based systems, some might be NT-based computers, and some might be Macintoshes, as well as a variety of other computers, and they all work and look different from one another. As a way to make things easier, many hosts use a menuing system that gives you access to their resources.

Telnet gives you a way to use those menuing systems by using something called *terminal emulation*. It lets you use your computer to emulate the type of keyboard and computer that each of the different computer systems expect. Different computers often require different kinds of terminal emulation, but one common kind is called VT-100 emulation, so if you use Telnet software and tell it to use VT-100 emulation, that's a safe emulation to use.

Telnet clients are available for all the major operating systems, including Linux, Unix, Macintosh, and all versions of Windows. If you use an Internet shell account instead of a SLIP/PPP connection, you'll typically use a Telnet client by simply typing the word **`Telnet`** followed by the Internet address of the computer you want to access. For example, if you wanted to gain access to a computer run by the federal government called Fed World that lets you access a great deal of government information, you'd type **`Telnet fedworld.gov`**.

A Windows- or Macintosh-based Telnet client is easier to use than a DOS- or Unix-based Telnet client because the former remembers hostnames for you. With clients, you can often keep an address book of hostnames so you can easily revisit them.

Understanding Telnet

1. To use Telnet, you need to know the Internet address of the host whose resources you want to use; your Telnet client contacts the host, using its Internet address.

Fedworld.gov

2. When you contact the host, the distant computer and your computer negotiate how they will communicate with each other. They decide which terminal emulation will be used. Terminal emulation determines how your keyboard will transmit information to the distant computer and how information will be displayed on your screen. It determines, for example, things such as how certain keys like the backspace key will work. VT-100 is the most common type of terminal emulation.

PC Running Telnet Software

3 When a client and a server communicate, they use the Telnet protocol. The Telnet protocol assumes that each end of the connection—the client and the server—is a network virtual terminal (NVT). Each NVT has a virtual "printer" and a virtual "keyboard" The keyboard sends data from one NVT to the other. When you type text on your keyboard, you're using the NVT keyboard. The printer is not really a printer at all—it receives and displays the data on the computer screen. When a distant Telnet connection sends you data and you display it on your screen, it is the printer that displays the information.

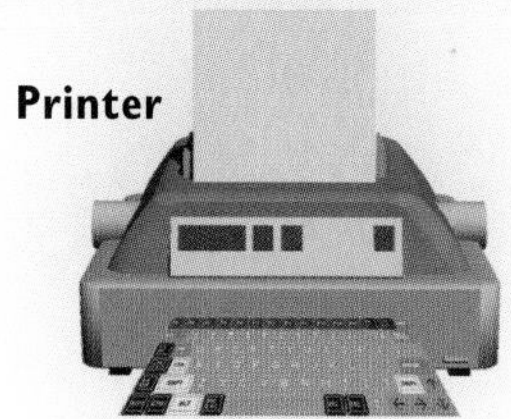

4 Typed text in a Telnet session accumulates in a buffer on your computer. When a complete line of data is ready for transmission, or when you give a command to transmit data (such as pressing the Enter key), the data is sent across the Internet from your NVT keyboard. Along with the data is the host's IP address, which ensures the packet is sent to the proper location.

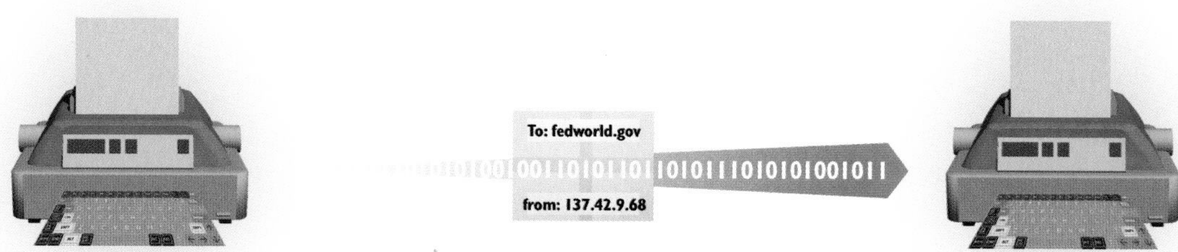

5 Your IP address is also sent, so that information can be routed back to you. Additionally, specific Telnet commands are sent that the other NVT uses to decide what to do with the data or how to respond to the data. For example, when data is sent from one NVT to another, and certain information must be sent back to the originating NVT for a process to proceed, the Telnet Go Ahead (GA) command is sent.

6 The Telnet host receives the data you've sent. It processes the data and returns to your screen (your NVT printer) the results of using the data or running the command on a distant computer. So, for example, if you type a series of keys with the letters `dir` and press Enter, the distant computer carries out the `dir` command. That computer also returns to your screen the `dir` command and sends the results of running that command on the distant computer.

7 Because packets must go through many Internet routers in each direction between your computer and the host, a delay might occur between the time you send a command and the time you see the results on your own computer screen.

CHAPTER

31

How FTP Downloading Works

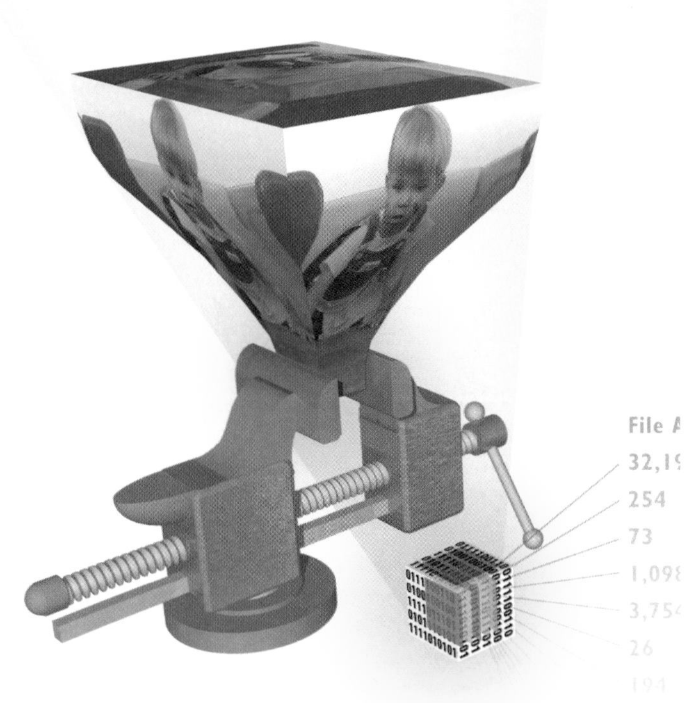

ONE of the most popular uses of the Internet is to download files—that is, transfer files from a computer on the Internet to your computer. These files can be of many types: programs that you can run on your own computer; graphics you can view; sounds and music you can listen to; or text files that you can read. Many tens of thousands of files are downloaded every day over the Internet. Frequently, using the Internet's File Transfer Protocol, commonly referred to as FTP. You can also use FTP to upload files from your computer to another computer on the Internet.

FTP, like many Internet resources, works on a client/server model. You run FTP client software on your computer to connect to an FTP server on the Internet. On the FTP server, a program called an FTP daemon (pronounced "demon") allows you to download and upload files.

To log on to an FTP site and download files, you must type in an account number (or username) and a password before the daemon will allow you to enter. Some sites allow anyone to enter and download files, but an account number (or username) and password must still be entered. Often, to get in, you use `anonymous` as your username and your e-mail address as your password. Because of this, these sites are often referred to as *anonymous FTP sites*. Some FTP sites are private and allow only certain people with the proper account number and password to enter.

FTP is fairly simple to use. When you log on to an FTP site, you can browse through the available files by changing directories and seeing a listing of all the files available in each directory. When you see a file you want to download, use your client software to instruct the FTP server to send you the file.

As the World Wide Web gained popularity, downloading software became even easier. You can use your Web browser and click links to files. Behind the scenes, FTP is often still downloading the files. FTP remains the most popular way to download files from the Web and the Internet. The HTTP protocol of the Web can be used for downloading files from the Web, but it's not as efficient as FTP, so it isn't used as frequently.

One problem with downloading files over the Internet is that some files are so large that it can take a tremendous amount of time to download them; especially if the connection is made via modem. Even at 56Kbps, downloading files can be slow. As a way to speed up file transfers and save space on the FTP server, files are commonly compressed, or shrunk in size using special compression software. Many different methods are used to compress files. Depending on the file type, files are usually compressed from 10%–50%. After downloading the files, you'll need to run the compression software on your own computer to decompress the files so you can use them.

How an FTP Session Works

1 FTP, like many other Internet services, runs on a client/server model. To use it you'll need client software on your computer. To begin an FTP session, run the FTP client software and contact the FTP server from which you want to download files. You can get FTP client software in hundreds of places on the Internet, such as ZDNet Downloads at `www.zdnet.com/downloads`. A command-line FTP program is also included on Windows-based computers, but is much harder to use than these FTP clients.

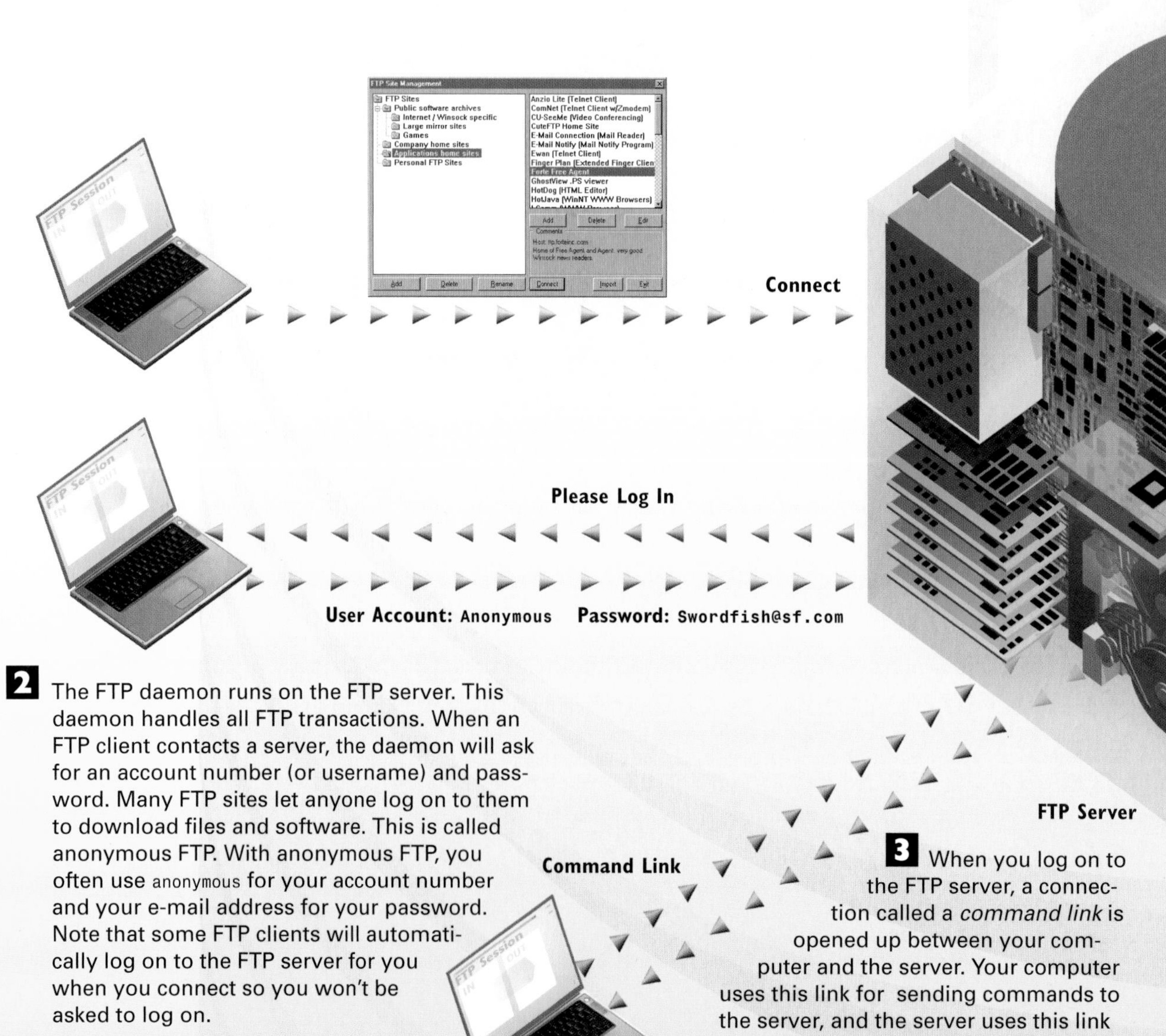

2 The FTP daemon runs on the FTP server. This daemon handles all FTP transactions. When an FTP client contacts a server, the daemon will ask for an account number (or username) and password. Many FTP sites let anyone log on to them to download files and software. This is called anonymous FTP. With anonymous FTP, you often use `anonymous` for your account number and your e-mail address for your password. Note that some FTP clients will automatically log on to the FTP server for you when you connect so you won't be asked to log on.

3 When you log on to the FTP server, a connection called a *command link* is opened up between your computer and the server. Your computer uses this link for sending commands to the server, and the server uses this link for sending messages and information back to your computer.

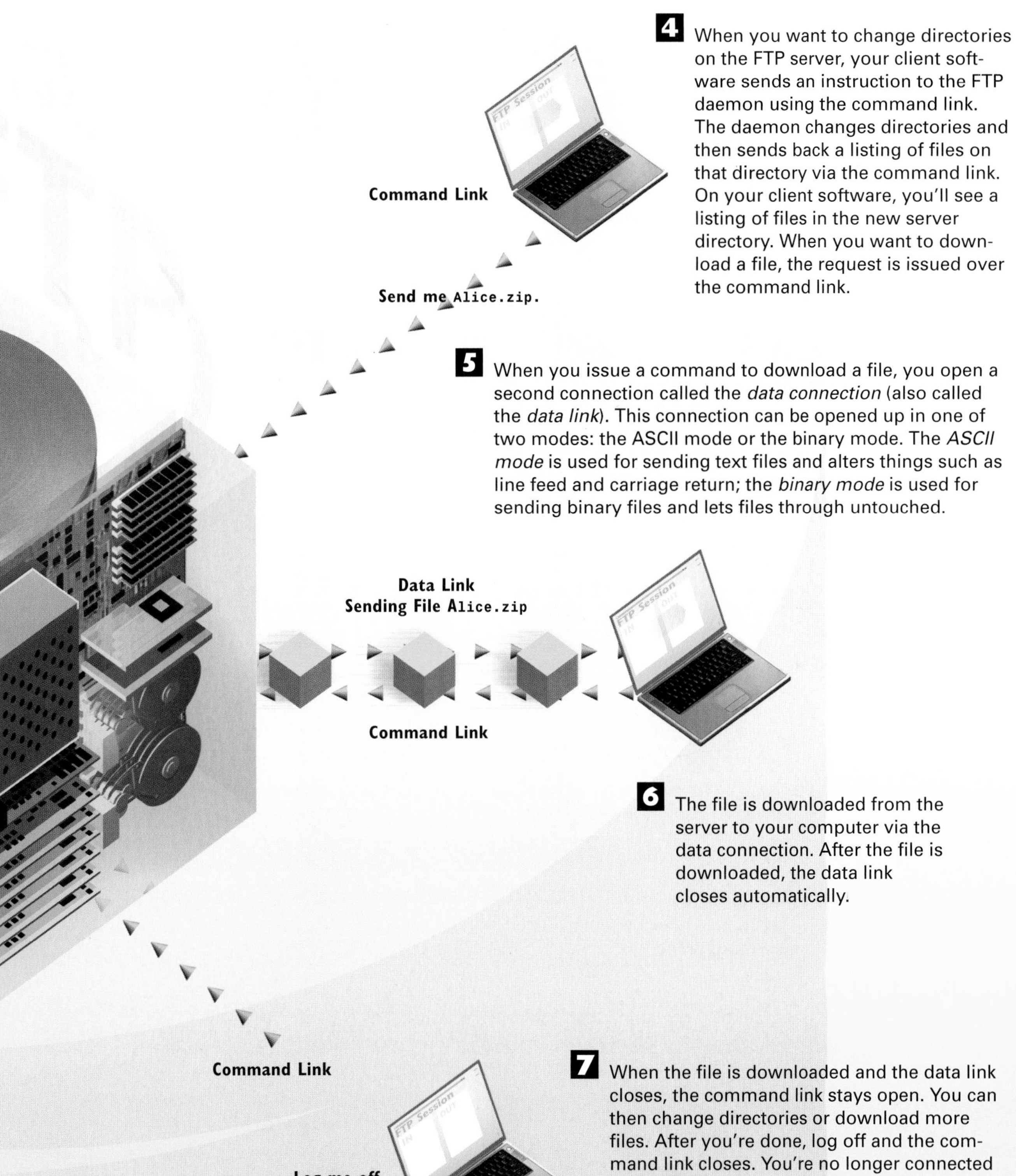

4 When you want to change directories on the FTP server, your client software sends an instruction to the FTP daemon using the command link. The daemon changes directories and then sends back a listing of files on that directory via the command link. On your client software, you'll see a listing of files in the new server directory. When you want to download a file, the request is issued over the command link.

5 When you issue a command to download a file, you open a second connection called the *data connection* (also called the *data link*). This connection can be opened up in one of two modes: the ASCII mode or the binary mode. The *ASCII mode* is used for sending text files and alters things such as line feed and carriage return; the *binary mode* is used for sending binary files and lets files through untouched.

6 The file is downloaded from the server to your computer via the data connection. After the file is downloaded, the data link closes automatically.

7 When the file is downloaded and the data link closes, the command link stays open. You can then change directories or download more files. After you're done, log off and the command link closes. You're no longer connected to the FTP server.

How File Compression Works

1. Compression programs use *algorithms*—complex mathematical formulas—to shrink files. In the first step in the process, the algorithm examines the file to be compressed and looks for repeating patterns of data.

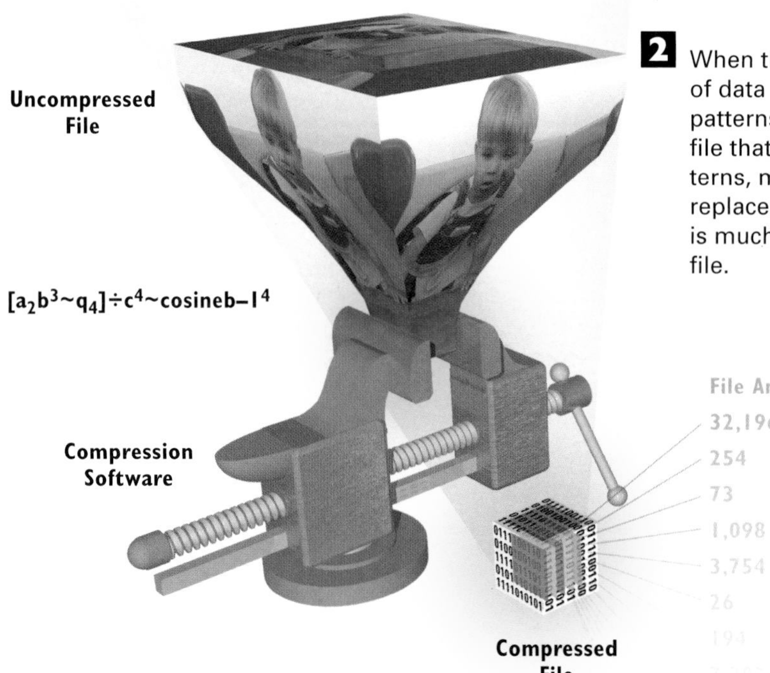

2. When the algorithm finds patterns of data that repeat, it replaces the patterns with smaller *tokens*. In a file that has many repeating patterns, many tokens are used to replace data so the compressed file is much smaller than the original file.

3. A *header* can also be added to the file as it is compressed. This header contains information about the file, such as the filename, the file size, and the compression method used. This information is used to help reconstruct the file when it is uncompressed.

7. File *extensions*, the letters that appear after the period at the end of a filename, tell you whether and how a file is compressed.

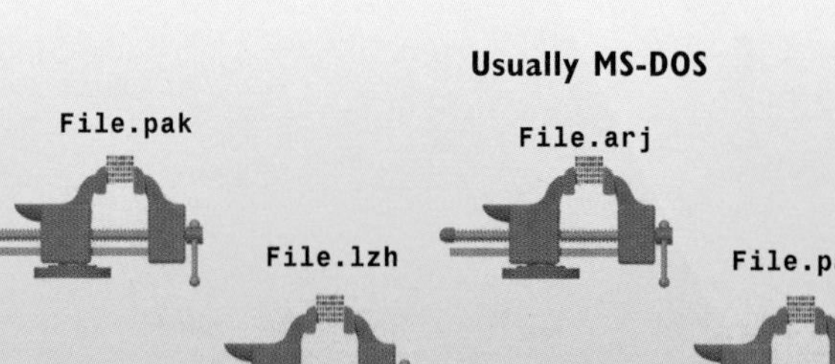

File.zoo

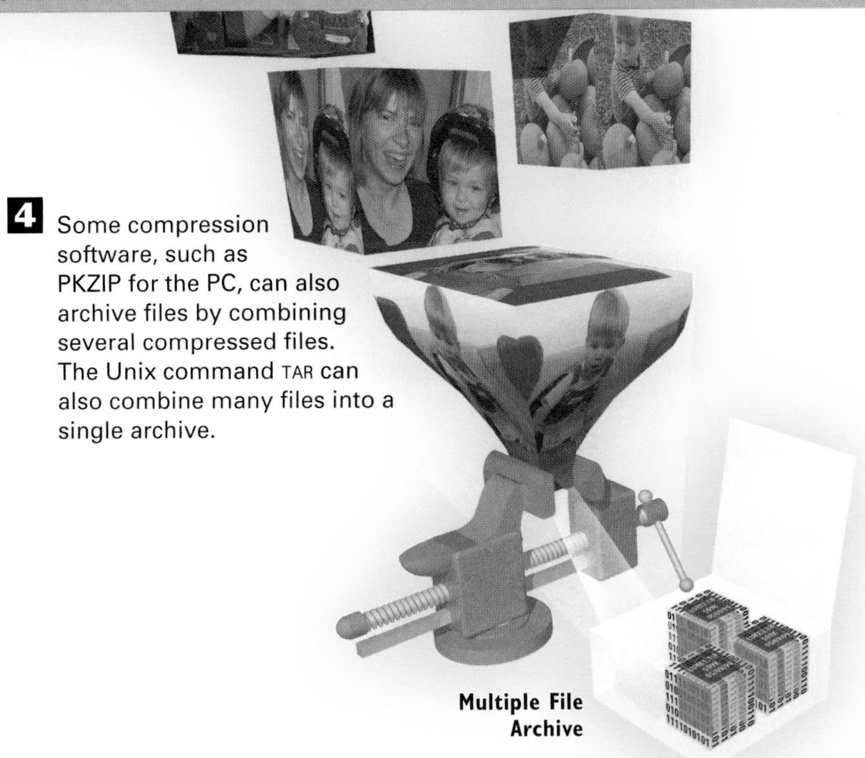

4 Some compression software, such as PKZIP for the PC, can also archive files by combining several compressed files. The Unix command TAR can also combine many files into a single archive.

5 When you want to use a compressed file you find on the Internet, transfer it over the Internet to your computer.

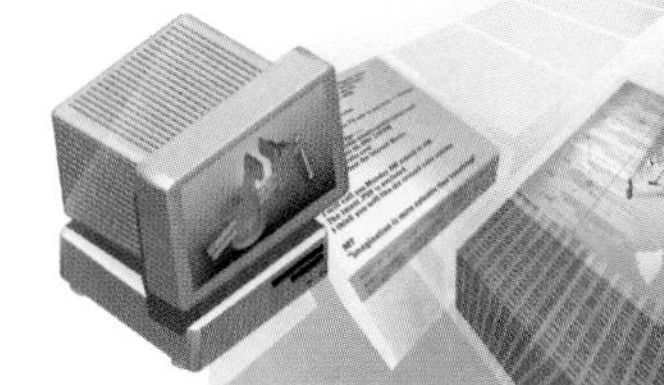

6 To use the file, you'll need decompression software on your computer. The decompression software looks into the file's header and examines the tokens in the file. The decompression software uses a decompression algorithm to reconstruct the original file which you can then use on your computer.

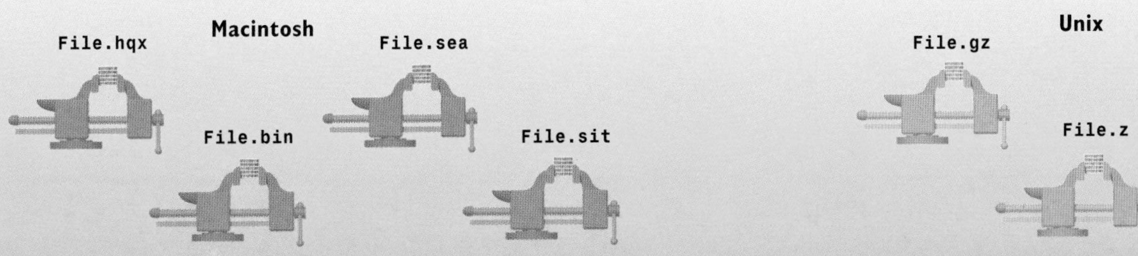

CHAPTER

32

How Internet Searching Works

SO much information is available on the Internet, but there is so little organization to the Internet that it can seem impossible to find the information or documents you want. A number of solutions have sprung up to solve the problem. The two most popular ones are indexes and search engines.

Indexes present a highly structured way to find information. They enable you to browse through information by categories, such as arts, computers, entertainment, sports, and so on. In a Web browser, you click a category, and you are then presented with a series of subcategories. Under sports, for example, you'll find baseball, basketball, football, hockey, and soccer. Depending on the size of the index, several layers of subcategories might be available. When you get to the subcategory you're interested in, you are presented with a list of relevant documents. To get to those documents, you click the links to them. Yahoo! (`http://www.yahoo.com/`) is the largest and most popular index on the Internet. Yahoo! and other indexes also enable you to search by typing words that describe the information you're looking for. You then get a set of search results—links to documents that match your search. To get the information, you click a link.

Another popular way of finding information is to use *search engines*, also called *search tools* and sometimes called *Web crawlers* or *spiders*. Search engines operate differently from indexes. They are essentially massive databases that cover wide swaths of the Internet. Search engines don't present information in a hierarchical fashion. Instead, you search through them as you would a database, by typing keywords that describe the information you want.

There are many popular Internet search engines, including Google, Lycos, Excite, and AltaVista. Although the specifics of how they operate differ somewhat, generally they are all composed of three parts: at least one spider, which crawls across the Internet gathering information; a database, which contains all the information the spiders gather; and a search tool, which people use to search through the database. Search engines are constantly updated to present the most up-to-date information, and they hold enormous amounts of information. Search engines extract and index information differently. Some index every word they find in a document, for example, and others index only the key 100 words in each document. Some index the size of the document; some index the title, headings, subheadings, and so on.

Additionally, each search engine returns results in a different way. Some weigh the results to show the relevance of the documents; some show the first several sentences of the document; and some show the title of the document as well as the URL.

Many search engines and indexes are on the Internet, each with its own strengths and weaknesses. To cast the widest possible net when looking for information, you should search as many of them as you can. The problem is that doing so is too time-consuming. So a type of software called *meta-search* software has been developed. With this software, such as Copernic, you type a search on your own computer. The software then submits the search to many Internet search engines and indexes simultaneously, compiles the results for you, and then delivers the results to your computer. To visit any resulting site, just click the link, the same as if you were on an index or a search engine site.

How Internet Search Engines Work

1 Each search engine uses a crawler or spider with its own set of rules guiding how documents are gathered. Some follow every link on every home page they find and then, in turn, examine every link on each of those new home pages, and so on. Some spiders ignore links that lead to graphics files, sound files, and animation files. Some ignore links to certain Internet resources, such as newsgroups, and some are instructed to look primarily for the most popular home pages. It can take a spider from several seconds to many minutes to crawl each site it finds, depending on the size and complexity of the site.

2 As the spider discovers documents and URLs, software agents are instructed to get the URLs and documents and send information about them to indexing software.

3 The indexing software receives the documents and URLs from the agent. The software extracts information from the documents and indexes it by putting the information into a database. Each search engine extracts and indexes different types of information. Some index every word in each document, for example, but others index only the key 100 words in each; some index the size of the document and the number of words in it; some index the title, headings and subheadings, and so on. The kind of index built determines which type of searching can be done with the search engine and how the information will be displayed.

6 When you click a link to one of the documents that interest you, you're sent straight to that document. The document itself is not in the database or on the search engine site.

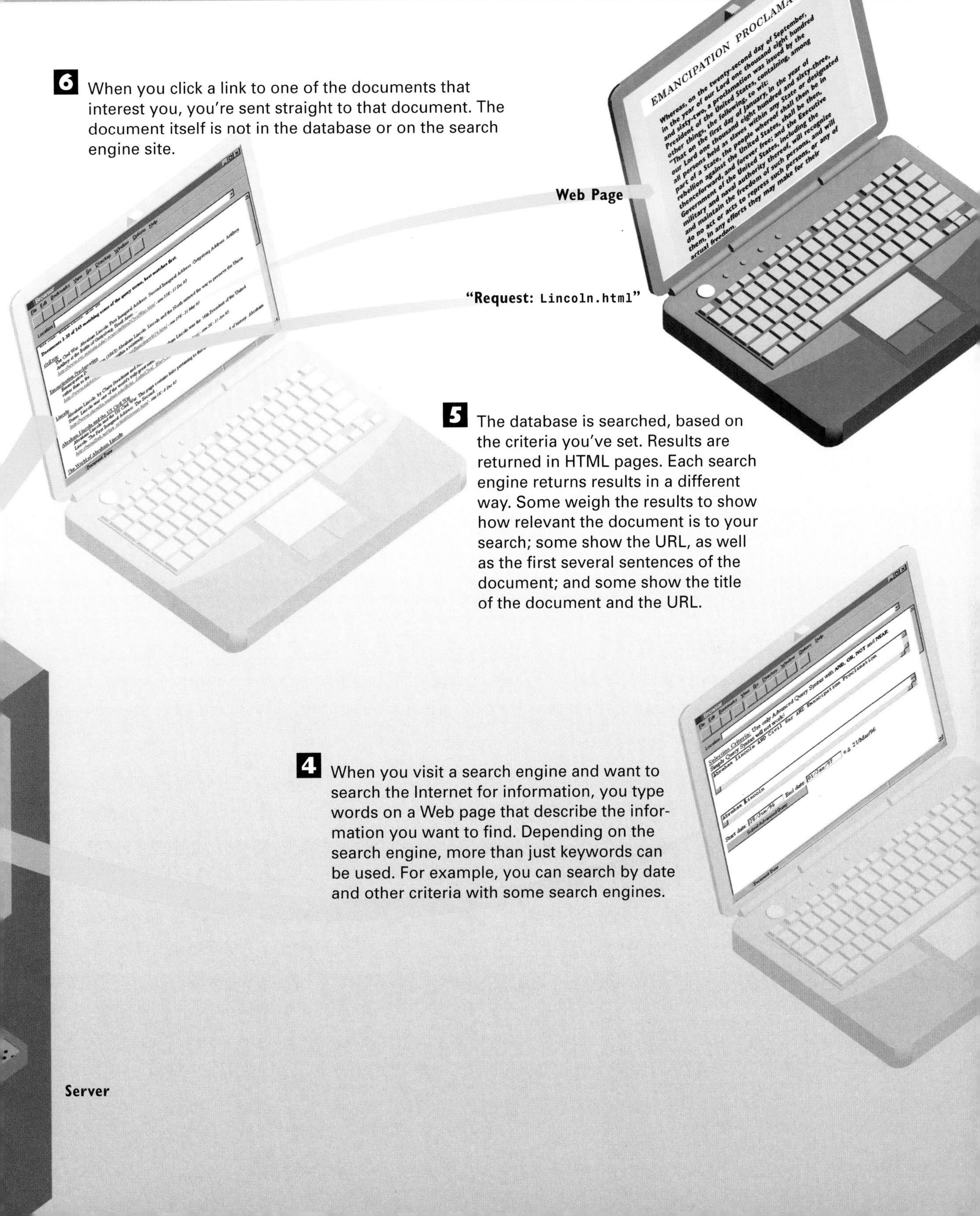

5 The database is searched, based on the criteria you've set. Results are returned in HTML pages. Each search engine returns results in a different way. Some weigh the results to show how relevant the document is to your search; some show the URL, as well as the first several sentences of the document; and some show the title of the document and the URL.

4 When you visit a search engine and want to search the Internet for information, you type words on a Web page that describe the information you want to find. Depending on the search engine, more than just keywords can be used. For example, you can search by date and other criteria with some search engines.

How Meta-Search Software Works

1 Meta-search software is software that sits on your computer and enables you to search through many Internet search engines simultaneously and to view and use the results. When you want to search for something on the Internet, you type descriptive words or a search term into the meta-search software.

Meta-Search Software

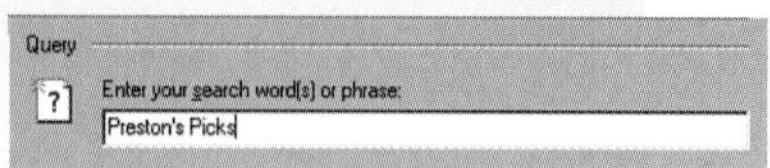

Preston's Picks

http://www.hotfiles/home.html
http://www.hotfiles/index.html
http://www.hotfiles/prespick/presmain.html

Preston's Picks

http://www.hotfiles/index.html
http://www.hotfiles/prespick/presmain.html

5 The agent sends the results back to the meta-search software. After the agent sends its report back to the meta-search software, it goes to another search engine and submits a search in that engine's proper syntax and again sends the results back to the meta-search software.

Preston's Picks

http://www.hotfiles/home.html
http://www.hotfiles/index.html
http://www.hotfiles/prespick/0401/pc.html

Preston's Picks

http://www.hotfiles/prespick/0401/pc.html
http://www.hotfiles/prespick/pres0401.html
http://www.hotfiles/prespick/0401/pc.html

6 The meta-search software takes all the results from all the search engines and examines them for duplicate results. If it finds duplicate results, it deletes them. It then displays the results of the search, ranking each *hit* by the likelihood that it contains the information you requested. It figures out the ranking by examining the title of the site found, the header information in the site, and the words on the site.

Results

Title	Address	Rank	Hit Count	Date Found
ZDNet Software Library - Top Rated Home & ...	http://www.hotfiles.com/home.html	8	2	5/8/98 4:16:10
write(''); Home & Education options Make the grade in math. You need not be a believer to appreciate Bible's poetry and parables.				
ZDNet Software Library - Top Rated Shareware	http://www.hotfiles.com/index.html	2	3	5/8/98 4:16:10
.leftnav2 { color: #FFFF00; } .leftnav { color: white; } = 3.0) {btype=1;} else if (browser_name == Microsoft Internet Explorer && browser_version = 3.0) {btype=1;} // popup window //interURL = url; if (btype==1) { var ApplyWindow = window. Our collection of top-rated b...				
ZDNet Software Library - Preston's Picks	http://www.hotfiles.com/prespick/presmain.html	1	5	5/8/98 4:16:10
Preston Gralla, ZDNet's "shareware guru," is executive editor of software for ZDNet. Each month, Preston selects his favorite new shareware programs from the ZDNet Software Library, giving you a chance to download the very best we have to offer.				
Preston's Picks for April	http://www.hotfiles.com/prespick/0498/pc.html	5	1	5/8/98 4:16:10
It also lets you create playlists of your files, so that you can in essence put together your own multimedia album. .. - Chris Wilson Fakalofa, Kia ora, Preston, ... - Sione My sympathies to owners of Win.				
Preston's Picks for April	http://www.hotfiles.com/prespick/.../pres0498.html	6	2	5/8/98 4:16:10
var cleargif_date=(new Date()). .. - Preston Gralla Clyde: We use cookies for our ... - Preston Gralla Just wanted to say THANKS for ... - Larry D. Stauffer Hey Clyde, you should have thr.				
ZDNet Software Library - Preston's Picks for ...	http://www.hotfiles.com/prespick/pres1097.html	6	1	5/8/98 4:16:10
ZDNet Software Library - Preston's Picks for October Join for FREE! Editors' Picks / Preston's Picks Downloads Internet Explorer 4.... 10/06/97				

2 The meta-search software sends many "agents" out onto the Internet simultaneously—depending on the speed of your connection, usually from 4 to 8, but it can be as many as 32 different agents. Each agent contacts one or more search engines or indexes, such as Yahoo!, Lycos, or Excite.

3 The agents are intelligent enough to know how each search engine functions—for example, whether a particular engine allows for Boolean searches (searching by using AND, OR, and other variables). The agents also know the exact syntax each engine requires. The agents put the search terms in the proper syntax required at each specific search engine and submit the search—they don't have to fill out forms, as users normally do at search engines.

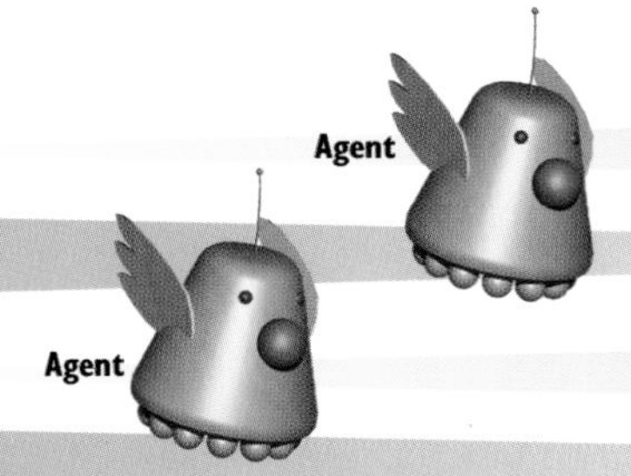

4 The search engines report the results of the search to each agent. The results typically include the URL of each site that matches the search, and often a summary of information found on the site, the date the site was last updated, and other data.

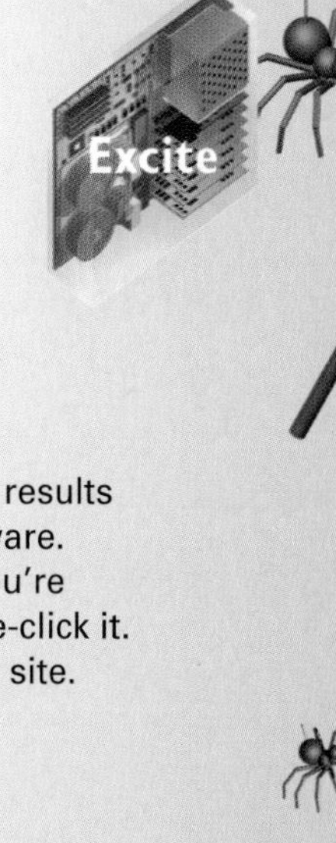

Web Page

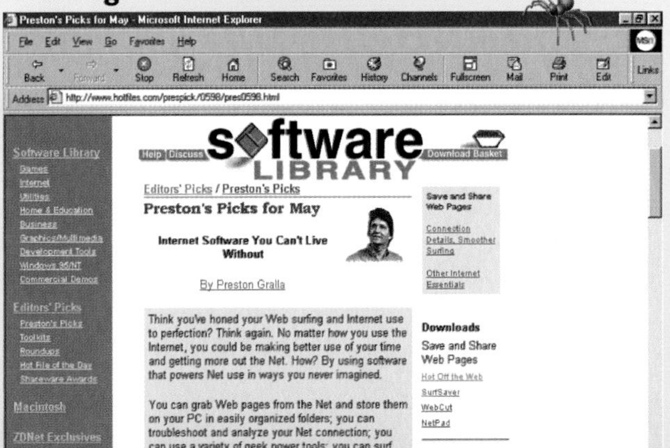

7 You browse through the results in the meta-search software. When you see a page you're interested in, you double-click it. You then are sent to that site.

CHAPTER 33 How Agents Work

THE Internet has grown so quickly and its resources are so vast that we need help navigating around it. We can now use special software called agents to help us access the Net's resources.

Although there are a lot of technical definitions for agents, put simply, agents are programs that do your bidding automatically. Many of them run over the Internet or on individual computers every day. Agents can find the latest news for you and download it to your computer; they can automatically monitor Internet traffic and report on its total usage; they can find you the best deal on the CD you want to buy; they can perform important Web maintenance tasks; and they can do far more. They are becoming so complex that systems are being developed to allow agents to interact with one another so they can perform jobs cooperatively.

On the Internet, agents are commonly called *spiders*, *robots* (often shortened to "bots"), and *knowbots*, among other terms. Those used for searching automatically create indexes of almost every resource on the Web and then allow people to search through those indexes to find things more quickly. Common search tools such as Lycos, Infoseek, and AltaVista use spiders in this way. This specialized use of spiders is discussed in Chapter 32, "How Internet Searches Work."

All these agents are software programs that are invisible to the user. You just determine the task you want done, and behind the scenes the agent automatically goes off and performs that task. A variety of programming languages can be used to write agent programs.

Agents might well alter the way we all use the Internet in the future. Not only do they respond to our requests, but they also "learn" from our requests the types of tasks and information that interest us. They then go off on their own and perform those tasks and get that information, even before we make these additional requests. As we use these types of agents more, they'll become even smarter and more efficient.

Robots and agents can cause problems for some Web sites. For example, they can overload Web servers by swamping them with too many requests in too short a time. That means users who try to get access to those Web pages will be denied access, or access will be exceedingly slow.

Another problem has to do with the way Web sites make money. Many Web sites sell ads to support themselves and charge advertisers based on the number of pages that have been viewed. If many of those pages "viewed" are in fact never seen by people and are instead accessed only by a computer via a robot, both advertisers and the Web site suffer.

Several ways exist to solve these problems and limit robot access. One way includes creating a file called `Robots.txt` that describes the areas that are off limits to robots, which the robots would automatically read, adhere to, and not visit. Another is to use a technology that automatically detects whether a robot or a human has visited a page and forgo charging advertisers whenever robots visit.

Agents on the Internet

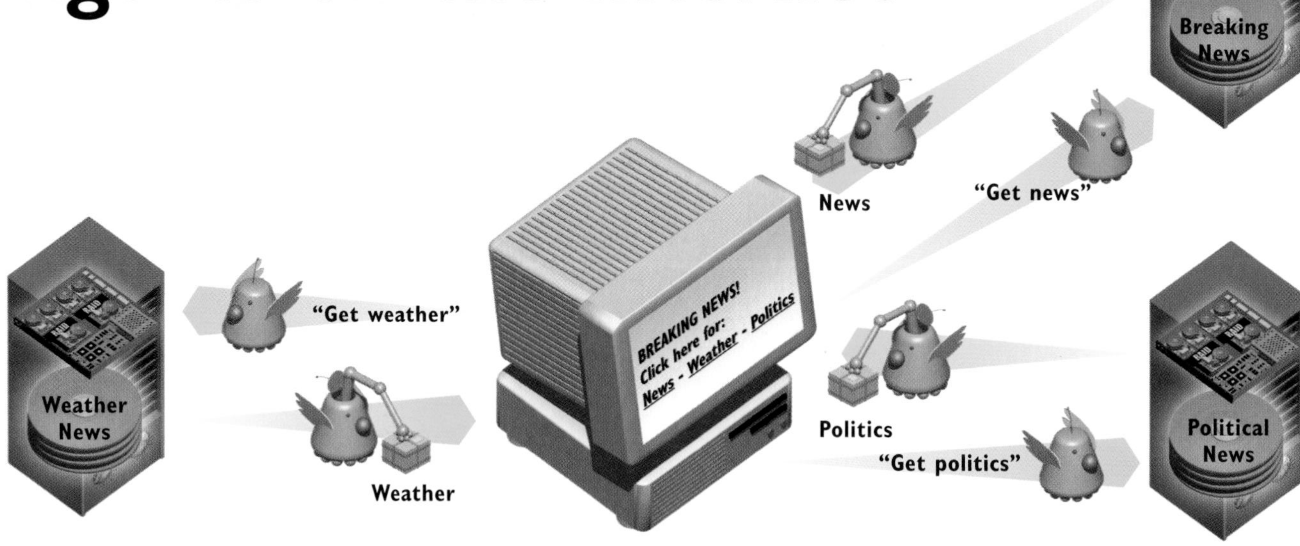

1 A simple Internet agent is one that gathers news from a variety of sources while you're not using your computer or while you are using your computer for another task. News agents can work in several ways. In the simplest example, you fill out a form saying which type of news you're interested in and on what schedule you want your news delivered. Based on that information, at preset intervals, the news agent connects to news sites around the Internet and downloads news stories to your computer, where you can read them as HTML pages.

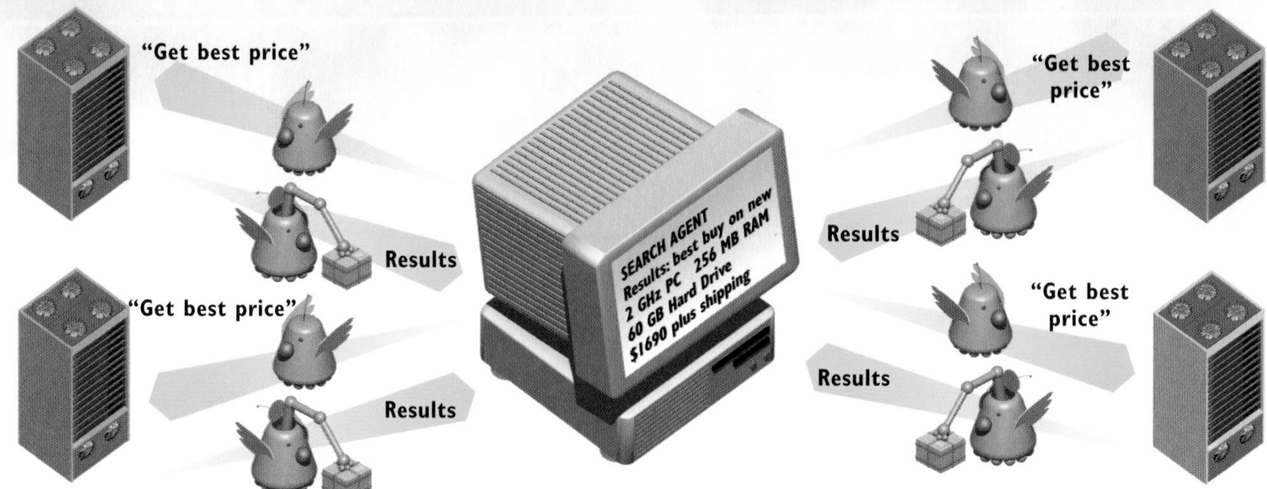

2 Shopping agents let you search through all of the Internet for the best bargains. On the Web, you fill out a form detailing the product you want to buy. When you submit the form, the shopping agent launches programs that search through a variety of shopping sites and databases on the Internet. The agent looks into the databases of those sites and finds the best prices. It then sends back to you the links to the sites so you can visit the sites with the best prices and order from there.

4 When robots and spiders do their work on a remote Internet site from where they were launched, they can put an extra load on the site's system resources—for example, by swamping the server with too many requests in too short a time. Because of this, some system administrators are interested in ways of excluding robots in certain circumstances, such as not allowing robots into certain Web directories. A variety of ways have been devised to limit robot access, including creating a file called `Robots.txt` that describes the areas off limits to robots, which the robots would read, adhere to, and not visit. But there is nothing that guarantees the robots must adhere to this rule. It's up to the good faith of the person writing the robot to adhere to it.

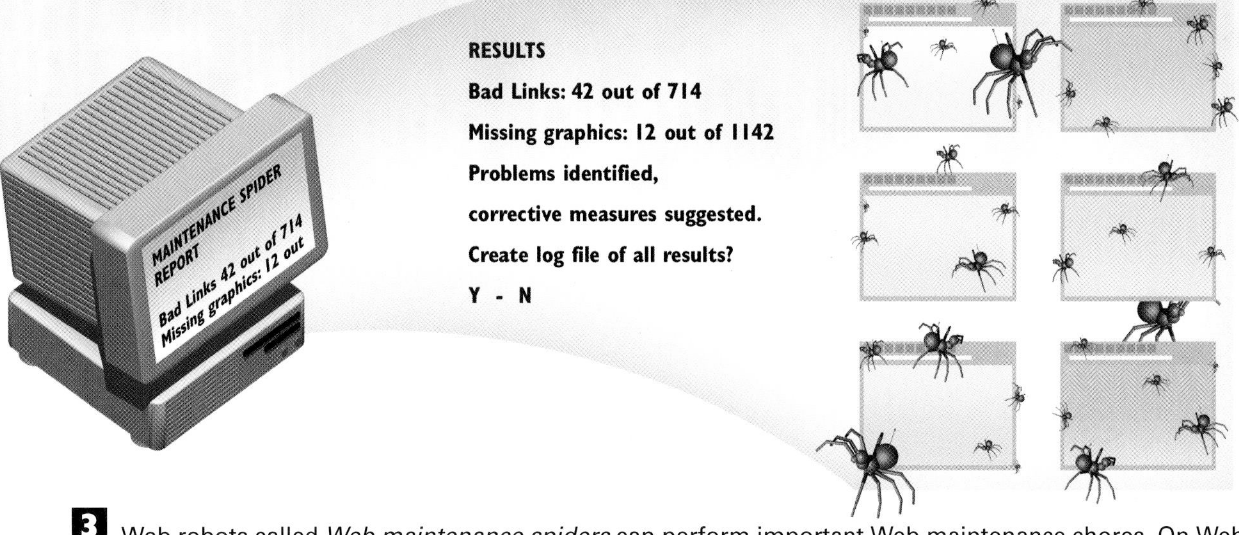

3 Web robots called *Web maintenance spiders* can perform important Web maintenance chores. On Web sites, particularly large ones, very often HTML pages can include links that become outdated. In other words, the object being linked to has been taken off the Internet. Whenever a user clicks the link, an error message is sent. A Web maintenance spider can look at every link on every HTML page on a Web site and trace each link to see whether the linked object still exists. It then generates a report of dead links. Based on that report, the system administrator can rewrite the HTML code, getting rid of the bad links.

CHAPTER 34

How Java, ActiveX, and JavaScript Work

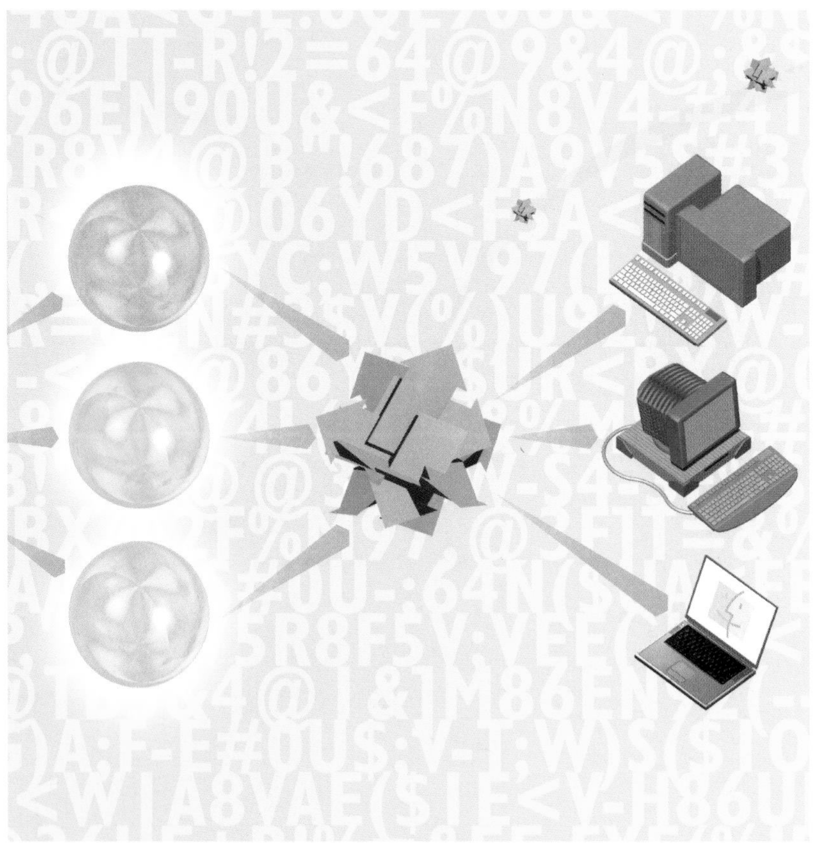

THE Internet is no longer a place that you visit with your computer and merely look at documents or gather information—increasingly, it is an extension of your computer. You can now run programs that reside on the Internet rather than on your own computer, and tools have been developed that enable your computer and the Internet to interact as if they were one large computer system. This allows for all kinds of things never before possible: news tickers that flash breaking news; interactive games; multimedia presentations combining animation, sound, and music; and much more.

The three most important programming tools associated with Web technology are Java, ActiveX, and JavaScript. *Java*, a computer language developed by Sun Microsystems, enables applications to be run from the Internet—the same as word processing and spreadsheet programs that are run on your computer. It is similar to the C++ computer programming language and is object-oriented, which means programs can be created by using many preexisting components instead of by a programmer writing the entire program from scratch. Although most Java programs are run from the Internet, they don't have to be and can be run just like any other type of program.

Java programs run inside your Web browser if you have a Java-enabled browser. Most browsers are Java-enabled. When Java programs are run inside a browser, they are called *applets*. You don't need to do anything to run a Java applet. When you visit a Web site that has a Java applet on it, the applet is downloaded automatically from a Web server and then run automatically in your browser. Java applets can be run on any computer, such as a PC, a Macintosh, or a Unix workstation.

ActiveX, a technology from Microsoft, enables Internet programmers to create programs—commonly referred to as ActiveX *controls* or *components*—that can essentially turn the Internet into an extension of your computer. Similar to Java applets, these controls are downloaded to your computer and run there. They can do anything a normal application can do, in addition to interacting with the Web, the Internet, and other computers connected to the Internet. To run these controls, a browser that supports ActiveX, such as Internet Explorer, is necessary.

One benefit of ActiveX controls is that they are written as components, which means they can be put together, much like building blocks, to build larger and more complex applications. Another benefit is that, because you have already downloaded a component, you won't ever need to download it again. So, when you visit a page with a complex ActiveX application on it, you might need to download only a small portion of it because you might already have the other components on your computer.

JavaScript is a scripting language that is less complex and therefore much easier to learn than Java and ActiveX. People without substantial programming experience can write scripts with JavaScript. It's also an interpreted language, which means that its commands are executed by the browser in the order in which the browser reads them. It's commonly used for things such as creating drop-down boxes, navigational aids, and interactive forms, although it can be used for creating more complex applications, as well.

How Java Works

1 Java is a compiled language, which means that after a Java program is written, the program must be run through a compiler to turn the program into a language a computer can read. Java differs from other compiled languages, however. In other compiled languages, computer-specific compilers create distinct executable binary code for all the different computers on which the program can run. In Java, by contrast, a single compiled version of the program—called Java *bytecode*—is created by a compiler. Interpreters on different computers, such as a PC, Macintosh, or SPARC workstation, understand the Java bytecode and run the program. In this way, a Java program can be created once and then used on many types of computers. Java programs designed to run inside a Web browser on the World Wide Web are called applets. Java-enabled browsers contain Java bytecode interpreters.

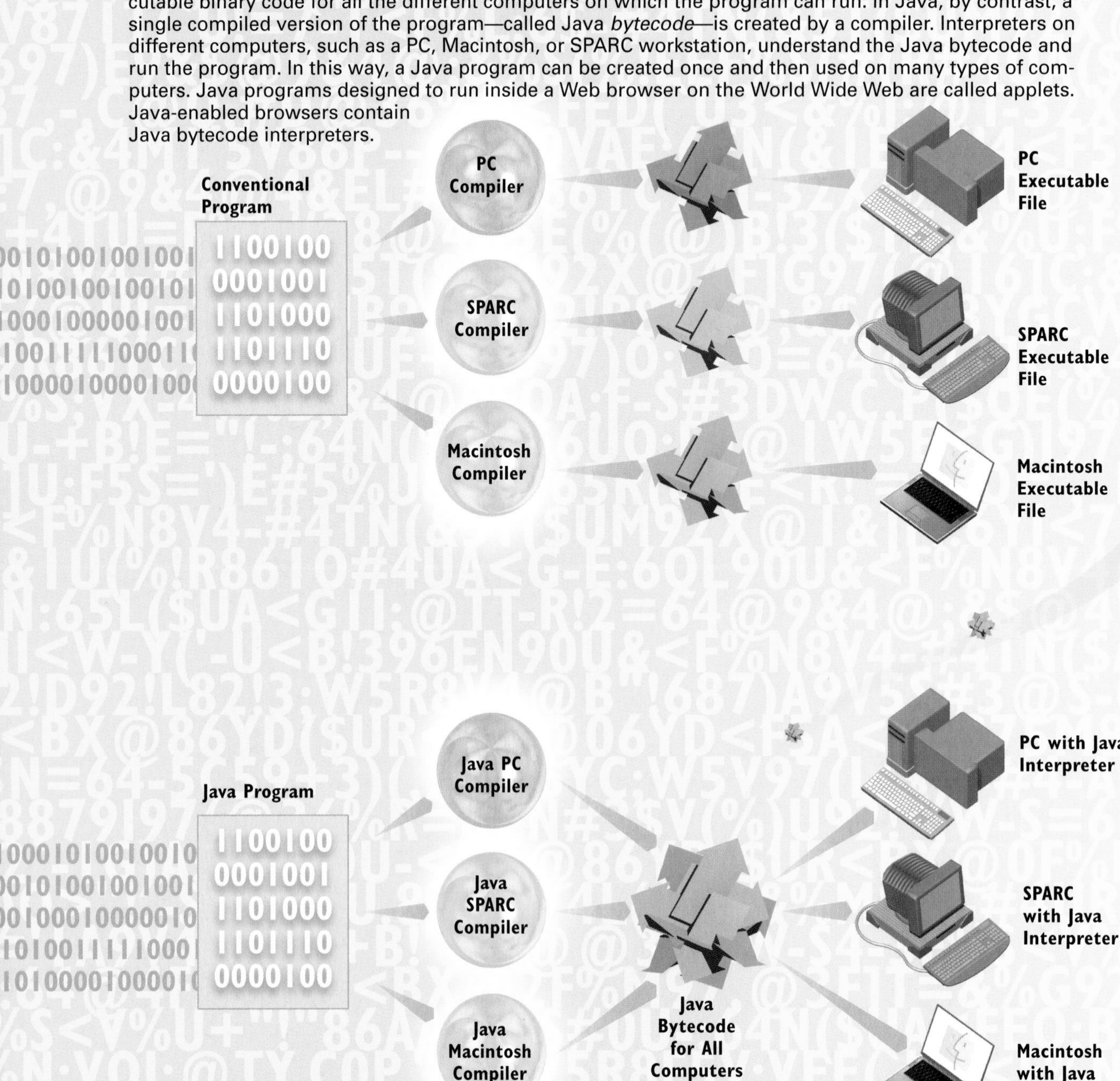

3 When you visit a home page with a Java applet on it, the applet downloads to your computer. To run the Java applet, you need a Web browser that has a bytecode interpreter that can run Java applets. Many browsers, such as Netscape Navigator, have these interpreters built into them.

2 After a Java program is compiled into bytecodes, it is put on a Web server.

6 The Java applet is run; because it allows for animations and interactivity, it opens many other kinds of multimedia possibilities.

5 After the bytecodes have been verified, they are put into a restricted area in your computer's memory and run. By putting the applet into this special area of your computer, further care is taken that no virus can harm your computer.

4 Because Java applets are programs that run on your computer, theoretically they could carry a virus just like any other computer program could. To help ensure that no viruses infect your computer, when a Java applet is downloaded to your computer, the applet first goes through a process of verification—a process that ensures that the bytecodes can be run safely.

How ActiveX Works

1 First, a programmer creates an ActiveX control. A variety of programming tools can be used to create controls, such as Visual Basic or the C programming language. A control can be as complex as a program that checks your computer for viruses and then eradicates them, or as simple as showing a Web site in an outline view. After the control is created, it is posted on a Web server, and information about the control is coded into the Web page through use of the HTML `<object>` tag.

10100100010001000101001001
00100100100010010100100100
11001001111010001000001001
00100101010010101001111100
01000001010111101000010000

ActiveX Control

2 When you visit a Web page that contains an ActiveX control, your browser sees the HTML `<object>` tag. This tells your browser that an ActiveX control is present. The tag contains a variety of information required to run the control. It can tell the browser where the control is located on the server, for example, and which type of file it is. It can point to the control (which has an .ocx extension); to an installation file (which has an .inf extension); to a compressed file (which has a .cab extension); or to a variety of other kinds of files.

```
<OBJECT ID="ourMenu"
WIDTH=0, HEIGHT=0
CLASS ID="CLSID:9BC24D87-
E21A-10DF-B7D2-180089E9610A
CODEBASE="http://www.que.com/
ActiveX/QueControls.CAB#
Version=1, 0, 8, 0">
```

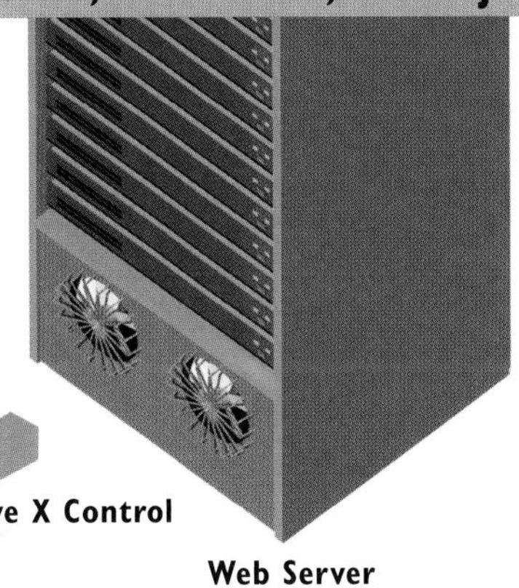

3 Some ActiveX controls need more than a single control to work. In that event, the HTML page contains multiple references to ActiveX controls needed to run the control on that page. The controls can be located on the same server, on a different server on the same Web site, or on another site and server on the Internet.

ActiveX Control

4 Using the information in the <object> tag, the browser starts to download the ActiveX controls. If you have set your browser to a certain level of security, you get a message asking whether you want to download the control. To ensure even more security, ActiveX controls can be digitally *signed* by a digital certificate authority, such as VeriSign. This signing assures you that the control you want to run was written by the person to whom it is attributed. If a problem occurs with the control, you will be able to contact that person.

Web Browser

WELCOME

Do you want to download control XYZ?

ActiveX Control

5 If you have low security set on your browser, or if you give the okay to download the control, the control and its related ActiveX controls are downloaded to your computer. Some of the controls already might be on your system, so you won't need to download them. After the control is downloaded, the file is decompressed (if it was compressed), information about it is put into the Windows Registry, and it is installed on your computer. The control then runs. An ActiveX control can do anything any other program can do. It can interact with your computer and with any Internet resource, such as the Web, FTP, Telnet, or virtually any other Internet resource. It can also directly use the Internet's TCP/IP protocols so that it need not ride on top of another Internet resource.

How JavaScript Works

JavaScript is an *object-oriented* language, which means that it works by manipulating objects on a Web page, such as windows, buttons, images, and documents. It groups these objects into hierarchies, which enables programmers to manipulate them more easily. It's also an *interpreted* language, which means that its commands are executed by the browser in the order in which the browser reads them.

Window
Document
Elements
Button
Check Box
File Upload
Password
Radio

2 JavaScript commands are put directly into the HTML file that creates a Web page. Depending on the script being run, the commands can be put into several places in the file. Often, the commands are put near the top of the file. Special codes set off the commands, alerting the browser that they're JavaScript commands. If the commands are put before the HTML `<body>` tag at the top of the file, the script can start executing while the HTML page is still loading.

<HTML>
<READ>
<SCRIPT LANGUAG
"javascript">
<!--Hide Script fr
older browsers
document.write

window.open
then
document.write
then
window.status=
"these are the times
that try men's souls"
then

3 The heart of the way JavaScript works is to take actions on objects. These actions are called *methods*. Using this basic concept, JavaScript can be used for a wide variety of sophisticated, interactive features, but we'll look at a simple script that opens a new browser window to a specified size, puts a specific Web page in it, and names the window. In the basic syntax of JavaScript, first the object is named, and then a period appears, followed by the action taken on the object—the method. So, the command to open a new window in JavaScript is `window.open`. In this instance, `window` is the object, and `open` is the method. This command opens a new browser window.

window.open

HTML PAGE

HTML HTML HTML HTML HTML HTML HTML

How JavaScript Works

window.open ("http://www.howitworks.com/jscript.html", "How_JavaScript_Works", "height=1750, width=150")

4 You can add further instructions to the `window.open` command. You do this by adding parameters after the command. You put all the parameters inside one set of parentheses, put each individual parameter inside quotation marks, and then separate the parameters by commas. So, the command `window.open("http://www.howitworks.com/jscript.html","How_JavaScript_Works","height=1750,width=150")` opens a new browser window 1750 pixels high and 150 pixels wide with the `http://www.howitworks.com/jscript.html` in it.

Blank Window

CHAPTER 35 How CGI Scripting Works

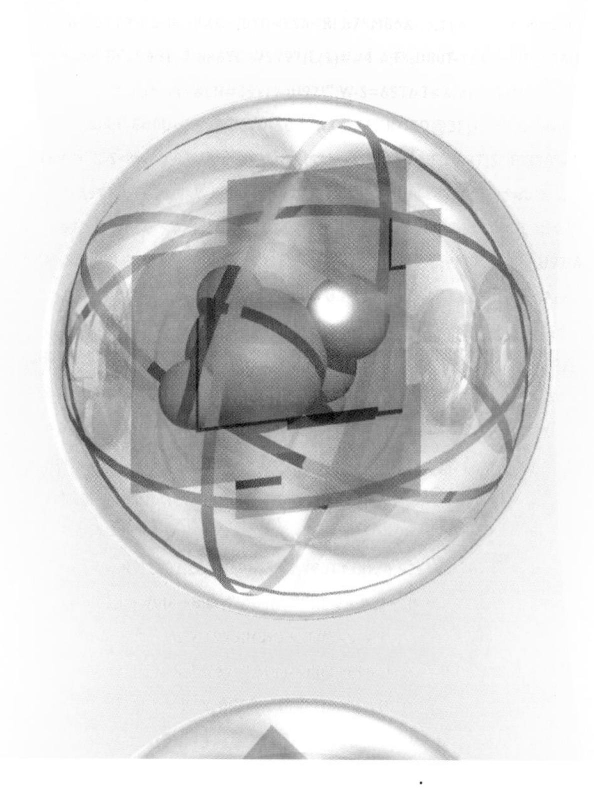

IF you browse the Web for very long, you are sure to come across the term CGI, or *Common Gateway Interface*. CGI refers to the communications protocol by which a Web server can communicate with other applications. For example, a CGI application, sometimes called a *script*, is often used to enable Web users to access databases or to get information from forms people fill out. CGI can also be used to create agents that do things such as check a Web site to see whether it has any broken links.

Essentially, CGI is a standard way in which the Web interacts with outside resources. Often, that outside resource is a database. You've probably run CGI scripts many times without knowing it. For example, if you've filled out a form on a Web page to register to use a site and then later received an e-mail notification with a password for you to use, you've probably run a CGI script. In that case, the CGI script probably took the information you filled in on the form and performed several actions on it, including putting the information in a database, automatically creating a password, and then sending you mail.

CGI and CGI applications are often confused. *CGI applications* receive data from the server and return the data via the Common Gateway Interface. CGI applications usually are written in a programming language called Perl (Practical Extraction and Reporting Language), although they can be written in C, C++, Pascal, AppleScript, or others as well. CGI itself is a standardized means of communicating between a CGI application and the HTTP server. It's the "doorway" of sorts through which the Web server sends requests and the CGI application collects and returns data.

In the example of providing information on a Web page designed to accept user input, CGI performs many tasks. First, you submit unique information—such as a name or e-mail address—to the server for processing. Next, the server redirects the information to a CGI application that is called by the form "submit." CGI scripts are activated by the server in response to an HTTP request from the client. Lastly, a CGI application might send form data to another computer program, such as a database; save it to a file; or even generate a unique HTML document in response to the user's request. This is known as an *interactive form*.

In the illustration that accompanies this chapter, we'll look at a CGI program that enables someone to search a movie database for information.

Understanding CGI Scripting

1 People who dial into the Web site don't need to know programming to access CGI programs. Instead, a programmer writes a CGI program. A number of languages can be used for CGI, such as C or C++, FORTRAN, Visual Basic, and AppleScript. An application written in a programming language such as C must be passed through a program called a *compiler* before it can be run. The compiler turns the application into a language CGI can understand. Other languages, called *scripting languages*, do not need to be compiled first. CGI scripts tend to be easier to debug, modify, and maintain than compiled programs so they are used more frequently. Perl is probably the most popular language used for writing CGI scripts.

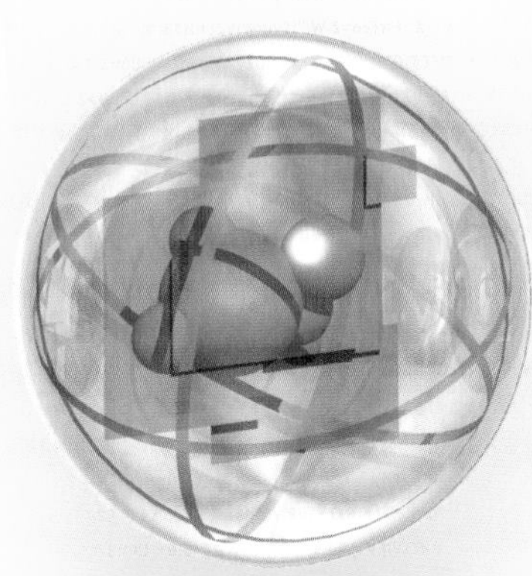

2 After the program is written and compiled, or the script is written, the program is put into a special directory on the Web server, such as `/cgi-bin`, where all the CGI programs are stored and maintained. The person in charge of the Web server determines which directory should hold CGI programs. If someone writes a program and doesn't put it in the proper directory, it won't run. This is a security feature. If there were many different directories people could use to store and run CGI programs, keeping track of them all would be difficult, and someone from the outside could create and post a program that could be dangerous to the software that's already there.

6 The CGI program receives the data from the database and formats it in a way that will be understandable to the user. For example, the program might take the information and put it into HTML format so the user can read it using her Web browser. The CGI program sends the results in HTML format to the user, who displays it in a Web browser. The user can then access that HTML page. She can click links to visit other pages, print pages, and view graphics and multimedia files.

5 The CGI program contacts a database and requests the information the user is looking for. The database sends the information to the CGI program. The information can be in a variety of formats, such as text, graphics, sound and video files, and URLs.

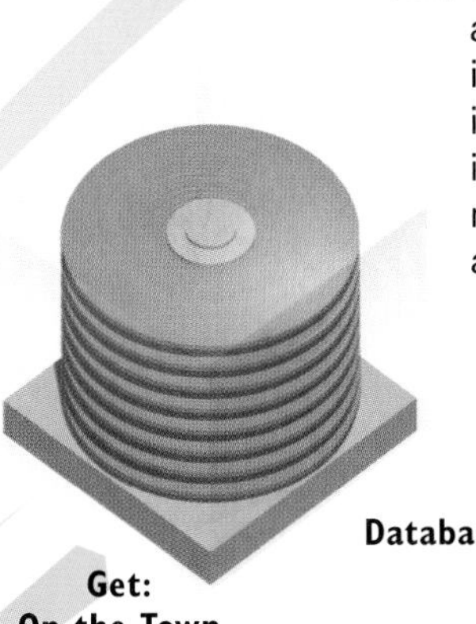

Database

Get:
On the Town

4 When you visit the Web site and click the URL, the CGI program is launched. If the CGI program allows you to search a database, for example, it sends a form in HTML format. You then fill out the form detailing what you want to find. When you finish the form and click Send, the data from the form is sent to the CGI program.

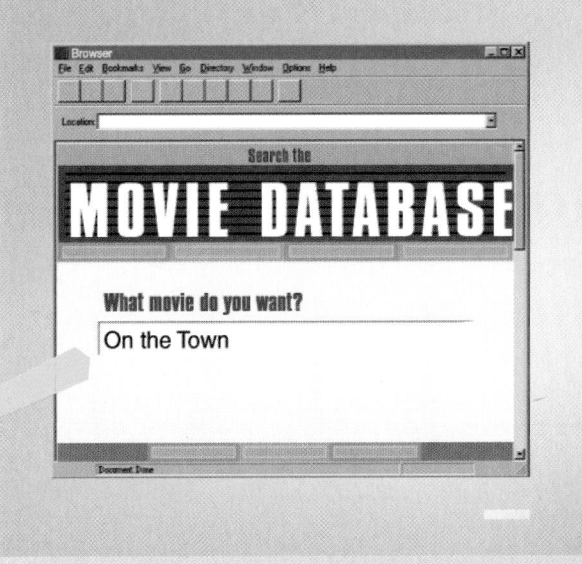

3 After the CGI program is posted to a special directory, a link to it is embedded in a URL on a Web page.

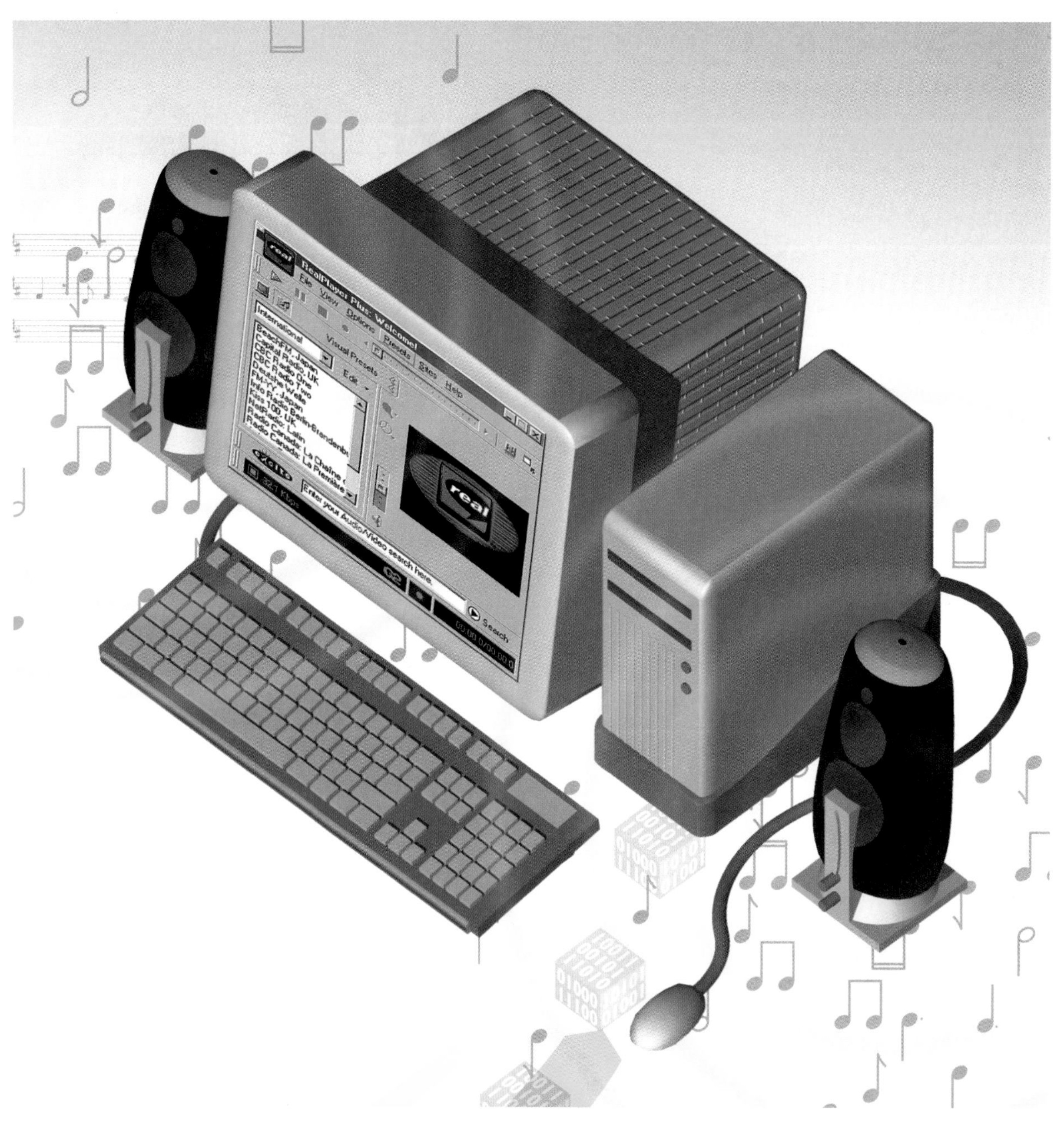
RealPlayer Plus: Welcome!
File View Options Presets Sites Help
International
Visual Presets
Edit
excite
Enter your Audio/Video search here.
Search
real

P A R T

ENJOYING ENTERTAINMENT AND MULTIMEDIA ON THE INTERNET

POSSIBLY the most dramatic and remarkable part of the Internet is the multimedia content and entertainment you can find there. You can listen to music, sound clips, and live radio stations from your computer. You can share your favorite music files with others all over the world. You can watch astronauts live while they're on the space shuttle. You can watch video clips of the news and other events. And you can even have live videoconferencing with people from all over the world.

You can do all that with the Internet's audio and video capabilities. You won't need specialized hardware and software to do it—and in many cases, you won't even need a very high-speed Internet connection. An ordinary dial-in connection to the Internet will do, although the sound and video quality will be better at higher speeds. And you'll only need free or inexpensive software, and a sound card and speakers that ship with most computers, or that are available separately.

The Internet's multimedia capabilities go beyond mere playing of audio and video clips and listening to Internet radio stations. You can participate in virtual worlds and join in virtual chat sessions in which you build your own online persona, called an *avatar*, which communicates with other avatars. The Internet enables the creation of remarkable online multimedia content, combining animation, sound, and programming via technologies such as streaming audio and video, Shockwave, and Multicast IP.

This section of the book discusses how every aspect of multimedia and entertainment on the Internet works. Chapter 36, "How Music and Audio Work on the Internet," covers audio and music. You'll see how audio files are sent to your computer and played. You'll look at how streaming audio works in detail. Streaming audio enables you to play sounds and music on your computer while the audio file is being transferred to your computer, so you don't have to wait for the file to download.

Chapter 36 also looks at the hottest new type of music on the Internet—music that can be downloaded and then played on a computer using a format called MP3. MP3 files are near-CD quality sound files, yet are small enough so they easily can be downloaded. This chapter also shows how Internet radio broadcasting works. Increasingly, radio stations broadcast live over the Internet so you can listen in using special software or just your browser. Many of these stations are Internet-only stations that broadcast only online, although many real-life radio stations around the world also broadcast over the Internet.

Chapter 37, "How Napster and File Sharing Work," looks at one of the most controversial uses of the Internet—the way music files can be shared with others. It shows you the inner workings of Napster, the file-sharing software that enables anyone to download their favorite music from other music lovers.

Chapter 38, "How Video on the Internet Works," details how video works. You'll learn how streaming video works, which (like streaming audio) lets you watch a video while it is being downloaded to your computer. Today, you're able to watch news broadcasts, music videos, and even live launches of the space shuttle through streaming video technology.

Chapter 38 also examines videoconferencing. Videoconferencing enables people from various parts of the world to see each other and talk to each other—all through their computers. The voices and images are transferred over the Internet.

In addition, Chapter 38 covers a lighter topic: how NetCams work. NetCams are cameras on the Internet that broadcast a photograph or digital animation at regular intervals. NetCams are all over the world, from the top of Pike's Peak to the streets of Hong Kong.

Chapter 39, "How Multicast IP and the MBone Work," looks at Multicast IP and the MBone. Multicast IP is a technique that enables videos to be broadcast to many thousands of people simultaneously, without clogging up the Internet's backbone. And the MBone is a high-speed Internet backbone used for transmitting Multicast IP video across the Internet.

Chapter 40, "How Virtual Reality Works," examines virtual reality. Virtual reality enables the creation of virtual worlds—3D creations on the Web through which you can walk or fly, interacting with your surroundings. As the bandwidth of the Internet increases, these virtual worlds might become increasingly popular.

Finally, Chapter 41, "Animation on the Web," looks at some of the most popular types of animation technologies, from the very simple to the very sophisticated. You'll learn how client pull and server push technologies enable the easy creation of simple animations. You'll also look at Shockwave, an extremely sophisticated way in which animation, audio, and other types of interactive technologies can be used to create powerful multimedia presentations on the Web. You'll even learn about the newest and most powerful kind of Web animation—Flash—which goes several steps beyond the capabilities of Shockwave.

CHAPTER

36

How Music and Audio Work on the Internet

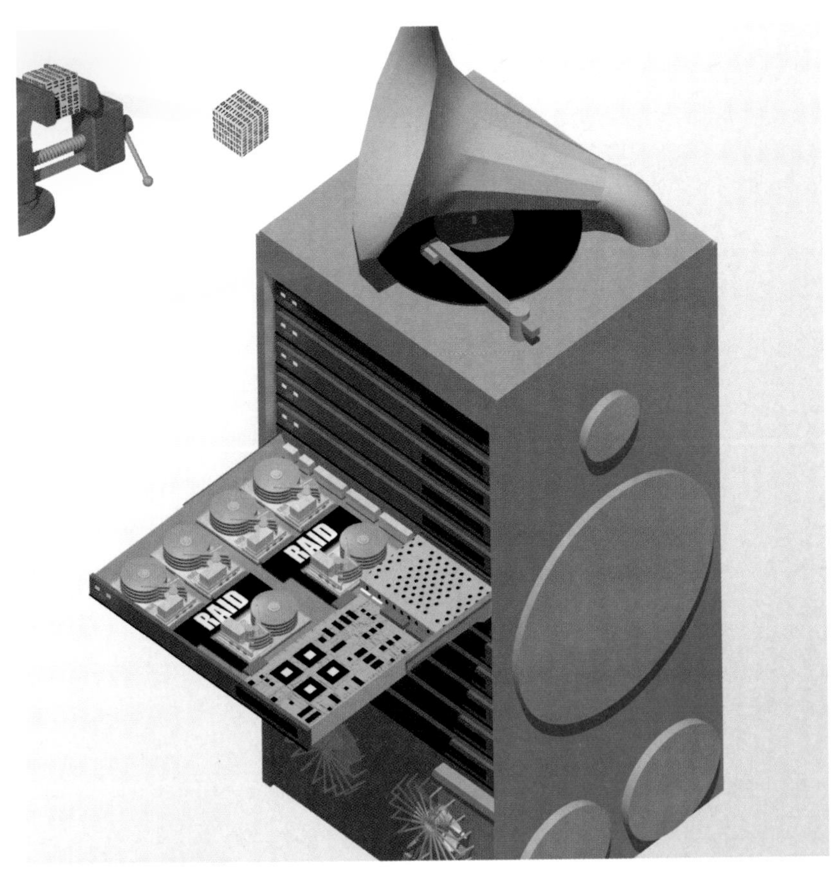

SOUNDS, voices, and music are now an everyday part of the Internet. Through the Internet, you can listen to radio stations, interviews, music, sound clips, and much more.

You can listen to all this music and sound by downloading *audio files*—files that have been digitized so that a computer can play them. You'll find many music files and sound clips in a variety of sound formats online. Each of these formats has a different extension associated with it, such as .WAV, .MP3, or .AU. To play these files, you'll first have to download them and then have audio-player software play them on your computer. Netscape and other browsers have some of these software players built in, as do many operating systems. For additional formats, you'll have to find and download the player and then configure your browser properly to play the files—or run special client software that can play them.

Most sound files tend to be quite large—even after being compressed. For some types of sound files, you won't be able to listen to them until you download the entire file, and this can take quite awhile. Downloading a sound file that has less than a minute of sound in it may take 15 minutes.

A far better and newer use of audio on the Internet is called *streaming audio*. It handles audio in a much more clever way. With streaming audio you don't have to wait until the entire audio file is downloaded to play it. Instead, you listen to the audio while it downloads to your computer. A variety of technologies allow for streaming audio. For all of them, you'll need to have the proper audio player for each specific kind of streaming audio. This chapter looks at the most popular audio streaming technology, called RealPlayer. Other kinds of streaming technologies exist, such as that used by the Windows Media Player. However, all streaming technologies work similarly.

One problem with streaming audio is that the sound quality generally isn't nearly as good as a music CD. However, MP3, a popular kind of audio file type, offers CD-quality audio. Furthermore, the MP3 files themselves aren't that large—usually less than 4MB or 5MB per song. With other kinds of computer music technology, these songs can take up 20MB and more. Technologies have been developed that enable MP3 files to be streamed so that you can listen to them as they download to your computer. This technology gives you the best of both worlds—high quality sound without having to wait for the whole file to download.

One of the more intriguing new audio uses of the Internet is the ability to listen to radio stations from all across the world. An increasing number of radio stations stream their live broadcasts over the Internet, and you can listen right from your browser or use software such as RealPlayer or the Windows Media Player. Entirely new radio stations have sprung up that broadcast only over the Internet.

How RealPlayer Streaming Audio Works

1. When you use your Web browser and click a link to a RealPlayer sound clip on a home page, the link doesn't lead directly to a sound file. Instead, your Web browser contacts the Web server, which then sends a file called a *RealPlayer metafile* back to your browser. This metafile is a small text file that has the true location—the URL—of the RealPlayer sound file you want to play. The metafile also has instructions telling your Web browser to launch the RealPlayer sound player, which is required to play the clip.

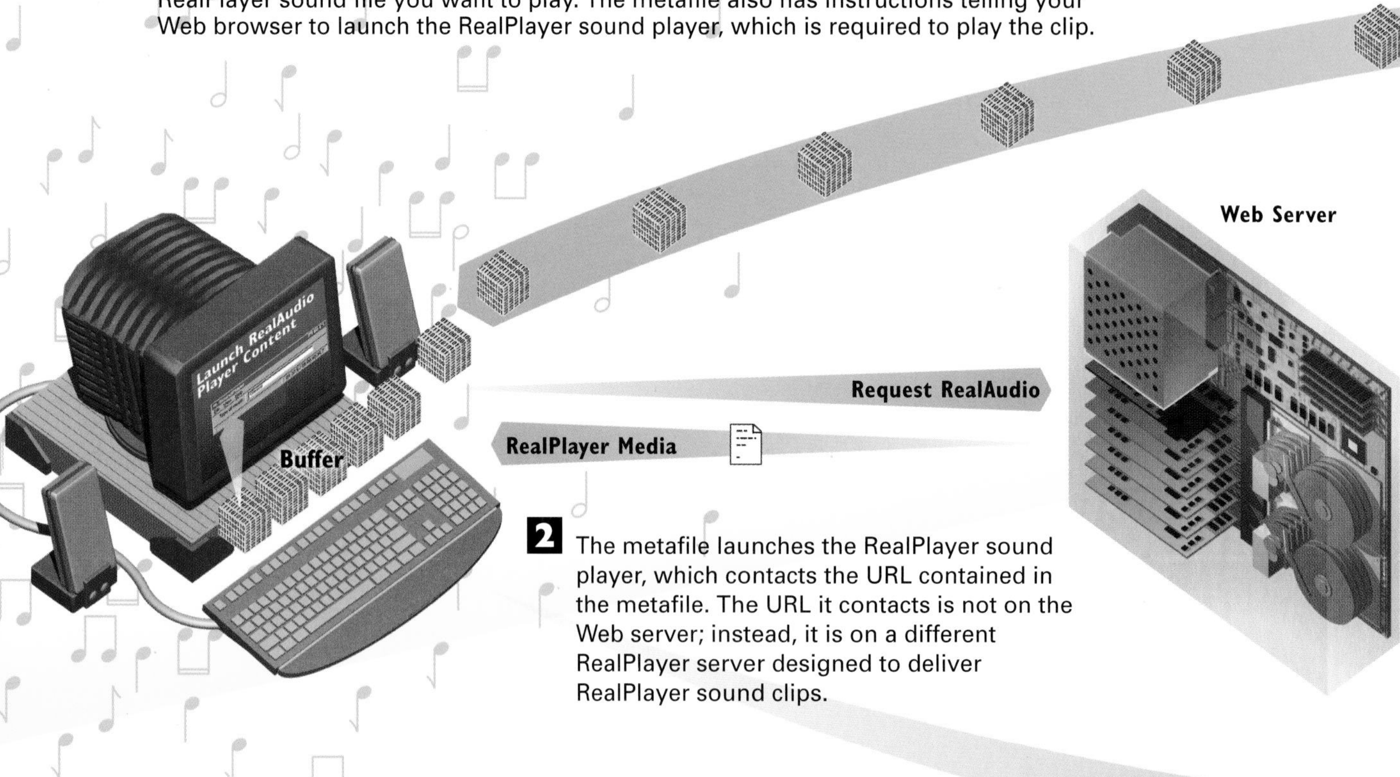

2. The metafile launches the RealPlayer sound player, which contacts the URL contained in the metafile. The URL it contacts is not on the Web server; instead, it is on a different RealPlayer server designed to deliver RealPlayer sound clips.

5. The packets are sent to a buffer on the receiving computer. When the packets exceed the capacity of the buffer, they are sent to the RealPlayer player, which then plays the sound file. RealPlayer allows you to jump ahead or back in a sound or music clip. When you move to a different place in the clip, the RealPlayer player contacts the server and tells it to start sending the file from that new place in the clip.

4 The RealPlayer clip is compressed and encoded. The sound file is too large and takes too long to send and play if it is not compressed. The clip is sent in IP packets using the UDP (User Datagram Protocol) instead of the Internet's normal TCP (Transmission Control Protocol). Unlike TCP, UDP doesn't keep resending packets if they are misplaced or other problems occur. If packets have to keep being re-sent, the sound player on the receiving end is constantly interrupted with packets and can not play the clip.

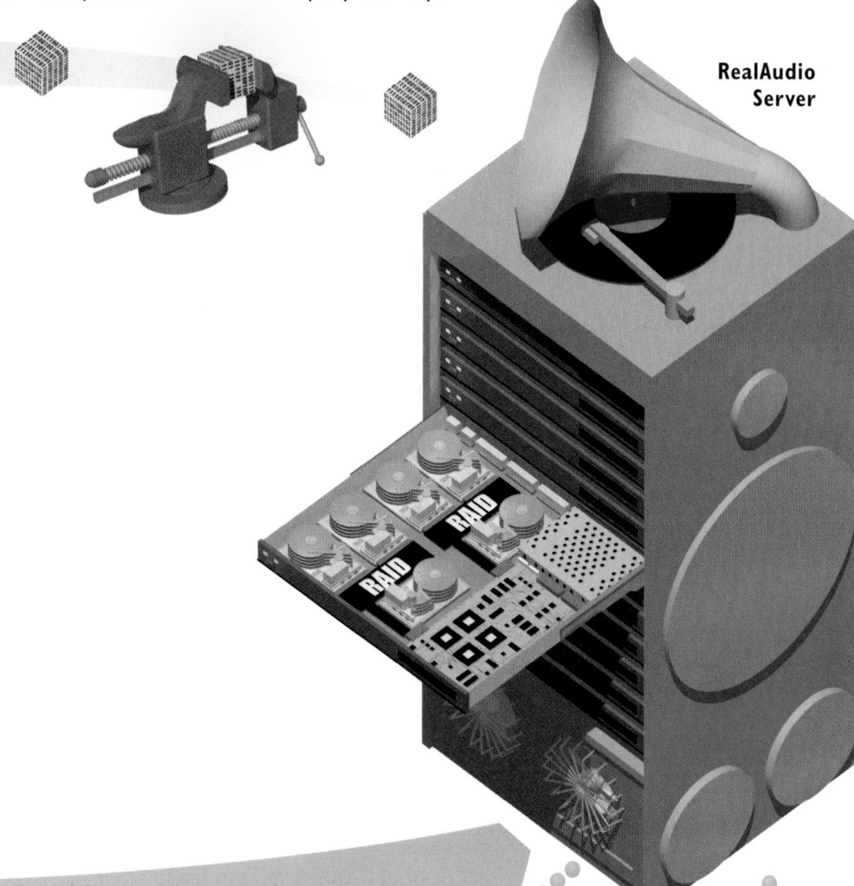

3 The RealPlayer server and the RealPlayer sound player "talk" to one another so that the server knows at what speed the user is connected to the Internet. If the connection is a low-speed connection, a smaller RealPlayer file is sent that contains less data. This file is of lesser quality than a file sent via a high-speed connection. If a high-speed connection is used, a larger, higher-quality sound file is sent. This provides for better sound quality.

How MP3 Music Files Work

1 One of the most popular ways to distribute music on the Internet is through the use of MP3 music files. The files use special algorithms that shrink the size of the files while retaining CD-like quality. Before MP3 files can be posted, however, the music has to be recorded. The music is recorded no differently than any other kind of music and is then put on a CD.

2 The music from the CD has to be converted to the MP3 format so that it can be posted on the Internet. A typical way to convert the music is to use a *ripper*—a piece of software that takes the music from the CD and converts it to MP3 format. The software uses special algorithms that shrink the size of the file dramatically so that a typical song is under 3MB and still maintains high quality. (In earlier kinds of PC music formats, those files would be 20MB and more.) This mix of small size and high quality is what sets the MP3 standard apart from other Internet music formats.

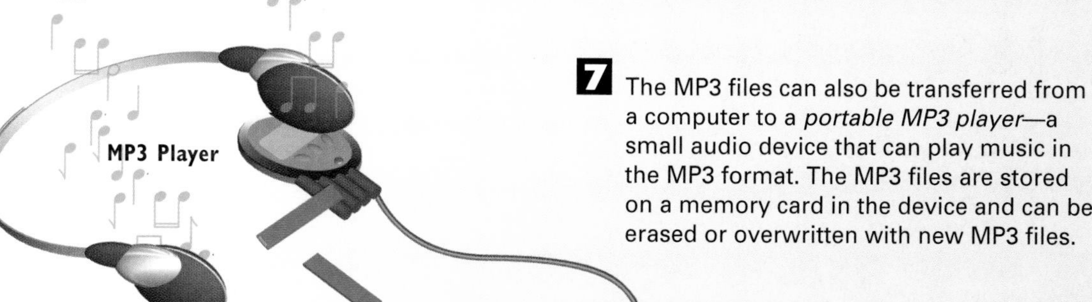

7 The MP3 files can also be transferred from a computer to a *portable MP3 player*—a small audio device that can play music in the MP3 format. The MP3 files are stored on a memory card in the device and can be erased or overwritten with new MP3 files.

6 One issue with MP3 files is that they can violate an artist's copyright—for example, if the file was created and posted without the artist's permission. In some instances, an MP3 player won't play an MP3 file if someone who didn't get the artist's permission ripped the file from a CD. In other instances, the file will play, but may contain copyright information about the MP3 file. However, in many instances, the file can be played and does not include copyright information.

4 When someone wants to download the MP3 file, he visits the Web site or FTP download site and downloads the file to his computer.

Get MP3 File

.MP3 File

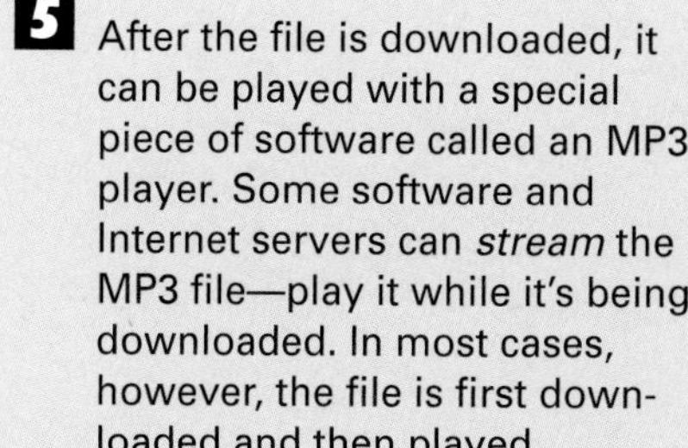

5 After the file is downloaded, it can be played with a special piece of software called an MP3 player. Some software and Internet servers can *stream* the MP3 file—play it while it's being downloaded. In most cases, however, the file is first downloaded and then played.

3 After the file has been converted to an MP3 format, it's posted to a site on the Internet where people can download it.

Web Server

How Internet Radio Broadcasting Works

1 Two main types of radio stations broadcast over the Internet—traditional radio stations that also broadcast over the airwaves as well as Internet-only broadcasts. In both instances, the radio station plays music, news, or offers other kinds of broadcasts in much the same way that a normal radio station does.

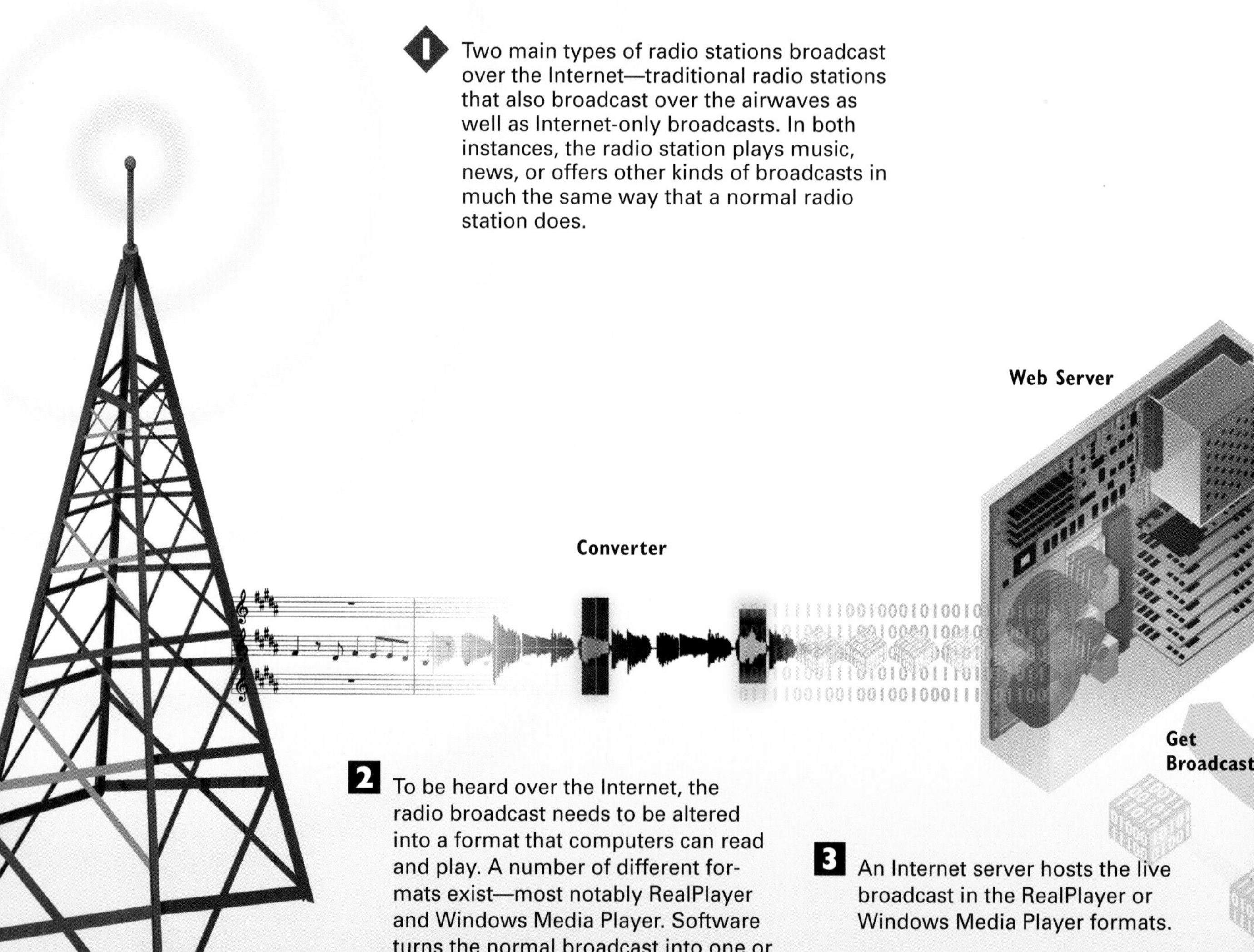

2 To be heard over the Internet, the radio broadcast needs to be altered into a format that computers can read and play. A number of different formats exist—most notably RealPlayer and Windows Media Player. Software turns the normal broadcast into one or both of those formats. (To get the RealPlayer, go to `www.realnetworks.com`. For the Windows Media Player, go to `www.microsoft.com`.)

3 An Internet server hosts the live broadcast in the RealPlayer or Windows Media Player formats.

6 The client software now plays the broadcast live on the person's computer. The broadcast can be controlled like a radio broadcast—the sound can be lowered or raised and, depending on the software used, the quality of the sound can be altered. Generally, the higher the speed of the connection between the PC and the Web server, the higher the audio quality of the broadcast.

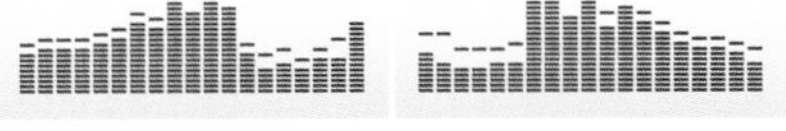

5 When the link is clicked, the client software contacts the server. The server sends the broadcast to the PC in a steady stream.

4 When someone wants to listen to a radio broadcast, he launches their client software radio player, such as RealPlayer. If he has Internet Explorer 5.0 or higher, he can also launch a radio toolbar that sits near the top of the browser window. From this toolbar, he can choose radio stations to listen to. To listen to a radio station, someone clicks a link in the player or in the browser. He can also visit a radio station site and click a link on the site.

CHAPTER 37 How Napster and File Sharing Work

EVERY once in a while a new feature or application takes the Internet by storm and not only changes the way many people use the Internet, but, at times, even changes the world beyond the Internet's borders.

Several years ago that's what Napster did. Not only did it change the way that many people used the Internet, but it also threatened the multi-billion dollar music industry. Napster forever changed the way people thought of and listen to music.

It did all this by putting into effect a very simple idea—letting people share their music with each other over the Internet. Despite all the hype, technology, and lawsuits, that's what it all comes down to.

People can make digital copies of their CDs by using a piece of *ripping* software that can turn CD tracks into digital files that can be played on a computer—most commonly files in the .MP3 music format. Napster isn't a ripper. Instead, it lets people find music in .MP3 format by searching through the music collections of thousands of other people. When someone finds a song he wants, he can download it to his computer from another person. Then he can listen to that song on his computer by transferring it to an MP3 player and listen to it there, or burn it onto a CD and listen to the song in a CD player.

The music industry cried "Foul!" and brought Napster to court on copyright violations. Napster was ordered to figure out a way to stop alleged copyright violations, while still allowing people to share music. The legal and technical fights continue, and it's unclear whether Napster will survive, and, if it does, whether it will remain free.

But no matter what happens, the genie is out of the bottle. Other software such as the Gnutella file-sharing network—software that lawyers and judges can't pursue—enables people to do the same thing.

This kind of technology, which enables people to share files directly with one another, is called *peer-to-peer*. Peer-to-peer has gone far beyond allowing people to share music—people can share any kind of files from spreadsheets to movies.

A whole new kind of application has sprung up in Napster's wake: business peer-to-peer software. The most notable example is called Groove—software that enables people in corporations to create their own private workspace where they can share files, messages, and software. Multi-billion dollar corporations have already signed on and are using the software. Ironically, a technology that started as guerilla music-sharing software might find fruition as a corporate mainstay.

How Napster Works

1. To use Napster, download and install it on your computer. After you've installed Napster, it compiles a database of all the music on your computer.

2. When you connect to the Internet and launch Napster, Napster contacts a Napster server. It tells the server all of the music on your computer, the location on your computer of that music, and your name and IP address.

6. You choose the song you want to download and from whose computer you want to download. You bypass Napster's servers and download the song directly from the person's computer.

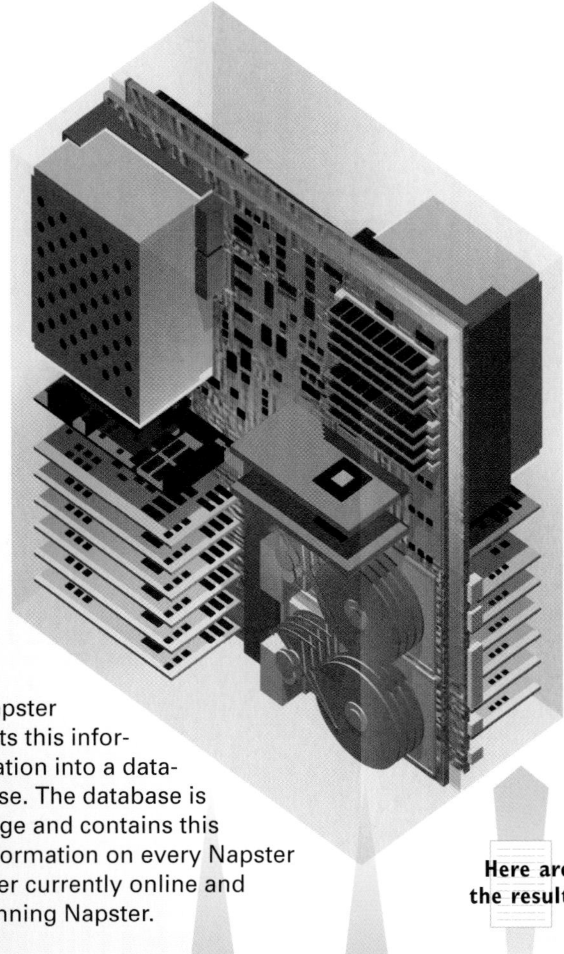

3 Napster puts this information into a database. The database is huge and contains this information on every Napster user currently online and running Napster.

Artist/Song	Name	IP Address
Dylan/Like a Rolling Stone	GIGiggey	168.1.12.123
Dylan/Tangled up in Blue	GIGiggey	168.1.12.123
Davis/Kind of Blue	JazzHound	123.4.89.143
Coltrane/My Favorite Things	JazzHound	123.4.89.143
Coltrane/Giant Steps	JazzHound	123.4.89.143
Mozart/Eine Kleine Nachtmusik	ClassEguy	168.23.12.123
Cage/The Seasons	ClassEguy	168.23.12.123
Spann/Cryin'Time	BluSe	156.23.34.456
Ball/Red Beans	BluSe	156.23.34.456
Wolf/I'm a Man	BluSe	156.23.34.456
Earle/Transcendental Blues	CoLliYou	124.78.1.234

4 When you want to search for music, type in the artist and song title for which you're looking in Napster.

5 The Napster client contacts the Napster server. The server looks in its database and finds the artist and song title for which you're looking. The server then sends a list to you of every copy of every artist and song and shows you on whose computer you can find each.

CHAPTER

38 How Video on the Internet Works

THE Internet began as a way for people to share text-based information such as e-mail, discussion groups, and file transfers. Today, however, the technology has advanced far beyond text. Currently on the Internet, you can have video conferences in which you talk live with someone and see them live on your computer screen. You can use whiteboard applications that let you see and talk to other people at their computers, and you can also work on a file together live on your computer screens. You can watch live video footage of astronauts from outer space. Plus, you can watch taped videos whenever you want—not when a national broadcaster says you must watch them.

To understand how all this works, you must understand three types of technologies. The first is called the *MBone (Multicast Backbone)*; it's a special Internet high-speed backbone capable of sending vast amounts of information. Many video transmissions—especially live ones—are sent across the MBone because of its high bandwidth. Turn to Chapter 39, "How Multicast IP and the MBone Work," for more information on the MBone.

The second technology is called streaming video. *Streaming video* solves a long-standing problem of sending video signals across the Internet. Video files tend to be extremely large because they have so much information packed into them. Because of that, sending video was never very practical—it could take hours to send a single video file to someone's computer. The person on the other end would have to wait until the entire file was downloaded and then play it—and it might play for only a few minutes.

Streaming video solves the problem in two ways. First, it compresses the video file dramatically so it is much smaller as it is transmitted across the Internet. Secondly, streaming video lets the receiving computer start playing the video while the file is being transmitted. So if you receive a streaming video file, you watch the video as you receive it—no waiting for the entire file to download. Streaming video files are not usually live broadcasts. Instead, they are often files created ahead of time and then posted on the Internet. You can watch the video by clicking its hypertext link. You need a special player to watch the video. A number of ways exist to send streaming video across the Internet and watch it as it comes to your computer.

The third piece of technology is *videoconferencing*. It lets you use your computer to have live videoconferences across the Internet. Videoconferencing is done live, although the technology can also be used to broadcast taped videos as well. NASA, the National Aeronautics and Space Administration, sometimes uses the technology to broadcast live from the Space Shuttle and also to broadcast taped videos about space exploration.

Webcams, also called *digital cameras*, are another intriguing use of video technology. A *Webcam* is a camera attached to the Internet that automatically broadcasts photographs of moving images at certain intervals. Photos can be downloaded or browsed with your Web browser. There are hundreds of Webcams on the Internet, sending live pictures from all over the world.

How Streaming Video Works

1 Streaming video refers to video you can play live on the Internet—you don't have to wait until the download is complete to see the video. Instead, you can play the video while it is being sent to your computer.

Analog Video Input

Digital Video Input

2 Before the video file is posted on the Internet, it is compressed and encoded in a special codec (coder/decoder)—an algorithm (mathematical formula) that compresses the video to a small size. This algorithm is required because without it, the video file would be so large that it would take an enormous amount of time to send it across the Internet.

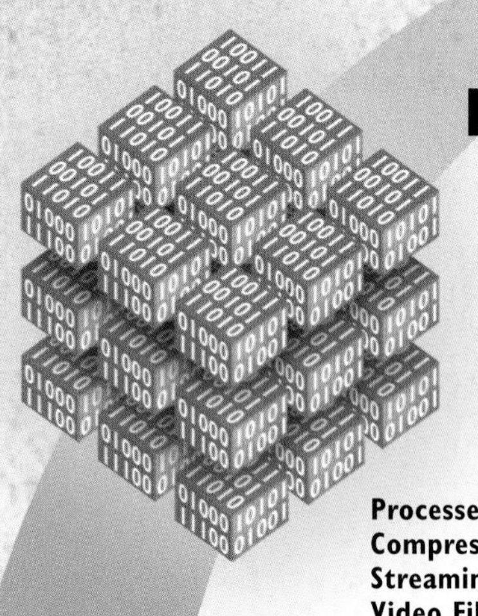

Processed and Compressed Streaming Video Files

Streaming Video Server

Play Video File

User Datagram Protocol

3 When you send a request to see the video by clicking an icon or a link on a World Wide Web page, you are sending a message from your computer to a server asking for the video file. The server sends the file to you in packets across the Internet, using the IP protocol. It does not use the normal Internet TCP, though. Instead, it uses the User Datagram Protocol (UDP). Unlike TCP, the UDP does not constantly check to see whether data has been sent, so it results in a more uninterrupted file transfer.

4 The video packets are sent to a buffer in your computer—an area of memory that ranges between 5KB and 30KB. The server can tell by how fast the buffer fills up which speed connection you have to the server. At higher speeds, it sends more video data and you get a smoother, more lifelike video. At lower speeds, it sends less data, which causes the video quality to suffer.

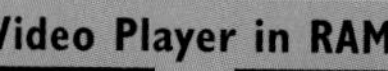

5 When the buffer fills up, which takes only a few seconds, a video player is launched on your computer. You can now watch the video on the player. As you watch the video, video packets are still being delivered to your buffer. Data from the buffer is continually sent to the player so you can watch an entire video. When all the video data has been sent, the video stops. The video file does not stay on your system; each section of the file is discarded after it is played.

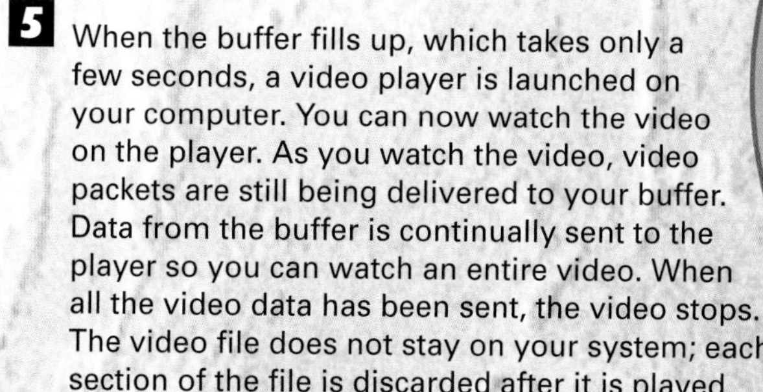

How Videoconferencing Works

1 There are a variety of ways for people to videoconference across the Internet. Most require client software that enables people to send and receive video and audio signals. Also involved are special types of server hardware and software (sometimes called *reflectors*) that host the videoconference and send the signals to everyone connected to the server.

2 When one person wants to videoconference with someone else, he uses client software to log into a reflector. A *reflector* is an Internet computer that hosts many live videoconferences people can join. When you log into a reflector, you can join any conference that exists. When someone is logged into a reflector, a signal goes out regularly from the person's computer to the reflector, telling everyone connected to the reflector that the person is logged in and available for a videoconference.

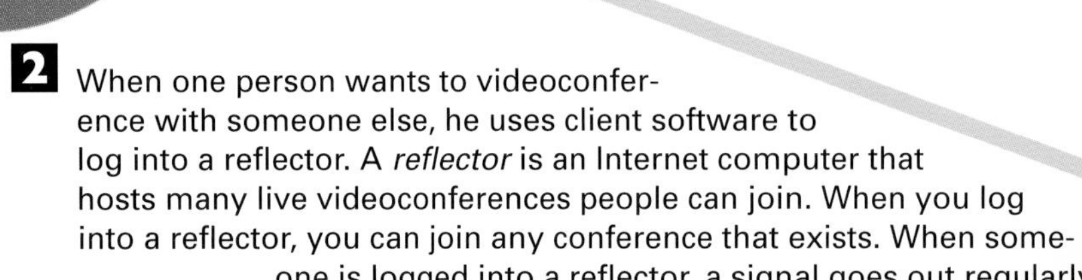

3 To be a live participant in a videoconference, you need a video camera and a microphone on your computer. (Sometimes the microphone is built into the camera.) The camera converts your video image into digital data. The client software then compresses and encodes that data, enabling it to be sent across the Internet. If the data were not compressed and encoded, it would be too large to be sent.

Some types of videoconferencing software also provide a way to videoconference without having to go through a reflector. If you know the IP address of someone who wants to videoconference, you can connect directly to that person without having to go through a reflector. In this case, you can participate only in one-on-one conferences rather than group videoconferences.

6 You and the person who wants to see your image both need the same client software. The software decodes the video image and displays it as video on the person's screen.

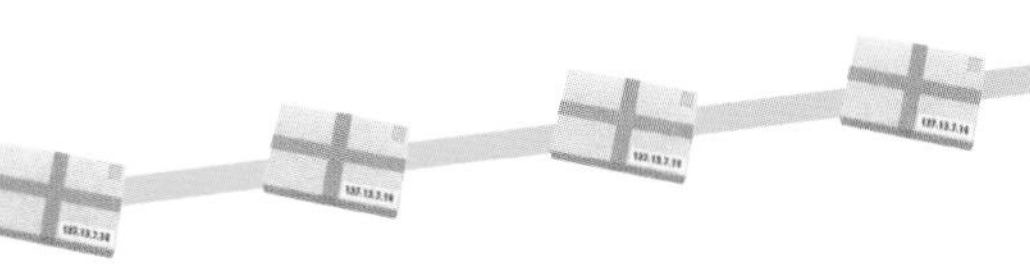

UDP Packets

5 The video data is sent across the Internet using UDP, which is more efficient than TCP when you are sending video data.

4 As another way of cutting down on the amount of data that needs to be sent across the Internet, some kinds of client software send only part of the screen and not the entire video image. They send only the part of the image that has changed. So, for example, if someone moves her head, it transmits only the head moving and not the background, which hasn't changed.

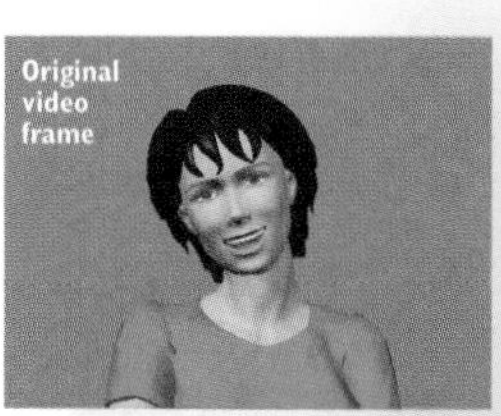

How WebCams Work

4 When someone clicks the link, the picture is sent to her Web browser and displayed. Some Webcams appear to send live video images, which means the Webcam image on your computer isn't a photograph, but instead appears to be a moving image. In fact, the "moving image" is a series of photographs sent every few seconds that give the illusion of movement. When you click the link to the image, the images automatically are sent to your Web browser as the video camera updates them.

A video camera is connected to a computer on the Internet. At regular intervals, one frame of the video is sent to a computer. It can be updated once every several seconds or once a day.

2 The picture is sent to the computer attached to the Internet. A video capture board or other hardware captures the image by converting it into binary format that computers can read. Typically, the picture is converted into the JPEG format—a graphics format that compresses the image while still retaining a high level of detail.

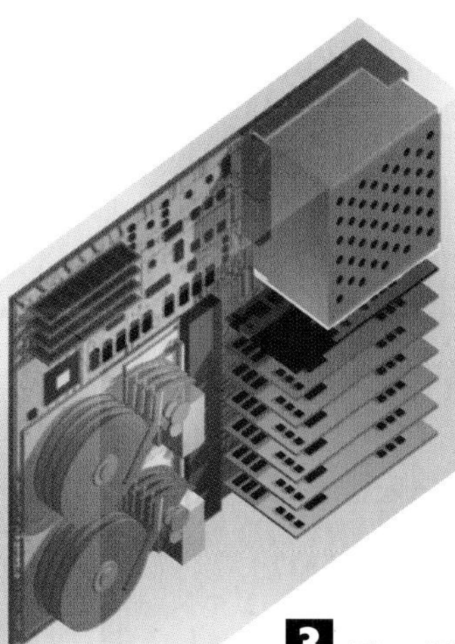

3 The JPEG image is linked to a specific URL on a Web home page. The link stays constant, even though the image itself changes regularly. That means whenever someone clicks the link, that person sees the most recent picture that was taken by the Webcam.

CHAPTER

39 How Multicast IP and the MBone Work

TO a great extent, the Internet of today is still in its infancy. Although multimedia elements can be found on the Internet, it's still largely made up of text and static pictures. These text and static pictures individually take up very little space—an entire Web page made up of text and pictures, for example, is often only 50 kilobytes (KB) or less.

The Internet of tomorrow, however, will be made up of a wide variety of multimedia elements: sound, video, animation, 3D objects, and more. Web pages will become interactive, and video-based shows might be broadcast over the Internet.

All this will cause serious congestion on the wires and networks that make up the Internet. (In fact, at times this congestion already occurs.) One more problem exists as well—there's no practical way for broadcasts to be sent out over the Internet because the files clog up the Internet. Suppose, for example, that someone wants to broadcast a telecast of a concert. The size of the file that contains that broadcast might be 50 megabytes (MB). Now imagine that 10,000 people want to watch the concert. That 50MB file needs to be sent individually to each of those 10,000 people. As you can imagine, that single broadcast could easily clog entire sections of the Internet, which would prevent the broadcast from being delivered.

A potential answer is on the horizon, however, called the Multicast Backbone, or the MBone. The *MBone* is a high-capacity Internet backbone for transmitting broadcasts using the IP multicast protocol. The MBone enables broadcasts to start out as a single transmission instead of, for example, 10,000 transmissions. Inside that single transmission are the addresses of all the people who want to see the broadcast. As the file is sent across the Internet, it eventually makes copies of itself when necessary and delivers the broadcast to the networks and individuals who want to see it.

Suppose that 100 people want to see a broadcast of a 50MB file. Fifty people who want to see it are connected to the Internet via the WorldNet Internet service provider, 25 people are on a corporate network at `zd.com`, and another 25 use the Internet Access Company Internet service provider. When the broadcast goes out, it goes out as one single file, not 100 separate files. The file then splits into three parts: One part goes to WorldNet, one part goes to `zd.com`, and one part goes to the Internet Access Company. After the file is on each of those separate networks, it is delivered to the people inside the networks who want to see it. The key here, however, is that instead of 100 files of 50MB traveling across the Internet—5 gigabytes (GB) of data—only three 50MB files travel, or 150MB of data. As you can see, the MBone can cut down tremendously the amount of traffic traveling across the Internet.

How Multicast IP Travels Along the MBone

1. The *MBone* (Multicast Backbone) is a high-speed Internet backbone capable of sending live video and audio broadcasts. It's a network of host computers that communicate with one another using a technique called IP (Internet Protocol) Multicast. An MBone multicast begins when a video signal is digitized and compressed so that it can be sent over the Internet. Without compression, the signal would be too large and take too long to deliver.

2. The compressed, digitized signal is sent in packets using the IP multicast protocol instead of the Internet's normal TCP protocol. The multicast protocol enables the signal to be sent to a number of sites on the Internet simultaneously. Normally, the Internet is *unicast*, which means that each signal can be sent only to a single, specific location.

3. A major advantage of the multicast protocol is that when the video packets are sent—for example, from Europe to the United States—they are sent only one time even though they might be sent to many destinations. Normally, TCP would have to send separate video packets for each destination. The multicast protocol solves the problem by putting information about the many Internet destinations into one packet. Later in the transmission, the video signals will be delivered to each of the destinations.

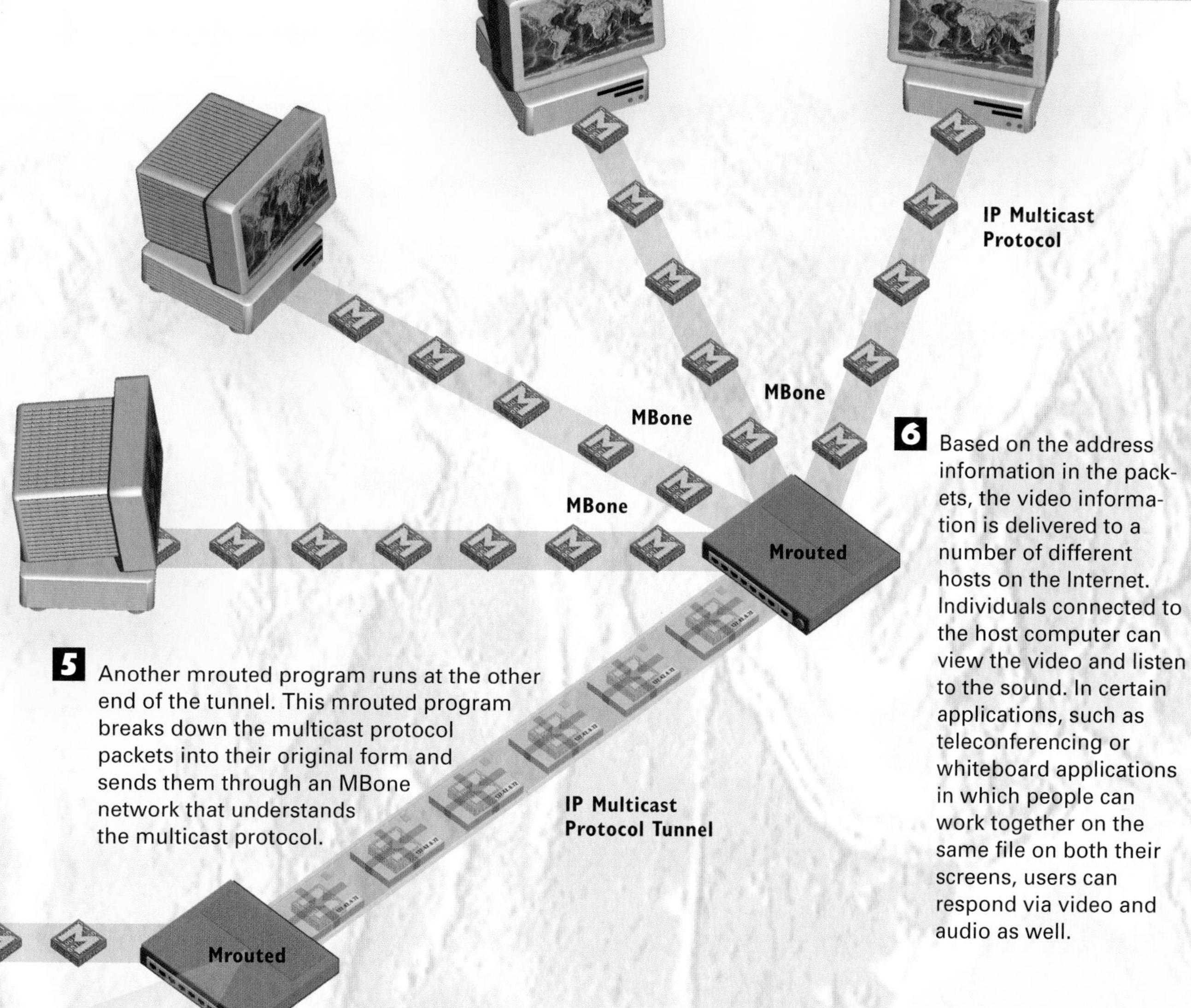

6 Based on the address information in the packets, the video information is delivered to a number of different hosts on the Internet. Individuals connected to the host computer can view the video and listen to the sound. In certain applications, such as teleconferencing or whiteboard applications in which people can work together on the same file on both their screens, users can respond via video and audio as well.

5 Another mrouted program runs at the other end of the tunnel. This mrouted program breaks down the multicast protocol packets into their original form and sends them through an MBone network that understands the multicast protocol.

4 The MBone understands the multicast protocol, but most networks and routers on the Internet do not. However, the MBone network often requires that data travel along normal Internet routes. To solve the problem, the MBone data travels in tunnels through existing Internet networks and routers. At one end of the tunnel is a Unix workstation that runs software called *mrouted* (multicast routing demon). This software encapsulates the multicast protocol packets inside normal TCP packets. To the Internet, the data now looks like normal TCP packets, and the data can be properly routed.

CHAPTER 40

How Virtual Reality Works

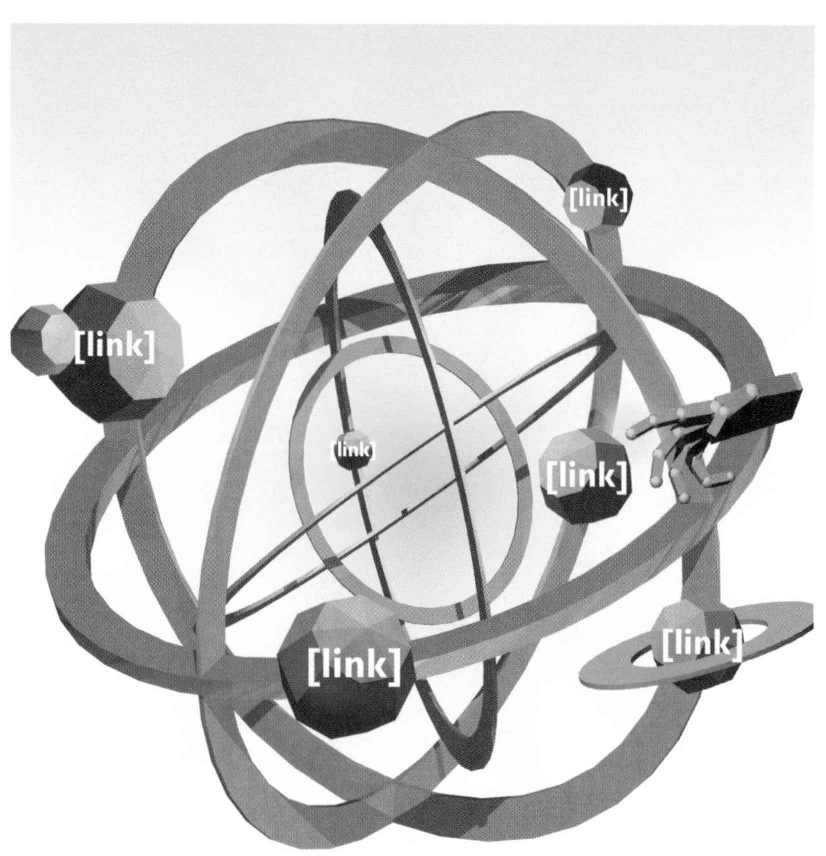

IMAGINE the Internet as a place where you could walk through three-dimensional worlds, pick up objects, examine them, and go to other Internet locations by flying or walking through doors. Picture home pages that were more than flat, two-dimensional surfaces that you could only read. What if you could be inside them, just like you can walk through a city or a building?

That's the promise of virtual reality (VR) on the Internet. In fact, it's more than just a promise—VR is already here. You'll find many virtual worlds you can explore on the Internet. You can walk through a giant computer, explore bizarre art galleries, visit outer space, go to the sites of what seem like ancient ruins, explore inside the human brain, and much more.

Virtual worlds are created using a computer language called Virtual Reality Modeling Language (VRML). This language instructs computers on how to build 3D geometric objects. Programmers and artists use the language to build complex worlds from these geometric objects. A VRML world is created by an ASCII text file containing VRML language commands—and for greater realism, graphics files can be added to this world as well. Because the virtual world is only an ASCII file, with perhaps a few graphics files, it can be downloaded quickly to your computer from the Internet, although some worlds with many graphics in them can be large.

When a virtual world is created, it is posted on an Internet server. When you want to visit that world, you either type in its URL or click a link to it, just as you do to visit any other location on the World Wide Web. To display the virtual world, you need a program capable of displaying the world—either a separate virtual reality browser, or more likely, a plug-in player that configures itself to your normal Web browser.

The VRML file describing the virtual world downloads to your computer. This can take a few minutes, or well over half an hour, depending on the size of the world and your connection speed. After the file is on your computer, your CPU computes the geometry of the world, based on the VRML commands in the file. Again, depending on the size of the world and the speed of your CPU, this can take only a minute or two, or up to ten minutes or more. After the world is computed, you can walk through it, fly through it, examine objects, and spin them. You can also visit other virtual worlds or places on the Internet by interacting with the world.

VR on the Internet is being used for far more than just creating virtual worlds people can walk through. For example, it has been used to create views of the brain and of molecules. It has been used by astronomers to show the rotation of molecular gas in a galaxy undergoing active star formation. Finally, as with everything else related to the Internet, VR will be eventually used for things that today none of us can imagine.

Despite all its appeal, one major problem with VR worlds is that they can be very large. Because of that, they can be very slow to load and interact with due to the current limited bandwidth of the Internet. As bandwidth increases, those problems might eventually go away.

How Virtual Reality Is Created by VRML

1 When someone wants to create a virtual world, she uses the Virtual Reality Modeling Language (VRML). VRML lets people create 3D worlds not by drawing them, but instead by using the VRML computer language to describe the geometry of a scene. VRML files are much smaller than graphics files. VRML files are simply text files that contain instructions for drawing the VRML world. VRML files end in a .WRL extension. After the world is created, it is posted on a Web server.

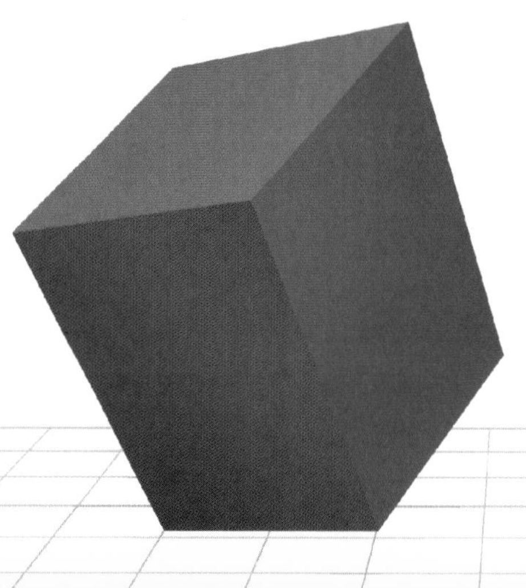

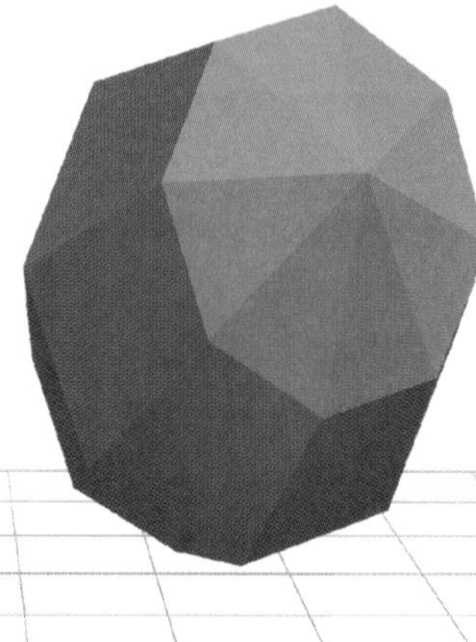

```
#VRML V1.Ø ascii
Separator {
  DirectionalLight {
    direction Ø Ø -1  # Light shining from viewer into scene
  }
  PerspectiveCamera {
    position   -8.6 2.1 5.6
    orientation -Ø.1352 -Ø.9831 -Ø.1233  1.1417
    focalDistance      1Ø.84
  }
  Separator {  # The red sphere
    Material {
      diffuseColor 1 Ø Ø  # Red
    }
    Translation { translation 3 Ø 1 }
    Sphere { radius 2.3 }
  }
  Separator {  # The blue cube
    Material {
      diffuseColor Ø Ø 1  # Blue
    }
    Transform {
      translation -2.4 .2 1
      rotation Ø 1 1  .9
    }
    Cube {}
  }
}
```

2 Here is an example of a VRML file describing a scene that has a red sphere and a blue cube in it, lit by a directional light.

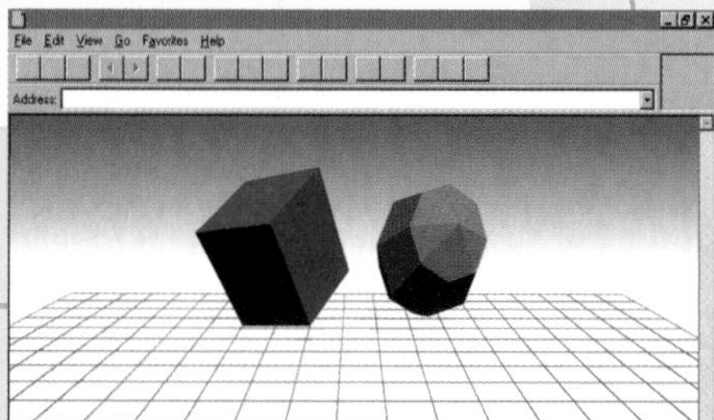

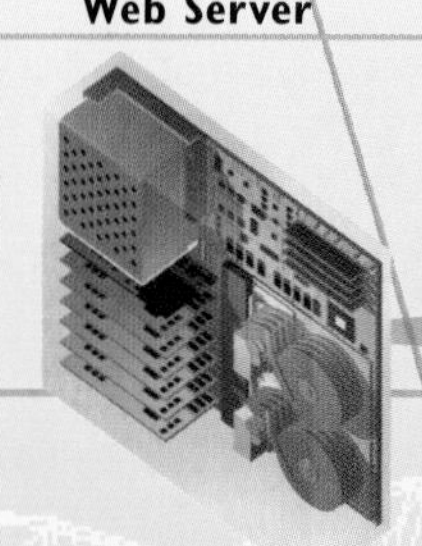

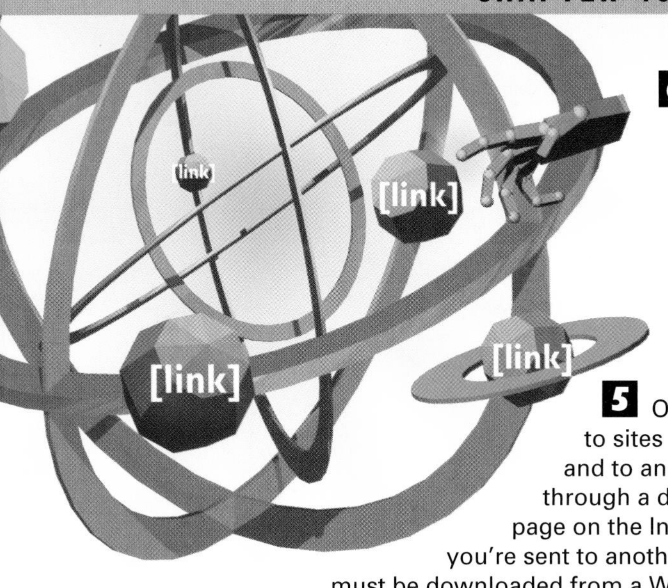

6 For greater realism and detail, graphics files can be "painted" on virtual reality objects—for example, to show paintings in an art gallery. When these graphics files are painted on objects, they must be downloaded along with the .wrl file as .gif or .jpeg files. When the browser displays the virtual world, it shows those graphics files on top of VR objects so they look like part of the scene.

5 Objects in the virtual world can be links to sites on the Web, to other virtual worlds, and to animations. So, for example, if you walk through a door, you might be sent to a home page on the Internet or to another virtual world. If you're sent to another virtual world, that virtual world must be downloaded from a Web server to your computer so your browser can compute the new world and you can interact with it.

4 As the file downloads, the VR plug-in is launched. It doesn't run separately from your Web browser. Instead, it takes over your Web browser while you're in the virtual world. After the file is downloaded, your VR plug-in creates the virtual world by taking the VRML commands in the file and having your computer compute the geometry of the scene. After the computation is done, the scene appears on your screen. The VRML file contains three-dimensional information that enables you to "walk" or "fly" through the scene using your browser. Depending on the complexity of the scene, your computer might have to do computations as you move through the scene.

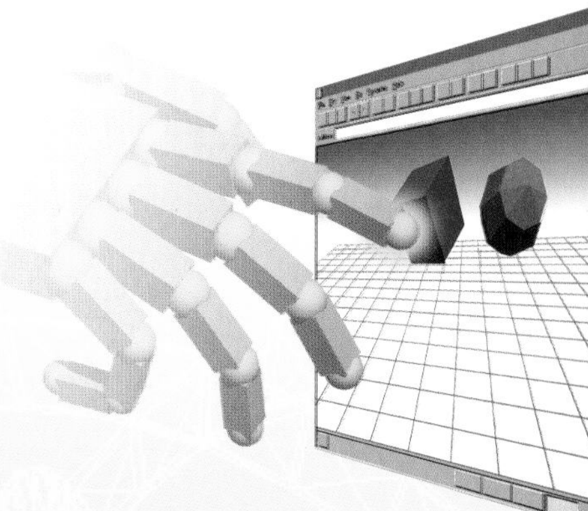

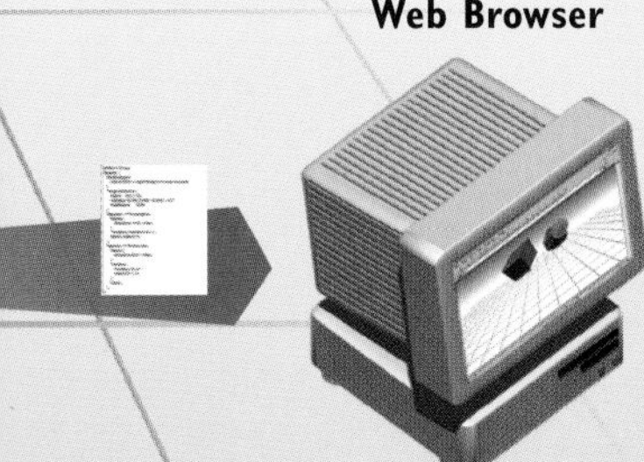

3 When you have a VR plug-in installed on your Web browser, you can visit a virtual world by clicking its URL. First, the VRML file is sent from the Web server to your computer. Depending on the size of the virtual world and your connection speed, the file can take from a few minutes to a half-hour or more to download to your computer.

CHAPTER

41

Animation on the Web

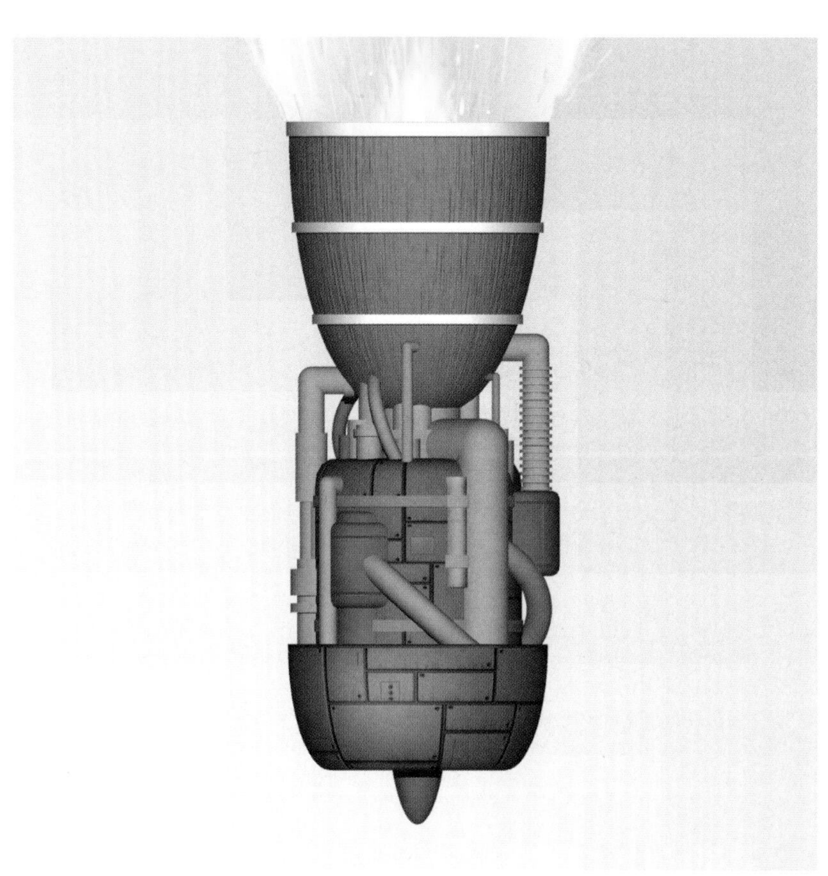

ANIMATION on the Web works no differently than animation anywhere else. Just like in a flip book, animation is a series of still images displayed in succession to create an illusion of fluid motion. The faster the frames advance, the more fluid the animation becomes. Unfortunately, the Web can be a very slow place, and an animation that should run quickly often crawls across the screen unless special technology is used.

A number of different ways exist for creating Web animations, including client pull, server push, animated GIFs, and the Shockwave and Flash multimedia plug-ins. In *client pull*, an HTML page gives the browser instructions to request and load another document automatically, similar to a slideshow. Web pages are displayed one after the other with a specified time delay in between. This feature is useful for step-by-step instructions. But client pull is slowed by the need to load a whole page rather than a single cell of animation, which prevents the illusion of fluid animation.

Client pull requests are embedded within the HTTP response header of a Web page that the server sends back to the client. The `<META>` tag inserts meta-information into a response header. *Meta-information* helps parse a Web page, but the browser does not display it. A *response header* is the beginning of each HTTP response that a server sends back to a client with the requested Web page.

Server push is a complement to client pull, although server push is the more complex of the two. Server push requires a *Common Gateway Interface (CGI)* script that tells the server when to automatically serve a new document or image. It also requires the client browser to be capable of recognizing the MIME-type, `multipart/x-mixed-replace`. This MIME-type enables multiple documents to be sent within one message. To understand how server push works, imagine an e-mail message with text, hypertext, a digital movie, and sound. You can see how multiple "documents" (media types) can be sent within a single message. The multipart message is simply a series of images that displays one image right after the other. The server sends, or *pushes*, each image. In this way, a small animation can be embedded among the text and images of an otherwise static Web page.

Animated GIFs are a series of graphical GIF images that roll up into a single image—much like the flip book seems to animate a series of drawings as you thumb through the pages. The animated GIFs load into a browser just like any GIF file, however, they load in a series to give the illusion of motion. Animated GIFs have the benefit of speed because images are cached on the client PC and loaded from memory rather than from the Internet. They represent an easy solution to adding motion to Web pages.

More complex multimedia animation has become possible using Macromedia's Shockwave and Flash plugs-in. Shockwave plays multimedia files that are created with Macromedia's popular Director and Authorware programs, whereas Flash uses its own special tools. You must first download and install the Shockwave and Flash plug-ins before you can view any Web pages that have Shockwave or Flash animations.

How Animation on the Web Works

Client Pull

Client pull is executed by the Refresh command. A refresh command is written into an HTML document using the <META> tag. The contents of the <META> tag are added to the header's meta-information that the server sends along with the HTTP response. During a client pull sequence, the browser reads this header information that instructs it to use your PC's internal clock to keep track of the time elapsed between pages retrieved. When the time has elapsed, the browser requests and displays the next page.

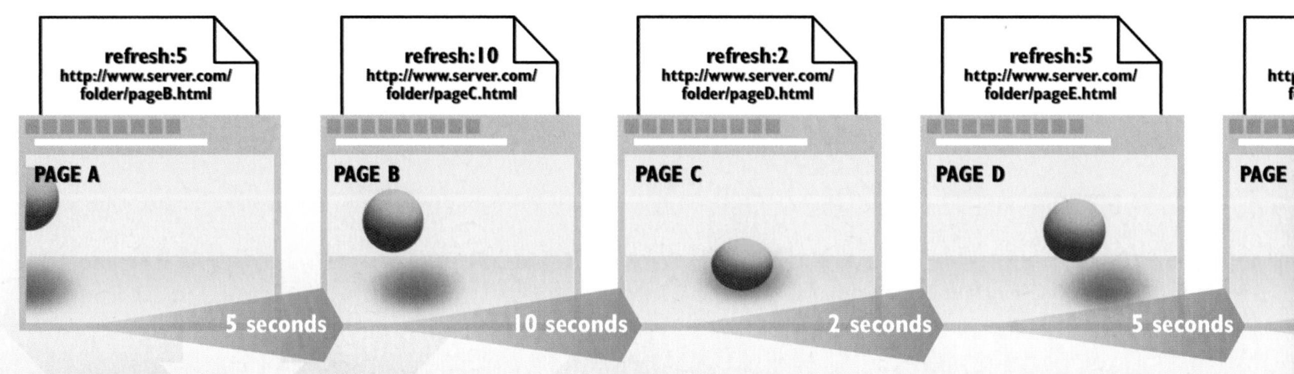

1. Each page in a client pull sequence can be located anywhere on the Web. The URL following the Refresh command might lead the browser to any active server. Page E is located on a different server than pages A–D, but is still requested automatically after five seconds.

2. If the next document to load also has a Refresh command in the header, the browser simply repeats the process. In this case, it retrieves and display page C after 10 seconds.

3. Whoever writes the HTML source code can specify how long it will be until the request for the next page is made. Page C refreshes after only 2 seconds, and page D follows.

4. The Refresh command does two things. First, it indicates the time before the next page request is sent or the same page reloads. For example, page A in the illustration refreshes after 5 seconds. Secondly, if the URL follows the number of seconds, a request for that page is sent automatically after 5 seconds. After the browser parses a document's meta-information and recognizes the Refresh command in the header, it knows to send a request for the page indicated by the URL following the command.

A client pull sequence might continue for as many or as few pages as the site designer wants. The last page will simply not have a Refresh command in the header. A user can stop the process manually by clicking the browser's Stop button.

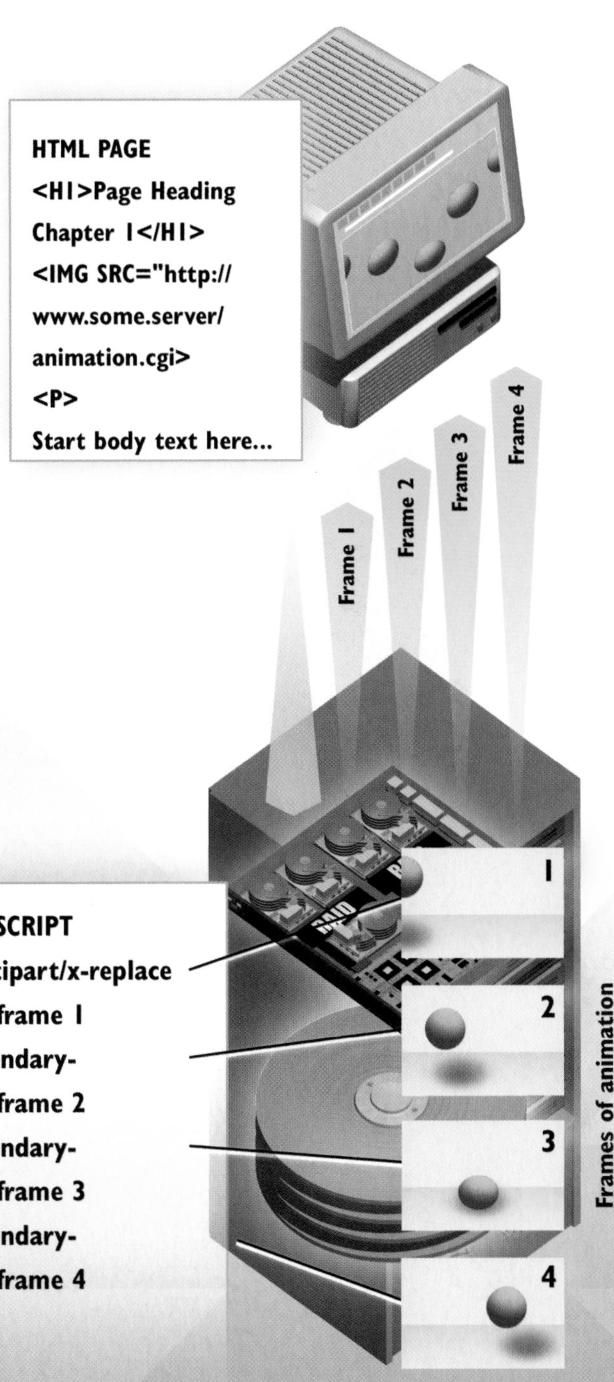

Server Push

Server push is more complicated than client pull, but it enables inline animation that does not require an entire Web page to load each animation frame.

1. The HTML source code for a server push animation is deceptively simple. The `<IMG>` (image) tag references the animation just like a static picture or icon.

2. When the browser recognizes the `<IMG>` tag, it makes a single request to the server for a file. But rather than retrieving an image file, the HTML reference tag `<IMG SCR=URL>` gives directions to a CGI script that runs the animation.

3. When the request arrives at the server, the CGI script is opened and executed. (Recall that a programmer must write a CGI script—similar to authoring other kinds of software.)

4. The CGI script takes advantage of the `multipart/x-mixed-replace` MIME type. This enables the CGI script to send, or push, a series of still images from the server to the client as if it were transferring a single file. In this illustration, the animation has four frames, and each frame is a separate file. Each new frame that arrives at the client replaces the old one, which gives the illusion of fluid movement.

The server and client make one connection that is open for as long as the CGI script runs. You can manually end a server push animation by clicking the browser's Stop button.

How Shockwave Works

1 The first step in a Shockwave animation happens in a multimedia-authoring program such as Director or Authorware. An animation designer must gather the raw materials, such as still images, music, and sound effects, necessary for a short and compelling animation.

2 The authoring program then helps arrange the elements frame by frame along a time line. It also enables the designer to match a sound effect with a particular action in the animation.

Director Software from Macromedia

4 Next, the movie file must be converted and compressed into a small file that can be quickly downloaded to a user's PC.

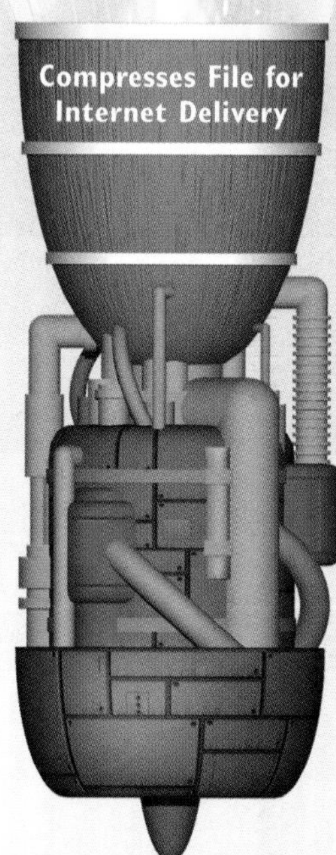

Converts Director File to Shockwave File

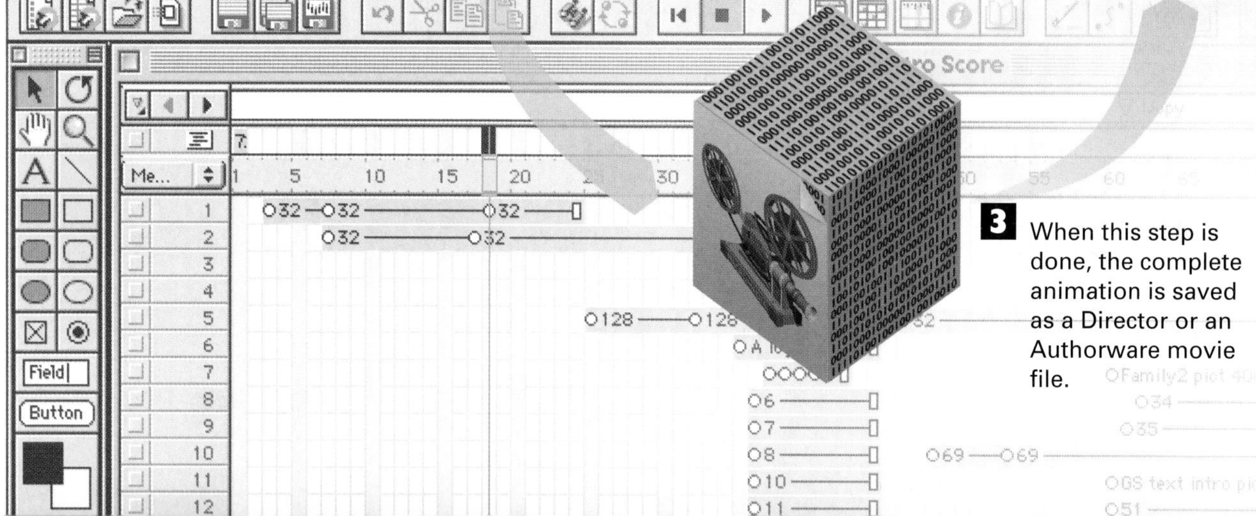

3 When this step is done, the complete animation is saved as a Director or an Authorware movie file.

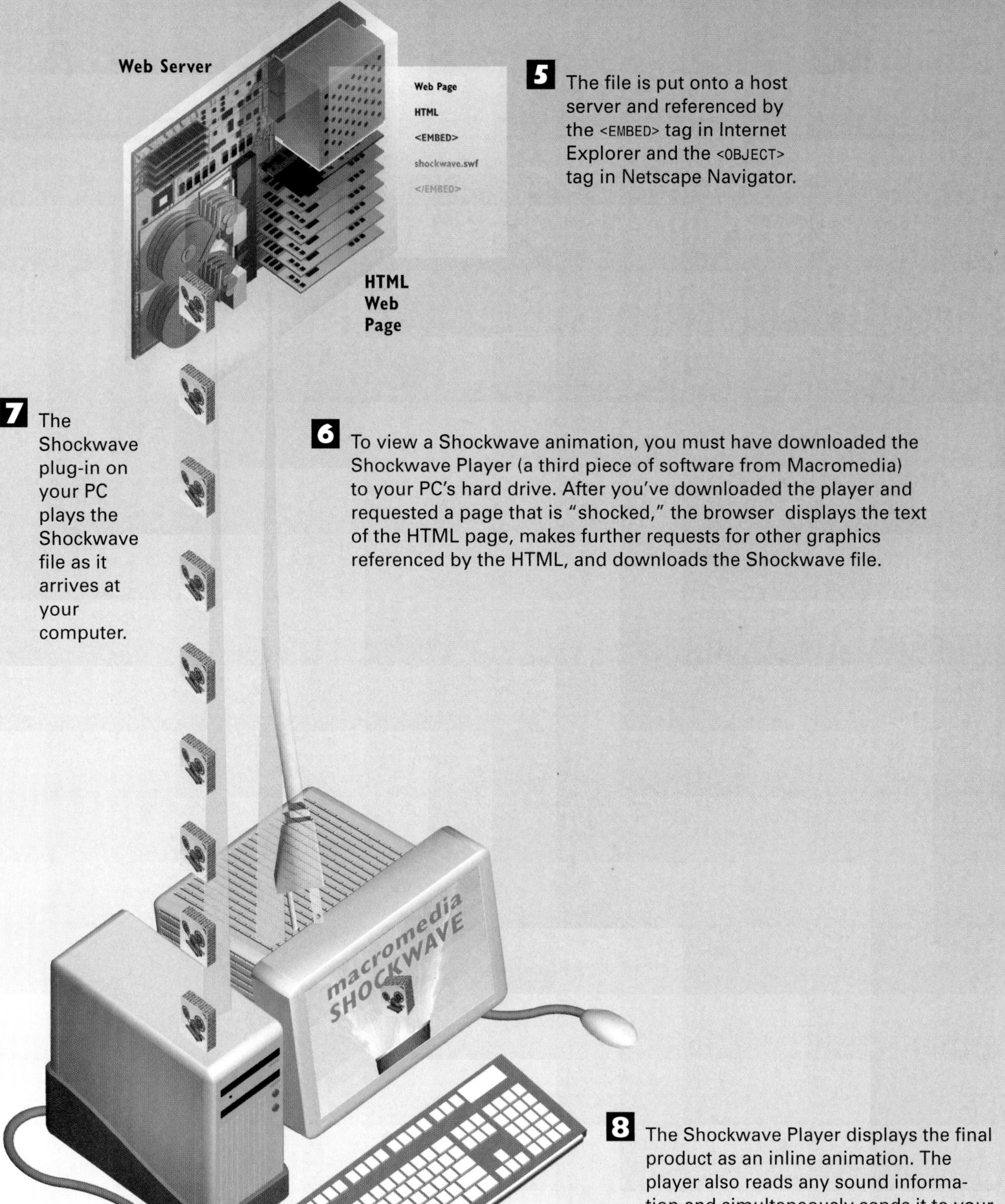

5 The file is put onto a host server and referenced by the <EMBED> tag in Internet Explorer and the <OBJECT> tag in Netscape Navigator.

6 To view a Shockwave animation, you must have downloaded the Shockwave Player (a third piece of software from Macromedia) to your PC's hard drive. After you've downloaded the player and requested a page that is "shocked," the browser displays the text of the HTML page, makes further requests for other graphics referenced by the HTML, and downloads the Shockwave file.

7 The Shockwave plug-in on your PC plays the Shockwave file as it arrives at your computer.

8 The Shockwave Player displays the final product as an inline animation. The player also reads any sound information and simultaneously sends it to your PC's audio hardware. Shockwave closes when it is no longer needed.

How Flash Works

1 Flash is an animation program that enables designers to add animation, sound, and interactivity to Web pages. Flash uses vector graphics instead of bit-mapped graphics. *Vector graphics* are mathematical descriptions of a shape, while a *bit-mapped* image is an actual pixel-by-pixel representation of the image. Not only are vector graphics smaller and more suitable to the Web because of reduced download time than bit-mapped images, but, unlike bit-mapped graphics, they can also be zoomed in on without any degradation in quality.

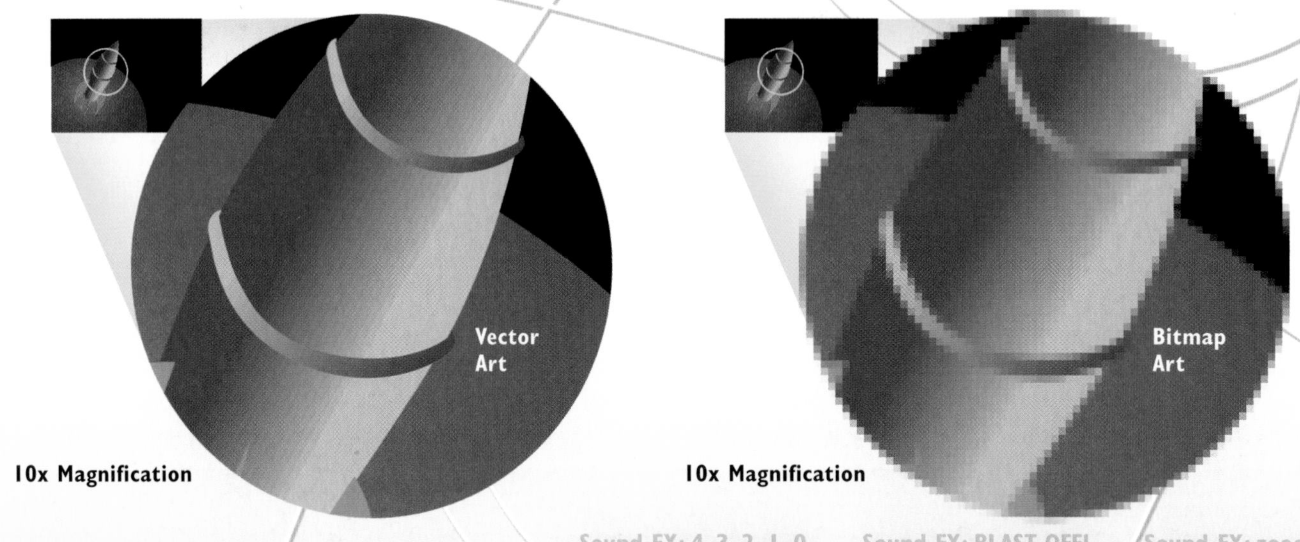

2 To create a Flash movie, a designer uses traditional animation techniques. He draws a picture in a frame, draws another picture slightly different than the first, then a third slightly different from the second, and so on.

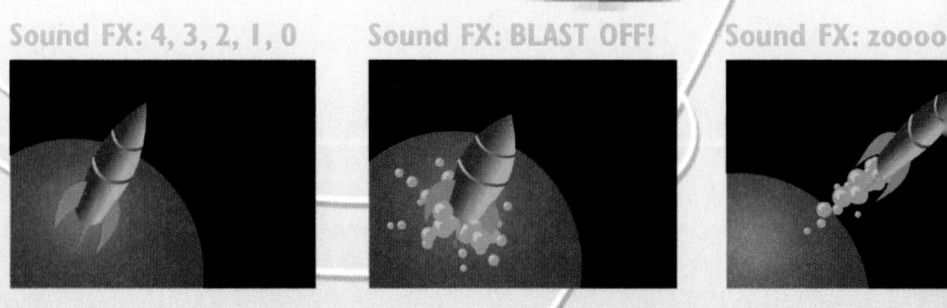

The art can change between frames with sound effects and more!

3 These pictures are all places on a Flash timeline and are displayed one after another—appearing to move. The animator has control over the speed at which the frames replace one another, or *frame rate*.

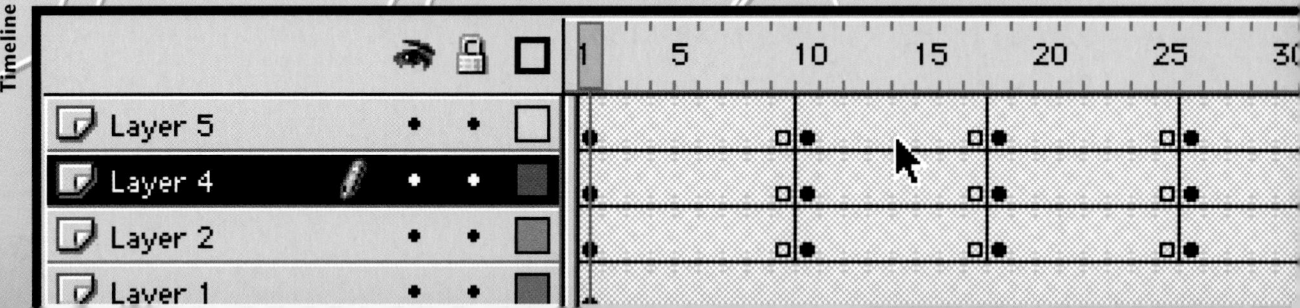

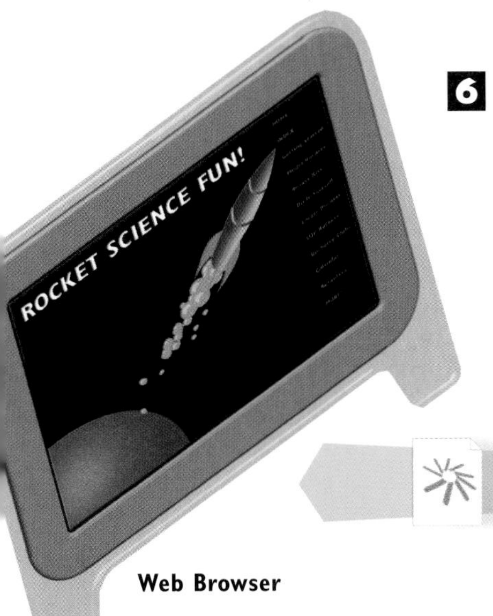

Web Browser

6 When someone visits a site with an HTML reference to the .swf file, the Flash movie begins to play. If the person doesn't have the Flash player, he is prompted to download it for free from the Macromedia site. The movie begins to play. A big benefit of Flash is that it *streams content*, which means that the movie can begin playing while the rest of the movie downloads in the background. This means that Flash movies can start playing very quickly even if they are very long ones.

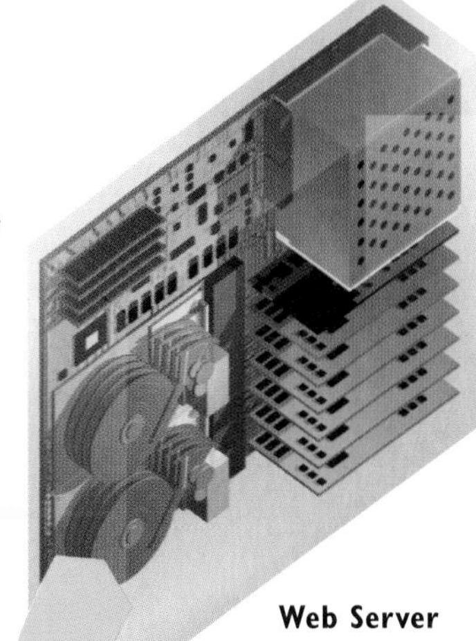
Web Server

5 When a designer finishes making a movie, it is compiled into a file with an .swf format and posted on a Web site. Anyone who views it needs a Flash player, which is available for free and is bundled into many versions of browsers.

Flash .swf File

Tool Bar

4 The timeline is used not just for images, but for sounds as well. To play sounds at specific times, the animator drops the sound into the timeline. The Flash movie can also include links to Web pages, JavaScript commands, and other kinds of interactivity. Again, all these are dropped into a timeline.

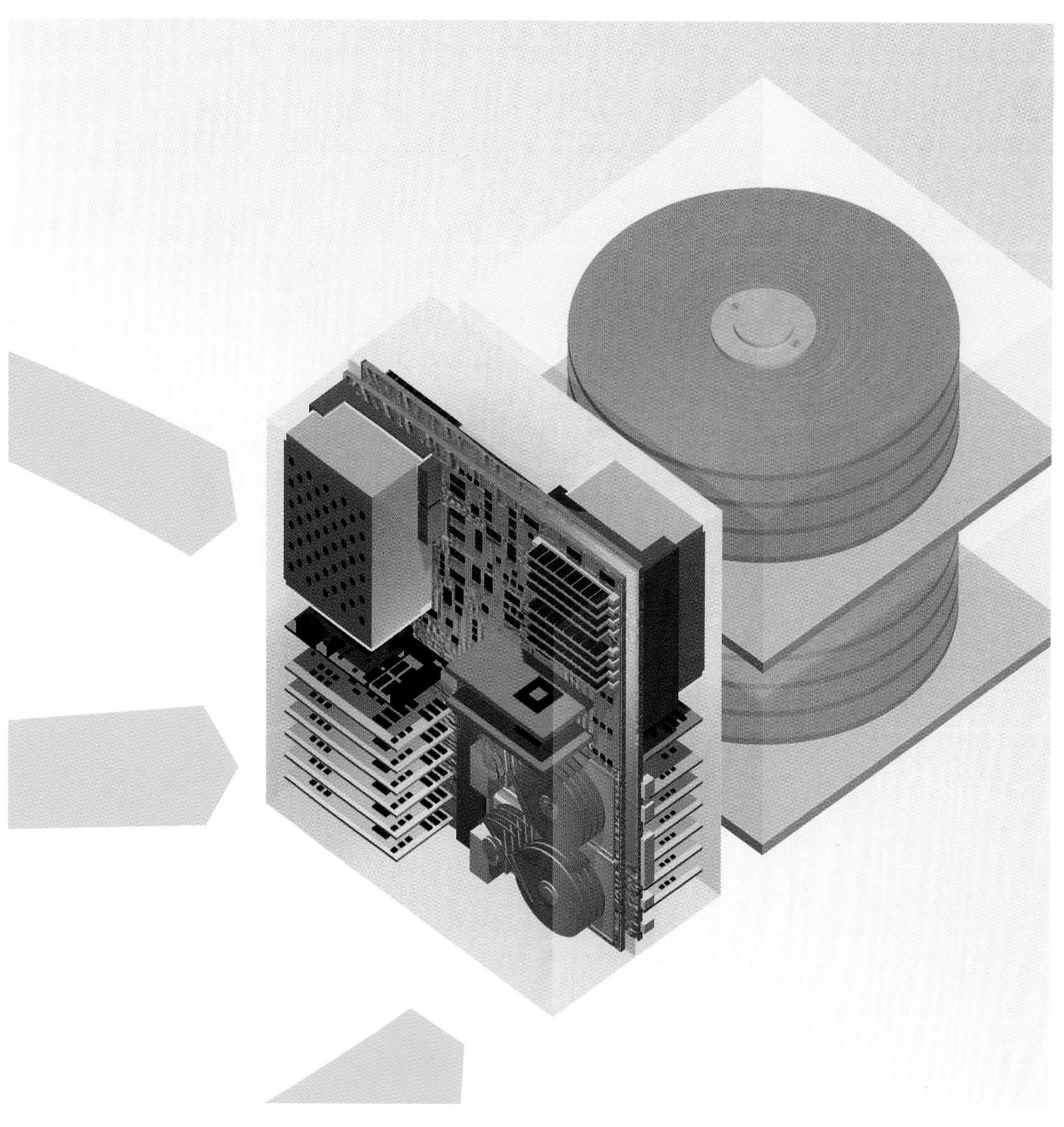

P A R T

SHOPPING AND DOING BUSINESS ON THE INTERNET

THE Internet is no longer a self-enclosed club with no connection to the outside world. It has become intimately tied to the way we live and work, and it will become more so with each passing year. At work, for entertainment, to get information, and to shop—the Internet is increasingly becoming a part of our daily lives.

The Internet might have its roots in the military and in academia, but its dramatic growth has been fueled in large part by business and consumers. The Internet might become one of the primary places in which businesses operate, and where hundreds of billions of dollars in goods and services will be bought and sold every year. In fact, already billions of dollars are spent every year in online shopping, and the use of the Internet has become a way of life at just about every business in the country.

Thousands of businesses use the Internet to market and sell their products, and many people buy things from home and from their places of business through the Internet instead of at retail stores. You can use the Internet to browse through catalogs and make purchases online; to buy and sell stock, mortgages, and insurance; and even to participate in online auctions. Companies are figuring out ways not only to sell online, but also to hook those online transactions into their internal computer and billing systems.

This part of the book looks at the various ways the Internet is used for business and shopping online. It covers how the Internet is being used by businesses as their primary corporate networks and how business and commerce are being conducted on the Internet every day.

Chapter 42, "How Intranets Work," covers intranets. Intranets are private networks set up by companies for their employees, using Internet technology. They're used for many purposes, including e-mail, group brainstorming, group scheduling, and access to corporate databases and documents, among others.

Although intranets use TCP/IP networks and technologies, the network and its resources are used only by the businesses and are not available to people outside the company. Intranets are separated from the Internet by firewalls that don't allow unauthorized access to the intranet. People who work in the company can access the intranet and use its resources, but intruders are kept out by the firewalls.

This chapter also looks at one of the most important parts of an intranet—workgroup software. This type of software ties together everyone in a corporation and enables them to work together better. Among other things, it enables people to share files and information; to cooperate more easily on projects; and in general, to work together in ways never before possible. It allows people to go beyond simply communicating and enables them to work together on shared documents.

This chapter also examines a variety of workgroup software. It covers messaging software that enables people to publicly participate in group discussions. It also looks at whiteboard software, which enables people to see what is on other people's computers and work together on documents. Several people could look at a spreadsheet together, for example, and one person could mark up the spreadsheet while everyone else sees what is being done.

Chapter 43, "Shopping on the Internet," covers what has become one of the most popular parts of the Internet—shopping online. Today, shopping on the Internet accounts for billions of dollars a year in revenue, and every year many more billions are spent. In fact, you can't turn on your television set or open a newspaper or magazine without being confronted by advertising for a variety of online shopping sites. Although many of the original shopping sites have gone out of business, they've been replaced by the very businesses they expected to supplant—existing retailers. So, today you'll find stores such as the Gap and Wal-Mart—so called bricks-and-mortar stores, or bricks-and-clicks—with big online shopping sites.

This chapter shows you what's going on behind the scenes when you shop online. It shows you how online shopping carts work—a technology that lets you gather together goods you're thinking of buying into a virtual shopping cart and then go through a checkout with them and pay by credit card. This chapter also details one of the newer and more intriguing shopping technologies—eWallets. When you use an eWallet, you don't need to put in personal and credit card information on the various sites where you shop; you just fill out the information once, in your eWallet, and that information is automatically sent to the shopping site when you want. Finally, this chapter covers one of the most popular ways to shop online—buying at online auctions. Every day, millions of people buy and sell millions of items through auction sites, such as the popular eBay, and through a variety of auctions powered by technology developed by a company called FairMarket. You'll see, in this chapter, how technology enables auctions to work.

CHAPTER 42 How Intranets Work

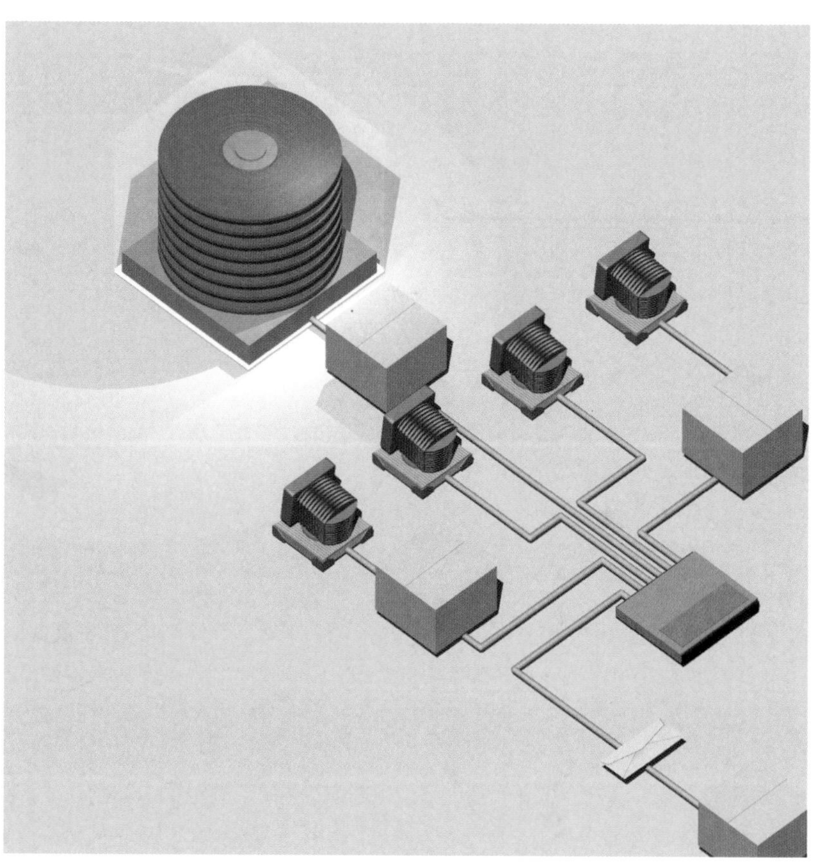

BUSINESSES increasingly use Internet technology to create private corporate networks called *intranets*. These intranets are used for a wide variety of purposes, such as e-mail, group brainstorming, group scheduling, access to corporate databases and documents, videoconferencing, and the buying and selling goods and services.

Intranets use TCP/IP networks and technologies as well as Internet resources such as the World Wide Web, e-mail, Telnet, and FTP. However, the network and its resources are used privately by businesses and are not available to people outside the company. An intranet is separated from the rest of the Internet by a *firewall*—a hardware and software combination that prohibits unauthorized access to the intranet. People who work in the company can access the Internet and use its resources, but firewalls keep out intruders. Turn to Chapter 44, "How Firewalls Work," to learn more about firewalls.

Intranets use a combination of off-the-shelf software, such as Web browsers, and customized software, such as database querying tools. Because intranets are based on Internet standard protocols, it will always be possible to quickly update them with the latest in network technologies.

In the long term, companies will make the most use of intranets in *workgroup applications*—software that enables people to work cooperatively with their computers. Many kinds of workgroup software exist. These programs enable people to participate in discussions and videoconferencing across the country and across the world, share databases, track documents, and much more.

The key to workgroup software is that it enables people to go beyond simply communicating and lets them work together on shared documents.

One of the most basic pieces of workgroup software is *messaging software*—programs that enable people to publicly participate in group discussions.

What makes intranet messaging software especially useful is the way it integrates with other Internet and intranet technologies. For example, some discussion software allows the use of Hypertext Markup Language (HTML) embedded inside messages. This means that from within a discussion, someone could embed a link to a Web page or other intranet resource.

A more sophisticated workgroup application is *desktop videoconferencing*. This application requires that everyone involved have computer-linked video cameras as well as hardware and software that enables computers to send and receive voice and sound. While sitting at computers, people can see and speak to one another.

A related technology is called whiteboard software. *Whiteboard software* lets people see what is on someone else's computer on an intranet while sitting at their own computers. This means people on the same intranet—whether they're on opposite sides of the country from one another—can easily comment on one another's work.

Document management software and workflow groupware are useful for intranets in companies that have complicated work procedures, or where many people must cooperatively put together a single document. These types of software streamline the way that work flows through a company and enable businesses to operate much more efficiently.

Using an Intranet Within a Company

1 An intranet is separated from the rest of the Internet by a *firewall*—a hardware/software combination that protects the corporate intranet from snooping eyes and malicious attacks. The firewall enables corporate employees to use the Internet and also enables certain parts of the intranet—such as areas designed for electronic commerce—to be accessed by outsiders.

2 A key component of an intranet is an internal e-mail system. The e-mail system works just like Internet e-mail. It can use normal Internet e-mail clients, but it is designed to route traffic within an organization, so the e-mail need not travel outside the intranet. Internal routers and mail servers send the mail to other corporate employees via the intranet. E-mail that travels to and from the Internet from the intranet must go through the firewall.

3 Corporate databases with important information can be made available over the intranet via Web-based HTML documents and search tools. Typically, searching those databases will require the creation of CGI scripts or Java programs. These databases will be available only to corporate employees, and like the rest of the intranet, the firewall protects them.

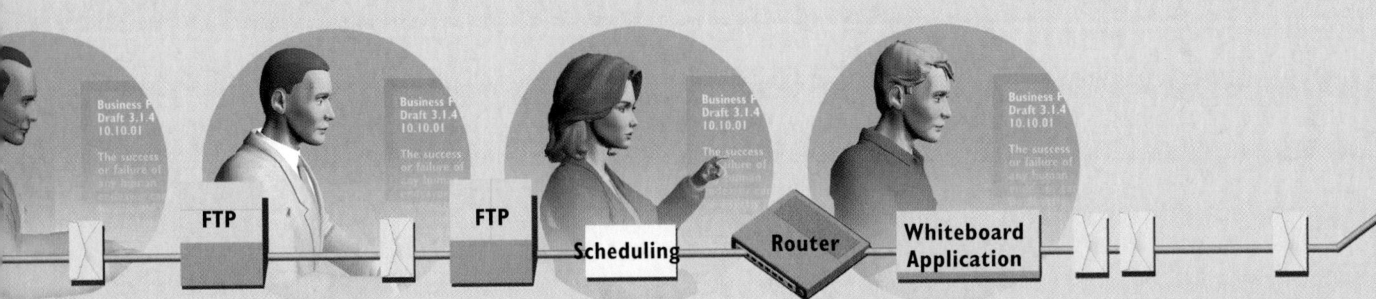

4 An intranet enables people to collaborate on their work electronically using groupware. *Groupware* enables people to have online brainstorming sessions, schedule group meetings, work on documents and plans together, create common databases, and perform other kinds of cooperative work.

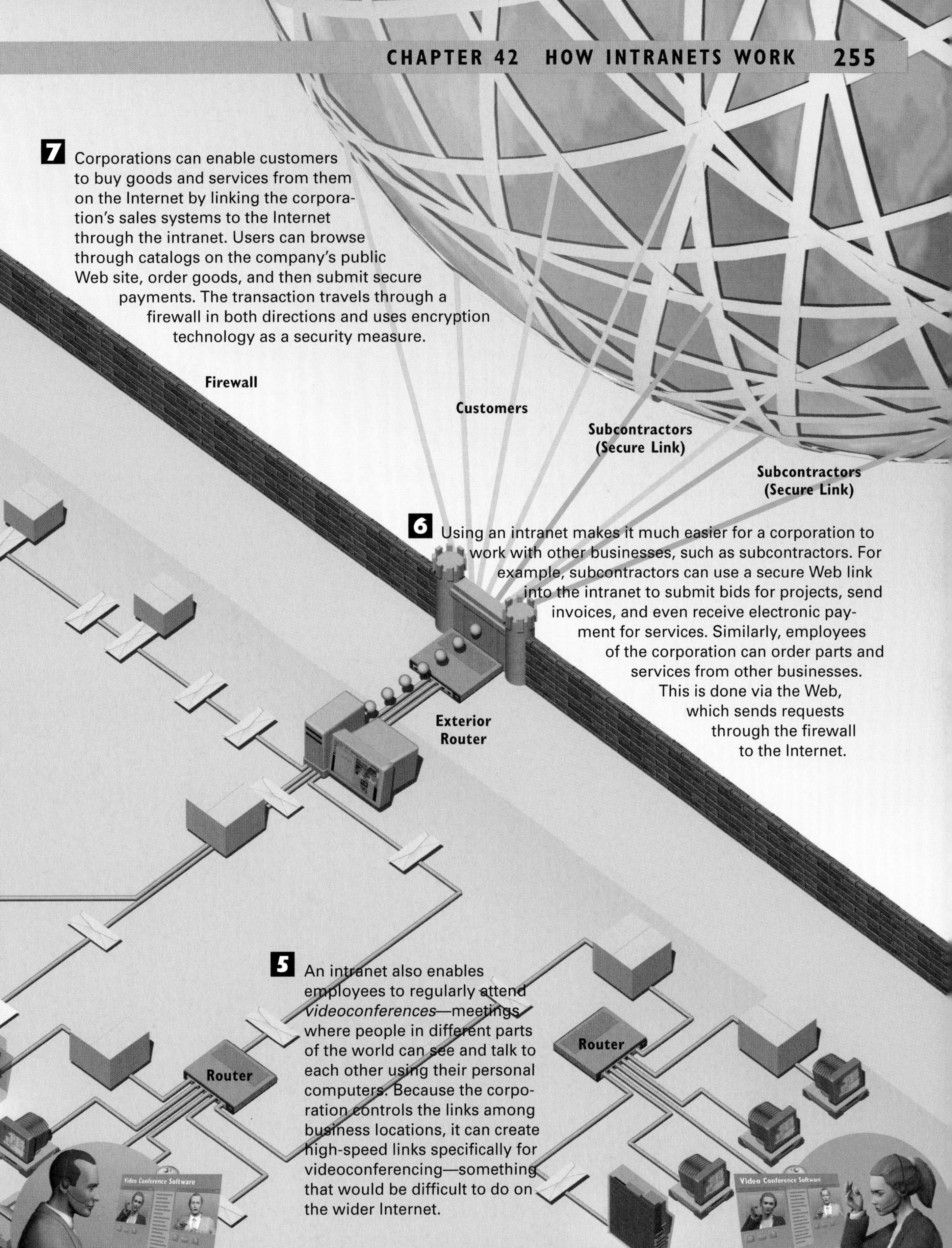
7 Corporations can enable customers to buy goods and services from them on the Internet by linking the corporation's sales systems to the Internet through the intranet. Users can browse through catalogs on the company's public Web site, order goods, and then submit secure payments. The transaction travels through a firewall in both directions and uses encryption technology as a security measure.
Firewall
Customers
Subcontractors (Secure Link)
Subcontractors (Secure Link)
6 Using an intranet makes it much easier for a corporation to work with other businesses, such as subcontractors. For example, subcontractors can use a secure Web link into the intranet to submit bids for projects, send invoices, and even receive electronic payment for services. Similarly, employees of the corporation can order parts and services from other businesses. This is done via the Web, which sends requests through the firewall to the Internet.
Exterior Router
5 An intranet also enables employees to regularly attend videoconferences—meetings where people in different parts of the world can see and talk to each other using their personal computers. Because the corporation controls the links among business locations, it can create high-speed links specifically for videoconferencing—something that would be difficult to do on the wider Internet.
Router
Router
Video Conference Software
Video Conference Software

How Workgroup Software Works

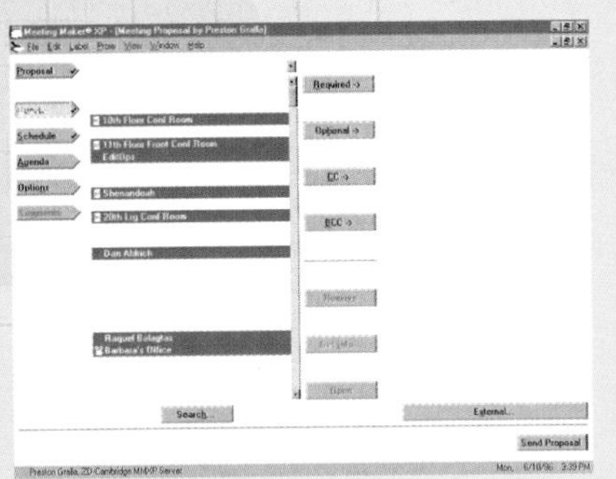

1 Discussion software enables people from within a corporation to exchange work and ideas. Links to other intranet resources are included in the software. From within a discussion, people can link out to a Web page on the Internet or intranet, or even link into intranet databases, servers, or shared applications. Additionally, software can replicate intranet discussions onto Internet newsgroups. From one discussion area, people on an intranet can hold discussions with people from within their company or people out on the Internet.

2 Document management software and workflow groupware enable intranet administrators to create systems that track and control access to documents through every aspect of their creation—for example, allowing only one person at a time to check a document out of a library. They can provide a *version history* of every document so anyone can see who has worked on a document along with the changes that person made. The administrators can also give certain people the right to lock the document so no further changes are allowed.

Whiteboard Software

5 Whiteboard applications will be a popular workgroup use of intranets. In a *whiteboard application*, two or more people can see and talk about what is on each other's computer screens across the intranet. Additionally, they can mark up what is displayed on each other's screens.

4 With intranet groupware, videoconferencing can finally be a corporate reality. Desktop-conferencing software enables two or more people to see and talk to each other on their computer screens as long as they have cameras connected to sound-equipped computers. Because intranets can be built using very high bandwidth connections, having a videoconference across an intranet is possible, although doing so across the Internet can be much more difficult because of the lower bandwidth of the Internet.

Video Conferencing

Desk-to-Desk Chat

3 Groupware can allow for desk-to-desk chats. People can sit at their computers and directly communicate with others sitting at their computers by typing on their keyboards. What one person types at the keyboard shows up on another person's computer screen and vice versa.

CHAPTER 43 Shopping on the Internet

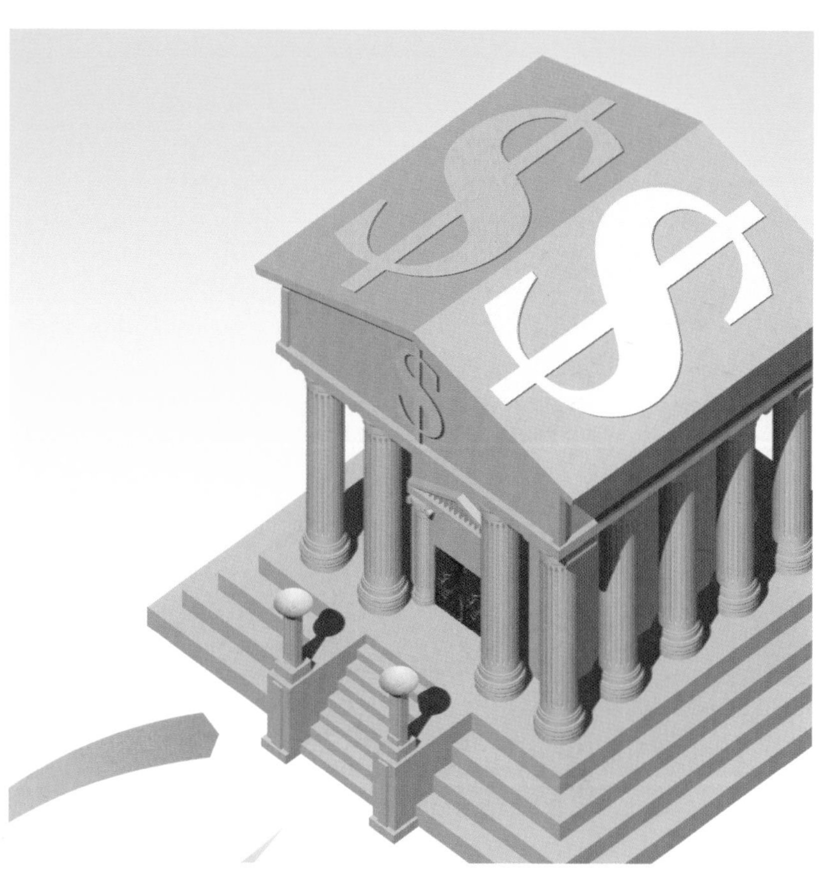

BILLIONS of dollars are spent every year shopping on the Internet—and if think tanks and market research firms are to be believed, that's only the beginning. The Internet will eventually revolutionize shopping in the same way it's revolutionized working, getting information, and communicating.

Online shopping is possible through the use of *encryption techniques*—the ability to scramble information as it's sent through the Internet so that no one can read it except the intended recipient. Encryption is used to scramble credit card information—the primary way that people pay when buying online. (For more information about encryption, and to see how encryption works, turn to Chapter 48, "Cryptography, Privacy, and Digital Certificates." To see how encryption can keep e-mail private, turn to Chapter 16, "How E-mail Works.")

Most of what you see when you visit a shopping site on the Internet is contained in databases on Web servers. These databases have information about the products for sale at the site—and they're also used to automatically generate the HTML pages that make up the shopping site. So, for example, when a new product becomes available, information about that product is put into a database, and CGI scripts and a Web server then work with the database to create a new item on a Web page describing the product. You, in turn, can look at that product and decide whether you want to buy it.

Databases and cookies are also used when you use *virtual shopping carts*—portions of a Web site where you place items you're considering buying. Before buying, you can take items out of the cart or can put new items in. *Cookies* track everything you put into and take out of the cart, and then *databases* work with the cookies, CGI scripts, and Web servers to complete the transaction when you want to buy something.

Web databases are also used to complete the shopping transaction when you buy. When you decide you want to buy something from a site, fill out a form, and send in your credit card information, that information is sent to a Web database. The database, in turn, checks the validity of your credit card. If it's valid, the database sends a confirmation to you and then sends off an order to a warehouse or other distribution method that ships the product to you. Databases can't do all this by themselves—they work in concert with CGI scripts, Web servers, and cookies.

This chapter looks at how online buying and virtual shopping carts work. This chapter also examines one of the newer shopping technologies—electronic wallets, or *ewallets*. Finally, you'll see how one of the most popular kinds of buying sites work—*online auctions*.

How Online Buying Works

1 Most shopping sites are built on top of databases, so when customers visit a Web site and browse or search for a product, they're actually searching through a database that is searched from the Web.

Product Listing

- VCRs
- Digital Cameras
- Video Cameras
- CD Players
- Printers
- Monitors

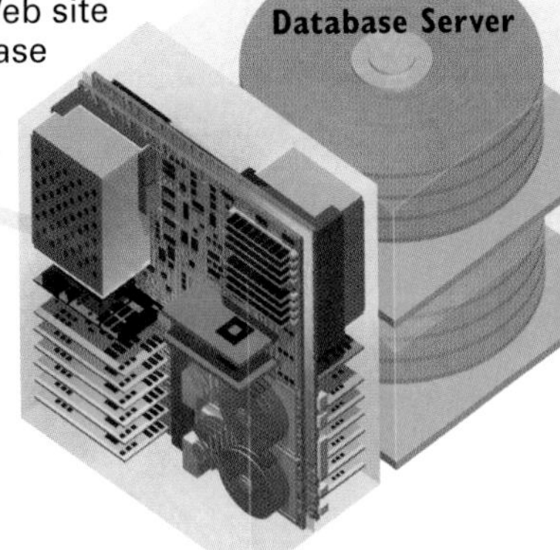

2 When customers see a product they want to buy, they'll usually pay by credit card. Before filling out a form with their credit card information, they're usually sent to a secure section of the Web site where encryption will be used to scramble the data.

6 The site confirms the order, and using CGI scripts, the Web page refreshes and displays a page that the customer can print out to confirm the order. Many sites also follow up by sending an e-mail message.

Thank you for your order.

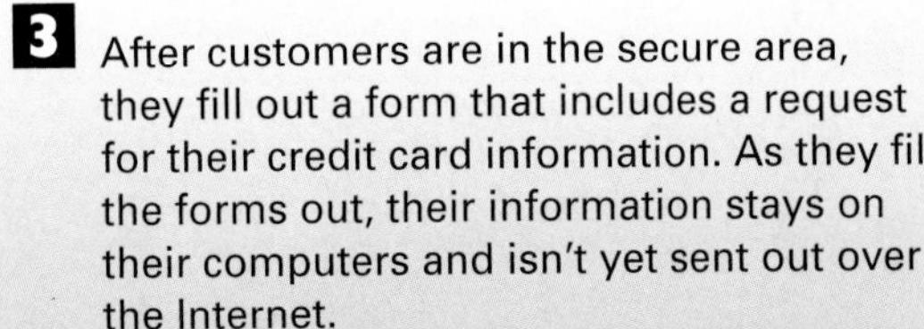

3 After customers are in the secure area, they fill out a form that includes a request for their credit card information. As they fill the forms out, their information stays on their computers and isn't yet sent out over the Internet.

5 The transaction server receives the encrypted information and decrypts it. It then checks with the credit card company to ensure that the card is valid and can be used, in a similar way to how a retail stores checks that your card is valid, except that it's usually done over the Internet.

Transaction Server

4 When the form is filled out, the customer clicks a Submit button, or something similar, to send the information from the customer's computer to the site's secure transaction server. As the information is sent out over the Internet, it's encrypted so that it's nearly impossible to read, except by the site itself.

Ok to accept?

OK

Ok to ship the goods.

7 The transaction server sends an order to the warehouse or other designated area that fills the order, and the order is completed as any other order is, by shipping via the mail or express mail service.

How Online Shopping Carts Work

2 When the person completes the registration form, it's sent to the Web database. The database creates a record for that person and sends the person a *cookie*—a small piece of data that sits on the person's hard disk and can be used to identify that person.

Cookie

4 The Web server in turn writes a new piece of data to the cookie, which identifies the item that the person wants to put in his shopping cart. More than one item can be put in the shopping cart in this way.

Change Cookie

ID#57329810
BUY ITEMS:
ID#10394
ID#794201

Ready

5 When the person is ready to check out his items, he goes to a Web page containing his shopping cart. When he goes to the page, the cookie tells the Web server what items to display on the page.

Before a shopping cart can be used, a person must register with the site by filling out such information as name, address, and other personal information. Sometimes a credit card number is required as well.

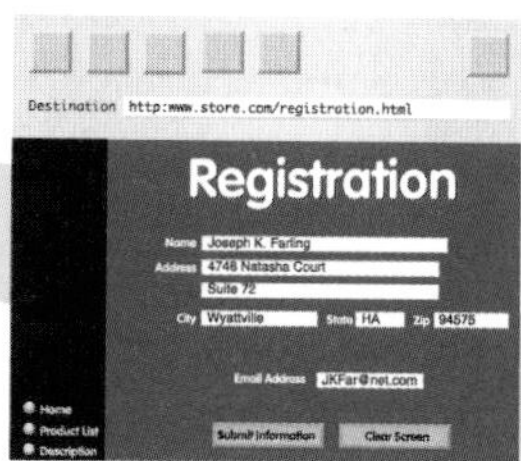

3 When the shopper thinks he wants to buy something, he clicks it, which puts it in his shopping cart. When he clicks an item, that information is sent to the Web server.

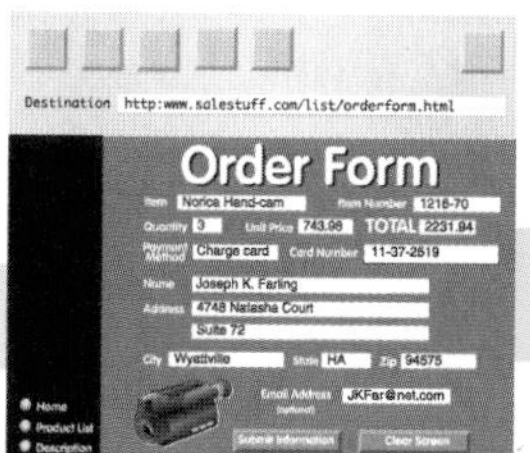

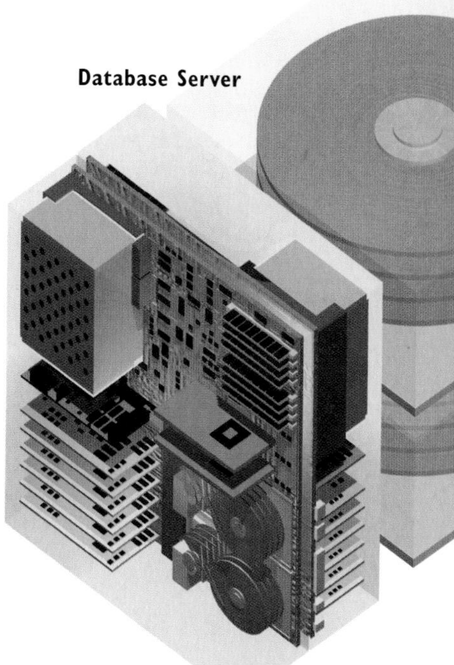

6 When someone decides to buy the items in the shopping cart, he sends in credit card information. When the items are bought, the server updates information about those items in the cookie. When the person visits his shopping cart, it is empty because the information about his purchases was deleted from the cookie, or else the cookie was designed so that it would expire after a certain amount of time.

How Electronic Wallets Work

1 Electronic wallets enable you to store information about your credit cards and similar information so that you don't need to fill out forms every time you want to buy something from a Web site. This illustration shows how one called eWallet works. *eWallet* is a piece of client software that runs on your computer. (Some electronic wallets, though not eWallet, run on Internet servers.) Typically, people either download eWallet from an Internet site, or it might be sent to them when they sign up for a credit card. The first step to using eWallet is to download the software and install it.

2 After installing the software, you enter a username and password that must be used to access the eWallet. That way, no one else can get at your credit card information. After entering a username and password, you enter information about the credit cards you'll be using to pay online.

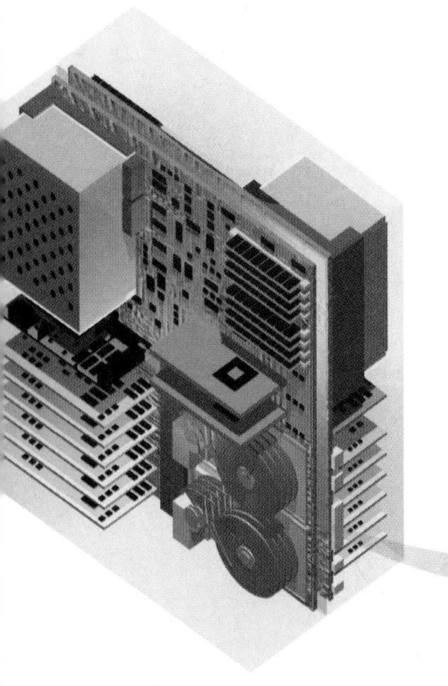

Web Server

Download Wallet

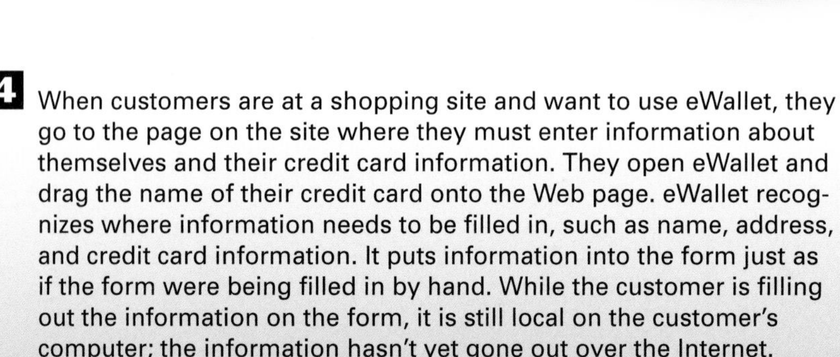

4 When customers are at a shopping site and want to use eWallet, they go to the page on the site where they must enter information about themselves and their credit card information. They open eWallet and drag the name of their credit card onto the Web page. eWallet recognizes where information needs to be filled in, such as name, address, and credit card information. It puts information into the form just as if the form were being filled in by hand. While the customer is filling out the information on the form, it is still local on the customer's computer; the information hasn't yet gone out over the Internet.

eWallet

3 All the information in the eWallet is encrypted and stored locally on the computer. That way, no one can get at the credit card and personal information except someone who has the user name and password for the eWallet.

Personal Data and Credit Card Info

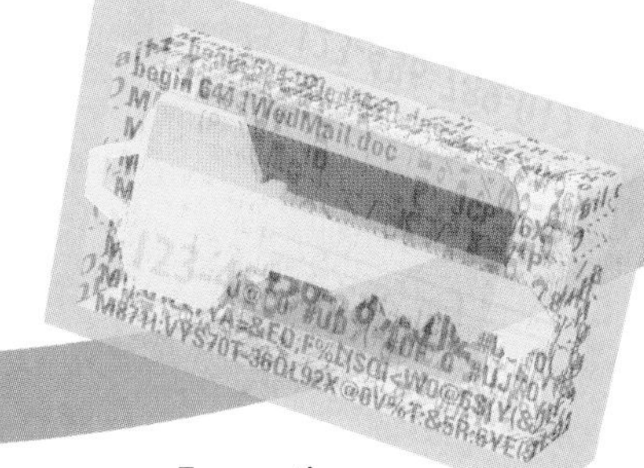

Encryption

Encryption

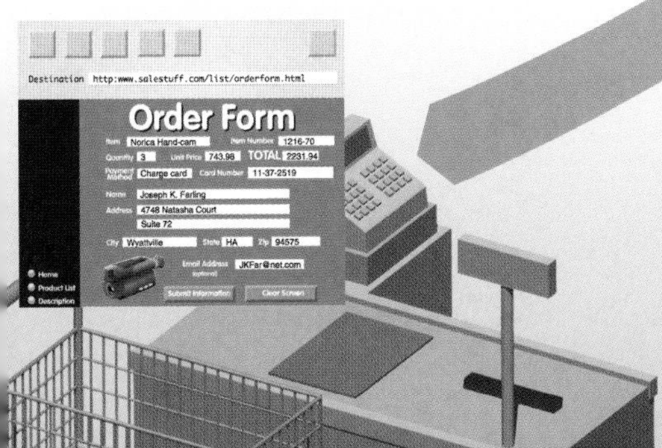

5 After the form is filled out, the customer clicks a button to place the order. As the credit card number and other information is sent over the Internet, it's encrypted by the shopping site so that no one can read it as it's sent. Only when the encrypted information is received by the shopping site can it be read.

How Online Auctions Work

Register Me

1 Before someone can put something up for sale or bid on an item, he has to register by filling out a form on the auction site. When he fills out that form, the information from the form is sent to the auction site's database, which creates a unique record for that person.

Will sell antique watch.

2 When the person wants to put an item up for sale, the site checks whether he's registered. This can be done via a piece of information put on the person's computer called a *cookie*. It can also be done by asking the person to enter his username and password. When the site confirms the person is registered, the person puts an item up for sale by filling out a form detailing the item to be put on sale. When he does this, a new record is created in the auction site's database.

3 A program or script takes information from the database and automatically creates a Web page on the auction site, which describes the item up for sale and information about it. The Web page is now available to anyone on the auction site looking to bid on an auction.

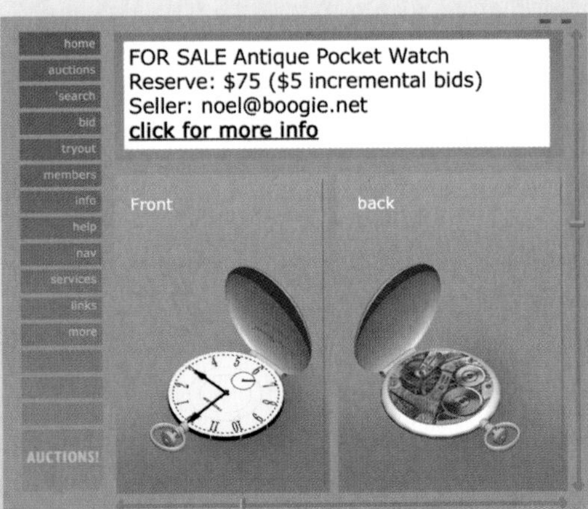

6 When the auction closes, the database checks to see which bidder has the highest bid. The database automatically sends an e-mail to the highest bidder notifying him that he has won and giving him contact information for the seller. The database also sends an e-mail to the person selling the item that gives the seller the name and contact information for the highest bidder. After the bidder and seller have each other's contact information, it's up to them to finish the sale. Payment and delivery of the goods are usually arranged privately between the seller and the highest bidder with no input from the auction site. However, at some sites, the auction site itself does the selling, and people pay the site directly.

5 The Web page describing the auction is again automatically updated—by scripting or similar technology—to reflect the new bid. New bidders keep coming in and adding new bids. Every time a new bid is placed, the database is updated, and the page is updated so that the newest information is always available.

4 When someone sees the item and wants to bid on it, he makes his bid by filling out a form. When he fills out the form, it updates the auction record in the database.

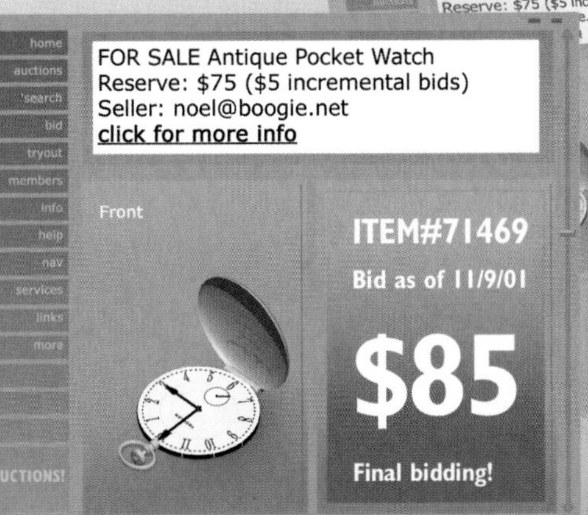

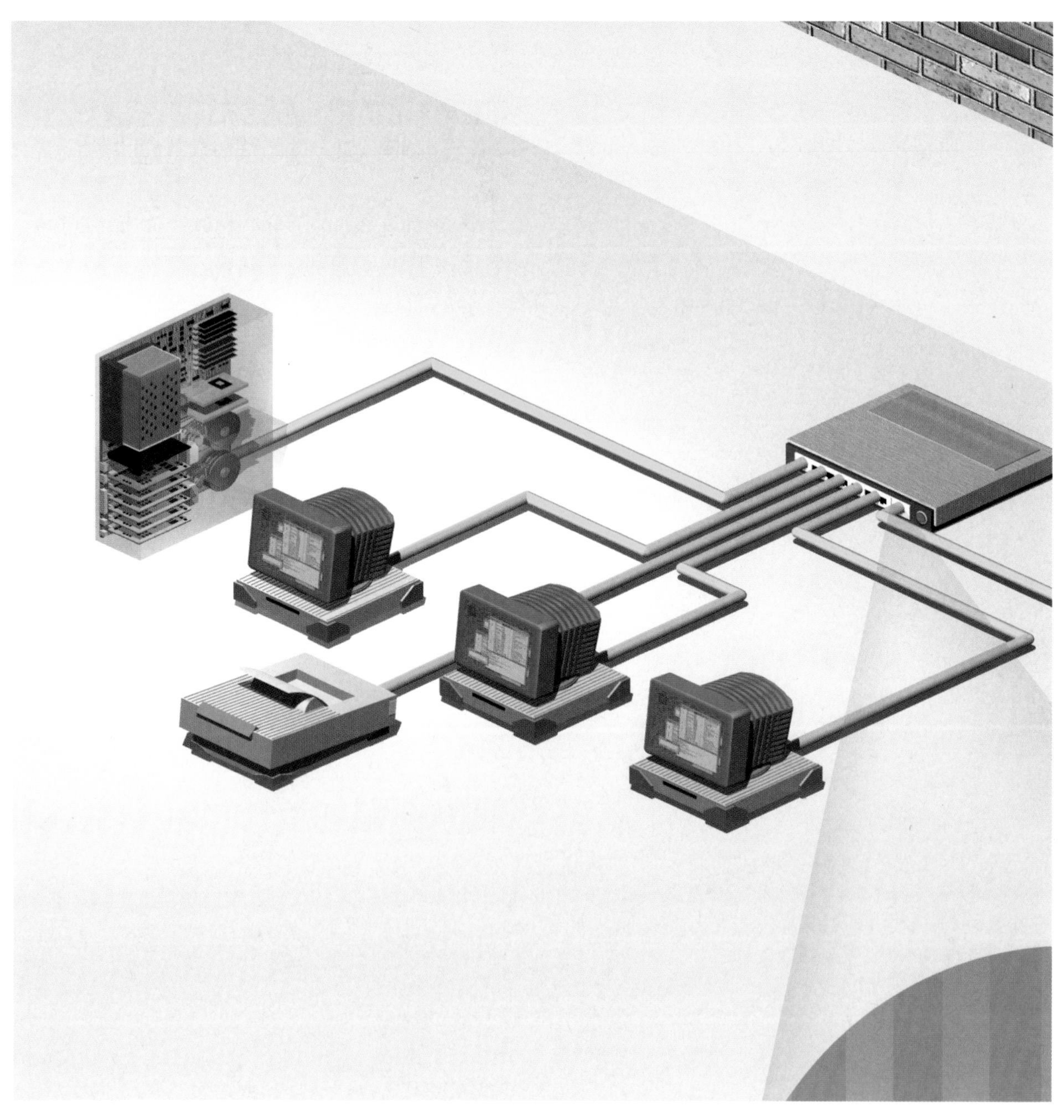

P A R T

PROTECTING YOURSELF ON THE INTERNET

THE very nature of the Internet makes it vulnerable to attack. It was designed to allow for the freest possible exchange of information, data, and files—and it has succeeded admirably, far beyond its designers' wildest expectations. However, that freedom carries a price: Hackers and virus writers try to attack the Internet and computers connected to the Internet; those who want to invade others' privacy attempt to crack databases of sensitive information or snoop on information as it travels across Internet routes; and distasteful and pornographic sites have sprung up on the Web and on Usenet newsgroups.

This section of the book looks at a variety of security-related issues. You'll see how various tools have been developed to make transactions on the Net more secure and to help companies protect their sensitive data. You'll examine the thorny issue of pornography versus free speech and see how software can block children from visiting obscene sites or getting obscene materials. You'll also learn about some of the more controversial technologies on the Internet, such as cookies, which enable Web servers to track you as you move through their sites. This section also takes an inside look at an even more controversial technology, the FBI's Carnivore program, which enables the federal government to do things such as read the private mail of people it's investigating. You'll also look at how viruses work and how hackers attack Internet service providers (ISPs).

Chapter 44, "How Firewalls Work," looks at firewalls. Many companies whose networks are connected to the Internet have a great deal of sensitive information on their networks and want to ensure that their data and computers are safe from attack. The answer is to use firewalls—systems that allow people from inside a company to use the Internet but also stop people on the Internet from getting at the company's computers. This chapter also discusses personal firewalls—software people can use at home to ensure that hackers can't invade their own computers.

Chapter 45, "How Hackers Can Cripple the Internet and Attack Your PC," looks at attacks launched by hackers that can cripple Internet service providers and attack your computer as well. In a smurf attack, also called *smurfing*, a hacker targets an ISP and floods it with so much "garbage" traffic that none of the ISP's customers can use the service. Smurfing is one of the most common types of hacking attacks on the Internet. This chapter also examines the various ways hackers can attack your PC.

Chapter 46, "How Viruses Work," looks at viruses and how they are detected. Any program you download from the Internet has the potential for being infected with a virus, and it could, in turn, infect your computer. You'll see just how these nasty data-killers work and look at antivirus tools that can detect and kill them. This chapter also examines how a special type of virus called a Trojan Horse works. Trojan Horse viruses are becoming increasingly common on the Internet, so you'll look at one of the most recent Trojan Horse viruses—Melissa—and how it affected the Internet. As of this writing, Melissa is the most famous Internet Trojan Horse of all time.

Chapter 47, "How Internet Sites Can Invade Your Privacy," explores controversial technologies that enable Web sites to track what you do when you're online. It covers cookies, Web tracking, and Web Bugs as well as a technology that can help preserve people's privacy—Internet passports. Some people worry that cookies and Web tracking can invade their privacy. Others disagree, saying that cookies and Web tracking can help customize the

Web to users' interests. Cookies are bits of data put on a hard disk when someone visits certain Web sites. That data can be used for many purposes. One common use is to make it easier for people to use Web sites that require a username and password by storing that information and then automatically sending the information whenever it's requested. Passports enable people to decide what type of information about them can be tracked by Web sites. Web tracking enables those who run Web sites to see how people use their sites. Web bugs are another technique for tracking people's Internet use.

Chapter 48, "Cryptography, Privacy, and Digital Certificates," examines cryptosystems and digital certificates. An enormous amount of information is sent across the Internet every day—everything from personal e-mail to corporate data to credit card information and other highly sensitive material. All that information is vulnerable to hackers and snoopers. Because the information is sent in packets along public routers, the possibility exists that someone could intercept and decipher it. As a way to ensure that the sensitive material can't be looked at, sophisticated cryptosystems have been developed so that only the sender and receiver know what's in the packets.

The chapter also looks at digital certificates. On the Internet, no face-to-face communication takes place, so knowing whether people really are who they say they are can be difficult. Digital certificates are used to absolutely identify someone. If someone sends you an e-mail, for example, a digital certificate will let you know that the person is who he says he is.

Chapter 49, "How the FBI's 'Carnivore' Program Works," details an extremely controversial program that enables the federal government to read people's e-mail and follow their Internet activity without people knowing about it.

Finally, Chapter 50, "Parental Controls on the Internet," takes a detailed look at the issues of pornography and free speech on the Internet. Explicit sexual material is posted on the Internet, and some people would like to fine and jail people and organizations that allow such material to be posted. Passing those types of laws raises a host of constitutional issues about free speech. As a way to solve the problem, companies create and sell software for parents that enables them to block their children from seeing obscene and violent material on the Internet. In this chapter, you'll see how one of the most popular pieces of parental control software works.

CHAPTER 44 How Firewalls Work

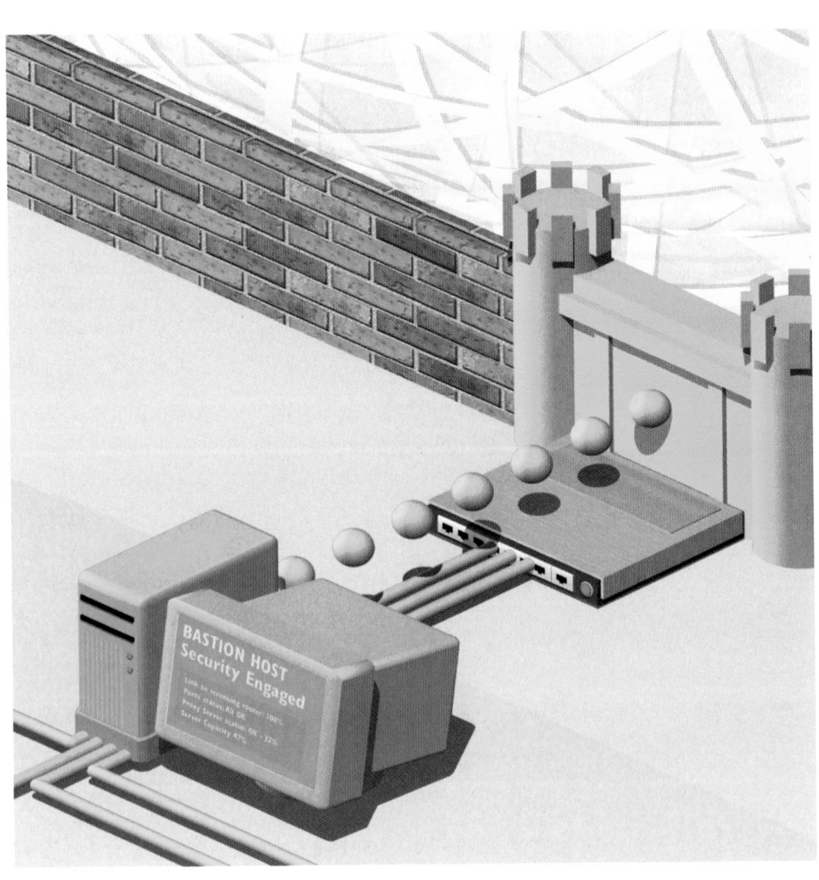

EVERY time a computer is connected to the Internet, it faces potential danger. Corporate Local Area Networks (LANs) connected to the Internet, as well as PCs at home—especially those connected to a high-speed cable modem or DSL modem—are likely targets for hackers.

Due to the Internet's openness, every corporate network connected to it is vulnerable to attack. Crackers on the Internet could theoretically break into the corporate network and do harm in a number of ways: They could steal or damage important data; damage individual computers or the entire network; use the corporate computer's resources; or use the corporate network and resources as a way of posing as a corporate employee. The solution isn't to cut off the network from the Internet. Instead, the company can build firewalls to protect its network. These firewalls enable anyone on the corporate network to access the Internet, but they stop crackers, hackers, and others on the Internet from gaining access to the corporate network and causing damage.

Corporate firewalls are hardware and software combinations that are built using routers, servers, and a variety of software. They sit at the most vulnerable point between a corporate network and the Internet and can be as simple or complex as system administrators want to build them.

One of the simplest kinds of firewalls utilizes packet filtering. In *packet filtering*, a screening router examines the header of every packet of data traveling between the Internet and the corporate network. Packet headers have information in them such as the IP address of the sender and receiver, the protocol being used to send the packet, and other similar information. Based on that information, the router knows what kind of Internet service—such as FTP or rlogin—is being used to send the data, as well as the identity of the sender and receiver of the data. (The command, rlogin, is similar to Telnet, which enables someone to log into a computer. It can be dangerous because it enables users to bypass having to type in a password.) After this information is determined, the router can bar certain packets from being sent between the Internet and the corporate network. For example, the router could block any traffic except for e-mail. Additionally, it could block traffic to and from suspicious destinations or from certain users.

Proxy servers are also commonly used in firewalls. A *proxy server* is server software that runs on a host in a firewall, such as a bastion host. Because only the single proxy server (instead of the many individual computers on the network) interacts with the Internet, security can be maintained. That single server can be kept more secure than can hundreds of individual computers on a network.

Home PCs connected to the Internet via high-speed cable modems or DSL modems are targets as well because if hackers can break into them, they can use them as launching pads for their attacks, while covering their tracks. *Personal firewalls* have become popular—software and hardware that sits on a home computer and protects the home computer in similar ways to how corporate firewalls protect corporate LANs.

How Firewalls Work

1. The *firewall* shields the internal corporate network from the Internet. The internal network works as networks normally do—servers provide internal services such as e-mail, access to corporate databases, and the capability to run programs from servers.

Internet Router (Choke Router)

Finance

2. When someone on the corporate network inside the firewall wants to access the Internet, the request and data must go through an internal screening router (sometimes called a *choke router*). This router examines all the packets of data traveling in both directions between the corporate network and the Internet. Information in the packets' headers gives the router important information, such as the source and destination of the packet, the kind of protocol being used to send the packet, and other identifying data.

3. Based on the information in the headers, the screening router allows certain packets to be sent or received, but blocks other packets. For example, it might not allow some services, such as rlogin, to be run. The router also might not allow packets to be sent to and from specific Internet locations because those locations have been found to be suspicious. Conceivably, a router could be set up to block every packet traveling between the Internet and the internal network except for e-mail. System administrators set the rules for determining which packets to allow in and which ones to block.

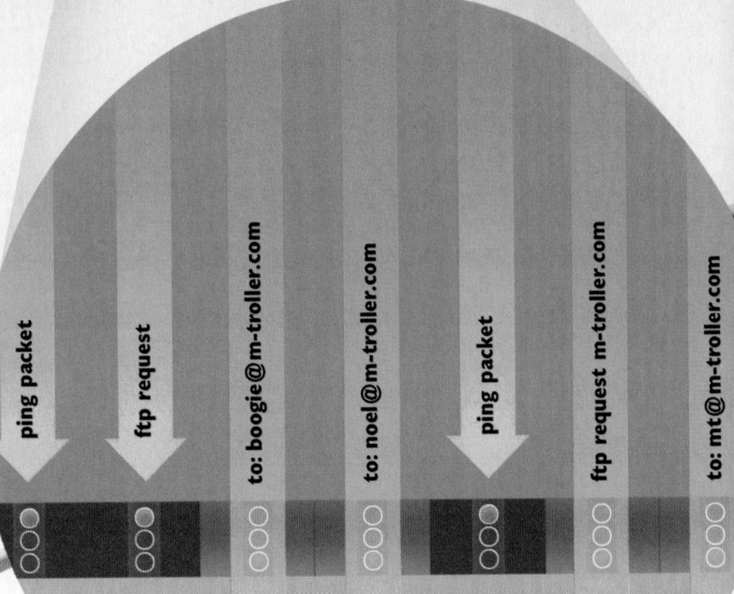

To Manufacturing

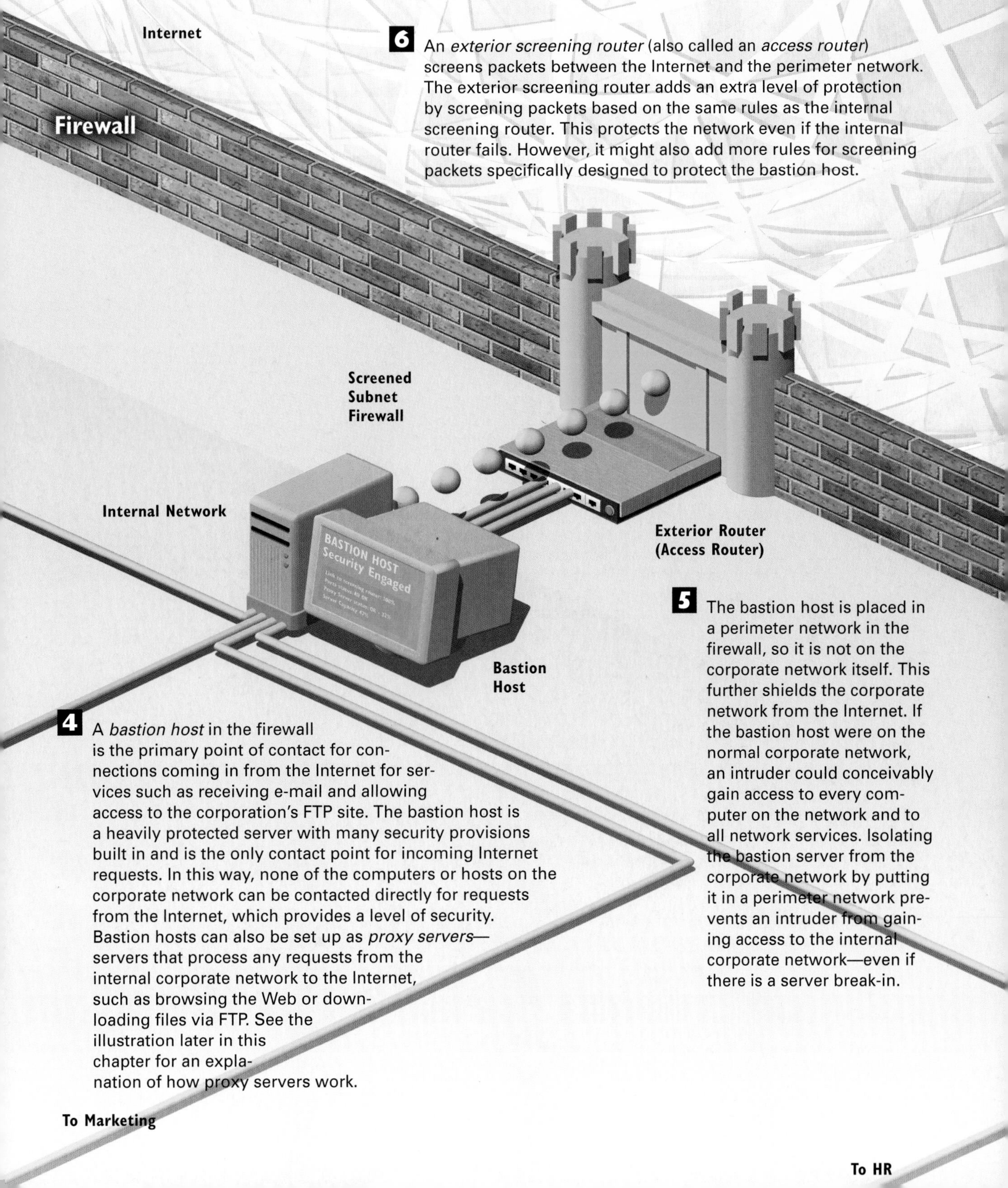

6 An *exterior screening router* (also called an *access router*) screens packets between the Internet and the perimeter network. The exterior screening router adds an extra level of protection by screening packets based on the same rules as the internal screening router. This protects the network even if the internal router fails. However, it might also add more rules for screening packets specifically designed to protect the bastion host.

5 The bastion host is placed in a perimeter network in the firewall, so it is not on the corporate network itself. This further shields the corporate network from the Internet. If the bastion host were on the normal corporate network, an intruder could conceivably gain access to every computer on the network and to all network services. Isolating the bastion server from the corporate network by putting it in a perimeter network prevents an intruder from gaining access to the internal corporate network—even if there is a server break-in.

4 A *bastion host* in the firewall is the primary point of contact for connections coming in from the Internet for services such as receiving e-mail and allowing access to the corporation's FTP site. The bastion host is a heavily protected server with many security provisions built in and is the only contact point for incoming Internet requests. In this way, none of the computers or hosts on the corporate network can be contacted directly for requests from the Internet, which provides a level of security. Bastion hosts can also be set up as *proxy servers*—servers that process any requests from the internal corporate network to the Internet, such as browsing the Web or downloading files via FTP. See the illustration later in this chapter for an explanation of how proxy servers work.

How Personal Firewalls Work

1 People who use high-speed connections such as cable modems at home might be prone to hackers' attacks because computers connected to the Internet in this way are more vulnerable and more enticing to the hackers. To protect home computers, many people have turned to *personal firewalls*—software that runs on the computer and protects the computer against Internet attacks. To understand how personal firewalls work, you first need to understand the concept of Internet ports. An *Internet port* isn't a physical device—rather it's a virtual entranceway between your computer and the Internet. When you make an Internet connection, many of these virtual connections are opened up, and each has its own number and purpose. For example, e-mail software usually uses port 110 on a mail server to get mail and uses port 25 on a mail server to send mail. FTP software usually connects to FTP servers using port 21.

2 Personal firewalls work by examining data packets your computer receives. These data packets have a great deal of information in them, such as the sending computer's IP address, your computer's IP address, the port over which the packet will be transmitted, and other pieces of information. Firewalls can filter out packets being sent to certain ports. For example, a firewall can block all packets being transmitted to port 21 so that an FTP program can't be used to attack your PC. Firewalls can block every single port to your PC, or they can block them selectively—for example, only blocking ports that are commonly used in hacker attacks, such as blocking port 31338, which is often used by the infamous Back Orifice Trojan horse.

3 One way that hackers can attack your computer is to plant a Trojan horse in it. That Trojan horse can then connect to a hacker on its own, which would give him complete control of your computer. Personal firewalls can tell you when programs from your PC attempt to connect to the Internet, and then only allow programs you know are safe to access the Internet—for example, your e-mail software.

4 Firewalls can also block specific IP addresses from contacting your computer. For example, if you know the IP of a hacker who has attacked you before, you can have your firewall block it from getting through to your computer.

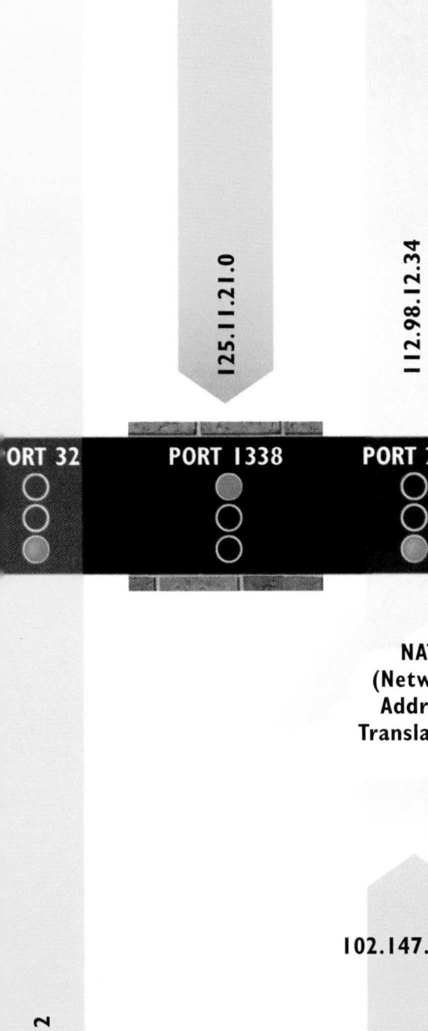

6 Many personal firewalls keep a running log of every attempt made to attack or probe your PC. These logs can be sent to your ISP, which can use them to try to track down the hackers and shut them down.

5 Many home network routers include a hardware-based personal firewall that protects you from the Internet using a technique called *Network Address Translation* (NAT). With NAT, your true IP address is shielded from the Internet—it can't be seen by anyone or any application outside your home network. In essence, it's invisible and can't be reached by hackers.

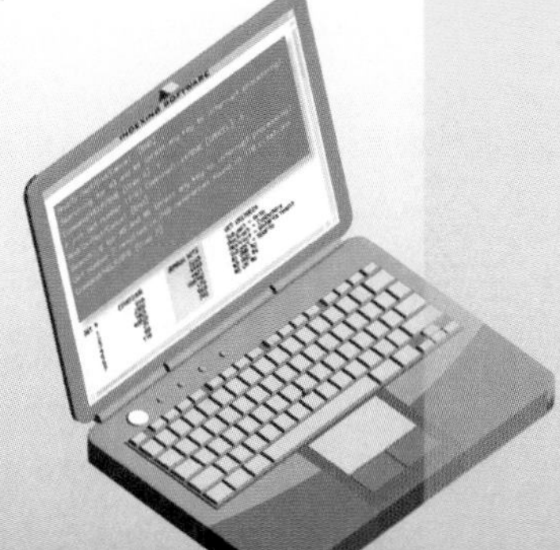

How Proxy Servers Work

1 System administrators can set up proxy servers to be used for many services, such as FTP, the Web, and Telnet. System administrators decide which Internet services must go through a proxy server. Specific proxy server software is required for each kind of Internet service.

2 When a computer from the corporate network makes a request to the Internet—such as to get a Web page from a Web server—it looks to that computer as if it were connected directly to the Web server on the Internet. In fact, however, the internal computer contacts the proxy server with its request, which in turn contacts the Internet server. The Internet server sends the Web page to the proxy server, which then forwards the page to the corporate computer.

3 Proxy servers can be used as a way to log the Internet traffic between an internal corporate network and the Internet. For example, a Telnet proxy server could track every single keystroke in every Telnet session—and could also track how the external server on the Internet reacts to those keystrokes. Proxy servers can log every IP address, date and time of access, URL, number of bytes downloaded, and so on. This information can be used to analyze any attacks launched against the network.

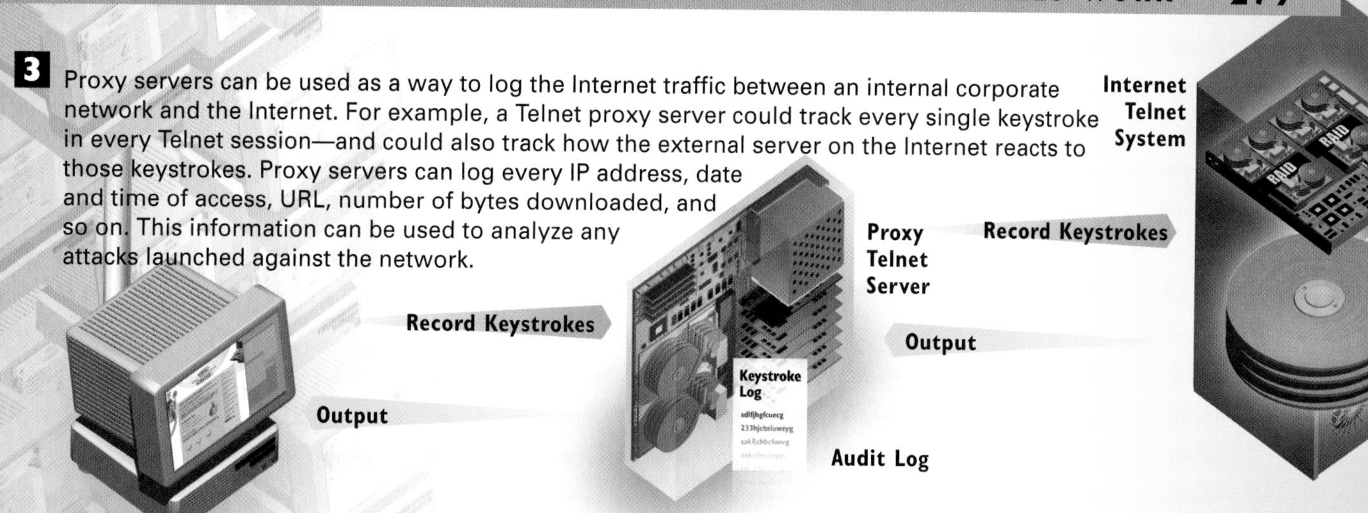

4 Proxy servers can do more than simply relay requests back and forth between a computer on a network and a server on the Internet. They can implement security schemes as well. For example, an FTP proxy server could enable files to be sent from the Internet to a computer on a corporate network, but not enable files to be sent from the corporate network out to the Internet, or vice versa.

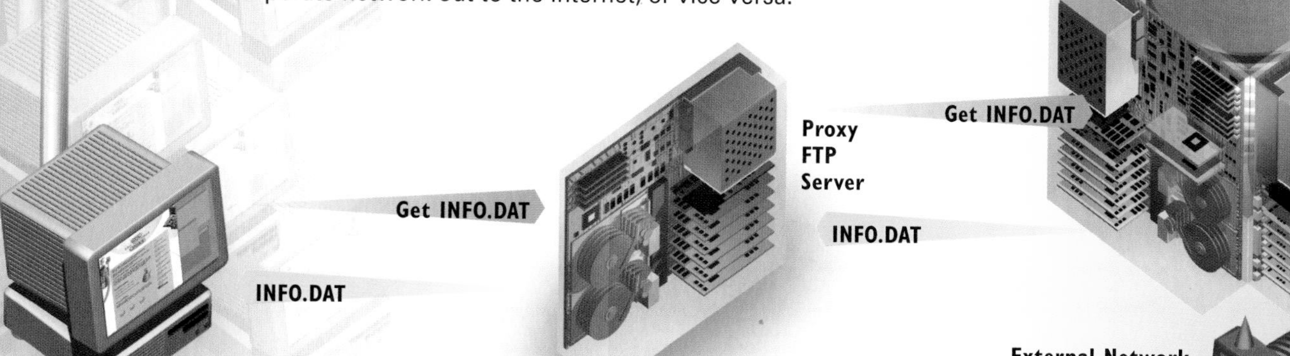

5 Proxy servers can also be used to speed up performance of some Internet services by *caching data*—keeping copies of the requested data. For example, a Web proxy server could cache many Web pages. Then, whenever someone from the internal corporate network wanted to get one of those Web pages, that person could get it directly from the server at a high speed instead of having to go out across the Internet and get the page at a lower speed.

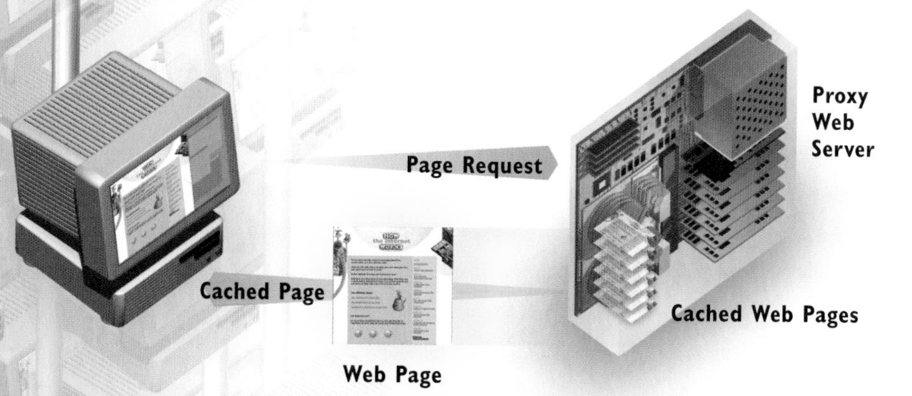

CHAPTER

45

How Hackers Can Cripple the Internet and Attack Your PC

HACKERS are equal opportunity attackers—they attack individuals as well as Web sites by using a variety of software and malicious programs. Among hackers' many targets are *Internet service providers* (ISPs)—companies that sell access to the Internet. A hacker might target an ISP for several reasons: He might be angry at the ISP or at someone using the ISP, or he might attack the ISP for the mere thrill of it.

One of the most common attacks against an ISP is called a *smurf attack*, or *smurfing*. (Smurfing is a kind of Denial of Service, or DOS attack. There are several ways that a hacker can launch a DOS attack; smurfing is one of the most popular ones.) In a smurf attack, a hacker floods the ISP with so many garbage packets that all the ISP's available bandwidth is used up. The ISP's customers can't send or receive data and can't use e-mail, browse the Web, or use any other Internet service.

In a smurf attack, hackers exploit a commonly used Internet service—ping (Pocket Internet Groper). People normally use *Ping* to see whether a particular computer or server is currently attached to the Internet and working. When a computer or server is sent a ping packet, it sends a return packet to the person who sent the ping, which in essence says, "Yes, I'm alive and attached to the Internet." In a smurf attack, hackers forge the return addresses on ping requests so that, instead of going back to them, the return packets go to the hackers' target ISP. The hackers are able to use networks attached to the Internet as a way of relaying their ping requests and magnifying each ping request many times. In this way, a hacker can use networks attached to the Internet to flood the ISP with so many return ping packets that the ISP's customers can't use the ISP's services. Hackers can use multiple networks attached to the Internet in a single smurf attack.

ISPs have difficulty fighting smurf attacks because the ping answering packets come from legitimate networks and not from the hacker. The ISP has to track down where the ping answering packets are coming from and then contact each of those networks to ask it to turn off the ping answering packets. Making this more difficult is that when an ISP goes down, often its customers will send ping requests to it to see whether it is alive and connected to the Internet. The ISP has a difficult time separating the legitimate ping packets from the smurf attack packets.

Smurf protection features and software have become available for ISPs and to put on Internet routers. But few companies are using those features and software because they have yet to gain widespread acceptance and not everyone recognizes how big a problem smurf attacks have become.

Hackers don't just target ISPs, of course. They attack individuals as well. As you'll see in the illustration later in this chapter, hackers can take over people's computers to delete and steal files, steal personal information and passwords, and even use the person's computer as a launch pad for attacks on ISPs and Web sites.

How Smurf Attacks and DOS Attacks Work

1 In a *smurf attack*, or "smurfing," and a *denial of service*, or DOS attack, a hacker targets an Internet service provider (ISP) and floods it with so much garbage traffic that none of the ISP's customers are able to use the service. Smurf attacks have become one of the most popular kinds of hacker attacks on the Internet. The attack starts when a hacker sends a series of *ping* (Packet Internet Groper) packets to a network attached to the Internet. Ping uses the *Internet Control Message Protocol*—a widely used protocol for, among other things, determining whether a particular computer is attached to the Internet and working properly. The network being pinged is not the target of the attack. Instead, it will be used as a way to attack the ISP.

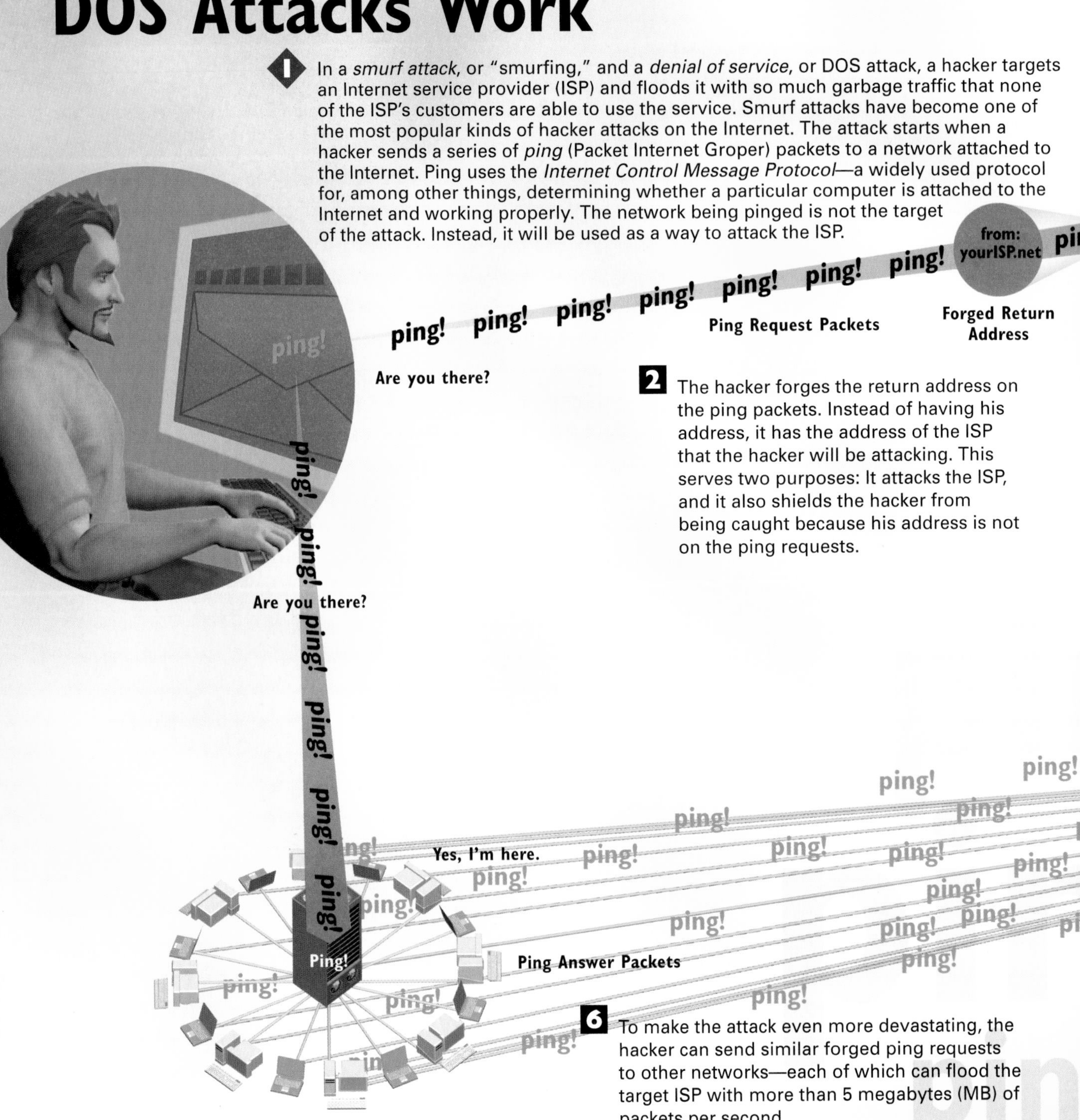

2 The hacker forges the return address on the ping packets. Instead of having his address, it has the address of the ISP that the hacker will be attacking. This serves two purposes: It attacks the ISP, and it also shields the hacker from being caught because his address is not on the ping requests.

6 To make the attack even more devastating, the hacker can send similar forged ping requests to other networks—each of which can flood the target ISP with more than 5 megabytes (MB) of packets per second.

3 The ping requests are sent in a constant stream to the network's *directed broadcast* address. This address, in turn, sends the ping requests to every computer attached to the network—which can be several hundred or more computers.

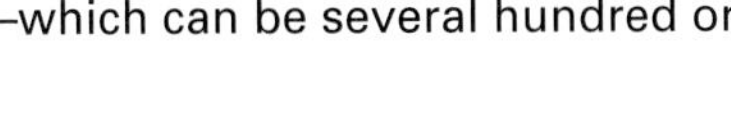

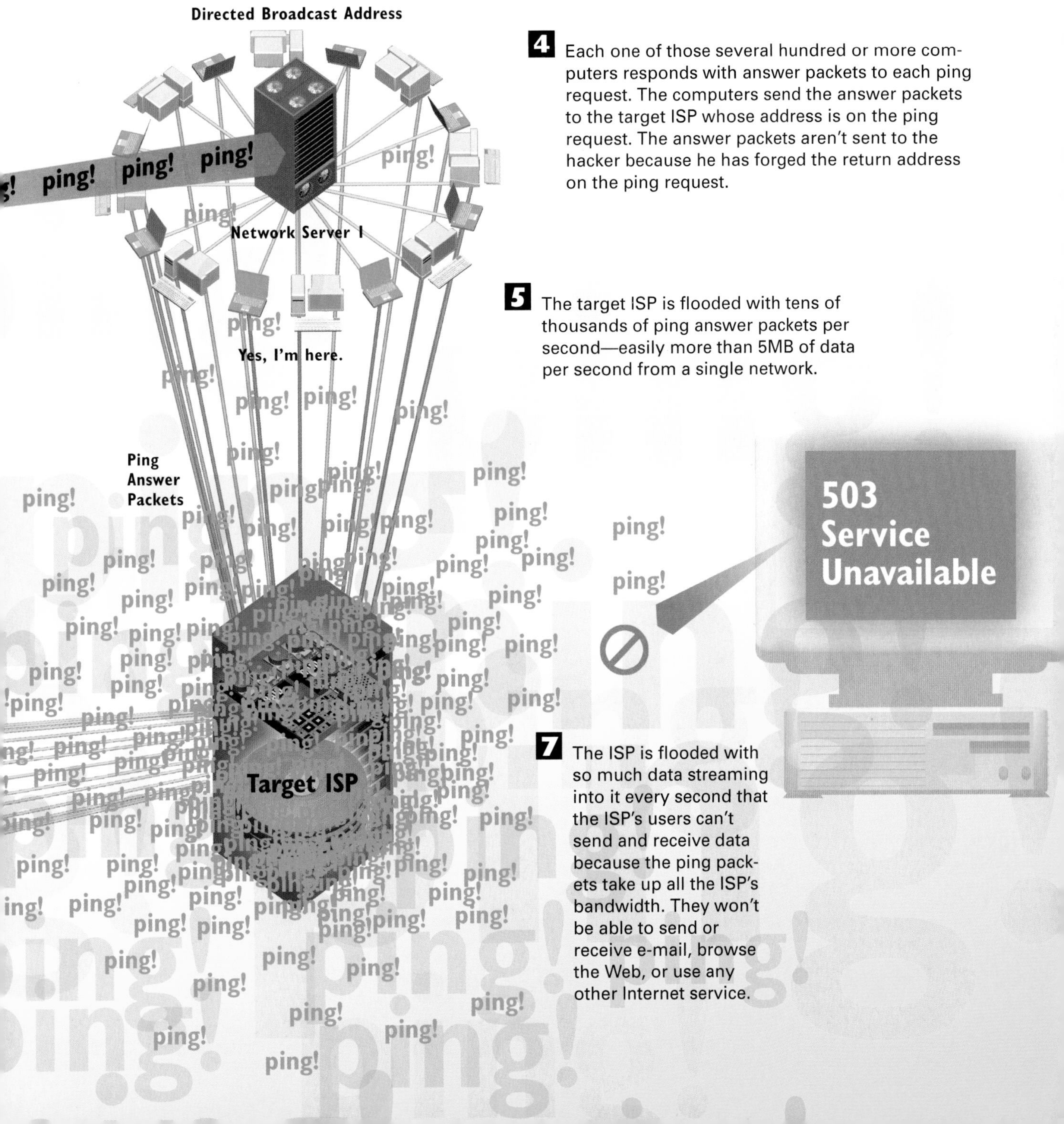

4 Each one of those several hundred or more computers responds with answer packets to each ping request. The computers send the answer packets to the target ISP whose address is on the ping request. The answer packets aren't sent to the hacker because he has forged the return address on the ping request.

5 The target ISP is flooded with tens of thousands of ping answer packets per second—easily more than 5MB of data per second from a single network.

7 The ISP is flooded with so much data streaming into it every second that the ISP's users can't send and receive data because the ping packets take up all the ISP's bandwidth. They won't be able to send or receive e-mail, browse the Web, or use any other Internet service.

How Hackers Can Attack Your Computer

1 Hackers not only attack big Web sites and corporations, but also individual computers in homes or businesses. Hackers can do damage and use your computer in many ways. As a start to many of hacker's nefarious deeds, they need access to your computer. One common way they gain it is through the use of a program called Back Orifice. Before the hackers can use the program, you have to get it on your computer. You can unwittingly get a copy of Back Orifice on your computer in many different ways—for example, you can open a file in an e-mail message and it can be installed to your computer without you realizing it, or you can be sent it when you use Internet's IRC chat protocol.

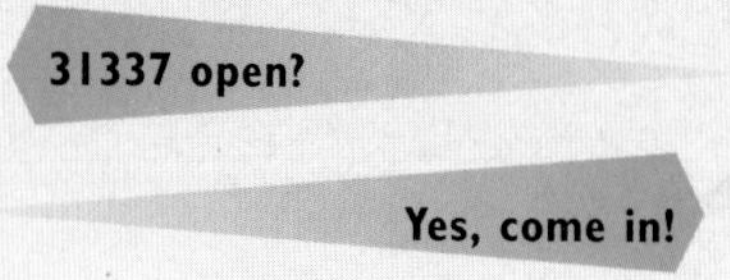

Hacker

2 Hackers have automated tools that scan thousands of different computers to see which ones have Back Orifice running on them. These tools send out *port probes*—packets that look at a specific virtual ports that all computers have when connected to the Internet. Back Orifice uses port 31337, and if it's running on a computer, it will open that port. A port probe will alert the hacker that port 31337 is open so that he knows he can take control of your PC.

3 The hacker can do many things when he takes control of your computer—in essence, it's as if he's sitting at your keyboard and monitor without you knowing about it. He can, for example, copy or delete all the files, data, and software on your computer.

4 He can find out personal information about you by looking through your files. For example, he might be able to gain access to your credit card number, bank account, and social security number, and then use that information illegally.

Amex, 101-11-33
$15,000 please.

Hacker

5 He can gain access to all your passwords, which would enable him to pose as you on Web sites and break into data on your computer that you've tried to protect with passwords.

6 He can upload any files to, or download any files from, your computer. For example, he could use your computer to store copies of illegally copied software and could even enable other hackers to then download those illegal copies.

7 Often, hackers use access to someone else's computer to launch attacks against corporations or Web pages. The hacker could launch an attack, and when the attack was traced, it wouldn't lead to the hacker's computer—it would lead to yours, and it would appear that you were the culprit.

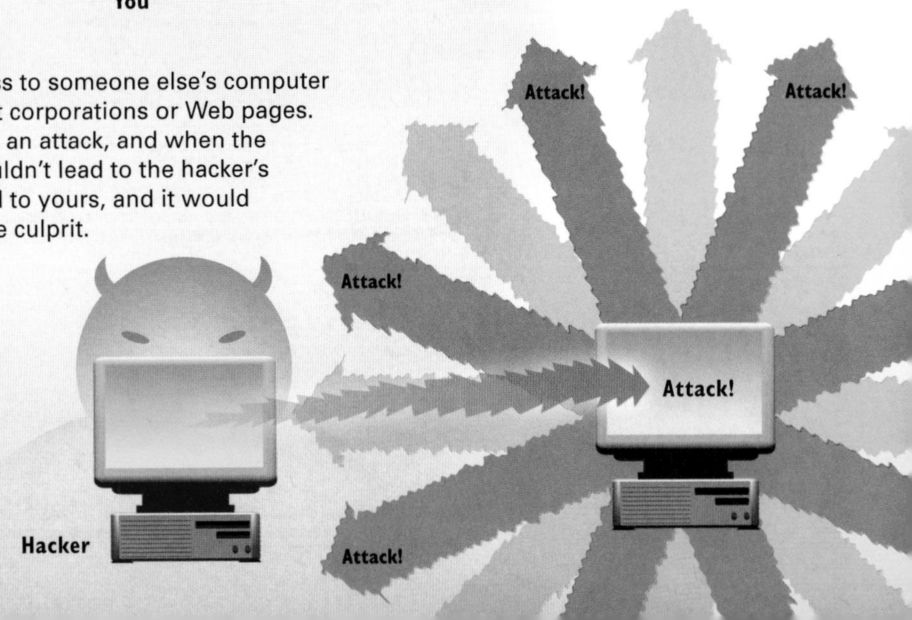

CHAPTER 46 How Viruses Work

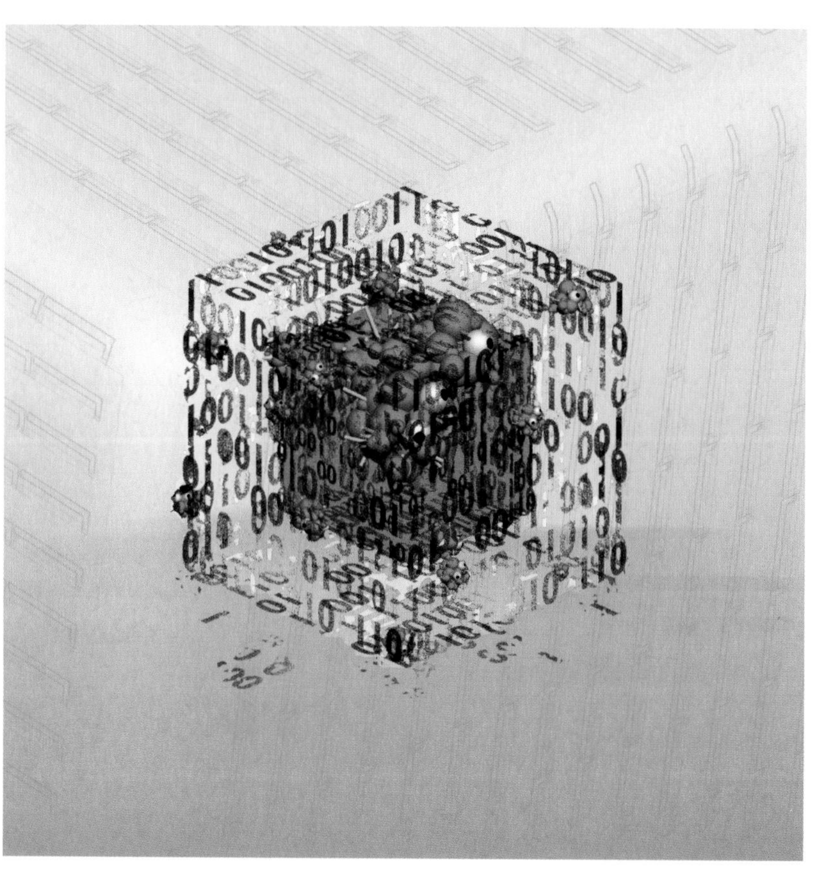

THE Internet, just like the rest of the world, is not a perfectly safe place to visit. If you download files from the Internet, there is a chance—a very small chance, but nonetheless a chance—that your computer could become infected with a virus.

Viruses are malicious programs that invade your computer. They can cause many different kinds of damage, such as deleting data files, erasing programs, or destroying everything they find on your hard disk. Not every virus causes damage; some simply flash annoying messages.

Although you can get a virus from the Internet by downloading files to your computer, the Internet is not the only place where viruses can be picked up. If you've sent files via e-mail or on your company's internal network, you can get viruses that way as well. Instances have occurred when commercially bought, shrink-wrapped software has contained viruses.

The term virus is a somewhat generic term applied to a wide variety of programs. Viruses are written for specific kinds of computers, such as PCs or Macintoshes, because the files they infect run only on one kind of computer.

Traditional viruses attach themselves to programs or data files, infect your computer, replicate themselves on your hard disk, and then damage your data, hard disk, or files. Viruses usually attack four parts of your computer: its executable program files; its file-directory system that tracks the location of all your computer's files (and without which, your computer won't work); its boot and system areas that are needed to start your computer; and its data files. At one time it was believed that data files could not be infected by viruses, but recently, viruses have been written that infect data files too. For example, some viruses attach themselves to Microsoft Word macros inside a Word data file and are launched whenever a particular macro is run.

Trojan horses are files or programs that disguise themselves as normal, helpful programs or files, but in fact are viruses. For example, if a program purported to be a financial calculator, but really deleted every file on your hard disk, that program would be called a Trojan horse. The most famous Trojan horse of all, Melissa, was disguised as a Word document sent via e-mail—and it wreaked enough havoc that it crashed many Internet and corporate mail servers by making use of the Outlook and Outlook Express e-mail programs.

Worms are programs designed to infect networks such as the Internet. They travel from networked computer to networked computer and replicate themselves along the way. The most infamous worm of all was released on November 2, 1988. The worm copied itself to many Internet host computers and eventually bringing the Internet to its knees.

The best way to protect your computer against viruses is to use antiviral software. Several kinds of antiviral software exist. A scanner checks to see if your computer has any files that have been infected; whereas an eradication program will wipe the virus from your hard disk. Sometimes eradication programs can kill the virus without having to delete the infected program or data file, while other times those infected files must be deleted. Still other programs, sometimes called *inoculators*, do not allow a program to be run if it contains a virus and stop your computer from being infected. Malicious e-mail programs can sometimes be stopped by disabling a built-in capability to run scripts in e-mail software.

How Viruses Infect Computers

1 A virus hides inside a legitimate program where it remains dormant until you run the infected program. The virus springs into action when you actually run the infected program. Sometimes the first thing the virus will do is infect other programs on your hard disk by copying itself into them.

Infected Application

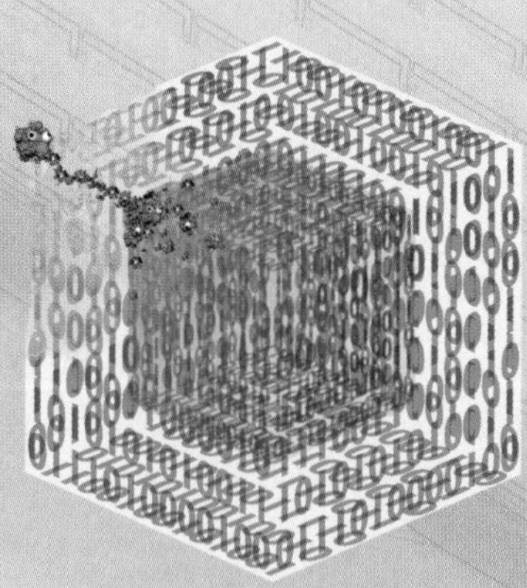
Newly Infected File

2 Some viruses place messages called *v-markers* or *virus markers* inside programs that they infect, and these messages help manage the viruses' activities. Each virus has a specific v-marker associated with it. If a virus encounters one of these markers in another program, it knows that the program is already infected so it doesn't replicate itself there. When a virus cannot find more unmarked files on a computer, that signals to the virus that there are no more files to be infected. At this point, the virus might begin to damage the computer and its data.

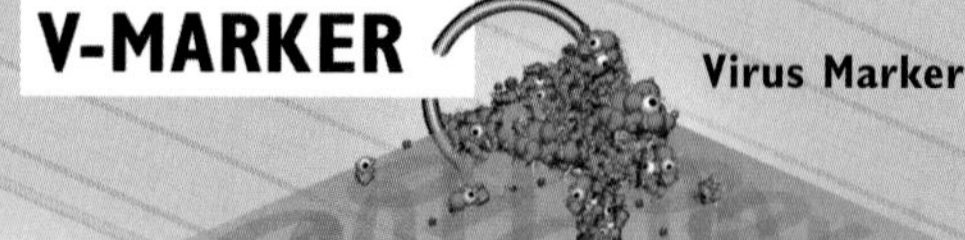

Virus Marker

Damaged File or Application

3 Viruses can corrupt program or data files so that they work oddly, not at all, or cause damage when they do run. They can destroy all the files on your computer, change the system files that your computer needs when it is turned on, and cause other types of damage.

4 Software programs called *scanners* check for viruses and alert you to the viruses' presence. They work in many different ways. One method of detection is to check your program files for telltale virus markers that indicate the presence of a virus. Other methods include checking to see whether a program's file size has changed. Some types of antiviral programs run continuously on your computer and check any program for the presence of a virus before the program is run or downloaded.

SCANNING FOR VIRUSES

5 *Eradication programs* disinfect, or remove, viruses from software. Sometimes they can eradicate the virus without damaging the program that the virus has infected. In other instances, they have to destroy the program as well as the virus.

How Trojan Horses Work

1 Trojan horses are programs that disguise themselves as normal, helpful programs or files, but in fact are viruses. The most well known Trojan horse of all time, called Melissa, used e-mail to spread itself, and damaged many Internet and corporate mail servers. Here's how it did its work.

2 Melissa arrived in people's e-mail inboxes—disguised as a normal e-mail message—with a Microsoft Word file as an attachment. The subject line of the e-mail read, "important message from," followed by a person's name—and that name might have been the name of a friend, acquaintance, or co-worker of the person receiving the message. The body of the e-mail read, "Here is that document you asked for...don't show anyone else."

3 When people opened the attached Word file, Melissa sprang to work. If the file wasn't opened, then Melissa could do no damage. The attached file appeared to be a normal Word file that contained a list of pornographic sites. However, when the file was opened, a *macro* ran without the user knowing it. A macro is a set of automated commands—much like a program.

4 The macro checked to see whether the person had Outlook on his computer. Outlook is a Microsoft e-mail program. If Outlook wasn't present, the macro wasn't able to do any damage. If Outlook was present, Melissa looked at the first 50 names in Outlook's address book, then made a copy of itself and mailed itself to all those 50 names without the person knowing this was happening. The e-mail sent to each of those people looked exactly like the e-mail the person received: The subject line of the email read, "important message from," followed by the name of the person who had been infected by Melissa. It appeared that the infected person was sending out a personal message.

125,000 Possible Infections

5 Each of these 50 people, in turn, received the infected e-mail and attached Word document. When he opened the attached file, Melissa did the same thing to him—automatically sent itself to 50 more people.

6 The volume of e-mail being sent quickly became so great that Internet and corporate e-mail servers were unable to keep up with the demand for sending and receiving messages—and many of them crashed. Many Internet and corporate mail servers were overwhelmed by the huge demand for sending and receiving e-mail, and so normal mail—not just Melissa-related mail—couldn't be sent or received. The problem was finally resolved when anti-virus software was updated to include features that could detect and kill Melissa.

CHAPTER

47

How Internet Sites Can Invade Your Privacy

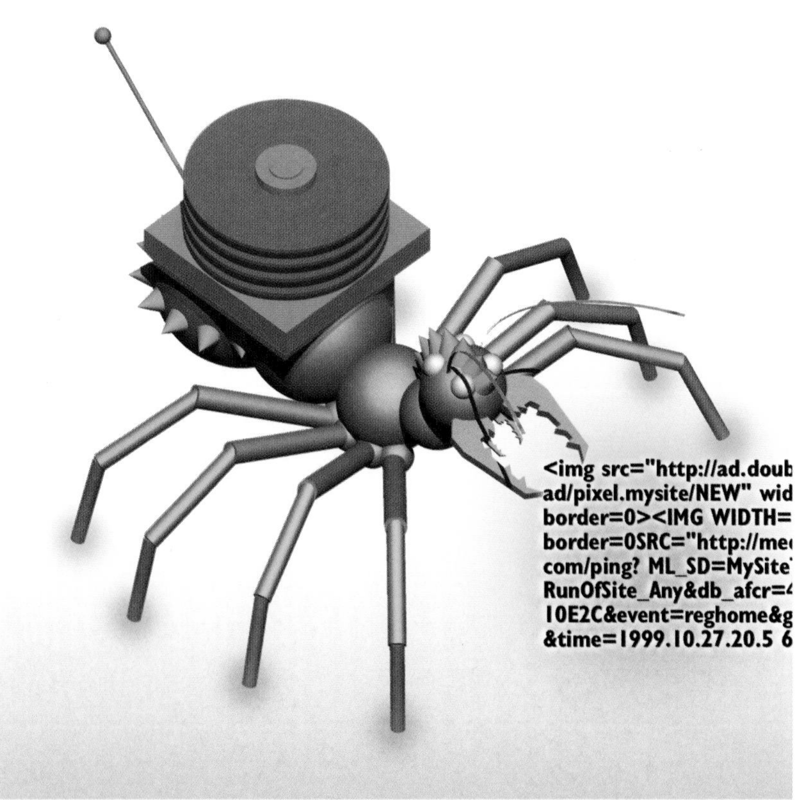

PRIVACY issues are a big concern on the Net. Much information can be gathered about people when they use the Net, and it's not always clear who will use that information or how it will be used. In particular, three technologies that concern people are cookies, Web tracking, and Web bugs. Cookies and Web tracking both serve useful purposes, but many people worry that there is a "Big Brother" aspect to them. Web bugs, on the other hand, can be used for nefarious purposes. One technology, Internet passports, might enable people to ensure that their privacy isn't invaded while still enabling Web sites to gather information that can be used to deliver specialized services to Web surfers.

Cookies are bits of data put on a hard disk when someone visits certain Web sites. The most common use of this data is to make it easier for people to use Web sites that require a username and password. The cookie on the hard disk has the username and password in it, so people don't have to log in to every page that requires that information. Instead, the cookie sends the information to the server, and the person can visit the page freely.

Cookies can contain virtually any kind of information, such as the last time a person visited the site, the person's favorite sites, and similar, customizable information. They can be used to track people as they go through a Web site and to help gain statistics about what types of pages people like to visit. Although some people view them as invaders of privacy, they can also make the Web a much better place to visit by doing things such as making it easier to conduct electronic commerce.

Although cookies can be used to track how people use a Web site, many other methods can be used, as well. In one method, Web server logs are examined in detail. This would make it possible, for example, to identify the most popular pages on the site, the sites people have just visited, how many pages people read in a typical visit, and similar information. Other methods include using software *sniffers* that examine every packet coming into or going out of a Web site. Webmasters can use this tracking information to help create better sites—but they can also use it to assemble demographic information to sell to advertisers. The second illustration in this chapter shows the functionality of Web tracking software from a company called Accrue.

Web bugs can also trace people's paths through a Web site. Web bugs get their name not in reference to an error in a program, but instead from the term *to bug* as in "to wiretap." More dangerously, Web bugs can be included in e-mail, and they can actually enable people to view some of your e-mail, as you'll see in the illustration later in this chapter.

To allay people's privacy concerns, a variety of technologies and standards are being developed. They include the Platform for Privacy Preferences (P3P), the Internet Content and Exchange standard (ICE), and the Open Profiling Standard (OPS). Generically, we'll call these Internet *passports*. These Internet passports let people control which information about themselves they'll allow to be released to Web sites—and how that information can be used. And they let people control what type of information can be gathered about their surfing and how that information can be used, as well. In general, the more information that people allow to be gathered about themselves, the more specialized services they'll gain on the Web, such as customized news feeds.

How Cookies Work

1 *Cookies* are pieces of data placed on a computer's hard drive by a Web server; they can be used for a variety of purposes. They can store usernames and passwords, for example, so that people don't have to continually log on to a site that requires registration; or they can enable people to fill electronic shopping carts with goods they want to buy. Cookies also store the name of the site that placed the cookie. Only that site can read the cookie information, so information from one site can't be shared with information from another site. Cookie information is put into a special file on a hard disk. The location and files vary according to the type of computer and the browser. On PCs using Netscape, for example, the information is put into a file called `COOKIES.TXT`. That single text file holds all the cookies, and each cookie is one line of data in the file.

Web Server

CGI Script

Password: pg
Username: who

www.buyshop.com

Buyshop.com cookie

2 When you visit a site, your browser examines the URL you're visiting and looks into your cookie file. If it finds a cookie associated with that URL, it sends that cookie information to the server. The server can now use that cookie information.

```
# Netscape HTTP Cookie File
# http://www.netscape.com/newsref/std/cookie_spec.html
# This is a generated file!  Do not edit.

.ad-up.com        TRUE   /~barryl/public_html   FALSE   946079999   Ad-UpUser   125181
www.lego.com      TRUE   /cgi-bin/pirat  FALSE   883699199   &r   &n=unknown&pf=&b=2&t=1&f=
.gowest.com       TRUE   /   FALSE   946684799   INTERSE   155.48.99.17113860849884657
.hotbot.com       TRUE   /   FALSE   937396800   ink   IU0DH12pE40A364005044800S3959C153
.focalink.com     TRUE   /   FALSE   946641600   SB_ID   ads03.21677849891891049315
.boston.com       TRUE   /   FALSE   946684799   INTERSE   mia.tiac.net27733850856212370
.netscape.com     TRUE   /   FALSE   1609372800   MOZILLA   MOZ_ID=DFGMKGIIRJSSPTS[-]MOZ_VERS
.netscape.com     TRUE   /   FALSE   1609372800   NS_IBD   IBD_SUBSCRIPTIONS=INC005|INC018|I
.realaudio.com    TRUE   /   FALSE   946684740   uid   19927924050346722865
.nytimes.com      TRUE   /   FALSE   946684799   PV   27.7270
.nytimes.com      TRUE   /   FALSE   946684799   ID   .7,=22=6
.nytimes.com      TRUE   /   FALSE   942189160   iibuser .7,=22=6
.nytimes.com      TRUE   /   FALSE   942189160   iibq   +6=,9'=,9cV,=22=cDZP9+c6/+8529+6
.netscape.com     TRUE   /   FALSE   946684799   NETSCAPE_ID   1000e010,13bf0f76
ad.doubleclick.net   FALSE   /   FALSE   942191940   IAF   1cecb58
.infoseek.com     TRUE   /   FALSE   882131378   InfoseekUserId   848BFC0465009557036 0E4A35
.software.net     TRUE   /   FALSE   946684799   ADURL   http://www.software.net/PKSH0203
.yahoo.com        TRUE   /   FALSE   883609200   IDAHO   domain=y&path=39312F31372F7
.wsj.com          TRUE   /   FALSE   946625010   user_type   subscribed
www.maricle.com FALSE   /   FALSE   1293753600   EGSOFT_ID   155.48.99.171-1175746720.
www.download.com   FALSE   /   FALSE   946598400   csr   /=/PC/FrontDoor/
.family.com       TRUE   /   FALSE   946681200   ck_stateID   49143.38564416.788
Buyshop.com                  TRUE   123702  132
```


3 If no cookie is associated with the URL, the server places a cookie inside the cookie file. Some sites might first ask a series of questions, such as name and password, and then place a cookie on the hard disk with that information in it. This is typical of sites that require registration. Commonly, a CGI script on the server takes the information the user has entered and then writes the cookie onto the hard disk.

4 As you travel through a Web site, more information might need to be put into your cookie. On a site where you can purchase goods online, for example, you might put goods into an electronic shopping cart. Every time you did this, new cookie information would be added, detailing the goods you wanted to buy. When new cookie information is put in, a CGI script deletes the old cookie information and puts in a new cookie. When you leave a site, your cookie information remains on your hard disk so the site can recognize you the next time you decide to visit—unless the cookie has specifically been written to expire when you leave the site.

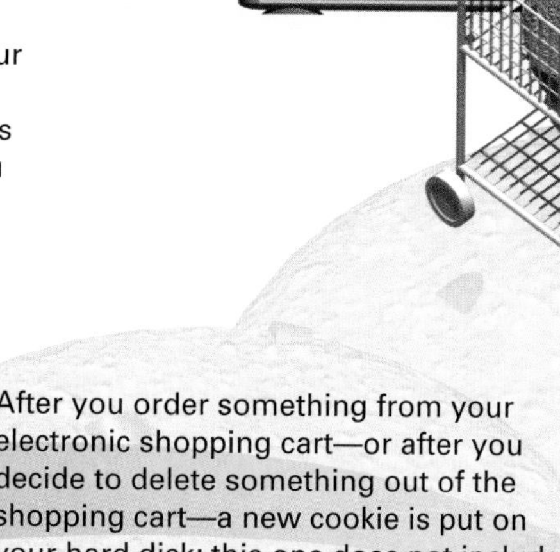

5 The server takes actions based on your cookies—for example, displaying your electronic shopping cart. If the site enables you to buy online, it might have asked for your credit card number. For security reasons, that number is not stored in your cookie. Instead, it is stored on a secure server. When you decide to buy something, you enter a secure area with your browser. Your cookie then sends an ID to the server that identifies you, and the server then displays your credit card information, enabling you to buy online.

6 After you order something from your electronic shopping cart—or after you decide to delete something out of the shopping cart—a new cookie is put on your hard disk; this one does not include the goods you bought or decided to take out of your shopping cart.

Web Server

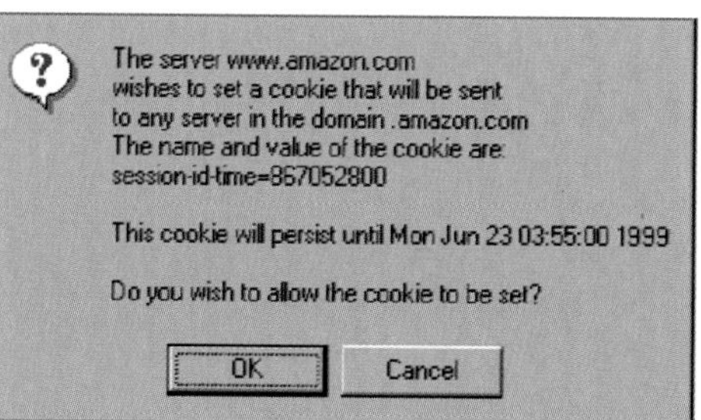
The server www.amazon.com
wishes to set a cookie that will be sent
to any server in the domain .amazon.com
The name and value of the cookie are:
session-id-time=867052800

This cookie will persist until Mon Jun 23 03:55:00 1999

Do you wish to allow the cookie to be set?

OK Cancel

7 Because some people don't like cookies to be placed on their hard disks, browsers give people control over whether to accept cookies, to not accept cookies, or to ask each time a cookie is being placed on the hard disk. Pictured is the message you get if you've asked to be told each time a cookie is placed on your hard disk.

How Web Tracking Works

1 Accrue's software doesn't rely on analyzing Web logs to figure out how a Web site is being used. Instead, a *sniffer* sits on the Internet and analyzes traffic to the site. This sniffer is a computer that runs software that examines all the TCP/IP packets coming in and out of the Web site.

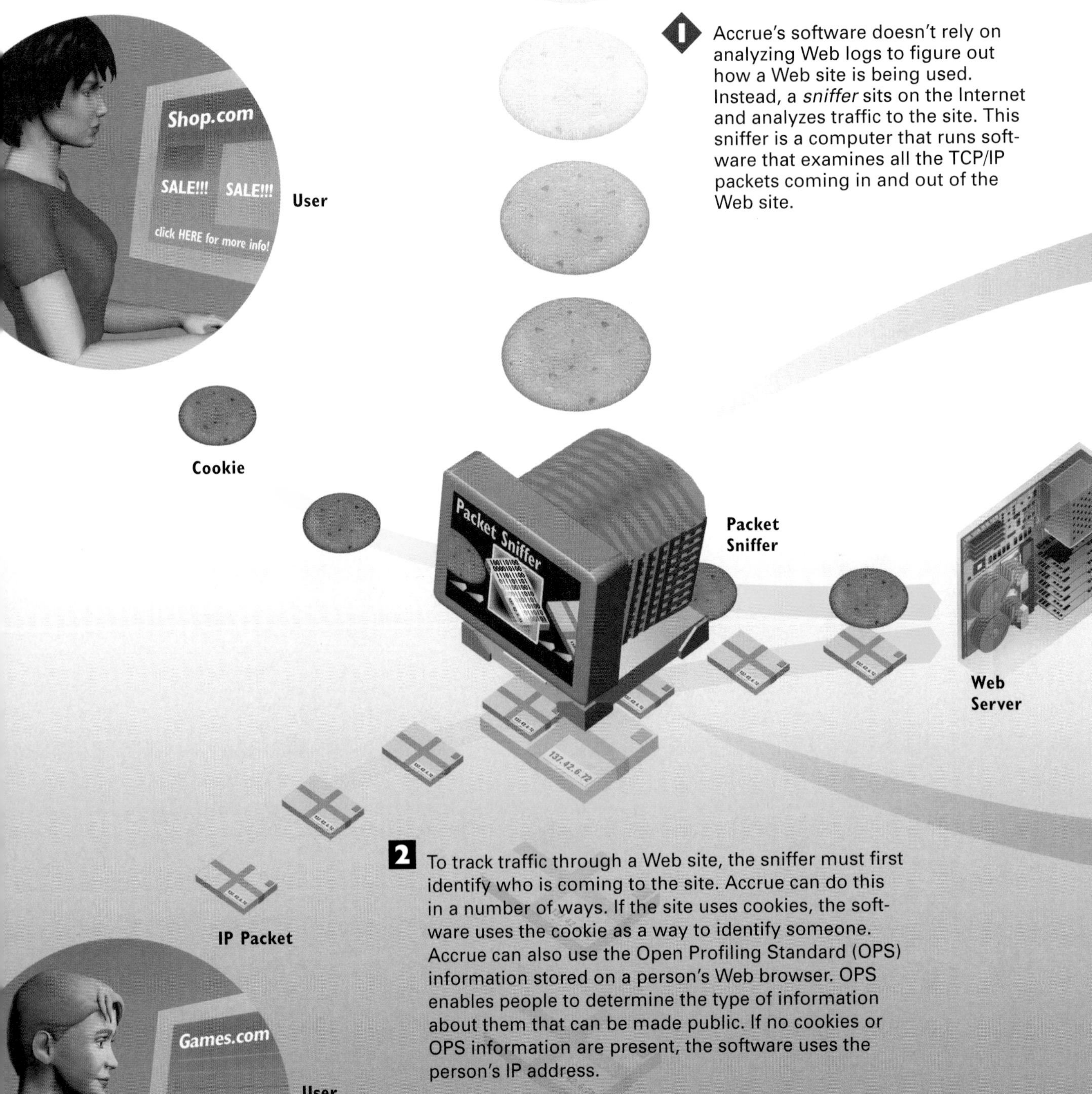

2 To track traffic through a Web site, the sniffer must first identify who is coming to the site. Accrue can do this in a number of ways. If the site uses cookies, the software uses the cookie as a way to identify someone. Accrue can also use the Open Profiling Standard (OPS) information stored on a person's Web browser. OPS enables people to determine the type of information about them that can be made public. If no cookies or OPS information are present, the software uses the person's IP address.

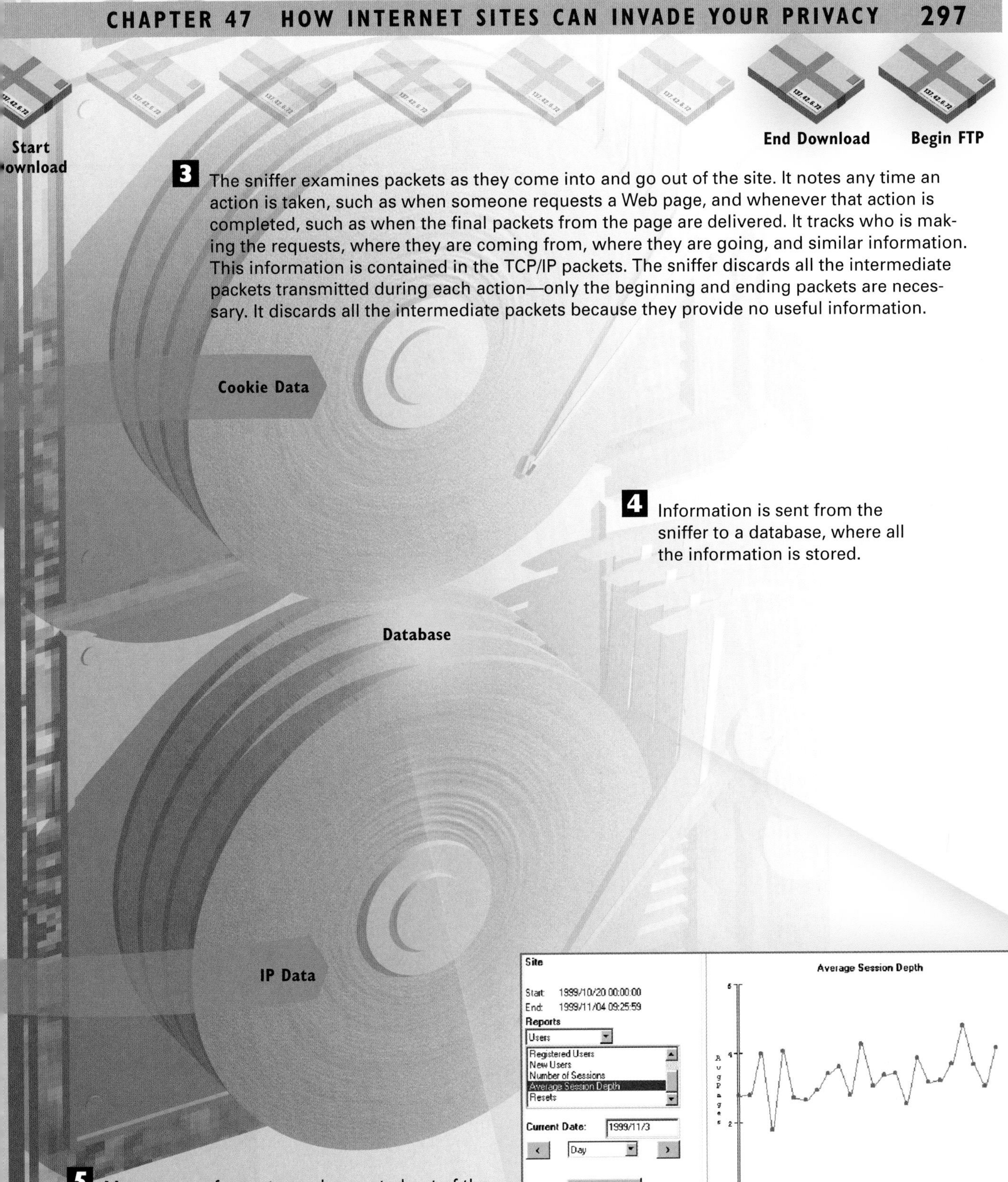

3 The sniffer examines packets as they come into and go out of the site. It notes any time an action is taken, such as when someone requests a Web page, and whenever that action is completed, such as when the final packets from the page are delivered. It tracks who is making the requests, where they are coming from, where they are going, and similar information. This information is contained in the TCP/IP packets. The sniffer discards all the intermediate packets transmitted during each action—only the beginning and ending packets are necessary. It discards all the intermediate packets because they provide no useful information.

4 Information is sent from the sniffer to a database, where all the information is stored.

5 Many types of reports can be created out of the database, such as the average amount of time people spend on a site, the average number of pages they read per visit, the most popular pages on a site, sites people have just visited, sites they're going to visit, and other information.

Server Traffic Analysis

How Web Bugs Can Invade Your Privacy

1 A *Web bug* is a piece of HTML code placed on Web pages or in e-mail messages that can be used to silently gather information about people, track their Internet travels, and even allow the creator of the bug to secretly read a person's e-mail. In this illustration we'll look at Web bugs used in e-mail. E-mail Web bugs can be placed only in HTML e-mail, so the person creating the bug must create an HTML-based e-mail message.

2 In the HTML code for the message, the person puts in a small piece of JavaScript code that has the capability to read the entire contents of an e-mail message.

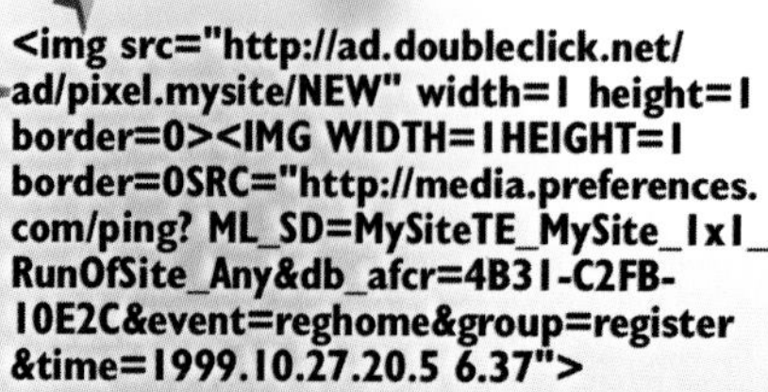

4 The person sends the e-mail message. The recipient opens the message in an HTML-enabled e-mail reader, such as Outlook. (Note: If the recipient doesn't have an e-mail reader, the Web bug won't work.)

3 The person also puts a Web bug into the e-mail message. The Web bug is an HTML reference to a tiny graphic—the smallest possible on a computer screen is one pixel by one pixel—that is transparent so that it can't be seen. This tiny graphic is also called a *clear gif* because *gif* refers to a common Web graphics format. When someone reads her HTML message, her computer gets the graphic from a server—and that server then can get information about the person's computer.

5 The JavaScript runs and reads the entire e-mail message. The person's e-mail software contacts the remote server to get the clear gif. It does more than get the gif, though—it also send identifying information about the computer, such as its IP address and the time the message is being read. It also sends the contents of the e-mail message, as taken by the JavaScript. At this point, that doesn't really matter because the sender of the message knows the contents of the message because she created it. But the sender now knows identifying information about the recipient of the mail.

Get Graphic

IP 47.32.21.2 read
5:10 09/12/02

Get
Graphic

IP 132.21.23.4
read 6:20 10/13/02

Cookie

clear.gif

6 The server sends the gif, but can also send a cookie along with it. It can match this cookie with the identifying information send via the Web bug, and with those pieces of information track a person's use of the Internet. For example, if the piece of mail that set all this in motion was a piece of junk mail, the sender would be able to know who responded to the offer, and track what he did in response—visiting a particular Web page or buying specific products, for example. That information could then be kept in a database.

7 If the recipient of the message sends the message along to someone else, and sends a message along with it, the whole process starts all over. Now, however, when the Web bug sends the contents of the e-mail message, it contains the person's comments—so the mail has effectively been wiretapped. This can keep continuing so that every time a new person gets the message, the wiretap continues.

Forwarded
E-mail

How Internet Passports Work

2 When the user visits a Web site, the information in the profile the person has put into his passport is sent to the site's Web server.

3 The server examines the information in the passport. In this instance, the profile includes a username and password—so the username and password are sent to the Web site, automatically logging the person in to a special portion of the site that allows only those who have already registered at the site. The server might then send a welcome message to the person logging in.

Web Server

Passport

1 Internet *passports* are designed to let people decide what personal information they will allow to be released to Web sites. A variety of technologies are involved with Internet passports, including the Platform for Privacy Preferences (P3P), the Internet Content and Exchange standard (ICE), and the Open Profiling Standard (OPS). The passport lives inside a Web browser. A user fills out a profile in the browser, determining what information can be made available to Web sites, such as name, address, occupation, username and password, and age. The user also decides which type of information about his surfing habits can be shared among Web sites—and which can't. In this instance, the person has decided that information about what news stories he reads can be shared, but not information about what products he buys.

4 While on the site, the person reads news about the latest sports scores, then buys an electric razor and a book about sailing. The Web site puts into the person's profile that he has read sports scores, but not that he has bought a razor and a book—because the person's profile said it would allow information about what news stories he reads to be shared but not information about what he buys.

5 The person visits another Web site. The information in the profile the person has put into his passport is sent to the site's Web server. The server sees that the person has recently read a story about sports scores, so it sends to him a daily digest of the latest sports news. Because the profile doesn't have any information about what the person has bought, it doesn't send any information about special sales on the site.

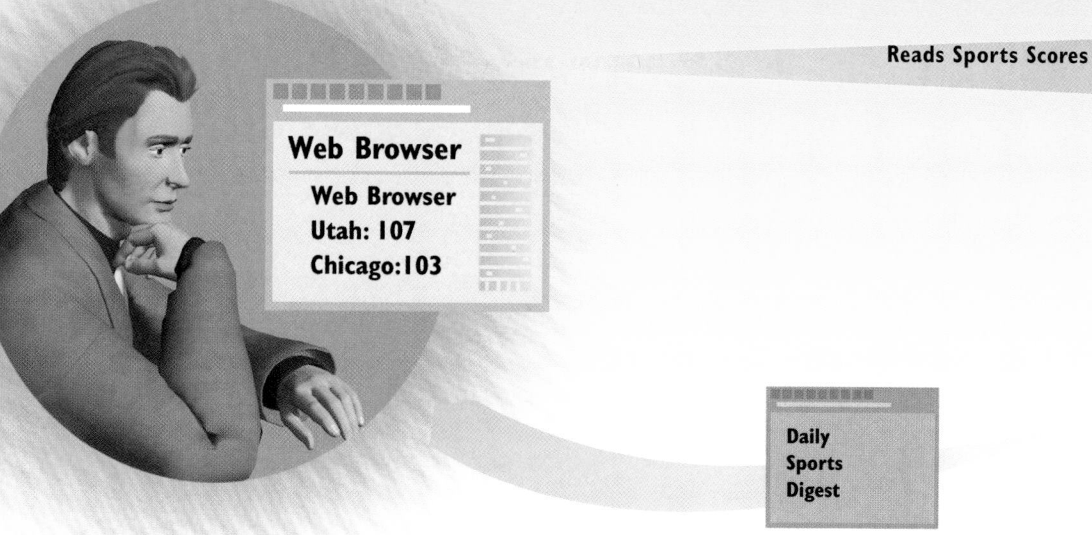

News Site

6 The person now surfs to a different Web site. This site allows in only people who have agreed, in their profiles, to allow their online buying habits to be shared among sites. Because the person has said he doesn't want that information to be shared, the person is not allowed onto the site.

Buying Site

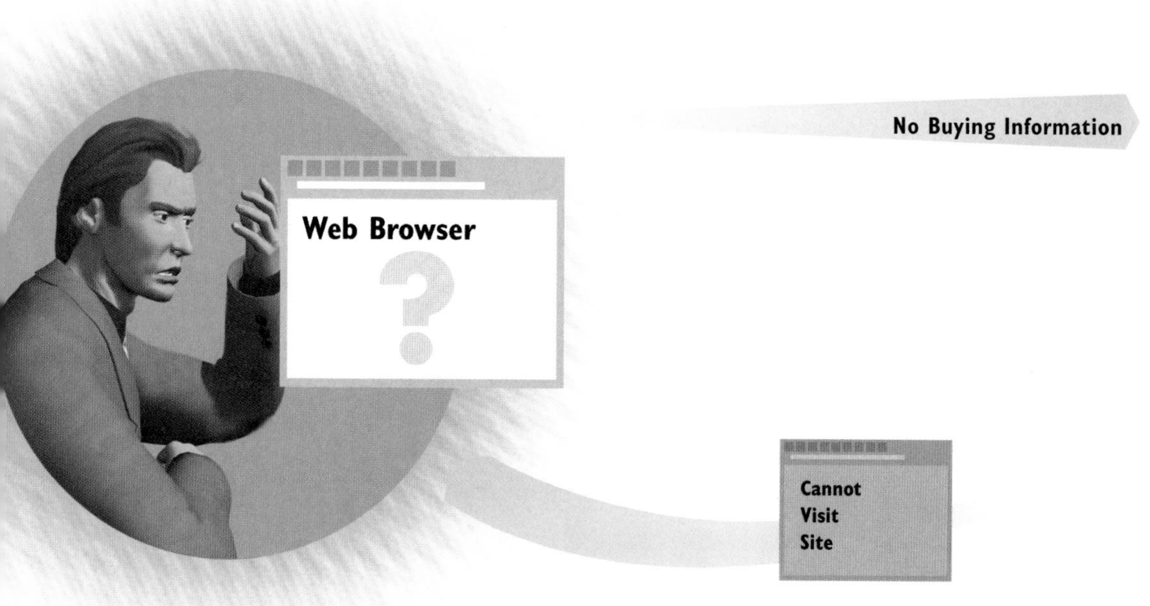

CHAPTER

48

Cryptography, Privacy, and Digital Certificates

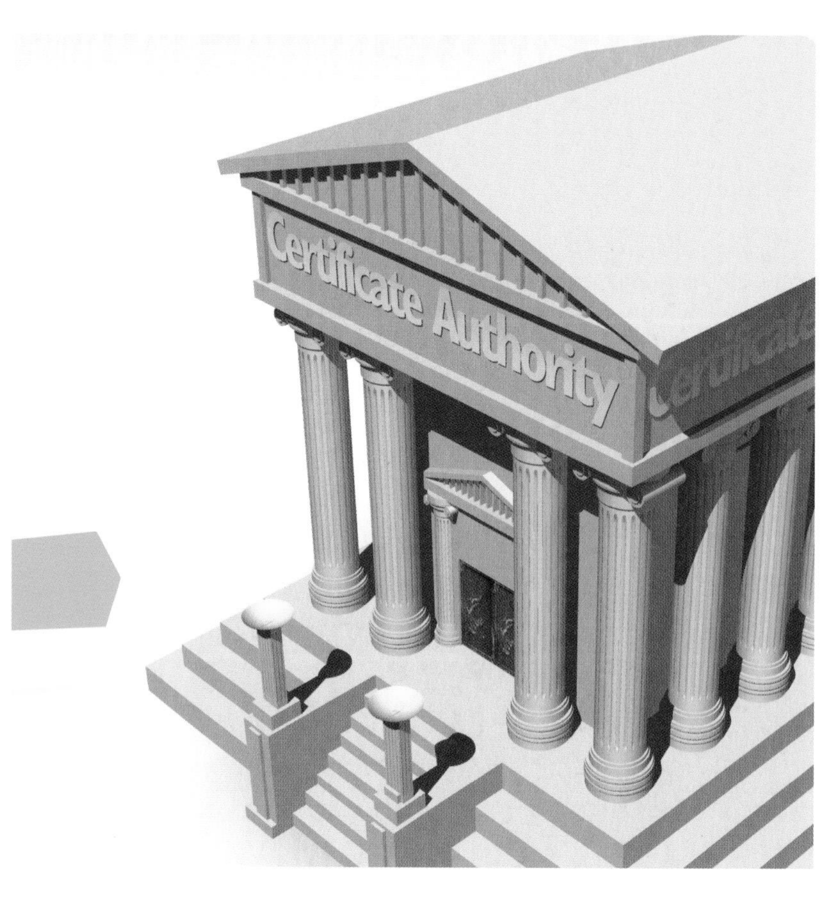

THE Internet is a notoriously insecure network. Anything you send across it can be easily snooped upon. This is of particular concern when highly confidential information, such as corporate data and credit card numbers, is transmitted across the Internet. Unless there is some way to protect that type of information, the Internet will never be a secure place to do business or send private, personal correspondence.

Another related concern is that knowing that the person sending the information across the Internet, such as credit card information, is really who he says he is can be impossible. There are ways for people to forge identities and steal credit card numbers, and financial institutions and other businesses require ways to know that the person sending information really is who he says he is.

Several ways have been developed to solve these problems. At the heart of them is *encryption*—a way of altering information so that to anyone other than the intended recipient it will look like meaningless garble. When the recipient gets the information, it needs to be *decrypted*—that is, turned back into the original message by the recipient, and *only* by the recipient. Many complex cryptosystems have been created to enable this type of encryption and decryption.

Cryptosystems use what are called *keys*—secret values computers use in concert with complex mathematical formulas called *algorithms* to encrypt and decrypt messages. If someone encrypts a message with a key, only someone else with a matching key will be able to decrypt the message.

There are two kinds of common encryption systems: secret-key cryptography and public-key cryptography, also called asymmetric cryptography. Public key cryptography is what is commonly used on the Internet.

In *public-key cryptography*, two keys are involved: a public key and a private key. Every person has both a public key and a private key. The public key is made freely available, whereas the private key is kept secret on the person's computer. The public key can encrypt messages, but only the private key can decrypt messages the public key has encrypted. If someone wants to send a message to you, for example, she would encrypt it with your public key. But only you, with your private key, would be able to decrypt the message and read it. Your public key could not decrypt it.

Digital certificates use encryption to verify that the person sending information—such as a credit card number, a message, or anything else over the Internet—really is who she says she is. The certificates place information on a person's hard disk and use encryption technology to create a unique digital certificate for each person. When someone with a digital certificate goes to a site or sends e-mail, that certificate is presented to the site or attached to the e-mail, and it verifies that the user is who she claims to be.

Digital certificates are issued by certificate authorities. These certificate authorities are private companies who charge either users or companies for the issuance of the certificates. You might be familiar with one such certificate authority, called VeriSign. Digital certificates contain information such as your name, the name of the certificate authority, the certificate's serial number, and similar information. The information has been encrypted in a way that makes it unique to you.

How Cryptosystems Work

1 Gabriel wants to send a confidential message over the Internet to Mia. Mia will need some way to decrypt the message as well as a way to guarantee that Gabriel—and not an imposter—has actually sent the message. First, Gabriel runs his message through an algorithm called a *hash function*. This produces a number known as the *message digest*. The message digest acts as a sort of "digital fingerprint" that Mia will use to ensure that no one has altered the message.

2 Gabriel now uses his private key to encrypt the message digest. This produces a unique digital signature that only he, with his private key, could have created.

3 Gabriel generates a new random key. He uses this key to encrypt his original message and his digital signature. Mia will need a copy of this random key to decrypt Gabriel's message. This random key is the only key in the world that can decrypt the message—and at this point, only Gabriel has the key.

4 Gabriel encrypts this new random key with Mia's public key. This encrypted random key is referred to as the *digital envelope*. Only Mia will be able to decrypt the random key because it was encrypted with her public key, so only her private key can decrypt it.

5 Gabriel sends a message to Mia over the Internet that is composed of several parts: the encrypted confidential message, the encrypted digital signature, and the encrypted digital envelope.

Original Message

Hash function

Message digest

Gabriel's public key

Gabriel's private key

Mia's public key

6 Mia gets the message. She decrypts the digital envelope with her private key and out of it gets the random key Gabriel used to encrypt the message.

7 Mia uses the random key to decrypt Gabriel's message. She can now read the confidential message he sent to her. However, she can't yet be sure that the message hasn't been altered en route to her or that Gabriel was definitely the sender.

8 Mia now uses the random key and Gabriel's public key to decrypt his encrypted digital signature. When she does this, she gets his message digest, the message's "digital fingerprint."

9 Mia uses this message digest to see whether Gabriel indeed sent the message and that it was not altered in any way. She takes the message she decrypted and runs it through the same algorithm—the *hash function*—that Gabriel ran the message through. This produces a new message digest.

10 Mia compares the message digest she calculated to the one she got out of Gabriel's digital signature. If the two match precisely, she can be sure that Gabriel signed the message and that it was not altered after he composed it. If they don't match, she knows that either he didn't compose the message or that someone altered the message after he wrote it.

Mia's private key

Digital signature

Random key

Encrypted message

Encrypted digital signature

Encrypted random key (digital envelope)

How Digital Certificates Ensure Internet Security

1 A digital certificate is used to guarantee that the person who sends information or e-mail over the Internet or who makes a financial transaction really is who he says he is. Digital certificates are issued by certificate authorities (CAs). To get a digital certificate, you typically visit a CA site and request a certificate. You then provide information about yourself, such as your name and other identifying information.

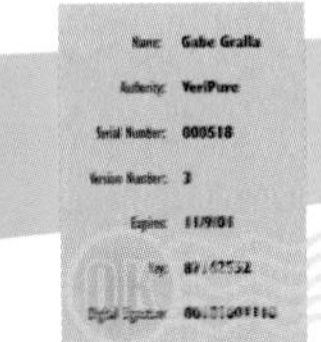

2 You are issued a digital certificate, which has been digitally signed to guarantee its authenticity. The certificate is data unique to you and is put on your hard disk, along with a private key.

Name: **Gabe Gralla**

Authority: **VeriPure**

Serial Number: **000518**

Version Number: **3**

Expires: **11/9/01**

Key: **87162552**

Digital Signature: **00101001110**

Secure Key

3 The digital certificate is composed of information such as your name, the name of the CA, the unique serial number of the certificate, the version number of the certificate, the expiration date of the certificate, your public key, and the digital signature of the CA. The exact format of the certificate is defined by a standard known as X.509.

Gabe Gralla Requests Certificate

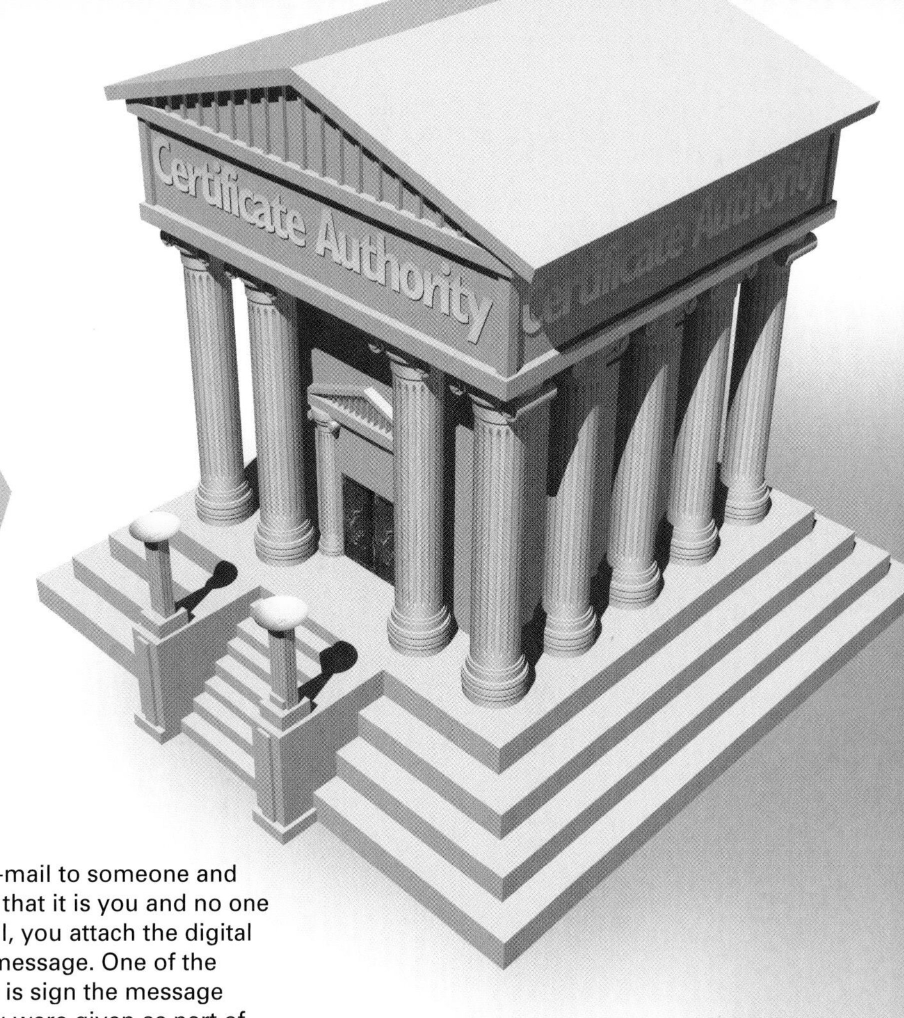

4 When you want to send e-mail to someone and have her know for certain that it is you and no one else who has sent the mail, you attach the digital certificate to your e-mail message. One of the things the certificate does is sign the message with a private key that you were given as part of the digital certificate.

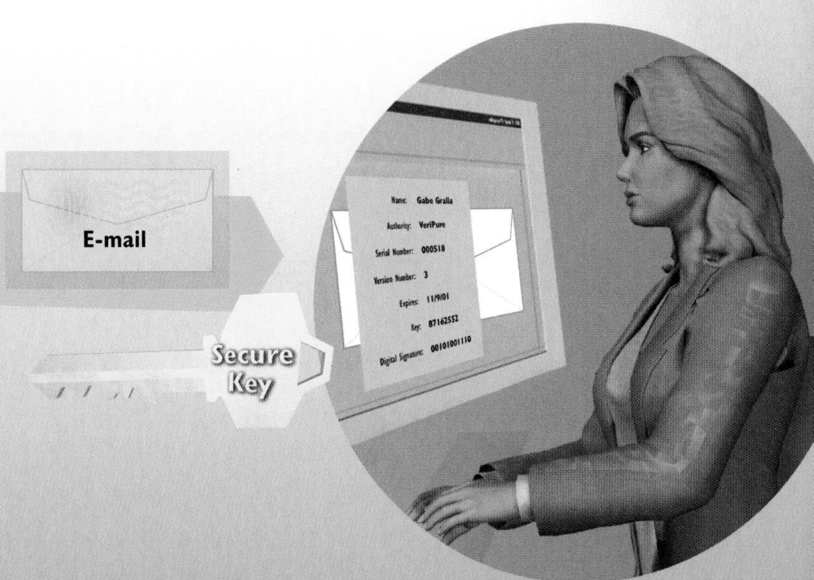

5 The person to whom you're sending e-mail gets your digital certificate along with your e-mail. The key is used to read the private key's signature. That signature matches information found in the digital certificate, so the receiver is assured that the message really came from you.

CHAPTER

49

How the FBI's "Carnivore" Program Works

THE most controversial law enforcement tool related to the Internet is the FBI's so-called Carnivore system. Carnivore is the Internet equivalent of a wiretap—it allows FBI agents to examine everything that a suspect does on the Internet, from sending and reading e-mail, to browsing the Web, sending and receiving files via FTP, and, in fact, anything else someone does. It literally allows agents to examine and keep copies of every bit of information sent to and from an individual.

Just as a special warrant is required for a law enforcement agency to obtain a wiretap, so is a special warrant required for the FBI to obtain a Carnivore tap.

With Carnivore, the FBI places a Pentium-class computer at the Internet service provider (ISP) of the target of the investigation. It then taps into the line of the ISP and examines all the ISP's Internet traffic, using filters and software to get copies of the target's traffic and discarding the rest. Depending on the warrant, the FBI might target only portions of the target's Internet usage—for example, e-mail but not FTP.

Although no public records about specific the use of Carnivore exist, indications are that law enforcement officials are increasingly asking for warrants to examine the activities of Internet users. Between 1997 and 1999, for example, an increase of more than 800% occurred in warrants served to America Online by state and local investigators investigating the online activities of America Online subscribers.

Civil libertarians and those concerned with privacy issues have criticized Carnivore. They worry that it can easily be abused, and they argue that the simple fact of tapping into someone's Internet usage is an invasion of privacy.

Chief among the concerns is that there is no way for people to ensure that Carnivore isn't being abused. The system can in fact examine every Internet packet of every subscriber in a given ISP. That means the federal government could have access to everything you see and do online and could keep a record of it. The FBI counters that it will not abuse its system and that it will adhere to the warrants it asks for. It claims that it asks for a Carnivore tap only in extreme circumstances, and that even in those circumstances, it limits the tap as much as possible.

But critics worry still. They point to the numerous problems the FBI has had in recent years—among them, not revealing thousands of documents it was required to by law in the Oklahoma bombing case. And they point to the FBI's past history of abuse of power in the 1960s and 1970s. The FBI says, however, that those incidents are deep in its past and that without the power to use Carnivore, it won't be able to protect the country against criminals and terrorists. In the end, it will be our country's usual democratic system of checks and balances that will determine how, when, and whether Carnivore will be used.

How Carnivore Can Invade Your Privacy

1 The FBI's system for tracking people's Internet use, including reading their e-mails and seeing what Web sites they visit, is called Carnivore. The data-gathering portion of Carnivore is a Pentium-based system, on which the Carnivore packet sniffing software runs. No keyboard or monitor is attached to the computer, so no one at the ISP can make use of it.

FBI

Dedicated Phone Line

CARNIVORE

2 The computer is attached via a dedicated phone line and a 56K modem to the FBI offices. The FBI runs an off-the-shelf program called PcAnywhere to enable it to control the Carnivore software and computer remotely. The dedicated connection is not connected to the Internet, and all data is encrypted, using both PcAnywhere's encryption and other encryption programs.

3 FBI agents have the right to monitor only someone against whom they've obtained a wiretap warrant. The warrant also might require that they gather only certain types of information about that person—for example, only his e-mail messages. They use the Carnivore software to set filters, which filter out all the data they don't want and focus only on the data they do want. So, for example, they set a filter that says only to track packets to and from a particular person, or only to examine his e-mail, or e-mail and Web usage.

Save all packets to and from IP 168.2.9.100

Discard all other packets

1 00001 1101001
10010 0 10 10 11
11 100 011 100
1010 1 1 00001
1101001 10010 0
10 10 11 11 100
011 100 1010 1
1010 1 1101001

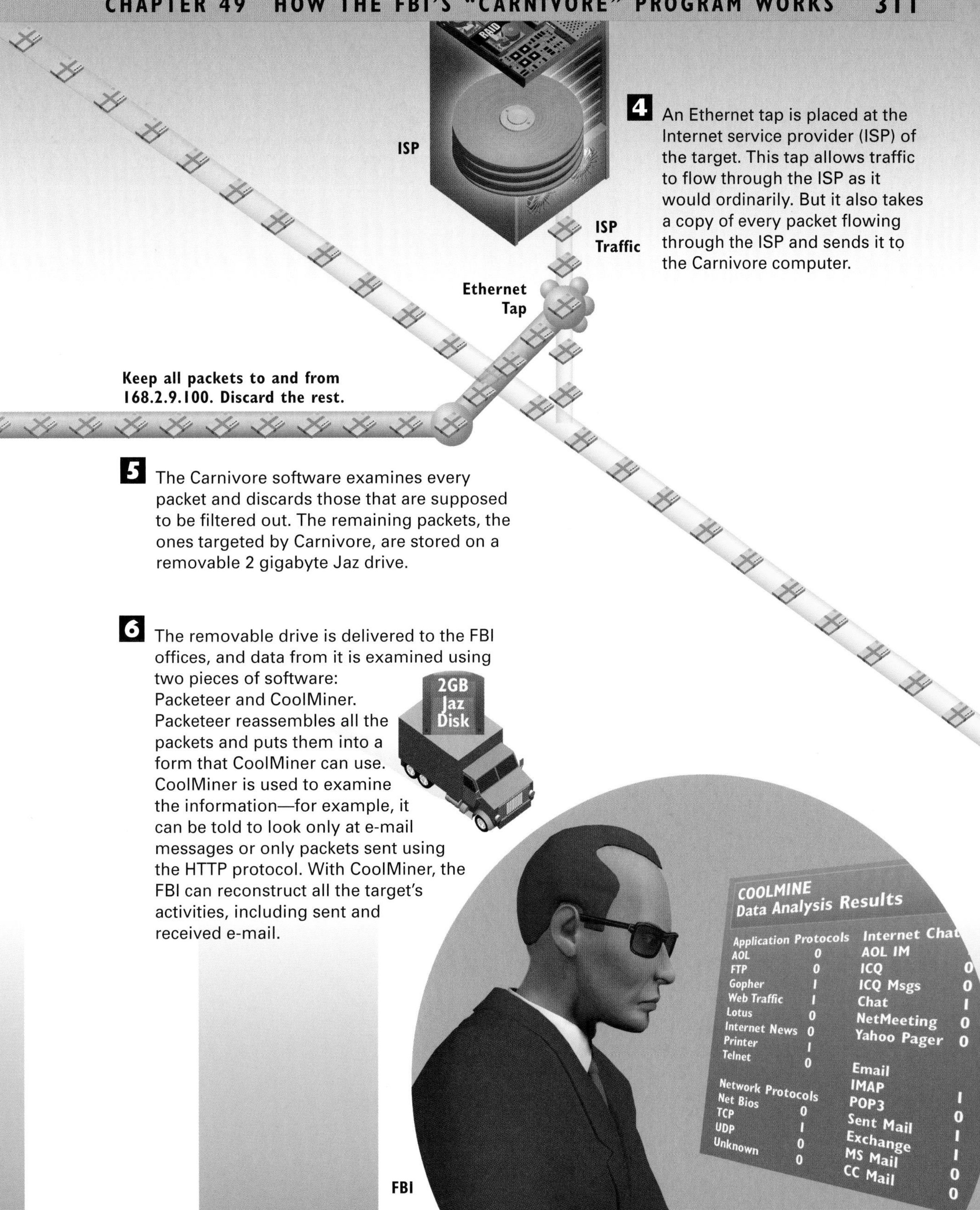

4 An Ethernet tap is placed at the Internet service provider (ISP) of the target. This tap allows traffic to flow through the ISP as it would ordinarily. But it also takes a copy of every packet flowing through the ISP and sends it to the Carnivore computer.

5 The Carnivore software examines every packet and discards those that are supposed to be filtered out. The remaining packets, the ones targeted by Carnivore, are stored on a removable 2 gigabyte Jaz drive.

6 The removable drive is delivered to the FBI offices, and data from it is examined using two pieces of software: Packeteer and CoolMiner. Packeteer reassembles all the packets and puts them into a form that CoolMiner can use. CoolMiner is used to examine the information—for example, it can be told to look only at e-mail messages or only packets sent using the HTTP protocol. With CoolMiner, the FBI can reconstruct all the target's activities, including sent and received e-mail.

CHAPTER 50 Parental Controls on the Internet

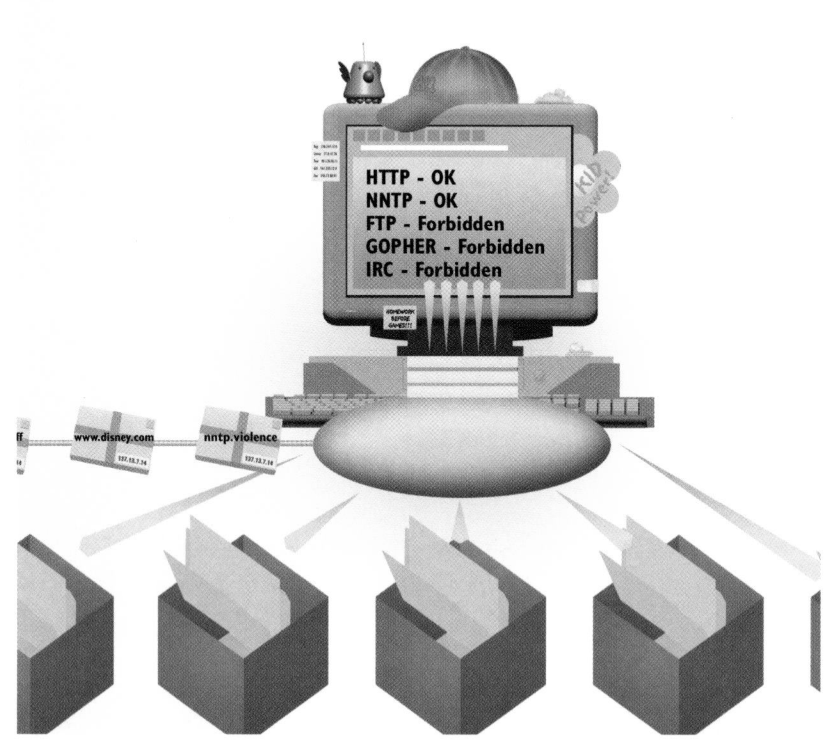

THE very nature of the Internet—the way it allows the free, unfettered flow of information among people—has gotten it a lot of bad publicity. Much has been made of the fact that erotic and pornographic information is available on the Internet, everything from pictures to discussions about subjects many people find objectionable. The truth is, that kind of content makes up a very small part of what's available on the Internet. Furthermore, the objectionable content is not exactly in public view—you have to do a bit of digging to find it.

However, just the fact that this type of information is available to anyone who wants to see it, including children, has made people uncomfortable. In fact, Congress and other legislative bodies have tried to take steps to ban certain types of content from being available on the Internet. As a result of these efforts, a controversial law was passed against online pornography. The law is called the Communications Decency Act, which the Supreme Court ruled unconstitutional.

The real answer to the problem, though, doesn't lie with legislation. The answer lies with technology—software that enables parents to ensure that their children are not seeing objectionable material. A number of companies make and sell software that will do this, such as SurfWatch, CyberNanny, and CyberPatrol. They each check sites for content and then bar children from getting to those sites containing content that is unsuitable for them. Some routers used for home networks also include filtering capabilities built into them.

Online services such as CompuServe and America Online have a variety of ways to block access to objectionable material on the Internet. Some allow parents to block children from using services such as the World Wide Web, chat, or newsgroups completely. Others, such as America Online, license technology from software makers, such as those that manufacture SurfWatch, to enable anyone on their service to block Internet sites they don't want their children to visit.

One group working on the issue is Platform for Internet Content Selection (PICS), which is trying to give parents control over the type of material to which their children have access. The group is trying to develop industry standards for technology that would allow the content of all sites and documents on the Internet to be rated according to its suitability for children. Additionally, the group would create standards to enable software to be developed for blocking sites based on those suitability ratings.

Businesses are also concerned with the type of Internet material their workers are accessing over corporate networks. There is a feeling that getting at and displaying sexual material could be interpreted as sexual harassment. Furthermore, some companies simply don't want their workers accessing that material on company time. Some companies now lease the same software parents are buying. Instead of installing the software on individual computers, though, the software is installed on a server, and it checks all incoming Internet traffic to every computer in the company.

How Parental Controls Work

1 The SurfWatch module examines the URL of every address coming toward the TCP/IP stack. It looks specifically for five types of URLs: https, nntps, ftps, gophers, and IRCs. It takes each of those five types of URLs and puts it in its own separate "box." It allows the rest of the Internet information coming in to go through. SurfWatch checks for these types of URLs because they are the ones that are the most likely to contain objectionable material.

2 SurfWatch software is installed on a computer a parent wants to monitor to ensure that children can't get to objectionable material on the Internet. When a child launches software to get onto the Internet, SurfWatch latches onto Winsock or MacTCP, depending on whether a PC or Macintosh is being used. A SurfWatch software module sits "in front" of Winsock or MacTCP (which we'll generically call a TCP/IP stack) and monitors the TCP/IP data stream coming to the TCP/IP stack from the Internet.

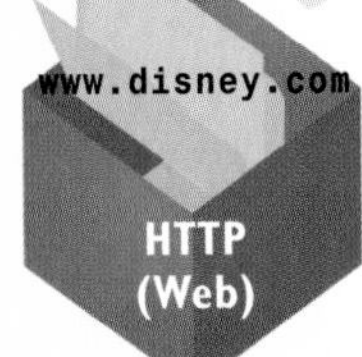

Objectionable URLs: meanstuff.com, naughtystuff.com, sexystuff.com, violentstuff.com

3 Every URL in each of the boxes is checked against a database of the URLs of objectionable sites. If SurfWatch finds that any of the URLs are from objectionable sites, it doesn't allow that information to be passed on to the TCP/IP stack, blocking the site and preventing information from being viewed. It alerts the child that the site has been blocked. SurfWatch checks thousands of sites and lists in its database the ones that are found to be objectionable.

Objectionable words: sex, violence, pornography, guns

4 If the URL is not in the database, SurfWatch does another check of the URL. This is called *pattern matching*. It looks at the words in the URL and checks them against a database of words to see whether any of them indicates a request for objectionable material. Often, people creating objectionable material put representative words in the URL to draw attention to the site. If SurfWatch finds a matching pattern, it doesn't allow that information to be passed on to the TCP/IP stack, blocking the site and preventing information from being viewed. It also alerts the child that the site has been blocked.

PICS

5 There is another way that SurfWatch eventually might check for objectionable sites. A rating system called PICS (Platform for Internet Content Selection) is being developed that will embed information about the content in its documents—saying, for example, whether objectionable material can be found there. If SurfWatch uses this system and finds that the URL is of a site containing objectionable material, it won't allow that information to be passed on to the TCP/IP stack, blocking the site and information from being viewed. It also will alert the child that the site has been blocked.

6 If the URL is not found to be of an objectionable site after the checks have been completed, the URL is passed to the TCP/IP stack and then to the Internet software, where the child can view it and interact with it. SurfWatch does all the checking practically instantly, so there is no apparent delay in getting material from the Internet.

7 Because the Internet is growing so quickly, and so many new sites are being created every month, the SurfWatch database of objectionable sites could become outdated. To solve the problem, SurfWatch automatically updates the database of sites every month. That way, the list of sites is always kept current.

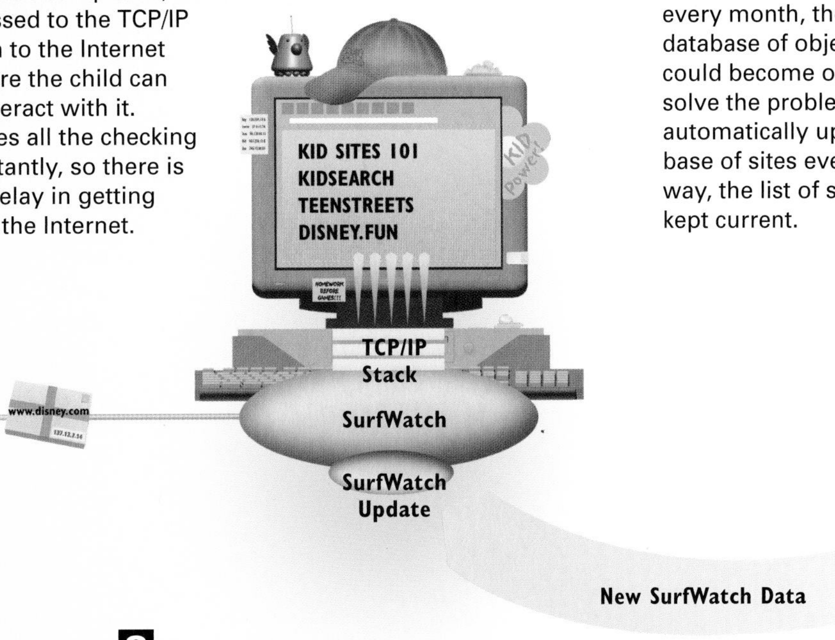

www.disney.com

New SurfWatch Data

8 Parents aren't the only people who want to filter out objectionable sites. Many businesses also might want to ensure that their workers aren't accessing objectionable sites over their corporate networks. Instead of having a copy of SurfWatch installed on every user's computer, the software is installed on a network server through which all Internet traffic must travel. At the server, the SurfWatch software checks for objectionable sites in the same way it does at individual machines. However, when SurfWatch is on a server, the software filters all Internet traffic for the entire company.

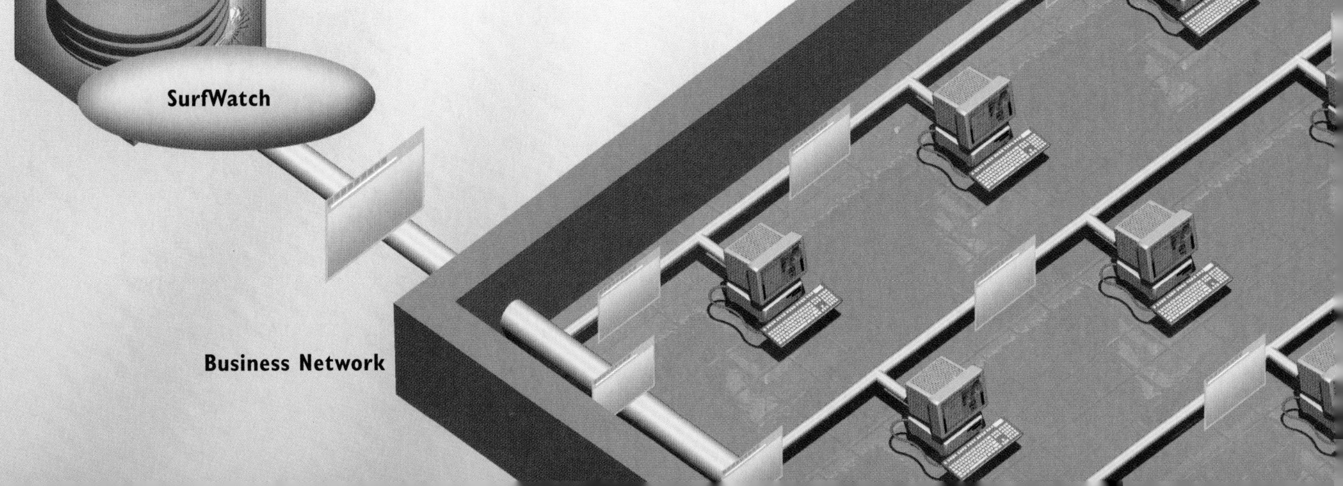

Network Server

SurfWatch

Business Network

Glossary

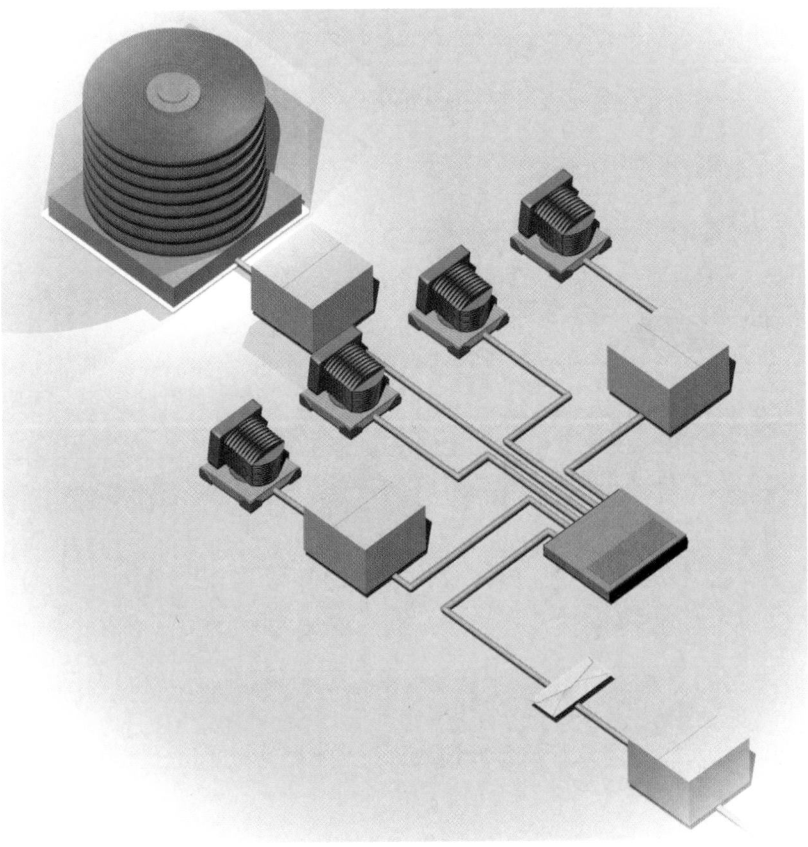

ActiveX A technology for Microsoft Internet Explorer that enables programs to be downloaded and run in your browser.

Address An Internet location, such as a URL, an IP address, or an e-mail address.

Agent A piece of software that goes out across the Internet and does a job for you—for example, finding the best prices on a product you want to buy.

Application service provider (ASP) A service that enables you to run software over the Internet without installing it on your computer. Many ASPs enable the software to run inside your Web browser when you visit a Web site.

ASCII characters Plain-text characters that you get by pressing keys on your keyboard.

Attachment See *File attachment.*

Audio file A file you can download or play from the Internet that has music or sounds in it.

Avatar A picture that represents you in picture-oriented chat rooms.

Bandwidth A measure of the amount of data that can be sent across an Internet connection over a unit of time.

Bluetooth A wireless networking standard that allows devices of many different kinds to communicate in a peer-to-peer fashion, that is, without having to use a server or other hardware to connect them.

Bridge A device that connects local area networks with each other.

Broadband connection A very fast Internet connection, such as via a cable modem, or DSL.

Browser See *Web browser.*

Buddy list In instant messaging software, a list of friends you create so that you are alerted whenever one of your "buddies" comes online.

Cable modem A device used to connect a computer to the Internet at very high speeds over cable TV lines. The device isn't a true modem, though, and uses a network card inside the computer to connect to the cable line.

Cache A place on a computer or server that temporarily stores items such as Web pages and graphics so they can be more quickly retrieved.

Carnivore An FBI hardware and software system that can be used to read people's e-mail and track everything they do when they are on the Internet.

Chat A way that two or more people can communicate in real-time by typing messages on their keyboards.

Chat room A location in cyberspace where people go to chat.

Client A piece of software running on a local computer or device that communicates with a central server.

Client pull animation A Web animation technique in which the Web browser requests a series of images that, when displayed one after another, appear to be animated.

Client/server architecture A model of computing in which clients on local computers cooperate with distant servers to compete tasks. The Internet is largely based on client/server architecture.

Coaxial cable The type of cable used for cable TV connections. It can also be used to provide high-speed access to the Internet, via cable modems.

Common Gateway Interface (CGI) A communications protocol that enables Web servers to communicate with applications, such as databases.

Cookies A bit of data put on your computer by a Web server that can be used to track what you do when you are on the Web.

Cryptosystems Systems used to encrypt data and then decrypt data so that only the intended recipient can read it.

Decryption A method of unscrambling encrypted data so that it can be understood.

Digital certificate A key used to encrypt and decrypt information; it can be used to guarantee that you're the sender of a message or to verify the authenticity of a person sending you a message.

Digital signature An encrypted electronic "signature" that identifies you as the sender of a message—and that can't be forged.

Digital subscriber line (DSL) A way of giving a computer high-speed access to the Internet using existing phone lines. A DSL modem is required.

Domain An area of the Internet owned by a company or person, such as `zdnet.com`.

Domain name server A server that translates Internet addresses, such as `www.zdnet.com`, into their IP addresses, such as `128.42.23.68`, and vice versa.

Domain Name System (DNS) The system that translates Internet addresses, such as `www.zdnet.com`, into their IP addresses, such as `128.42.23.68`, and vice versa.

Download To transfer information or files from the Internet to your computer.

Dynamic Host Configuration Protocol (DHCP) A protocol used to renew an IP address or provide a new IP address to a computer when it connects to a server. When you connect to the Internet using an Internet service provider, you usually are given a different IP address every time you connect.

Dynamic HTML (DHTML) A group of HTML-related technologies that allows for greater interactivity and animation on Web pages.

Dynamic IP address An IP address delivered via DHCP; with a dynamic IP address, the IP address of a computer will be different each time it goes onto the Internet.

E-mail filter A way of automatically sorting incoming e-mail so that some are automatically routed to certain folders or deleted, based on the sender and the content of the message. E-mail filters can be used to cut down on spam sent to you.

E-mail reader A piece of software used to send and receive e-mail.

Encryption A method of scrambling data so that it can be read only by its intended recipient.

Ethernet The most common local area networking standard.

Ewallet An electronic wallet that contains your credit card information or electronic money so that you can use it to easily shop at many online shopping sites.

eXtensible Markup Language (XML) An extension of HTML that separates the content of a Web page from its display. It can be used to allow designers to easily create Web pages to be displayed on many different devices, such as computers, cell phones, and PDAs.

File attachment A file attached to an e-mail message or a newsgroup posting. Any type of file can be attached to e-mail or newsgroup postings.

File compression Shrinking the size of a file down so that it can be transferred more quickly over the Internet.

File extension The letters on the end of a filename that are used to identify the type of file it is. For example, files with .doc extensions are Microsoft Word files.

Firewall A hardware or hardware/software combination that protects computers on a network from being attacked by hackers or snoopers.

Flash movie An animated movie played over the Web, created using Macromedia's Flash software.

FTP (File Transfer Protocol) A way of downloading files on the Internet. See also *Download.*

Gateway A device that connects local area networks with each other and can translate data from one network to another.

GIF (Graphics Interchange Format) A common graphics format used on Web pages. Files in this format end in .gif.

Helper application See *Plug-in.*

Hops The number of times a packet of information needs to be sent to different routers before reaching its destination.

Host See *Server.*

HTML (Hypertext Markup Language) The computer language that forms the basis of the World Wide Web. Web browsers interpret HTML commands and display Web pages based on the HTML commands.

HTTP (Hypertext Transfer Protocol) An Internet protocol that defines the way Web browsers and Web servers communicate with each other.

Hub A device that connects several computers to one another on a network.

Hub/Router A combination of a hub and router that connects computers, routes data among them, and provides access to the Internet or other networks. Home networks commonly use a hub/router.

Hyperlink A link on a Web page that sends you to another Web page or resource.

Hypertext Text that, when clicked, sends you to another piece of text or location.

Image map A static image that has been turned into a clickable image with different clickable parts.

Instant message A chat-like message sent to another individual in a private, one-on-one conversation.

Instant messaging software Software that enables people to know when their friends are online and lets them send person-to-person messages.

Internet-enhanced TV The use of Internet technologies to add interactivity and Web links to television broadcasts.

Internet service provider (ISP) A company that provides dial-in or some other type of access to the Internet for a monthly fee.

Internet telephony The use of the Internet to make telephone calls.

Intranet A private network inside a corporation that uses Internet technology.

IP address An Internet address that is a series of four numbers separate by dots, such as `155.40.112.23`. Every time you go onto the Internet, you use an IP address; without it you can't do things such as surf the Web.

IRC (Internet Relay Chat) A standard that enables people to chat with each other over the Internet. You need special IRC software to chat via IRC.

ISDN (Integrated Services Digital Network) A method of establishing a high-speed connection to the Internet using telephone lines. Special lines and modems are needed for ISDN.

Java A programming language used to create programs that can be run inside Web browsers or on a variety of computers. The strength of Java-written programs is that they can be written once and can then run as is in a variety of computers.

JavaScript A technology that enables Web designers to use a variety of interactive features on Web pages.

JPEG (Joint Photographic Experts Group) A common graphics format used for Web pages. Files in this format end in .jpg.

Key A piece of data used to encrypt or decrypt information.

Lightweight Directory Access Protocol (LDAP) A protocol that enables the creation of Internet white pages, which let people look up other people's e-mail addresses.

listserv A type of software that manages sending and receiving e-mail broadcasts and discussions. The term often is used generically to describe an e-mail broadcast.

Local area network (LAN) A network that connects computers to each other so they can easily communicate.

MacTCP Software for Macintosh computers that interprets TCP/IP commands.

Mail header The part of an e-mail message that contains the subject line, the sender, the receiver, and similar information.

Mail server A server that delivers or receives e-mail.

Mailing list See *listserv*.

MBone (Multicast backbone) A high-capacity Internet backbone used for transmitting broadcasts using the Multicast IP protocol.

Message board A public area online where people can read and send messages.

Metasearch software Software that can search through many search engines simultaneously and report back the results.

Microbrowser A browser that a cell phone or similar device uses to browse the World Wide Web.

Microsoft Outlook A popular e-mail program.

Moderated newsgroup A newsgroup in which all postings first have to go through a moderator before being posted.

MP3 file A special music format that's of almost CD quality, but that produces files that aren't very large and so don't take a long time to download.

Multicast IP A protocol that enables video and audio broadcasts to take place, while using a minimum of bandwidth.

Name server A server that translates Internet addresses, such as `www.zdnet.com`, into their IP addresses, such as `145.45.23.45`.

Napster A popular program used for sharing music files in the MP3 format with others.

NetCam A video camera that attaches to a computer and often is used for Internet videoconferencing or videochat.

Network address translation (NAT) A technique in a local area network that provides an internal IP address to computers inside the network, while masking the IP address to the outside world. It also enables several computers on the local area network to share an external IP address.

Network card An add-in card put into a computer so that it can get onto a network.

Newsgroup A discussion area on the Internet.

Newsgroup reader A piece of software used to read newsgroups.

Node A portion of a network through which many computers are connected.

Online auction Just like a real-life auction, except that it's done online.

Opt out A policy that lets you say you don't want to receive junk mail or similar information.

Packet A piece of data that has been broken down into pieces for transmitting over the Internet or another network.

Packet switched network A network in which there is no unbroken connection between sender and receiver; instead data is broken into packets, sent, and then reassembled when received. The Internet is a packet switched network.

Palm Query Application (PQA) A small piece of software on a wireless Palm device that enables it to get information from the Internet using Web clipping.

Palmtop computer A small computer, such as the Palm, that fits in the palm of your hand and is often used for keeping track of schedules, to-do lists, and a calendar; it also can be used for wireless communications.

Parental controls/content filtering A feature of America Online, some routers, and some add-in software that lets parents decide where kids can go on America Online and the Internet and how they can use America Online and the Internet.

Passport A technique that enables people to determine what information to give to Web sites and what information to keep private.

Password A set of private letters and numbers or words you type in to give you access to a service or site.

Peer-to-peer network A network that enables computers or other devices to connect directly with one another without having to use a server or other hardware to connect them.

Personal Digital Assistant (PDA) A small handheld computer, such as a Palm device or Windows CE device.

Personal firewall A hardware or hardware/software combination that protects an individual computer from being attacked by hackers or snoopers.

Piconet A network formed by the connection of two or more Bluetooth devices with one another.

Plug-in A piece of software that installs in a browser or works in concert with a browser, such as for displaying different types of video.

Point-to-Point Protocol (PPP) A protocol for computers to connect to the Internet using dial-up modems.

POP 3 (Post Office 3) A communications protocol used by e-mail servers to deliver e-mail.

Pretty Good Privacy (PGP) A program used to encrypt and decrypt information. It's especially useful for sending out private e-mail that only the sender and recipient can understand.

Private key Someone's key in an encryption scheme that only one person can use. It's used in concert with that individual's public key to encrypt and decrypt information. See also *Key* and *Public key*.

Proxy server A server located between a client, such as a Web browser, and the server the client is trying to contact, and which tries to fulfill the request before sending it to the server. For example, a proxy server could be used to speed up the delivery of Web pages.

Public key Someone's key in an encryption scheme that anyone can use. It's used in concert with that individual's private key to encrypt and decrypt information. See also *Key* and *Private key*.

RealPlayer A popular piece of software that plays video and audio files.

Registrars Private companies that accept payment from companies and individuals who buy Internet domains.

Router A piece of hardware that sends packets to their proper destinations on the Internet.

Routing table A database in a router that details the various paths packets can take en route to their destinations.

Search engine A Web site that lets you perform searches throughout the Internet.

Secure site A site that encrypts your credit card information as it's sent across the Internet so the credit card number can't be stolen.

Serial Line Internet Protocol (SLIP) A protocol for computers to connect to the Internet using dial-up modems. It's not as effective as a similar protocol, called PPP.

Server A computer that performs some task for other computers, such as sending or receiving e-mail or delivering Web pages.

Server push animation A Web animation technique in which a server sends a series of images to a browser that, when displayed one after another, appear to be animated.

SET (Secure Electronic Transactions) The electronic encryption and payment standard that a group of companies, including Microsoft, Netscape, VISA, and MasterCard, is pushing to become the standard for doing electronic commerce on the Internet.

Shockwave An animated movie played over the Web, created using Macromedia's Director software.

Shopping cart A list of items someone wants to buy when at a online store.

SMTP (Simple Mail Transfer Protocol) A communications protocol used to send e-mail.

Smurf attack A method hackers use to attack Internet service providers or Web sites.

Socket Software that understands and interprets TCP/IP commands.

Spam Junk e-mail sent to people who haven't requested it. Most spam are commercial offers and can also be fraudulent.

Spam filter Software that can filter out spam before it is received.

Spamoflauge The act of hiding of a spammer's true e-mail address so that the true sender of the spam can't be traced.

Spider Software that gathers information from the Web and puts it into a large database that can be searched by search engines.

SSL (Secure Sockets Layer) A technology that scrambles information as it's sent across the Internet so hackers can't read it.

Static IP address A fixed IP address that never changes. Unlike a dynamic IP address, it is permanent, so the IP address of the computer never changes whenever it goes onto the Internet.

Streaming audio See *Streaming media.*

Streaming media A technique that enables you to view and listen to audio and video files from the Internet while they're still downloading to your computer. With streaming media, you can view and listen to audio and video files only a few seconds after you click them.

Streaming video See *Streaming media.*

T1 line A high-speed line that can carry data at a rate of 1.544Mbps.

T3 line A high-speed line that can carry data at a rate of 44.746Mbps.

TCP/IP (Transmission Control Protocol/Internet Protocol) The communications protocols that underlie the Internet.

TCP/IP stack See *Socket.*

Telnet A way of controlling a host computer from your own computer over the Internet.

Trojan horse A malicious program that appears to be benign, but in fact is doing damage to your computer. Some Trojan horses can give hackers complete access to the computers of people who run them.

TRUSTe A company that sets voluntary standards for privacy on the Internet and that gives out "seals" that companies can post on their Web sites if the companies adhere to those privacy rules.

Uniform resource locator (URL) An address on the Internet, such as `www.zdnet.com`, that enables computers and other devices to visit it.

Universal Serial Bus (USB) A technology that enables many devices to connect to a computer, such as NetCams, scanners, and digital cameras. The devices can be attached to one another in daisy-chain fashion, allowing many to be connected at once.

Unmoderated newsgroup A newsgroup in which postings don't have to go through a moderator before being posted.

Upload To transfer a file from your computer to another computer or to a server.

Usenet An Internet service for newsgroups.

Videoconference A conference among several people in which they can talk to one another and see each other using video cameras over the Internet.

Virtual Private Network (VPN) A encryption technique that enables people to connect to their corporation's network over the Internet, while protecting the data from being seen by anyone else.

Virtual reality (VR) The simulation of reality on a computer screen or over the Internet.

Virtual Reality Modeling Language (VRML) The language used to create Virtual reality Web sites.

Virus A malicious program that attacks a computer.

WAP Transaction Protocol (WTP) A communications protocol, part of the Wireless Access Protocol (WAP), that is the equivalent of the Internet's TCP/IP protocols and enables cell phones and similar devices to access the Internet.

Web browser A piece of software that enables people to browse the World Wide Web.

Web bug A technique that enables Web sites or people to track people's activities when they visit the Web or use e-mail.

WebCam A video camera that sends live still or video images to a Web site.

Web clipping A technique that enables Palm devices to get information from the Internet.

Web page template A preformatted design for a Web page that includes colors, fonts, layout, and other elements. Templates make creating Web pages easy—you only have to put in your own words, pictures, and content.

Web tracking A technique used by Web sites that tracks what people do when they visit a Web site.

WebTV A product that lets you get access to the Web on your television set.

Web white pages Web sites that contains information that can be searched through, for identifying information such as e-mail addresses, phone numbers, and addresses.

Whiteboard In videoconferencing, an application that enables several people to work on the same screen simultaneously.

Winsock Software for Windows that interprets TCP/IP commands.

Wireless access point A device that connects wireless devices, such as a computer equipped with a wireless network card, to a network.

Wireless access protocol (WAP) An Internet protocol that defines the way cell phones and similar devices can access the Internet.

Wireless Markup Language (WML) A markup language related to HTML that is used to create Web sites that cell phones and similar devices can visit.

WMLScript A scripting language that enables interaction between cell phones and the Internet.

Workgroup software Software that enables groups in a corporation to work more closely and effectively with each other and does things such as route documents among people and allow people to run whiteboard applications.

World Wide Web The most popular portion of the Internet, it allows you to view pages that include text, pictures, video, sound, and various forms of interactivity.

World Wide Web Consortium (W3C) The group that develops standards for the evolution of the World Wide Web.

Index

Symbols

A

B

J-K

L

M

N

O

P

Q-R

T

X-Z